Giles Block

Giles Block was educated at Dulwich College and at St Catherine's College, Oxford. For reasons now lost in time, and at a ridiculously early age, he announced that he was going to become an actor. But he had to wait until he was thirteen before landing his first role in the school play as Prince Arthur in Shakespeare's *King John*. Other parts followed: he became a member of Michael Croft's Youth Theatre – and many more Shakespearian roles – and acting for the OUDS provided yet more. By the time he left Oxford in 1963, and started life as a professional actor, he'd appeared in about a dozen of Shakespeare's plays – some of them more than once. By 1970 he had also begun directing, and after another seven years – by which time he had appeared in over thirty Shakespeare plays – directing became his main focus. In 1977 he joined the National Theatre as a Staff Director, and in 1981 was appointed Director of Platforms, and went on to direct two main-house productions, *The Fawn* (John Marston) and *She Stoops to Conquer* in 1983/4. Between 1982 and 2003, he regularly visited Japan, directing, for the Japanese theatre company Shochiku, some twenty plays, including productions of *Macbeth*, *King Lear*, *Hamlet* and *Richard III*, the first two of which, were televised by NHK.

By the early 1990s he was increasingly drawn to wondering why Shakespeare's writing developed in the way it did, and why his verse contained so many irregularities. He felt that the answer had to be that this was exactly how Shakespeare 'heard' his characters speaking; and in 1995 Richard Eyre, then Artistic Director at the National Theatre, invited him to run some workshops at the National Theatre Studio to investigate this further. It was these workshops that, indirectly, led him in 1999 to taking up a post at Shakespeare's Globe Theatre. For the last fifteen seasons he has been leading the Globe Company's text work, while in those early years he also directed *Antony and Cleopatra*, *Hamlet* and *Troilus and Cressida*. More recently he has directed *The Tempest*, *Henry V* and *The Comedy of Errors* at the Blackfriars Theatre in Virginia. He has taught Shakespeare to countless groups in the UK and abroad, running workshops in America, Canada and Japan. In 2008 he was Shakespeare Consultant on the film *Me and Orson Welles*, directed by Richard Linklater. In 2011 he received the Sam Wanamaker Award in recognition of his work at the Globe.

Giles Block

SPEAKING THE SPEECH

An Actor's Guide to Shakespeare

Foreword by Mark Rylance

NICK HERN BOOKS
London
www.nickhernbooks.co.uk

A Nick Hern Book

Speaking the Speech
first published in Great Britain in 2013
by Nick Hern Books Limited,
The Glasshouse, 49a Goldhawk Road, London W12 8QP
in association with Shakespeare's Globe

Reprinted 2014

Cover photo: Timothy Walker as Malvolio in *Twelfth Night*,
Shakespeare's Globe, 2002, photographed by John Tramper
Cover design by Nick Hern Books

Typeset by Nick Hern Books, London
Printed and bound in Great Britain by
Ashford Colour Press Ltd, Gosport, Hampshire

A CIP catalogue record for this book is available from the British Library

ISBN 978 1 84842 191 2

*To Penny and Sam
With love, and ever thanks...*

I knew when seven Justices could not take up a quarrel, but when the parties were met themselves, one of them thought but of an if; as if you said so, then I said so: and they shook hands, and swore brothers. Your if, is the only peace-maker: much virtue in if.

Touchstone, *As You Like It*: Act 5, Scene 4

Contents

Foreword
Mark Rylance

I think we speak like a speedboat careering across a deep loch. So many different forces are at work to create the way we speak. Memories alone are constantly rising up or pulling us down. Stuff we have read rises high all around us. Stuff we have experienced too rears up like mountain peaks. Creating or simulating all those forces spontaneously, as we speak Shakespeare, is the difficult work of the actor, and is expressed through the sound of the word and the little silences thereby accentuated.

I heard wonderful verse-speakers at the RSC when I was growing up. Judi Dench particularly comes to mind. She always sounded so natural, so present. I gradually realised that there were different styles of speaking. Some were very musical or impressive. I came to love it most when the person sounded like a person I might meet off the stage in the actual world. I then grew interested in the relationship, off the stage, between my thinking and speaking and realised that, while I always had a genuine need to speak about a certain subject, I rarely knew how I was going to express myself until I was doing so and even then my mind got distracted as different connected subjects appeared. Only if I quoted someone did I know what I was going to say, or if I had waited a long time to say what I wanted to say. How to achieve this discovered sound of speech and yet honour the verse became a concern.

People sometimes ask me how I learn the lines, but forgetting them is the real work. Forgetting what you are going to say next, so you discover the text as you would your own thoughts.

Of course the next question was the relationship between my thoughts and the wordless desires that give them form. Anyway, all these considerations made me suspicious of conscious verse-speaking. I feared it would kill spontaneity and liveliness and innocence. I found that directors were happy with the way I spoke, on the whole, if I found the meaning and the need to speak. With Shakespeare the lines are written so naturally that the true sense usually leads you to the accurate verse. So I muddled along.

But, in the back of my mind, I was unsettled. The author had clearly taken enormous trouble to place some lines in verse and some in prose. Why? Should one not treat the verse differently therefore from the prose? What was different? The line endings, rhymes, and rhythm: why was the author using these rhetorical forms? Would they just look after themselves?

Still, I was wary of rules and laws about verse-speaking. One director told me the rules were meant for the actors in the ensemble, who might not have the talent of the leads, but if they followed the rules they would all be the same and of a certain standard. I wonder if this was just a trick to make the leads sound better. Why shouldn't every character be as true as each other? Does Shakespeare treat any of the characters with less humanity? Does nature?

I told myself that laws are only formed when love has ceased; that if I loved the language, if I listened to it, thought about it, I would find my way without the need for law.

It was about that time, when I was forty, that I met Giles Block, and I knew he loved the language more than I did and therefore knew what I needed to know.

I have always been fascinated by the working relationship in theatre between the director and the actor. I have witnessed some directors empower an actor to play and others, without necessarily meaning to, disempower an actor. When I have directed and acted myself, I have also experienced this first-hand. As soon as I became Artistic Director at Shakespeare's Globe Theatre, I copied the ballet companies I knew of, and introduced an hour three times a week, which was devoted to the actors' skills; movement, voice, and the words, verse and prose. Directors of Shakespeare know about these things, but they have a more important responsibility for the story and the audience; and I felt that we as actors should turn up for rehearsal, as ballet dancers do, with our skills ready. Many actors would come to us with little or distant experience of the dreaded verse-speaking. Also, with Shakespeare's plays, we are working with such an exquisite consciousness of words and rhythm and expression, that a space to share what we all perceived seemed essential. I needed a particular person to lead this work, as I did not want the actors disempowered by a strict set of 'laws', or a teacher-student relationship, or an atmosphere where the actor's own experience was discounted in favour of the leader of the work. I also did not want the directors to feel challenged or disempowered by another voice working directly with the actors on their lines. On the contrary, I wanted the directors to feel liberated, particularly in the final weeks of a production, when they are very concerned with the whole production, by knowing there was a pair of ears solely focused on the liveliness and accuracy of the actors' speaking: the Master of the Word.

Giles was the perfect 'Master of the Word'. I remember saying to the company that he was a master not of slaves or of a particular skill, he was master because of the quality of his love for Shakespeare's words. Giles never offended any director – or actor – to my knowledge. He survived my time as Artistic Director of Shakespeare's Globe and works closely with Dominic Dromgoole, the Globe's current AD, to this day. He is priceless.

When he directed me in the last production of *Hamlet* I did, at the Globe, he revealed to me the additions to the text he thought Burbage had made when playing Hamlet, and which had been considered so good that the creators of the First Folio had included them in that edition of the play. This was fascinating evidence of the aural nature of the plays; how they may have developed in the actors' hands; in their sense of the vernacular. In my experience, Giles only ever offers options and choices when carefully going through the text together with the actors, but you gradually realise the witty and close attention Shakespeare pays to the way people speak at different points in their emotional and thoughtful lives. You also become aware of how Shakespeare's writing changed to reflect his growing awareness of how people actually speak and his growing confidence in making the literal form serve the natural force.

The greatest delights of working with Giles is his coloured scripts, which one receives as soon as one starts to run the play in the rehearsal room, and then throughout previews. In a careful handwriting with marks and symbols, and a bright fluorescent colour, Giles tells you where you went wrong on the words, circling, writing out the misquote, sometimes suggesting a different stress, if so, always with a 'Let's talk' next to it. If you make the same mistake the next time, the same symbol or remark is made in a different fluorescent colour. I can achieve rainbows on some pages before I get it right.

Giles deepened my love for Shakespeare and for the way we all speak. I trust you will have a similar experience reading his book.

Author's Note

The First Folio of 1623

All the quotations from Shakespeare in this book are, whenever possible, based on the First Folio of Shakespeare's plays.

The First Folio came into being because sometime after Shakespeare's death in 1616, two of his old theatre colleagues, John Heminge and Henry Condell, organised the publication of thirty-six of his plays, and this, the First Folio, was finally published in 1623, seven years after the playwright's death at the early age of fifty-two. Earlier, during Shakespeare's lifetime, eighteen of his plays had been published in single volumes (these are known as Quartos: their pages being a quarter of the size of the Folio's). Some of these Quartos were full of errors, and so the Folio is of immediate value for the better editions of these plays that it gives us. But the major importance of the First Folio is that it prints *for the first time* eighteen of Shakespeare's plays. Without the First Folio, and the efforts of Heminge and Condell, we would be without *Macbeth*, *As You Like It*, *The Tempest*, *Julius Caesar*, *Antony and Cleopatra*, *The Winter's Tale* and *Twelfth Night*, to name but seven of the eighteen.

Our debt to Heminge and Condell has to be matched by that we owe to subsequent editors, who, through the intervening years, have cleared up many of the textual puzzles and errors the First Folio contains. But while I acknowledge and accept their insightful discoveries, I am constantly drawn back to the First Folio, because I know working from it takes me as close to Shakespeare as I can get. And sometimes, just sometimes, I find there a line changed by modern editors, that maybe doesn't need to be, or is one that could be altered in a better way.[1]

But I also use the First Folio, because I believe that the *original punctuation* (which, as it happens, most editors change rather freely) is invaluable for actors, as it can help them to discover points of emphasis, and ways of phrasing.

However, in keeping with most of the editions that are on sale today, I modernise the spelling, which includes the spelling of characters' names, remove *most* of the capitalisation the Folio gives to certain key-words, and the italics it gives to proper names. Also, like modern editions, I think it is helpful, when one character finishes another's verse line, to indent the second speaker's line, in order to show how the rhythm of these two lines are connected.

You will find more information about the First Folio and the value I place on its punctuation in Chapters 9 and 14.

You'll find a couple of symbols used occasionally throughout this book:

A speech bubble indicates that I am asking you to turn back to an earlier passage to work on a particular speech, and once you've done so to return to this place.

A book directs you, on a handful of occasions, to read some passages from a copy of your own.

Superscript numbers (like the [1] above) direct you to the end notes starting on page 344.

* Asterisks indicate words that are glossed at the bottom of the page.

Introduction

The First Folio of 1623 includes a delightful preface by Heminge and Condell, urging people to buy copies of the book, and addressing them by the happy phrase, '*To the great variety of readers*'. I have been mindful that this, my book, may also find its way into the hands of 'a great variety of readers'. Some of you may well have no prior knowledge of Shakespeare, whereas others may already be well versed in these matters. I am hoping that this book will be able to satisfy you all: to the first group I am confident that the opening pages should present you with no difficulties; and to the second, I hope you might feel that I am approaching Shakespeare's writing from a new angle – as if some experienced traveller to some great city decided for once not to arrive by rail or road, but to reach it by water – and to come across the familiar by a route they had not taken before.

I have been in the theatre all my adult life, and for the last fourteen years I have had the most perfect job: working with actors at Shakespeare's Globe Theatre. I have been involved with more than fifty productions, and my thinking as to how our actors might best approach the texts of these great plays has had time to develop gradually, little by little. So I have to thank Mark Rylance who first invited me to join the company in 1999, and Dominic Dromgoole who asked me to stay on, when he took over from Mark as Artistic Director in 2006. I also have to thank Globe Education, with its Director Patrick Spottiswoode; they have enabled me to share my thoughts with hundreds of students, and as so often happens, it has been by talking to them, and listening to them, that I have learnt yet more.

Shakespeare has been a part of my life for as long as I can remember –
one of my earliest memories of my father is how he would quote great
chunks from *Julius Caesar* – and while this is not the place to try and recall
all those who have influenced me over the years, one occasion stands out.
I was in New York – sitting in the 46th Street Theatre late in 1989, with a
company of actors, listening to Peter Hall talking about the importance of
Shakespeare's line endings. I realised in that moment that I had never
thought much about this before, and yet knew instantly that it brought
everything about the form of Shakespeare's verse into focus. I date my own
journey of trying to unravel the question as to why Shakespeare writes in
the way he does from that afternoon.[1]

So the aim of this book is to answer two simple questions – 'Why does
Shakespeare write in the way he does, and secondly, how can actors get
the most out of these incomparable plays?'

Maybe the first thing we should remember is that Shakespeare was an
actor, writing for other actors. Actors, or 'players' as they were then also
called, were his friends and his colleagues: he spent his life watching them
at work; listening to them. He wrote to their skills – whether it was the verbal dexterity of his clowns, or the power and presence of his tragedians.
Sometimes their performances blew him away:

> Is it not monstrous that this player here,
> But in a fiction, in a dream of passion,
> Could force his soul so to his whole conceit,
> That from her working, all his visage wann'd;
> Tears in his eyes, distraction in's aspect,
> A broken voice, and his whole function suiting
> With forms, to his conceit? And all for nothing?
>
> *Hamlet*: Act 2, Scene 2

Shakespeare uses the word 'monstrous' here to mean something unnatural. That the actor should be capable of becoming another person is, in
Hamlet's mind at this moment, something close to devilish – though
Hamlet is about to use their 'devilish' skills in order to trap his own father's
murderer.

For Shakespeare, though, seeing what these 'players' were capable of
has to be one of the reasons why his writing develops in the extraordinary
way it does – his writing was, you could say, 'actor-driven' – and the way
he continually breaks new ground, developing and refining, his earlier
work, is one of the themes running through this book.

If you were to ask me 'What makes Shakespeare so great?', high on my
list would be his extraordinary ability to bring his characters to life by a

simple turn of phrase, by a breath they take, by a pause they mark. He achieves this by the total identification he makes with each and every one of his characters. They are born in his imagination, and he lends them his own voice so they can speak. Being their creator, he knows them better than they know themselves; he knows that much is concealed from them, that they are frequently lost, unsure. But he reads their thoughts; he hears their breathing; he recognises how their emotions make them hesitate, shaping the expression of a particular thought into several parts.

And all this – the breaks, the new breaths – he is able to record and fix within his lines, and these clues lie there waiting for you to discover them, to understand them, and to use them. My wish is that you will look at all these wonderful words, spoken by Hamlet and Viola, Falstaff and Beatrice, King Lear and Lady Macbeth, and the hundred or so others that find their way into this book, and that you'll begin to hear their voices lifting off the page and speaking into your ear. Though finally you'll discover, it'll be you who are speaking for them.

This book begins by looking at Shakespeare's blank, or unrhymed verse; then moves on to his use of prose and rhymed verse. We'll look in some detail at all the 'irregularities' that are found in his verse lines; we'll also take time to consider how valuable his 'original punctuation' could be for us. Towards the end of our journey we will look in depth at *Macbeth* and *The Winter's Tale*, and use these plays to review and refine all we have learnt.

Occasionally I shall ask you to read a scene that I have not printed out in full, and so it would be a good idea for you to have a collected edition of Shakespeare's plays to hand.[2]

By the end of the book I want each of you to feel that you have found *your* way to approach these wonderful plays with confidence, so that they no longer seem mysterious, difficult or daunting, but that they become for you the most exciting and rewarding of plays to take part in. There are countless passages in this book for you to try out for yourselves, and I hope that whenever you can, you will say his lines out loud. Until they vibrate around you they will not live again, and begin to fulfil Shakespeare's purpose in writing them.

Giles Block
January 2013

One

Why Verse?

ORLANDO. Good day, and happiness, dear Rosalind.
JAQUES. Nay then God buy you, and you talk in blank
verse.

As You Like It: Act 4, Scene 1

Shakespeare's plays are written in blank verse, rhymed verse and prose. But the proportions of each of these in each of the plays are rarely even similar. A couple of plays have no prose at all, some others almost none; whereas a handful have more prose than verse. Some plays have virtually no rhymed verse, yet there are two plays in which nearly half of all the lines rhyme. But all of his plays have some blank verse in them, and most have more blank verse in them than anything else; so it's with blank, or unrhymed, verse that we must begin.

But why does he write in verse at all? Wouldn't his plays be more life-like, more real, if his characters spoke in prose?

To begin to answer this I want to look at a part of a very brief scene from Act 5, Scene 4 of *Julius Caesar*.

It's hard to be sure of any of the facts surrounding Shakespeare's life, though it seems likely that he was writing *Julius Caesar* in 1599, when he was 35 years old – in the same year that the Globe Theatre was erected on the south bank of the Thames.[1] But we can say some things about him with greater certainty. I believe, for example, that as he wrote Act 5, Scene 4 of

5

Julius Caesar, besides having his pen, ink and papers to hand, he also had a book open beside him, which he was glancing at from time to time. And I can say this with some confidence because it is clear that, not only was he reading this book, but he was also copying some of it straight into his scene. The book was a little background reading. It was Thomas North's Translation of Plutarch's *Life of Brutus*.

If we look at the way he was using this book – a book written in prose, as you might expect from the title – we'll begin to understand why Shakespeare writes in verse. So let's, as it were, look over his shoulder and watch him at work and hopefully begin to understand why he does what he does. And why this verse can be said to be 'more real' – more like our own normal speech patterns, than prose.

The situation in this short scene – it is only about thirty lines long – is that the war is going badly for Brutus's forces, and they are at the point of final defeat at the hands of Antony and Octavius. To give Brutus a chance of outwitting his foes, Lucilius, one of his friends and fellow soldiers, tells the enemy that he is Brutus and allows himself to be captured. The incident comes straight out of North's Plutarch. Here it is in North's words:

> Amongst them there was one of Brutus' friends called Lucilius, who seeing a troupe of barbarous men… going all together right against Brutus, he determined to stay them with the hazard of his life, and… told them he was Brutus… These barbarous men… sent some before unto Antonius to tell him of their coming… Lucilius was brought to him who stoutly with a bold countenance said 'Antonius, I dare assure thee, that no enemy have taken, nor shall take Marcus Brutus alive: and I beseech God keep him from that fortune. For wheresoever he be found, alive or dead, he will be found like himself.'

Now here is this same episode in Shakespeare's play:

SOLDIER. Yield, or thou diest.

LUCILIUS.   Only I yield to die:
There is so much, that thou wilt kill me straight:
Kill Brutus, and be honour'd in his death.[2]

SOLDIER. We must not: a noble prisoner.

Enter ANTONY.

2 SOLDIER. Room ho:* tell Antony, Brutus is tane.*

Room ho – make space
tane – taken

6

1 SOLDIER. I'll tell thee news. Here comes the general,
    Brutus is tane, Brutus is tane my lord.

ANTONY. Where is he?

LUCILIUS. Safe Antony, Brutus is safe enough:
    I dare assure thee, that no enemy
    Shall ever take alive the noble Brutus:
    The gods defend him from so great a shame,
    When you do find him, or alive, or dead,
    He will be found like Brutus, like himself.

Julius Caesar: Act 5, Scene 4

It is this last six-line speech of Lucilius's that I want to focus on.

Immediately you'll see the great similarities between Shakespeare's words and those of North's. In particular the second of Shakespeare's six lines follows North word for word,

    I dare assure thee, that no enemy

and the final line differs only in that Shakespeare adds the words 'like Brutus' to North's shorter phrase,

    he will be found like himself.

So it's pretty clear what Shakespeare is doing: he's rewriting North's prose into verse, but he doesn't need to change some of it because, coincidentally, it already fits into the verse pattern that Shakespeare wants. And this coincidence should alert us to the fact that this simple rhythm that Shakespeare is after, is all around us – all the time. It is not so special. It is not solely the language of poets. It is the way we all speak and write on occasions.

I pick up a newspaper (I was working in Virginia at the time) and within less than a minute I find this headline:

A BIT OF EDEN IN YOUR OWN BACKYARD.

The Washington Post, 28 January 2010

Shakespeare would have been absolutely happy with the rhythm of these ten syllables: it's basically the same rhythm as all the lines in the scene above. In fact it immediately reminds me of a line he actually wrote.

    This other Eden, demi paradise,

Richard II: Act 2, Scene 1

Say these two lines out loud, the one from the newspaper and the one from *Richard II*, and then the ten syllables that Shakespeare didn't need to change from North's prose:

> I dare assure thee, that no enemy

The simple rhythm that they all have in common is clear to see and hear. And only one of the three was actually *written* as 'verse'.

All these lines have ten syllables with the stresses gently falling on the alternating syllables – that is on the second, fourth, sixth, eight and tenth syllables. And as you may well know, this particular rhythm of un-stress/stress is called '*iambic*'.

With all the other lines from North, Shakespeare has reshaped North's words (with one exception) to make them fall into this same *iambic* pattern.[3] He has also, at the same time, made some of the phrases seem more direct and colloquial. But it is the rhythm that is his main concern.

Why is Shakespeare after this particular rhythm? Well, it's useful to him in many ways.

Perhaps the first thing we should say about this rhythm is that it sounds quite natural – quite speech-like. But the rhythm also seems to be toppling us forward through to the end of the line. This gives the line a feeling of movement and urgency. The *iambic* rhythm has therefore something persuasive about it. It's a rhythm that captures the sound of a voice that has something urgent or important to say. And in plays, having something important to say is almost always the case.

Of course this rhythm is also like the beating of our own hearts. So the very lines, with these heartbeats threaded through them, sound alive and vibrant. When we hear someone speaking in this rhythm, subliminally we are reminded of our common humanity. The lines sound human.

So, as actors, how does this work to our advantage in practice?

Well, it certainly won't work to our advantage if we sound it out in any obvious or heavy-handed way. It would simply be a turn-off for our audiences. All must sound natural, and every moment should sound new.

I like to call it our 'secret rhythm', not one which the audience is really conscious of, but one which, beating in time with the audience's own hearts, subliminally creates a sympathetic bond between audience and actor. We listen to the characters sympathetically because the rhythm of their words sounds familiar, purposeful and heart-felt. When someone speaks in this way, we hear the emotion that lies under whatever thought is being expressed.

If we want to describe our own heartbeat, we would probably say it was regular, consistent, reliable. Of course it can run faster and slower as it responds to different situations, but this doesn't take away from its reliability. Our heartbeat is dependable. So another message that is carried subliminally to the audience by the *iambic* rhythm is a sense of dependability. We listen to such a speaker and we feel that they mean what they say.

Shakespeare's blank verse is 'the sound of sincerity'.

It is also a careful and considered way of speaking. The iambic rhythm is easy to listen to; the stressed syllables are evenly spaced. We listen to someone speaking in this rhythm, and even if we can't hear the actual words they are using, the sound of the rhythm will convey to us an emotional need. With Shakespeare's words added, it has the power to move us; those speaking it sound sincere, as if they are expressing things that are dear to them. All the more terrible then are those characters, like Iago in *Othello*, whose lines of verse sound so sincere, yet whose intentions are anything but.

The satirist, Joseph Hall, describing an actor performing Marlowe's Tamburlaine, writes:[4]

> He vaunts his voice upon a hired stage,
> With high-set steps and princely carriage;
> Now swooping inside robes of royalty,
> That erst* did scrub in lousy brokery.*
> There if he can with terms Italianate,
> Big-sounding sentences and words of state,
> Fair patch me up his pure *iambic verse*,
> He *ravishes* the gazing scaffolders:*   (*My italics.*)

The authorities of law and order in sixteenth-century England were clearly aware of the power of this rhythmic language to move audiences, and they were worried by it. Just as in more recent times others have feared the power of popular music. And audiences are still being *ravished* by Shakespeare's verse today.

Let's look at those six lines of Lucilius's in more detail to see if what I've been saying makes good sense. Here they are again:

erst – formerly
brokery – dealing in second-hand goods
scaffolders – those sitting in the galleries of the theatres

LUCILIUS. Safe Antony, Brutus is safe enough:
    I dare assure thee, that no enemy
    Shall ever take alive the noble Brutus:
    The gods defend him from so great a shame,
    When you do find him, or alive, or dead,
    He will be found like Brutus, like himself.

(As I've said in the introduction to this book, always say these lines out loud if you can.)

I hope you will feel the courage and integrity of the man shining out of these lines. He has a confidence about what he wants to say. He speaks with clarity and intent. It is not a major moment in the play, but for this minor character, Lucilius, it is *his* moment and Shakespeare gives it to him. For these six lines the play is his.

My point has been so far that it is the rhythm that has given a special power to these words. Rhythm points to stress. The use of stress in speech is vital. Without it, it is hard to understand what someone is saying. But stress also reveals our *commitment* to what we are saying; it reveals those things that are important to *us*. Someone speaking without any stress at all is close to despair.

Let's look at the stress/rhythm of that third line.

Shall ever take alive the noble Brutus:

And don't worry too much about how to say it. Mostly just look at the words and say them as you'd instinctively want to say them. But it can be a useful exercise to ask yourself where the five stressed syllables fall. And then it's up to you to decide which of those words in the stressed positions will most persuade those listening to you of the rightness of your argument. Because we speak in order to persuade; we speak to change the minds of others.

Because this line is *iambic* the first stress is on the 'ev' of 'ever'. 'Ever' is an 'extreme' word. It admits of no other possibility. Lucilius is saying that it is just *not possible* that Brutus will allow the enemy to capture him alive. The next couple of stresses – on 'take' and on the '*live*' part of 'alive' – complete the phrase, though these probably need no more special stress than that they are said with clarity.

Usually, but not always, the last stress in the line, and when the thought carries on, the first stress in the line that follows, are of particular importance. And we don't want to stress anything needlessly. Too much stressing just confuses our listeners. Also take care that my use of the word 'stress' doesn't encourage you to be too heavy-handed. Stress lightly and that will normally still be sufficient to release the power your words contain.

This line ends with the words 'the noble Brutus'. 'Noble' is a word that Shakespeare has added – it is not in North – and it lets us feel how much Lucilius honours and admires Brutus. The name 'Brutus' ends the line, and because the word 'Brutus' is naturally stressed on the first syllable, the '*us*' at the end of his name means that the line has an extra un-stressed eleventh syllable. Such a line, and there are many of them in Shakespeare, is a common variation and is called a 'weak' or 'feminine' ending. But I'm sure none of this caused you any problems when you said the line out loud.

The next line but one is somewhat similar to North's, but like the previous line has been rewritten.

When you do find him, or alive, or dead,

whereas North has:

For wheresoever he be found, alive or dead,

North's words here fall into another 'coincidental' iambic pattern, so here Shakespeare changes North's words for a couple of different reasons.

The first is that North's iambic line is twelve syllables long, and for reasons that we'll go into in a moment, Shakespeare doesn't want a line of that length suddenly introduced in the middle of this speech.

But more importantly, I think, Shakespeare wants something simpler and more direct than that 'for wheresoever he be found' and so he writes 'When you do find him'; but then in order to maintain the new iambic pattern he is creating, Shakespeare has to add another syllable to 'alive or dead' and so it becomes '*or* alive or dead'.

Shakespeare frequently adds words like this to maintain the iambic rhythm and the emotional power that comes with it. But here the added '*or*' brings something else into play.

For Lucilius just to have said, 'When you do find him alive or dead', somehow sounds less caring. By saying '*or* alive or dead' we feel that Lucilius is keenly imagining both possibilities and both touch him. I suppose if Brutus were still to be alive when his enemies catch up with him, Lucilius is anticipating that Brutus would then kill himself in front of them.

And all this strength of feeling comes from this simply stressed line that echoes the movement of our own hearts and beats at a similar pace.

If we finally compare the effect of North's account and Shakespeare's six-line speech on an audience, by reading them both out loud, what would our conclusion be?

'Antonius, I dare assure thee, that no enemy have taken, nor shall take Marcus Brutus alive: and I beseech God keep him from that fortune. For wheresoever he be found, alive or dead, he will be found like himself.'

LUCILIUS. Safe Antony, Brutus is safe enough:
    I dare assure thee, that no enemy
    Shall ever take alive the noble Brutus:
    The gods defend him from so great a shame,
    When you do find him, or alive, or dead,
    He will be found like Brutus, like himself.

I know it's unfair to compare these two. North is not pretending to write words for an actor to say. Also he is translating from Plutarch and may not have felt he should strike out on his own too much. But nevertheless I find the effect of the two speeches interestingly different.

North's Lucilius is more reserved: his words sound more like an official report made by one soldier to another; whereas I feel that Shakespeare in writing this scene has been moved by what Lucilius is doing: he sees this moment of human daring and defiance, and he captures the emotional sound of the moment in and *by* his verse. Unlike North's 'report', Shakespeare's Lucilius sounds emotional and his love for Brutus shines through everything he says.

And yet Shakespeare has used most of the same words as North.

He does use Brutus's name three times as opposed to only once by North and that ups the emotional pull of the speech. Also in that last line, where Shakespeare has added the words 'like Brutus,' he gives Lucilius's final statement a fuller sense of completion – as if he has used every ounce of his breath to accompany his final utterance.

Also that word 'ever' in the third line –

    Shall *ever* take

– is worth remembering. It is so much more telling and direct than North's pedantic 'have taken, nor shall take'.

As I said before, 'ever' is the first stressed word in that line, and it is an 'extreme' word. Shakespeare's plays are full of them – 'never' and 'ever'; 'all' and 'none'. They are one of the reasons that his plays have such an impact on us. In big ways but also in small ways he takes us and his characters into extreme positions, and we should respond to the strength of these little words as we utter them.

So comparing the two, Shakespeare's words are more telling and pull more emotional strings, but ultimately we identify more with Shakespeare's characters, not because he has changed some words, but because of the secret power of the verse.

This is quite a minor moment in a deeply emotional play, and yet the incident comes alive. The pulse of the line gathers the syllables together and fills the utterance with a need, which is the same need that the speaker has – to be listened to and understood.

One result is that Antony himself seems moved by what his enemy, Lucilius, has said.

> ANTONY.   keep this man safe,
> Give him all kindness. I had rather have
> Such men my friends, than enemies.

Julius Caesar: Act 5, Scene 4

The most extraordinary thing about all this is that we might have thought at the beginning of this chapter that verse has to be a more artificial way of speaking and more removed from life than prose. After all, verse is often described as a 'heightened language', but I find that an unhelpful way to describe it.

Verse captures a certain way of speaking that we find familiar when we hear it.

Our own everyday speech is more patterned and less plain than we think it is. Also when we hear verse spoken on stage we shouldn't hear 'poetry', rather we should hear someone speaking with commitment and feeling.[5] Rather than calling verse 'a heightened language', I prefer to say that it is 'a language appropriate for a heightened situation'. That's much easier to deal with. Not nearly so scary!

Dramatic verse in Shakespeare captures both the thought, and the feel-ings that the speaker of that thought has, at one and the same time.

Verse is the emotional expression of thought.

There is still much more to be said, but don't worry for now: we will be returning to all these issues many times. We do, however, need to address one more factor here.

So far, in talking about blank verse, we have mainly been concerned with the rhythm of the line. We noticed in passing that one of North's phrases was longer that the lines that Shakespeare was writing for Lucilius, but we have not stopped to consider why Shakespeare's lines are the length they are.

We will come across lines in Shakespeare that are shorter and occa-sionally those that are longer, but most of them, like the ones we have been looking at, are what are called *pentameters*, which means five pairs of syllables. Or, in other words, a line consisting of ten, or if it has a feminine ending, eleven syllables in length.

But why this length? The short answer is that lines of this length sound more like speech; more like the way we all speak.

And the way we speak is dependent on the way we breathe.

If we continue talking for any length of time we have to breathe. Breathing every ten or eleven syllables is probably the norm. Of course we can speak for longer on one breath; we can take an especially deep breath and say a few more words because of it, but usually, especially when we are speaking spontaneously, we don't.

Sometimes Shakespeare does write a longer line. In *Measure for Measure*, written a few years after *Julius Caesar*, there is a moment when the heroine, Isabella, driven to distraction, has a slightly longer line than usual. She is confronting Angelo, who has condemned her brother, Claudio, to death for sleeping with his fiancée before they are married. Yet Angelo has suggested to Isabella, who is about to become a nun, that he will pardon her brother if she agrees to sleep with him. Isabella, outraged, immediately feels she has the advantage over Angelo and she says:

> ISABELLA. Sign me a present pardon for my brother,
> Or with an out-stretch'd throat I'll tell the world aloud
> What man thou art.

Measure for Measure: Act 2, Scene 4

The middle line is long. It has twelve syllables in it and you can feel the effort behind Isabella's utterance of it. If you took out the word 'aloud' at the end of the line, it would be a line of normal length, but Isabella doesn't only want to let the whole world know of Angelo's depravity, she wants to shout it from the rooftops. And so the line seems to call for an 'outstretch'd throat' in order to say it all, and needs a deeper than normal breath in order to achieve this.

So Shakespeare's verse is based on two things: a line length that corresponds with our breathing, and an underlying rhythm that corresponds with our heartbeat. So although the idea of a play in verse might at first have seemed somewhat intimidating, it is simply a mimicking of those two vital forces that are keeping us alive – our pulse and our breath.

But the effects of this are far reaching.

We could say that the 'form' of the verse, the actual shape it makes on the page, is like a frame on to which Shakespeare will find, as his writing develops, that he can place all the many ways in which we speak and express ourselves, from the simplest utterance to the most knotty and complex, because this frame is based on *us*. We should look at these pages of verse and 'see' our breath and our pulse running through each line of it.

It is now time to move on and look at how we can approach this verse in more practical ways.

Two

Thoughts and Thought-units

Love's heralds should be thoughts,
Which ten times faster glides than the sun's beams,
Driving back shadows over low'ring hills.
Romeo and Juliet: Act 2, Scene 4

Before we speak, we have a thought. We can 'see' someone having a thought; we see them take a breath. They take the breath so as to express the thought, though in practice our thoughts come so thick and fast that many of them never make it into words.

Juliet, in the lines quoted above, is saying that thoughts are the speediest things she knows of, faster than the way the shadows of clouds race over a hillside when the sun comes out. And she's wishing that her nurse could bring her news from Romeo just as swiftly.

The purpose of the previous chapter was to persuade you that the verse is speech-like and that its rhythmic charge supports the emotion you'll need to find in order to act convincingly.

That is what acting is all about. Do we believe that you mean what you say? Do we believe that what you are saying is important to you? Do we believe that these are your words?

But now let's consider what it means to us as actors, that before the words there has to have been a thought.

It's worth remembering the obvious. We speak in order to bring about a change. Silence frequently implies agreement. Speaking is an action; it is designed to have an effect. Of course we can speak idly sometimes;

though idle talk may well point to something that is not being said, something that is being kept hidden, a thought that has been censored, with the result that now something else, something idle, has taken its place to camouflage whatever is missing.

This happens in plays, as in life, but more often than not in Shakespeare we are speaking in order to convince other characters that our point of view is the correct one; that it is important to our character that what we say is accepted. In a good play if, say, you have five characters on stage, there will be five different views being expressed. Drama is the clash of opinions held by different characters all doing what they can to promote their own cause. In plays it is usually the one who has the best words who comes out on top.

Shakespeare has given us the words we need to say, so we don't have to make them up for ourselves when we act. However, in order to be 'convincing', we must understand what we are saying, so an excellent first step is to take the 'thought' that Shakespeare has given us and to put it into our own words: to paraphrase it.

Paraphrasing

I have directed three of Shakespeare's plays at the Blackfriars Theatre in Staunton, Virginia.[1] Exceptionally, at that theatre, before the director arrives, the actors have already learnt their lines and they have also paraphrased them. And during the first few rehearsals everyone reads out their paraphrased lines, which enables all the actors to check that they have correctly understood the thoughts that each of the other characters in the scene is expressing. It's also an excellent way for the director to check that each actor knows what they are saying too!

It is too easy to be seduced by how wonderful Shakespeare sounds and not pay enough attention to what is actually being said. (It's that rhythm that seduces us!) It is too easy for one actor to be listening to another on stage and not really know what is being said to *them*. And if *you* don't know what you are actually saying, then what chance has the audience? We must never allow audiences to think that they come to Shakespeare merely to bathe in the sound of all these wonderful words, because if so they'll probably only understand a fraction of what they hear.

The act of paraphrasing can be tough, for sometimes there are many possible meanings behind the words. Which is the correct one? Or are they all correct? Or is one meaning for one person to hear and another for another to understand? But the best thing about paraphrasing is that it gets you *thinking* the thoughts for yourself. It puts you in the same place as Shakespeare was when he was thinking about a particular part of the story, but before he had put pen to paper and given expression to those thoughts in words. Because as an actor you should feel the thought arising in you as you begin to speak.

We, in the audience, hear your words, but we should also *see* you thinking.

I am reminded of what Claudius, the king, says in *Hamlet* when he is trying to pray:

> My words fly up, my thoughts remain below,
> Words without thoughts, never to heaven go.
>
> Act 3, Scene 3

Here's a man who doesn't believe in his own performance! To act convincingly we have to subscribe to the thoughts behind our words. So how can we help ourselves to do that?

Thought-units

Let us go back to the passage that we must almost know by heart now – those lines of Lucilius's from *Julius Caesar* – and now let's consider whether these six lines contain more than one thought.

> LUCILIUS. Safe Antony, Brutus is safe enough:
> I dare assure thee, that no enemy
> Shall ever take alive the noble Brutus:
> The gods defend him from so great a shame,
> When you do find him, or alive, or dead,
> He will be found like Brutus, like himself.

Clearly these six lines are a unit, and by the last line Lucilius has delivered himself of all he wants to say. But because he is speaking 'spontaneously', or 'in the moment', he doesn't know what words are going to come out of his mouth until he actually says them. This is the same for all of us almost all the time, but it doesn't follow that we speak *hesitantly* because of it.

Antony, coming onto the stage, has asked his soldiers 'Where is he?' meaning 'where is Brutus?' because he looks around and doesn't see him. Then, probably after a pause, Lucilius replies, 'Safe Antony'.[2]

Now it could be that that is all he feels he needs to say; but it's such a surprising moment for those that hear it and such a triumphant moment for Lucilius that we understand why he'd want to allow his moment of glory to last a bit longer. And so to ram home what he's just said to all the open mouths around him, Lucilius says the same thing again, but in a slightly different way.

> Safe Antony, Brutus is safe enough.

I would call this line a 'thought-unit'.

And I'm now going to suggest that we divide up the other five lines into 'thought-units' as well. This is not an exact science, and there's no absolute right and wrong about it, but it's a useful exercise. My thought-units would run like this:

> LUCILIUS. Safe Antony, Brutus is safe enough:
>
> I dare assure thee, that no enemy
> Shall ever take alive the noble Brutus:
>
> The gods defend him from so great a shame,
>
> When you do find him, or alive, or dead,
> He will be found like Brutus, like himself.

Now this is simple and rather obvious I know. But that's good. We've now divided this six-line speech into four 'thought-units'. What we achieve immediately by doing this is some *variety*. And *variety* is the stuff of life and therefore should be the stuff of our acting too.

Here the variety we have achieved is that in place of a 'six-line speech' we now have four thoughts: two thoughts of one line each and two thoughts which are each two lines long.

This doesn't mean that Lucilius is now encouraged to hesitate three times in these six lines. Remember Juliet and her take on the speed of thoughts. It's just that we have *differentiated* these four thoughts from each other so that we can begin to think about *how* they differ.

In life or in a play every moment is different. One of Shakespeare's greatest instincts is to keep every moment alive by continual variation. Even a single line can change its 'colour and feel' as it moves through those ten brief syllables. Within a scene or an act his dramas can move from comedy to tragedy, from romance to farce in the twinkling of an eye. Seek out variety. Never be content to give a speech a single emotional wash. Think rather of speeches as being composed like a mosaic, of many different impulses that come together to form a whole picture. This is what is happening here. Look at that fourth line:

> The gods defend him from so great a shame.

Who is that spoken to? Maybe it's directly to the gods. If so the actor might raise his eyes away from Antony, to that upper part of the theatre we sometimes now call 'the gods', and say the line as a quick, heartfelt prayer; or he might say the line more to himself; or to the whole audience. Whatever he chooses to do, this line will have popped out of the other six as if it's something unplanned and spontaneous.

Let's call this a 'pop-up thought'. Now we have identified one, you will find them everywhere and finding them will make the delivery of your speeches more true to life, more varied, more filled with the unexpected.

By saying that the thought-units don't suggest hesitation might be slightly, but only slightly, misleading. What Lucilius has here is the *time* to express these four thoughts fully because of the impact that his first statement has created. He has fooled all the other characters on stage. No, he is not hesitant, but nor is he rushed. He's created his space in which to have his say, and his four thought-units, all coloured slightly differently, together form a larger unit that is now filled with more movement and vitality.

You should now sound it again and see if you can feel this happening to you.

You remember we were saying that there is something about the rhythm of the line, the iambic rhythm, that seems to propel us forward. It's like the gallop of a horse. Glynn McDonald, who is a Globe Associate and the movement guru at Shakespeare's Globe Theatre, always gives the companies and the students she is working with an exercise, which is to gallop across the stage as if on horseback. She does this to get this rhythm in their blood and in their brains and for them to feel the surging power of it.

The rhythm bears us to the end of the line. Of course we can break the line, sometimes we may feel we need to; but if we listen to people speaking, especially when they are saying things that are important to them, their utterances are not normally full of gaps.

When we have something that we want to say we have this desire, not to rush it, for that would undervalue it, but to finish the thought. It is only once the thought has been expressed that others might then act upon it. And our speeches, which are 'actions', are therefore designed to produce 'reactions'.

In these plays there is always a 'clock on the scene'. The plot demands that we solve the problem *soon*, that we get sorted what needs sorting *soon*.

So as actors we need to be energised sufficiently to convince our audiences that we are trying to achieve whatever it is we need to achieve as efficiently and as deftly and as *soon* as we can. The toppling forward rhythm of the galloping line encourages us in this; our thought-units work for us in a similar way.

We have identified two of Lucilius's single lines as a couple of thought-units. So with these, with thought and line running together, it's easy to feel that need to get not only to the end of the line, but also to the end of the thought, because they are one and the same place.

> Safe Antony, Brutus is safe enough:
>
> The gods defend him from so great a shame,

The other two thoughts in this speech are each two lines long, but again, once the actor/character feels these thoughts coming into consciousness, he, or she, will have a similar desire to complete this longer thought as well:

> When you do find him, or alive, or dead,
> He will be found like Brutus, like himself.

The 'shape' of this thought is therefore two lines long. As you say it, we will 'hear' its shape. It will have a beginning, a middle and an end. A two-line thought takes a fraction less time to say than two single-line thoughts would, because you will have 'packaged' the thought differently. The 'packaging' has come about because of your desire to get to the end of the thought. The same would be true for a seven-line thought-unit. It would just be a longer shape and a bigger package. Now it is this 'shaping' of a thought that helps to make it comprehensible to others.

Shaping the thought

When we listen to a good speaker we follow their thoughts because of the way they shape them. They tell us by the tone they use that here we have a new thought beginning; here, the thought is being developed; and here the thought is being concluded.

Now you could say this two-line thought-unit all on one breath; it would be possible. But I believe it would undervalue the thought. Why?

The short answer would be because if Lucilius said these two lines on one breath he would sound less caring. To convey to others how *much* we care we have to look after our words with care. We also have to have enough breath to be able to colour those words, most important to our argument, effectively.

When we are speaking ourselves, we are unaware of how much we use our breathing to *shape* the way we phrase the expression of any thought; all we are focusing on is getting our thought across. Our breathing looks after itself. Similarly, when others are speaking, all our attention is on following what they are saying, rather than *how* they are saying it, whether and when they are breathing, and so on.

The line length has this correspondence with the breath. To put it really simply, if we take this line of Lucilius's,

> The gods defend him from so great a shame,

we can all say that easily on one breath, and once any one of us had said it we would all do the same thing: we would all take another breath in order to go on speaking some more.

If however you tried to do the next *two* lines on one breath,

> When you do find him, or alive, or dead,
> He will be found like Brutus, like himself.

– well, it would be possible, but you would probably feel that you were getting a little short of breath by the end of the second line, in a way that doesn't really happen to you in everyday life. But more importantly it would have sounded as if you were a little less emotionally involved. The lines and the thoughts within them would have sounded less caring. It would also have sounded less spontaneous, as if you knew what words you were going to say before you spoke them.

Now try it like this: I've added a little symbol before the second of these lines to indicate that you might try topping up your breath there.

> When you do find him, or alive, or dead,
> ˇ He will be found like Brutus, like himself.

Now this breath is in no way special. It's not something you do because you are on stage and no one, not the audience or your fellow actors, should even notice what you've done. In the end you shouldn't even be aware of it yourself. But you do it so that, when you come to say that second line, the words in it sound as if you are creating them, choosing them, *as* you are speaking. These words are expressing Lucilius's love for Brutus, and to convey that love we need to give colour and emotional strength to his key words. And this needs the right amount of breath. But we need no more breath than that which is natural to the situation. We breathe in order to speak, and we breathe again in order to go on speaking, and Shakespeare's lines show us where to do that.

Now I know you can't act and be thinking where to breathe at the same time. So what you must do is to let the 'form' of the verse – that is, where one line ends and another begins – help you to *shape* how you express your thoughts and then your breathing should take care of itself. Learning where to breathe is therefore part of your *rehearsal* process – by the time you come to performance, taking a 'top-up' breath in order to say the new line should have become instinctive.

Line endings

In verse the part of the line that generally has most 'prominence' is at the end of it.

And this is probably because in learning to speak we have come to realise that, before we take a 'top-up' breath in order to go on speaking, it's best to leave our listeners with something that grabs their attention.

So we should now see that where a line is reaching to, where the line ends, where we have been carried to, will be a little climax, or a surprise, or a turning point. Look at the ends of our six lines:

> 'safe enough'
> 'no enemy'
> 'noble Brutus'
> 'great a shame'
> 'alive, or dead'
> 'like himself'

These phrases reveal the whole point of the line. This is absolutely the case when the line is a single thought. Where the thought continues on into the next line, then the phrases at the end mark a crucial stage in the shaping of that thought.

It is also one of the patterns of our English speech. 'I want you to come home <u>now</u>.' 'Let's meet on <u>Thursday</u>.' 'I never want to see you <u>again</u>.' Or, 'I never want to see you again, <u>ever</u>.'

Now in my list of six line endings I could have just given you the last stressed word, (shame; dead; self), but I think it's more valuable to think in terms of phrases rather than single words.

It is because of the importance of the line ending, that the second half of lines have more 'juice' in them than the first. Often inexperienced actors give the beginning of the line too much emphasis and let the second half tail away.

Always ask yourself why the line ends where it does. There will always be a reason. It will be to do with emphasis, or some antithesis, or in Shakespeare's later plays, some highlighting of something that is to *follow* in the line to come.

Shakespeare's line endings are never arbitrary.

When the thought is longer than a single line, the line endings are clearly not the conclusion of a thought, but they always mark an important stage in the development of that thought.

> I dare assure thee, that no enemy
> Shall ever take alive the noble Brutus:

The heart of what is being said here is that no wretched *enemy* will ever defeat *Brutus*.

In order to make that comparison clear, Lucilius puts those two words in as prominent a place as possible so that we savour the difference between them. The 'pattern' of speech here would be similar to saying something like, 'I don't know if you've thought about this <u>at all</u>, because it sounds as if you've just <u>made it up.</u>'

Because verse carries with it this inbuilt rhythm (*iambic*) and this other longer rhythm of line upon line (*pentameter*), Shakespeare can use the 'form' of the verse to 'capture' the *particular* sound of his characters' voices. Just suppose he had written these lines like this instead:

> I dare assure thee that
> No enemy shall ever take alive
> The noble Brutus:

(If you haven't already said these words out loud, do so now, and see if you can detect how the meaning behind the words has changed with the altered line endings.)

Here the force of the thought mainly falls on the word 'alive': the comparison he was making between 'Brutus' and the 'enemy' is now not so strong or noticeable. But the words are the same, and the lines still maintain the iambic beat. So why hasn't Shakespeare written them like this? Because stressing 'alive' is not the point he wants Lucilius to make here. Or maybe, as I'd prefer to say, not the point Lucilius wants to make.

Thus Shakespeare is able to bring out the precise meaning his characters are aiming at, by what he chooses to put at the end of the line.

Shakespeare's verse 'captures' the sounds of these voices as he first heard them.

Carrying the thought from line to line

Thoughts always bring two things together. Simple thoughts like

> The gods defend him from so great a shame,

can be accommodated in a single line. Anything more complex needs greater space.

> I dare assure thee, that no enemy
> Shall ever take alive the noble Brutus:

The nub of the thought here is that 'no enemy' (the first part of the thought) shall 'ever' overcome 'Brutus' (the conclusion of the thought). Both halves need to be expressed with clarity and it is to achieve this that Shakespeare places them on separate lines, as he will do with countless other lines that we have yet to encounter.

But there is something else: when the thought travels through one line into the next, not only do the ends of the lines ('enemy', 'Brutus') need stressing – thus making the comparison between the two obvious to all – but so does the *first* stress in the second line. Because, it is almost a general characteristic of speech, that when something is powerfully stressed – and yet is not the end of the thought – this will be followed by something else of particular weight. And in this instance the first stress in that second line is this magical, little, yet so powerful word, 'ever'.

Whenever the thought continues from one line into the next, be on the lookout for this double emphasis – on the last stress of the first line and the first stress of the next line. Rhythmically it can be exciting and fun to perform, while at the same time you'll find it uncannily mimics the rhythms of natural speech. Now try the following two examples out loud for yourself.

> I dare assure thee, that no enemy
> Shall *ever* take alive the noble Brutus:

The first stress in the subsequent line can be very telling and, if you use it well, can release a strong emotional charge. If we run the two lines into one, we will have undervalued the thought.

> When you do find him, or alive, or dead,
> He *will* be found like Brutus, like himself.

The word 'will' is not so obviously an 'extreme' word, as that 'ever' in the earlier line, so you might not have seen what effect it could have here. But Lucilius's 'will' is another expression of certainty and can be used, with care and discretion, to good effect.

We will talk much more about speaking and breathing as this book develops, partly because Shakespeare's verse form undergoes such dramatic developments itself, and we'll need to consider why, and what the implications of this are. But I hope by now it's become clear that there is a vital correlation between the line of verse and a breath; that it's possible to say any line with a single breath; and that to try to say more lines with one breath would be to strip that thought of some of its emotional force.

One way to make this entirely natural process of line and breath seem even more natural to you is to make sure that the last word in the line gets its due stress. *Because by emphasising it, you use up more breath.* If you do that and then feel you are choosing and using the first stress in the new line, you will find that topping up your breath before the second line is the most natural thing to do.

Here are those two lines again with the key words in bold plus the suggested 'breath mark'.

> When you do find him, or alive, or **dead**,
> ˇ He **will** be found like Brutus, like him**self**.

So now we are ready to tackle some longer passages of Shakespeare's early verse.

Thought-units in longer speeches

Here is a speech rather longer than six lines. It comes from one of Shakespeare's earliest plays, *Henry VI, Part Two*. It's Act 3, Scene 1, and in it Queen Margaret is trying to rouse her husband, King Henry, and the English court against the Duke of Gloucester. As I'll be suggesting, with all speeches whatever their length, the first thing to do once you've read it through, is to divide it up into 'thought-units'.

Below are mine. Basically, but not entirely, I have divided the speech up at the major marks of punctuation. We might all make different choices, but the point is to try to separate the thoughts out; to discover where a new phase of the speech arises. One result of this exercise is that the speech immediately starts to look more manageable.

The scene begins with a three-line speech from the King which Margaret then responds to. And I hope whether you are male or female you will all sound out all of the speeches that you'll come across from now on.

HENRY. I muse my lord of Gloucester is not come:

> 'Tis not his wont to be the hindmost man,
> What e'er occasion keeps him from us now.

MARGARET. Can you not see? or will ye not observe

> The strangeness of his alter'd countenance?
> With what a majesty he bears himself,
> How insolent of late he is become,
> How proud, how peremptory, and unlike himself.
>
> We know the time since he was mild and affable,
> And if we did but glance a far-off look,
> Immediately he was upon his knee,
> That all the court admir'd him for submission.
>
> But meet him now, and be it in the morn,
> When every one will give the time of day,
> He knits his brow, and shows an angry eye,
> And passeth by with stiff unbowed knee,
> Disdaining duty that to us belongs.
>
> Small curs are not regarded when they grin,
> But great men tremble when the lion roars,
> And Humphrey is no little man in England.
>
> First note, that he is near you in descent,
> And should you fall, he is the next will mount.
> Me seemeth then, it is no policy,
> Respecting what a rancorous mind he bears,
> And his advantage following your decease,
> That he should come about your royal person,
> Or be admitted to your highness' council.
>
> By flattery hath he won the commons' hearts:
> And when he please to make commotion,
> 'Tis to be fear'd they all will follow him.
>
> Now 'tis the spring, and weeds are shallow-rooted,
> Suffer them now, and they'll o'er-grow the garden,
> And choke the herbs for want of husbandry.

The reverent care I bear unto my lord,
Made me collect these dangers in the duke.
If it be fond, call it a woman's fear:
Which fear, if better reasons can supplant,
I will subscribe, and say I wrong'd the duke.

My Lord of Suffolk, Buckingham, and York,
Reprove my allegation, if you can,
 Or else conclude my words effectual.

Henry VI, Part Two: Act 3, Scene 1

The thought-units have given us variety. Instead of a speech of almost forty lines, we now have nine connected thoughts of different line lengths (5,4,5,3,7,3,3,5,3). We will now need to find a different colour for each of these units and to enjoy airing these differently coloured thoughts for different lengths of time.

See if you can find a way to describe, or a mood to give to each of these 'thought-units'.[3]

It is an exercise worth doing with all Shakespeare's speeches, but with these early plays it has a special virtue. The later plays, as we shall discover, are written in a more fragmented way, the verse is more obviously like a mosaic of thoughts that curl back on themselves, of self-interruptions and interruptions by others. By contrast the early dramas are noted for long, uninterrupted speeches, so making a conscious effort to find satisfying thought breaks will begin to tame and humanise them. We always want to find all the variety we can.

I think it's now time for you to sound Margaret's speech out with the thought-units I have suggested, or with others that seemed more suitable to you. And if you can, remember that the lines are like a breath and that each new line needs and deserves a breath that has been 'topped up' afresh.

Try the speech out now.

I trust your thought-units were interestingly varied, and I also hope you were able to observe the importance of the line endings and felt the strength throughout of that persuasive iambic rhythm.

I also hope in saying these lines out loud that you remembered to keep breathing as you spoke them and found that delightful 'release' you can give to each new line by topping up your breath before speaking it. If you're not sure whether that happened or not, go back over it again with that in mind. However, always remember that what we are trying to achieve is a naturalness of delivery (and a natural way of breathing too), even if what we are saying is grand and dramatic.

End stopping

Why do characters like Margaret sometimes speak at such length?

Partly it is to avoid anyone else taking over before they feel that their argument has won the day; they want to keep control and like a filibuster to wear the others down. Sometimes people speak at length to keep a feeling alive. Lovers at parting will do this, as will Queen Margaret herself in the very next scene when she is forced to part with her lover, who as it happens, is not her husband the King, but the Duke of Suffolk.

The speech you have just sounded out will sometimes be described as 'end-stopped', because all the heavy punctuation marks come at the ends of the lines. It is usually a sign that the play was written early in Shakespeare's career. And so these early plays have a special sound to them which comes from the form in which they are written.

To be able to speak as Margaret does here is quite an achievement. We see her filling line after line with a new thought, or if not a whole thought, certainly with a well turned grammatical phrase. It's a tribute to her eloquence and command of language. But it also shows that she is confident and sure of her opinions. It is something that all the characters in these early plays have in common with each other.

End-stopped verse is 'the sound of confidence'.

But Shakespeare still manages to find variety within these long end-stopped speeches. One way he achieves this is by finding natural ways to vary the rhythm of his lines. Not all lines are simply *iambic*. Sometimes a beat in the line will be *trochaic* – which is the exact opposite of the *iambic* rhythm.

Trochees

If the first syllable in the line is stressed then the line has what we call a *trochaic* first *foot. Foot* simply means a pair of syllables, and a *trochee* is the opposite of an *iamb*. So a word like 'begin' is an *iamb*, whereas the word 'finish' is a *trochee* because 'finish' is stressed on the first of its two syllables and 'begin' is stressed on the second.

In Margaret's speech above I've found four examples of a *trochaic* first *foot* and a couple of these happen in the two lines I've printed out again here:

> Now 'tis the spring, and weeds are shallow-rooted,
> Suffer them now, and they'll o'ergrow the garden,

Say these lines just as you'd instinctively want to say them and you'll probably stress the first syllables of both lines. Then you'll no doubt have stressed the fourth syllables in each of these lines too, so the two phrases have a similar rhythm to each other. '**Now** 'tis the **spring**' and then '**Suffer** them **now**'. We also have here a rather catchy repeat of the word 'now', plus the fact that 'spring' and 'suffer' both begin with an *s*, which go to make the phrases sound even catchier. Part of what makes for a successfully persuasive speech is to speak somehow *memorably*. I think this pair of phrases could be said to fall into this category.

The rhythm in these two lines presents a common Shakespearian variation: a *trochee* followed by an *iamb*.

Now we mustn't worry about these fancy words or for that matter that, for a moment, we have lost that powerful emotional iambic rhythm that we have talked so much about. Shakespeare will always revert to the iambic: it is his default setting. But in this long speech of Margaret's these few trochees bring variety.

The trochee injects a moment of surprise into her speech because the stress comes before we are expecting it; the trochee is assertive and makes us 'sit up and listen'; which is just what Queen Margaret wants her audience, both on stage and in the theatre, to do. These trochees also come in a 'thought-unit' that I felt sounded a bit 'teacher-like'; maybe it was the trochees that made me think so.

I had a maths teacher who liked to say as he pointed out sums on the blackboard,

> **Just** watch the **board** while I run **through** it.

His name was Mr Lax and he repeated this phrase often. The phrase is actually just one syllable short of a pentameter; if he had added the word 'now' to the end of it, it would have made up a verse line identical in rhythm to thousands of Shakespeare's.

Mr Lax didn't give us a pentameter, but what he gave us eight-year-olds, apart from a laugh each time he said it, was a *trochee*, to make us sit up and listen, followed by three iambs plus an extra unstressed syllable.[4]

A further rhythmic variation

A minor point, which it would be good to notice now, is that there are occasions when the last stress in the line is not the most important word in the line. It's when that word has already become the *subject* of the thought being expressed. In Margaret's speech, take the words 'himself' and 'knee', which both appear twice in the lines I've printed again below. The second time both these words are mentioned they have become qualified by another word.

In the fifth line it's important to see how the word 'unlike' in the phrase 'unlike himself' contrasts with the earlier 'himself'. Also how the 'knee' in the eighth line, becomes an 'unbowèd knee' five lines later. The word 'unbowed' here needs to be said as three syllables: 'un-bow-èd'. The sounded 'ed' is a common variant Shakespeare allows himself as a way of maintaining the power of the iambic rhythm.

Note the way the Folio prints the past tense of verbs: 'alter'd' but 'unbowed'

The Folio is also really very helpful to us in these situations. When it prints a word like 'altered' as 'alter'd', as it does in the second line below, it's indicating that the 'ed' should *not* be pronounced as a separate syllable – in which case this word will be said just as we would say the word today. But where later in this speech we have this word 'unbowed', printed as it would be today, this is telling us that this 'ed' *is* pronounced as a separate syllable, and that therefore this word should be pronounced with three syllables, rather than as we would say it today with only two.

Now in the passage below you can practise both how on occasion the last word in a line has been qualified by another, and also how sometimes we need that final 'ed' to be pronounced, to maintain the *iambic* rhythm, and sometimes not:

> MARGARET. Can you not see? or will ye not observe
> The strangeness of his alter'd countenance?
> With what a majesty he bears himself,
> How insolent of late he is become,
> How proud, how peremptory, and *unlike* himself?
>
> We know the time since he was mild and affable,
> And if we did but glance a far-off look,
> Immediately he was upon his knee,
> That all the court admir'd him for submission:

> But meet him now, and be it in the morn,
> When every one will give the time of day,
> He knits his brow, and shows an angry eye,
> And passeth by with stiff *unbowed* knee,
> Disdaining duty that to us belongs.

Just as we had to add an extra syllable to 'unbowed' there is a line some dozen lines further on that might have sounded 'unfinished' to you.

> And when he please to make commotion,

And it is unfinished unless we realise that words ending with '*tion*', especially in these early plays, would have also been sounded with an extra syllable, in this case to make it 'co-mmo-ti-on'.

Now that sounds strange to our ears, so I would suggest one solution for us might be to say 'commotion' as we say it today, but to make the smallest of hesitations before the word as if you are making a point of 'coining' the word. This suggestion is a bit of a cheat, but it will disguise the fact that the rhythm no longer works with modern pronunciation. Most of these 'ti-on' words will be found, by the way, at the ends of lines. However, you might well be working with a director one day who loves the sound of this original pronunciation. And if it is done subtly I rather like it myself.

To sum up: characters like Queen Margaret are powerful and their 'end-stopped' lines ring with the sound of command and confidence. They are surrounded, in these early plays, by others that have different agendas, different goals, which they also confidently proclaim. They all like the sound of their own voices. They are not much affected by what others say. Even a 'weak' character like Margaret's husband, King Henry VI, is still confident he knows what is right. There is not much self-doubt about the end-stopped line. And if people are not to be swayed by the words of others, the only recourse left sometimes is to kill them. And at the end of the *Henry VI* trilogy, Henry is finally murdered by the Duke of Gloucester, the future Richard III.

In this scene Richard and Henry have been trading insults with each other for over 50 lines, and neither of them is going to change their mind over anything that the other might say. And neither wants to stop talking either. So finally Henry is killed in mid-speech: nothing but death can silence him.

Folio stage directions

The text here is interesting too. You'll see that the Folio includes the stage-direction '*Stabs him.*' Stage directions are rather rare in the Folio – more frequently you are left to work out from the text itself exactly when something happens – but has the Folio got the positioning of this one in the right place? Sound out these lines and see what you think:

> HENRY. Teeth had'st thou in thy head, when thou wast born,
>   To signify, thou cam'st to bite the world:
>   And if the rest be true, which I have heard,
>   Thou cam'st –
>
> RICHARD. I'll hear no more: Die prophet in thy speech,   *Stabs him.*
>   For this (amongst the rest) was I ordain'd.
>
>   *Henry VI, Part Three*: Act 5, Scene 6

Our apparent difficulty is that Henry seems to have been stabbed as he says, 'Thou cam'st' – with the dash after his words indicating that he can speak no more; yet on the other hand it seems correct that the stage direction, '*Stabs him*' should accompany Richard's phrase, 'Die prophet in thy speech'. I suppose you could say that Henry stops speaking when he does, because he's seen Richard draw his dagger – but then Richard wouldn't have killed him, as he says he does, *while* Henry was still speaking.

I think the solution is, that occasionally characters speak over the top of what another character is saying, and I think this is what happens here. For Henry to be killed while speaking – and so honour the exact words that Richard uses – Richard will have to begin his speech immediately Henry says, 'And if the rest be true'. If we allow such an overlap to happen, the stage direction, Richard's words, and Henry being suddenly cut off in mid-flow work perfectly. Throughout this book we'll see that the text rewards close attention to details like this.

In the detail lies the life of these plays.

The protagonists in these early plays give no quarter, they fight for supremacy. In the end of course almost all of them die early without achieving it. But they are all convinced of the rightness of their opinions. We have to wait a few more years before we meet characters in Shakespeare who question and doubt themselves.

Three

The Thought Breaks

And midst the sentence so her accent breaks,
That twice she doth begin ere once she speaks.

The Rape of Lucrece: lines 566–7

We heard in the end-stopped line the sound of a confident character, and we noted that we would find such characters most frequently in Shakespeare's early plays. As a result the end-stopped line finds it difficult to capture the sound of doubt or emotional upheaval. To give you an extreme example of lines that are not 'end-stopped', here are the first few lines of Hermione's opening speech in the trial scene from *The Winter's Tale*.

In this play, one of the last that Shakespeare wrote, Hermione is wrongly accused by her husband Leontes, of having had an adulterous relationship with his friend Polixenes. She is arrested, and the child she gives birth to in prison is taken from her and carried away to be left to die in some deserted place. Her young son falls gravely ill. She is then brought to trial:

HERMIONE. Since what I am to say, must be but that
　　　　Which contradicts my accusation, and
　　　　The testimony on my part, no other
　　　　But what comes from my self, it shall scarce boot me*
　　　　To say, Not guilty: mine integrity

boot me – advantage me

34

> Being counted falsehood, shall (as I express it)
> Be so receiv'd.

The Winter's Tale: Act 3, Scene 2

It would be wrong to say that Hermione is not confident; she is completely confident in her own innocence. But she has certainly been subjected to a series of traumatic shocks. She is deeply distressed.

You might be experiencing some shocks of your own as you look at this example of Shakespeare's late verse; especially when you look at the line endings which probably seem haphazard in the extreme, as if the line can now end anywhere except at the end of a phrase or sentence, or as if Shakespeare now simply starts a new line whenever he comes to the tenth or eleventh syllable.

By the end of this chapter I hope I will have begun to show you that (as Polonius says of Hamlet) 'though this be madness, yet there is method in't'. Shakespeare's verse develops in this extraordinary way, not because he's got lazy or careless, but because he wants to capture the sounds of some emotional states in a way that the end-stopped line fails to do for him.

Hermione v. Othello: the 'ragged line'

The end-stopped line had given Shakespeare and his contemporaries, Marlowe and Kyd, a line that conferred an aura of powerful authority on those who spoke its rhythms.[1] They seemed to be characters well fitted to play their parts on the world's stages. Queen Margaret's speech in the previous chapter was one example.

But a character like Hermione is different. True she is also a queen and her husband is a king, and sometimes, even in this trial scene, she speaks with the authority that we might expect from a 'queenly character'. And when she does so, the verse captures this sound by employing a less haphazard form:

> The Emperor of Russia was my father.
> O that he were alive, and here beholding
> His daughter's trial:

The Winter's Tale: Act 3, Scene 2

But Shakespeare's Hermione is also a wife and mother; a woman who has been forced to give birth in prison; a woman who is then hurried to a trial, presided over by her deranged husband, and made to stand, falsely accused, in public and in the open air.[2] No wonder Shakespeare wants to capture vocal tones and rhythms which reveal the ordeals she has been enduring.

By way of comparison, though, let us look at the same time at part of a speech from *Othello*. Here Othello is not exactly on trial, but he is being asked to give an account of his actions before the Duke and the Venetian Senate. *Othello* is a play of Shakespeare's maturity, not as late in date as *The Winter's Tale*, but written maybe a dozen years or more after the *Henry VI* plays.

In this scene Othello shows supreme confidence when asked to explain to the Senate whether it is true that he has seduced, drugged and stolen Brabantio's daughter, Desdemona, from her father's house and under cover of darkness. Watch the line endings here; they are similar to the ones we have been looking at up until now.

> OTHELLO. Most potent, grave, and reverend signiors,
> My very noble, and approv'd good masters;
> That I have ta'en away this old man's daughter,
> It is most true: true I have married her;
> The very head, and front of my offending,
> Hath this extent; no more.
>
> *Othello*: Act 1, Scene 3

Sound out Othello's lines now and you will find he is measured and unruffled; he is in control. Let's compare these line endings with those from Hermione's opening speech and notice too how Hermione's line endings, by contrast, are all *unpunctuated*:

'reverend signiors,'	'must be but that'
'good masters;'	'and'
'old man's daughter,'	'no other'
'married her;'	'scarce boot me'
'my offending,'	'mine integrity'

Othello's line endings all seem to crystallise round an important phrase; they help to set out his argument clearly, naming all the major characters involved: the members of the Senate, Brabantio, Desdemona and himself. Othello feels in complete control of the situation; he feels in no danger.

By contrast Hermione has lost everything. Her son, from whom she is barred, is dangerously ill; her baby of a few days old has been taken away to be killed; and her husband, the King, wants her dead. All she has left is the desire to clear her name. Unlike Othello's speech, hers opens with a lengthy preamble through which she proceeds hesitantly, as if each step is a painful one. The line endings don't seem to be adding clarity at all. What are we to do – just ignore the way it is written?

I expect you've guessed that that is not the answer. What, in fact, is happening here is that Hermione's thoughts and the lines are no longer running smoothly together. The line still has the same correlation with the breath of the speaker that we noticed in Chapter 1, but the thoughts and the breath are now somehow at odds. You might say she is 'breathless'; or that her breathing is interrupting the expression of her thoughts. Or you might say that what is happening to Hermione physically and emotionally is making everything that she wants and needs to say doubly and triply hard to achieve. Whatever we choose to say, it is the 'ragged' appearance of these lines, *the absence of punctuation at the end of them*, that is capturing the sound of all this pain.

'Ragged form' captures the sound of emotional disturbance.

Being able to 'see' how the form of the verse can put us in touch with the emotions that lie behind the thoughts is one of the most important things I want to convey in this book. We are so conditioned, understandably so, to making sense of all the words that run from line to line that it's easy to ignore how the run of the lines themselves, partitioning and shaping the thoughts, are there to point us to the emotional truth about the moment that is being expressed.

But we have lots of time. We don't have to achieve everything at once and between the *Henry VI* plays and *The Winter's Tale* lies all the rest of Shakespeare's works. Were we to examine them one by one, which is not the purpose of this book, we would find that his verse line is in a constant state of development, capturing more and more variedly all those nuances and subtleties that reflect our human condition and the ways we express ourselves as we are subjected to a myriad of conflicting emotional states. This book plans to leap-frog over many of his plays, landing at certain places where we might perceive these developments with greatest clarity.

Lucrece v. Lavinia

In 1594 the plague, which visited London most years, was so bad that the theatres were closed for much of the time.[3] The same had been true of the previous year as well. And during those two years, when theatrical activity stalled, and there must have seemed little point in writing a new play, Shakespeare appears to have written his two long poems: *Venus and Adonis* in 1593 and in the following year *The Rape of Lucrece*.

This chapter began with a couple of lines from *The Rape of Lucrece*.
Here's the whole of that stanza:

> Her pity-pleading eyes are sadly fixed
> In the remorseless wrinkles of his face.
> Her modest eloquence with sighs is mixed
> Which to her oratory adds more grace.
> She puts the period often from his place,
>   And midst the sentence so her accent breaks,
>   That twice she doth begin ere once she speaks.
>
> *The Rape of Lucrece*: lines 561–7

It's a long poem; almost twice as long as *Venus and Adonis*. It's actually about the same length as Shakespeare's shortest play, *The Comedy of Errors*. I want to look at it because I believe writing it may have given Shakespeare a new insight into how people express themselves in a crisis. While composing this poem, Shakespeare's imagination becomes fixated on the desperate plight of this woman who is about to be raped, and on its aftermath.

A little earlier, Shakespeare had imagined a similar scene, when he wrote *Titus Andronicus*, the earliest of his tragedies.

In that play Titus's daughter Lavinia is raped by Tamora's two sons and then mutilated: they cut off her hands and cut out her tongue to prevent her revealing the identity of her rapists. Before she is raped, Lavinia pleads with Tamora, begging her to kill her rather than hand her over to the lust of her sons. Here are the lines with my 'thought breaks' indicated as I will continue to do throughout this book:

LAVINIA. 'Tis present death I beg, and one thing more,
That womanhood denies my tongue to tell:

O keep me from their worse than killing lust,
And tumble me into some loathsome pit,
Where never man's eye may behold my body,

Do this, and be a charitable murderer.

TAMORA. So should I rob my sweet sons of their fee,
No let them satisfy their lust on thee.

DEMETRIUS. Away, for thou hast stay'd us here too long.

LAVINIA. No grace, no womanhood? Ah beastly creature,
The blot and enemy to our general name,
Confusion fall –

But as with Richard's murder of King Henry VI that we looked at earlier, so here they will not let Lavinia continue speaking. The other son interrupts her line:

CHIRON.   Nay then I'll stop your mouth…

Titus Andronicus: Act 2, Scene 3

Amongst these fairly regular lines you might have discovered that Tamora's two lines are a rhyming couplet (the rhyme adding here a sound of sadistic pleasure to her words) and they have, I'd suggest, trochaic stresses in their opening feet, which also rhyme: 'So… No.' There are strong line endings throughout.

Lavinia's pleas begin coherently and display an amazing degree of control. Only in her later line

No grace, no womanhood? Ah beastly creature,

with three thoughts crammed into the one line, does Shakespeare capture something of the sound of her rising terror.

(Although this line contains three statements, I don't think that necessarily means that these are invitations for the actress playing the part to pause. Generally when a line contains two or more thoughts, it's better to consider in the first place that the subsequent thoughts *overwhelm* the earlier ones. All lines are different and there will be exceptions to this, but if you don't need to break a line, don't. And don't rush it either.)

If we compare these two violent assaults, Shakespeare's feelings for Lucrece seem to drive him into a deeper and darker part of his imagination. To Lavinia's ordeal, while she is an object of our pity, he seems more of an observer. But with Lucrece he seems to be living through her ordeal moment by moment.

Maybe it's because he's now a few years older. Maybe the length of the poem gives Shakespeare longer to contemplate what terrors Lucrece must be feeling as she pleads for Tarquin to spare her. Certainly the poem allows him to contemplate the rape and its aftermath for longer than he does in the play.

Tarquin rapes Lavinia in the 97th stanza; he runs from her house in the 106th stanza. But the poem continues for another 161 stanzas. These all detail the varying and conflicting emotions that Lucrece is assailed by until her husband's return; when eventually he's fetched home from his army posting, she tells him what has happened and then kills herself.

The rape itself in *Titus* happens off stage, whereas in the poem, Lucrece and what is happening to her physically remains before our eyes.

Shakespeare imagines not only what she says, and how her body is reacting to her terror, but how that terror in its turn affects *the way* she speaks.

> She puts the period* often from his place,
> And midst the sentence so her accent breaks,
> That twice she doth begin ere once she speaks.

Later he writes,

> With untun'd tongue she hoarsely calls her maid,
> Whose swift obedience to her mistress hies…
>
> lines 1214–15

> Poor Lucrece' cheeks unto her maid seem so,
> As winter meads when sun doth melt their snow.
>
> lines 1217–18

And then Lucrece asks the maid,

> But tell me girl, when went (and there she stay'd,
> Till after a deep groan) Tarquin from hence,
> Madam ere I was up, (replied the maid,)
>
> lines 1275–7

So Shakespeare continues to imagine how the after-effects of the terror continue hours later, encompassing more and more of Lucrece's world with its staining horror. It produces the hoarse un-tuned voice; the tear-stained cheeks; the deep groans interrupting her speech. And continues still as later Lucrece begins to attempt to write to her husband,

> Her maid is gone, and she prepares to write,
> First hovering o'er the paper with her quill:
> Conceit* and grief an eager combat fight,
> What wit sets down is blotted straight with will.
> This is too curious good, this blunt and ill,
> > Much like a press of people at a door,
> > Throng her inventions which shall go before.
>
> lines 1296–1302

Finally when her husband eventually returns home and she tells him what has happened to her, *his* grief is such that he is *unable* to speak. The horror continues:

period – full stop
conceit – thoughts

40

Lo here the hopeless merchant of this loss,
With head declin'd, and voice damm'd up with woe,
With sad set eyes and wretched arms across,
From lips new waxen pale, begins to blow
The grief away, that stops his answer so.
    But wretched as he is he strives in vain,
    What he breathes out, his breath drinks up again.

lines 1660–66

Even so his sighs, his sorrows make a saw,
To push grief on, and back the same grief draw.

lines 1672–3

I have quoted so much of this because I am struck by how accurately in Shakespeare's imagination he sees the far-reaching effects of grief, not only in Lucrece, but in her husband as well.

Graphically Shakespeare describes how this husband is trying to get control over his grief; how he seems to be struggling to expel the grief from his body, by forcing the sobs out; but how the sobs get gasped back in with his next intake of breath. And there is a brilliance about Shakespeare's image of the saw.

Shakespeare uses the image of a saw to draw a vivid parallel: how the movements and sounds of grief are weirdly similar to those accompanying someone sawing through a piece of wood; one body rocking in anguish, the other with the physical effort; the saw's rasps even mimicking the awful noises of human despair.

In imagining all this and remembering no doubt all the violence that he'd ever seen in that violent world of sixteenth-century London (the public executions, the heads on spikes), he realises perhaps more acutely than ever before that something happens to the breath of those in terror and those consumed with grief; how they can't get the words out; how sighs and other non-verbal noises take the place of words; how sentences get strangled in mid flow.

The 'Lucrece moment'

It could be said that Shakespeare's early writing for the stage, before *Lucrece* and the plague years of 1593/4, was heavily influenced by his contemporaries such as Marlowe and Kyd. It would also be fair to say that all their great 'end-stopped' plays are wonderfully theatrical and still have great appeal today, but that the characters in them speak more like characters who could only be found *within* a play, rather than sounding like individuals who are caught up in a drama of their own.

So maybe those two years when Shakespeare's focus shifted to writing his two long poems were a godsend to him. It might be that the insights his imagination gives him in writing *Lucrece* is the reason why the form of his verse undergoes the seismic shift which eventually leads to speeches like those of Hermione in her trial.

But his problem is: how can dramatic verse, which is composed of words, capture distraction and the absence of words? Because if he wants to dramatise all sorts of stories, all aspects of human behaviour, he has to find ways to achieve that as well.

I'm suggesting he finds what he is looking for in the 'breaks' his imagination observed in Lucrece's agonising speech patterns.

> And **midst the sentence** so her accent breaks,
> That twice she doth begin ere once she speaks.

And in the verse of his plays, he finds it in places where he can *allow* a verse line to break as well.

Either he will allow himself a short line so that the pulse of that moment continues in silence; or much more commonly he'll find it at that place where all lines break: after the tenth or eleventh syllable, before the thought continues in the *line that follows*.

We will come across examples of short lines later in this book, but for now let us look once more at those lines of Hermione's with which we began this chapter, and see, if by sounding them out now, you can get a pre-taste of things to come. And I've marked in bold those important last and first line stresses. But remember stress them lightly!

> HERMIONE. Since what I am to say, must be but **that**
> Which **contradicts** my accusation, **and**
> The **testimony** on my part, no **other**
> But **what** comes from my self, it shall scarce **boot** me
> To **say**, Not guilty: mine integrity
> Being **counted** falsehood, shall (as I **express** it)
> Be **so** receiv'd.

> *The Winter's Tale*: Act 3, Scene 2

The image of sawing again comes to my mind. If we describe someone sawing a plank of wood, we say they are sawing; we don't say they are sawing now, but now they've stopped, and now they are sawing again, with each forward and backward movement of the blade. So it is with the lines;

they run continuously; but one line runs and then the next line takes over. But there is a moment in between both the movements of the saw and the run of the lines that our eye and ear fail to catch.

And in both those 'moments' a breath will be taken.

Breathing correctly is the key to playing Shakespeare's verse.

But *Lucrece* is 1594 and *The Winter's Tale* is some sixteen years off. The immediate results of his '*Lucrece* moment', as I shall call it, can begin to be seen in a play written much closer to 1594. It is *The Merchant of Venice* probably written around 1596-7.

Four

The Merchant of Venice
The Creation of a New Verse Form

Tarry a little, there is something else,
The Merchant of Venice: Act 4, Scene 1

1594, when *The Rape of Lucrece* was published, was also the year when Roderigo Lopez, a Portuguese Jew living in England, was executed for treason – publicly of course. And some have wondered if Shakespeare witnessed this gruesome event and if so whether it influenced him when he came to write Shylock, the Jew who is such a major character in *The Merchant of Venice*.

But *The Merchant of Venice* is a comedy and steers clear of allowing Shylock to suffer a comparable fate. Nor indeed does it take us into scenes such as we were forced to dwell on in *The Rape of Lucrece*. On the contrary, many would say that the scenes in Belmont where Portia lives, the place to which many of the characters are drawn, is bathed in a golden light, which comes not from Portia's fabulous wealth, but much more from the emotional lives that are joyously played out there.

It's true too, though, that the other half of the play takes place in Venice, which is seen to be a place of racial hatred, of Christian against Jew, of Jew against Christian; a place where money rules; a place of jails and courtrooms. But it is also the city to which Portia in her turn is drawn; drawn there to save her marriage and at the same time to save the play from a disastrous and unfitting climax.

The connection we can make between this play and Shakespeare's *Lucrece* is in the complexity of emotions that both investigate. Although the play is based on two or three old folk tales, and maybe elements of it do strain our credulity, the characters in no way appear two-dimensional; they are complex, multilayered and behave in surprising ways.

The play is full of ambiguity. The characters' motives are open to many different interpretations. This is also the first play of Shakespeare's that seems on the face of it to express doubt in its opening lines. They are spoken by Antonio, who is the merchant of the play's title.

> *Enter* ANTONIO, SALERIO *and* SOLANIO.
>
> ANTONIO. In sooth I know not why I am so sad,
>   It wearies me: you say it wearies you;
>   But how I caught it, found it, or came by it,
>   What stuff 'tis made of, whereof it is born,
>   I am to learn:
>
> *The Merchant of Venice*: Act 1, Scene 1

Or actually does he know why he's so sad? And is he happy to keep the mystery from others, while indulging the very feelings he is expressing? It is so beautifully phrased. The first line full of 'o', 'i', and 's' sounds; in the next line two 'w's'; and in the next more stressed vowels. The line endings all speak of control and ease of expression. Not much disturbance here.

Watching out for the sounds of the words that your character chooses to use can give you insights into their moods and characters.[1]

Later in the play, Solanio, one of the two characters that Antonio is addressing in that first speech, says of Antonio's feelings for Bassanio,

> SOLANIO. I think he only loves the world for him,
>
> *The Merchant of Venice*: Act 2, Scene 8

So probably he and Salerio, Solanio's companion at the beginning of the play, also know all along why Antonio is so sad.

The relationships are full of ambiguity. Antonio loves Bassanio, giving him a small fortune so he can go and woo Portia, yet doesn't want to lose him. Shylock loves his daughter, but treats her like a prisoner. The terms of Portia's dead father's will compel her to accept any man as her husband that opens the right casket in the lottery which he has set up for her.

But the younger people, Bassanio and Jessica, and especially Portia, want to live freely; to live life to the full; to follow their instincts and understand who they are and what they want out of the time they have on this earth. And in this play they express these feelings in voices that seem new, intimate and delicate, and the form of the verse takes on *new forms* to capture these new sounds.

A new verse form

Portia's speeches are different from anything that has gone before. Here is her speech (divided up into thought-units) reassuring Bassanio, who has just won the lottery of the caskets and with it her hand in marriage.

> PORTIA. You see me Lord Bassanio where I stand,
>   Such as I am;
>
>   though for my self alone
>   I would not be ambitious in my wish,
>   To wish my self much better, yet for you,
>   I would be trebled twenty times my self,
>   A thousand times more fair, ten thousand times more rich,
>   That only to stand high in your account,
>   I might in virtues, beauties, livings, friends,
>   Exceed account:
>
>   but the full sum of me
>   Is sum of nothing: which to term in gross,
>   Is an unlesson'd girl, unschool'd, unpractis'd,
>   Happy in this, she is not yet so old
>   But she may learn: happier than this,[2]
>   She is not bred so dull but she can learn;
>   Happiest of all, is that her gentle spirit
>   Commits it self to yours to be directed,
>   As from her lord, her governor, her king.
>
>   My self, and what is mine, to you and yours
>   Is now converted.
>
>   But now I was the lord
>   Of this fair mansion, master of my servants,
>   Queen o'er my self: and even now, but now,
>   This house, these servants, and this same my self
>   Are yours, my lord,
>
>   I give them with this ring,
>   Which when you part from, lose, or give away,
>   Let it presage the ruin of your love,
>   And be my vantage to exclaim on you.

The Merchant of Venice: Act 3, Scene 2

What we have again achieved, by dividing up this speech into thought-units, as we did with Margaret's speech, is variety of length of thought. Or, rather, we have now made those varying lengths of thoughts more obviously apparent.

We should have noticed something else too, something decidedly new. All but one of the thought-units end not at the end of a line, as they did in *Henry VI*, but in the middle. The 'form' of the verse has changed.

But look at these lines:

> But now I was the lord
> Of this fair mansion, master of my servants,
> Queen o'er my self: and even now, but now,
> This house, these servants, and this same my self
> Are yours, my lord,

You will see that it's not simply where a thought now starts that is different, but the whole movement of the words from one line to the next has a different feel to it. Two of the lines have no punctuation at the end of them and the 'heaviest' punctuation mark, the colon after 'my self', occurs mid-line.[3] This is no longer the 'end-stopped' verse form of Shakespeare's earliest plays.

It's now time to sound the whole of Portia's speech out for yourself, but bear in mind that you are about to experience the most radical development in Shakespeare's writing of verse.

Did you feel this new sense of delicacy and intimacy?

Here we understand that Portia is saying something which is precious to her, fragile, and new. There is also something domestic about it. The words are not in any way 'grand'. A few of the lines are monosyllabic, and many more almost so. (Though maybe the oddest line, 'Is an unlesson'd girl, unschool'd, unpractis'd,' sounds like she's just made those words up and that they amuse her.) The whole speech brims with her happiness and a desire to handle the moment with tact and care. But this is conveyed, not just by her words, but in the 'form' in which these words are cast.

My hope is that you found the speech beautiful yet simple. But you may have wondered where you were supposed to breathe. You may have occasionally run out of breath.

Breathing these newly arranged lines

With the 'end-stopped' verse of *Henry VI* it was fairly clear to see that there was this connection between the length of the line and what you could easily say on one breath. Also the way the thoughts in the sequence of those earlier lines progressed meant that it was quite natural (after you'd taken a breath in order to express the initial thought) that when you came to the next line with its new thought (or it might have been a development of the previous one) you topped up your breath *before* this line in order to carry on speaking. But what are you to do now when all the thoughts are tumbling over from one line to the next? Does this development in Shakespeare's verse writing mean that there is no longer this same connection with the line and the breath? The answer is no.

The connection with the line and the breath remains; what has changed (as we saw briefly with those lines of Hermione's from *The Winter's Tale* in the previous chapter) is that the *thoughts* are no longer lying so calmly and securely *within* the lines. And that is because the characters we are now beginning to look at are themselves not so calm, nor as totally confident, as those from the earlier plays.

One thing that happens to us all when we are unsure, or emotional about something, is that our breathing alters. It might become shallower, or deeper; we might breathe more frequently. But whatever happens, our emotions, be they happy or sad, will have an effect on *how we speak*. This is what Shakespeare realised as he was writing *The Rape of Lucrece* and from now on this effects the way he writes everything else.

Let's look at these lines again:

> But now I was the lord
> Of this fair mansion, master of my servants,
> Queen o'er my self: and even now, but now,
> This house, these servants, and this same my self
> Are yours, my lord,

The thoughts are all moving from one line to the next; though interestingly the first statement *could* well have made a complete line all by itself. Instead of writing –

> But now I was the lord
> Of this fair mansion,

– Shakespeare could have written:

> But now I was the lord of this fair mansion,

– which would have made a perfectly good iambic pentameter.

Sound these two lines out loud. Do you hear the difference any between them? Do you see how the complete line, the one Shakespeare *didn't* write, sounds more confident? It sounds grander. It sounds somewhat like Portia is boasting about her wonderful house. But the broken line, as Shakespeare wrote it, is different, it sounds as if Portia is considering, reflecting on what she is saying *as* she says it.

Crucially of course with the broken line, the line ending is different. What Portia was, until a moment ago – 'the lord' – now receives from her that scrutiny that the ends of lines always need. Portia, therefore, ponders on that 'I was the lord' *as* she speaks. And in so doing she realises that now Bassanio has 'won' her, her relationship with her own house is changing. She is expressing a single thought, but the two halves of the thought come apart a little, as she views both parts of them afresh.

Technically, I am simply suggesting that the second half of the thought should be preceded by a topped-up breath, with which to fully investigate the newness of the phrase's completion. But if you are *feeling* how happy she is, the new breath will just come to you, naturally, and the expression of this thought will be 'ruffled' and alive with all these joyous feelings.

At the end of the previous chapter I said that the way the lines follow each other remind me of the action of someone sawing. They have this in common: they both *seem* to be continuous actions. Yet we neither see the moment when the saw is still, nor should the audience be *aware* of where you breathe. In the playing of Shakespeare, this movement from line to line, from breath to breath, is, mostly, ignored. And yet, when we speak spontaneously ourselves, this is how our speech sounds: fractured by breath. We talk, and to continue talking we need to breathe, but where we *choose* to breathe will make a difference to how our words sound, and how they are understood.

Phrases expressed in parts

Portia certainly isn't wanting to appear boastful about her 'fair mansion'; she is striving for almost the opposite effect. So Shakespeare purposefully, to capture that 'sound' in her voice, gives her a statement that she expresses in two parts. And this two-part statement will have been preceded by many others like it, and followed by many others too, all of them straddling a pair of lines:

'the lord / of this fair mansion'
'but now / this house'
'this same my self / are yours'.

One result of this is that the stresses either side of the breath are played more thoughtfully, with more investigation and care, because they are so separated. All these phrases are bringing two different entities together.

Say them now like this *without* any separation:

'the lord of this fair mansion'
'but now this house'
'this same my self are yours'

and they seem plainer, more matter-of-fact. But playing them with that topped-up breath and finding how the stresses fall from one line to the next will bring out your meaning with this added sense – that you are discovering the appropriateness of what you are saying *as* you are saying it:

'the *lord* / of *this* fair *mansion*'
'but *now* / this *house*'
'this *same* my *self* / are *yours*':

This way the phrases come alive and touch our hearts; our audiences are not aware of the 'separation' as such, they are only aware of the uniqueness of the moment. And if you really desire to express the new line – the continuation of the thought – creatively, *choosing* which words to stress, you should find that the need to breathe in order to do so will come naturally to you.

Let's now stand back a little from these phrases and look at one of her thought-units:

though for my self alone
I would not be ambitious in my wish,
To wish my self much better, yet for you,
I would be trebled twenty times my self,
A thousand times more fair, ten thousand times more rich,
That only to stand high in your account,
I might in virtues, beauties, livings, friends,
Exceed account:

The 'patterns' in speech

Whenever we are working on a piece of text we want to look out for the 'speech-patterns' that lie within it; because these patterns reveal how a character is choosing to *shape* the expression of their thoughts, which in turn will reveal where that character is breathing. What do we find here?

Many thoughts, and especially those we find in Shakespeare, are built on comparing one thing with another. We call this 'antithesis', and here we have an antithesis between 'my self alone' and 'you'. And we can see that both appear, conspicuously, at the end of a line, as if standing there, just waiting to be compared with each other. The line and a half between them (what Portia says she doesn't 'wish') should move quite swiftly, because, to make the comparison between 'my self' and 'you' work most effectively, once you've alerted us to the importance of the phrase 'my self alone', we will be waiting eagerly for that 'you' to complete the thought.

There is another similar 'pattern' at the end of this thought-unit – we have 'your account' and 'Exceed account'. The first is again at the end of the line, while the second is also prominently placed – at the beginning of the next line but one. Again, the line in between these should tumble forward quite freely, so that the comparison between 'your account' and 'Exceed account' rings out clearly and makes the difference between them apparent.

So these 'speech-patterns' are telling us that while the comparisons need some emphasis, the lines between them should be released without hesitation. And to achieve both these things you'll find you'll need to 'top up' your breath, at the beginning of the new lines – like this:

> though for my **self alone**
> ˇ I would not be ambitious in my wish,
> ˇ To wish my self much better, **yet** for **you**…
>
> That only to stand high in **your account**,
> ˇ I might in virtues, beauties, livings, friends,
> ˇ Exceed account:

The breath taken separates the moment of stress from the moment of releasing, and should sound – as in fact it is – just like natural speech. In our own lives we are constantly 'shaping' the expression of our thoughts so that they will be clearly understood.

Maybe speaking could be likened to riding a horse, or driving a car: you know where you are headed, but you're always aware of the terrain in front of you, and which you have to adapt to, as your journey proceeds. As we are speaking, we become aware that here I need to hurry up to make this comparison work effectively, but here I need to steady my pace. And

Shakespeare's lines show you when, and how, to achieve this. Here's Portia seeing what's ahead:

> To wish my self much better, yet for **you**,
> ˘ I would be trebled twenty times my self,
> ˘ A thousand times more fair, ten thousand times more rich,

As she says, '**yet** for **you**,' she senses – though she doesn't know what words are going to come out of her mouth – that she has got a whole breath-full of loving things to say to Bassanio, which would be *diminished* if she hadn't topped up her breath in order to say it all, and had to breathe in the middle of the line and disrupt the thought. It wouldn't matter how long we were all 'held' by that '**you**': we will wait happily for the thought to be continued; for if Portia, in this moment, holds her own breath, because of the happiness of the moment, before snatching another breath in order to deliver this next line, my guess is that we in the audience will be holding our breath too.

And did you notice that the very next line is extra-long, just like we found earlier with Isabella and her '*outstretch'd throat*'? It's a twelve-syllable line which has six stresses. If she had just said, '*ten times more rich*', the line would have been like all the others, but this fabulously rich woman wants for Bassanio's sake to be 'ten *thousand* times more rich'. Fabulous indeed! And again, as Portia would have been approaching this line, just like a rider coming up to a big jump, she would have prepared for it, by sensing that she now needs to take an even bigger breath.

By contrast look at this little moment which follows on from where we left off:

> but the full sum of me
> Is sum of nothing:

Here we get from her a short witticism – 'What I amount to is nothing'. Here's another line that if it hadn't been broken by the line ending would have made a perfectly good pentameter –

> but the full sum of me is sum of nothing:

– but do you see how the line *needs* to be broken by a breath in order to take us by surprise, and make us smile – which is what Portia is aiming at?

What I have been trying to do is to show you how we 'shape' our thoughts *as* we express them, and the shaping is achieved simply by where we choose to take a breath. The line ending prepares us for what is to follow – and we have seen that sometimes the line ending prepares us for something of length – a complete line – and sometimes it surprises us with something punchy and short.

Now we will move on and look at two more of these Portia thought-units:

> My self, and what is mine, to you and yours
> Is now converted.

>   But now, I was the lord
> Of this fair mansion, master of my servants,
> Queen o'er my self: and even now, but now,
> This house, these servants, and this same my self
> Are yours, my lord,

An 'added' comma

But here I have done something cheeky – I have added a comma to the lines above, and I've put it in bold so you can find it. And I've done this because I believe a comma *should* be there, though I acknowledge that there is no comma in the Folio, nor have I ever seen one in any modern edition. But I'm putting it there because I believe Shakespeare might have wanted it there too. Because this little comma changes the meaning of the line.

Let's look at the line in question and find its rhythm – first without the comma, and then with:

> Is **now** converted. But **now** I was the **lord**

> Is **now** converted. But **now,** I was the **lord**

(This line is actually unusual for yet another reason – because if you look you'll see it has an extra unstressed syllable in the middle of it. Later in this book we shall look at such lines in much more detail. For now I'll just say it's as if the line pauses at the full stop.[4])

The added comma, surprising us with its trochaic beat – the 'I' rather than the 'was' being stressed – means that the thought-unit now makes total sense.[5] The beginning and end of it become a perfect antithesis: 'Portia' was the lord, and now Bassanio is the lord – the thought-unit is now perfectly formed – the end is connected to the beginning:

>   But now, I was the **lord**
> Of this fair mansion, master of my servants,
> Queen o'er my self: and even now, but now,
> This house, these servants, and this same my self
> Are **yours**, my **lord**,

I have tried to 'mark up' these lines below – bold for the stresses; an <u>under-line</u> for that 'but', which seems to need some little individual help; and finally a set of these ˇ-marks to indicate where I feel you should, or might need, to top up your breath. I feel that you *should* top up your breath at the beginning of the lines, and you *might* want to top up again mid-line.

> ˇ But **now,** I was the **lord**
> ˇ Of **this** fair **mansion, master of** my **servants,**
> ˇ **Queen** o'er my **self:** ˇ and even **now,** <u>but</u> **now,**
> ˇ This **house,** these **servants, and** this **same** my **self**
> ˇ Are **yours,** my **lord,**

It looks rather complicated I know; but try to remember that the result should seem effortlessly natural and spontaneous. And you should sound out these lines now.

Speaking is almost always an enjoyable activity, and if you are playing Portia you must enjoy the words '*now*' and '*house*' and '*yours*' because in this situation these little words carry so much meaning. And especially note how Portia, who was the 'lord', is at the end of these few lines acknowledging that from now on Bassanio is *her* 'lord'.

The line endings divide up the expression of the thoughts into parts. And the result is they sound the richer, more delightful, because they are being so expressed. And we hear that the expression of these thoughts is being coloured by the way Portia is feeling and *breathing*. And she is breathing in this way *because* she is happy and excited.

Curiously, for the actor, following how these broken thoughts lie in and across the lines puts you more creatively in control. Look again at that last line and a half, and in particular at the last stress in the first line and the first stress that follows it:

> This house, these servants, and this same my **self**
> ˇ Are **yours,** my lord,

It is up to you to choose how that moment between 'my *self*' plays into 'Are *yours*'. Is it a sudden rush of joy from 'self' to 'yours', or is it more delightful if there is some delay between the two? Both will have a topped-up breath there, but your choice here will make a great difference. With a broken thought you choose the tempo with which it is delivered.

Sometimes the stress you choose might not be iambic, but its opposite, trochaic. I think the previous line begins with a trochaic foot – '**Queen** o'er my **self**' – and this assertive trochee gives us a slightly different sound: a kind of surprise.

Touch these words gently; the rest will happen by itself. These are single thoughts but they come in parts. The audience hears single thoughts, beautifully phrased, and they are not aware of how this is achieved. It's a mystery: ours and Shakespeare's. But it really shouldn't be a mystery at all, as it's the way we all speak. Just listen to the people around you: all their longer thoughts come divided up, frequently not at grammatical junctures, but in the middle of phrases.

Our added comma has now made something else clear too – and that is that this thought-unit is also about two *different* 'now's. All *three* 'now's' are each followed by a comma, all of them receiving that weight of emphasis that the comma gives, and so distinguishing clearly between the first and second 'now' moments. For Portia is saying that there was then, and there was another 'then', which happened just a moment after.

The first was the first '*But now,*' when everything was still hers, but that was followed by '*even now,*' when Bassanio opened the leaden casket; the '*even*' being the little word that differentiates the two moments. But somehow '*even now,*' on its own seems too vague, and so, to be more precise, she once more adds the phrase '*but now,*' to the '*even now,*' and the second '*but now,*' becomes, by contrast with the first, an even more precise moment which has only *just* happened, the '*but*' here meaning 'just' – 'just now'.

And notice how the two '*but now,*' phrases are differently stressed: the first is straightforwardly iambic with the stress on the '*now*'; the second, needs the '*but*' to be given some prominence, 'ruffling' the rhythm somewhat in the process.

It's not quite like what we found in a couple of lines from that long speech of Queen Margaret's. There we found occasions when the final word of the line (which would usually be one of the major stresses in the line) had become the 'subject' of the line and so needed the major stress to land elsewhere. This final '*now*' from Portia still receives some stress, but in the delicacy of expression that we are finding in *The Merchant of Venice* maybe not so much as you might expect.

I said that there is something domestic about the language in this play. And in these lines of Portia's you can see something of what I mean:

> This house, these servants, and this same my self
> Are yours, my lord,

Shakespeare's plays are full of 'things' that are pointed to and indicated. They seem to ask for an appropriate gesture to accompany the words. And here those 'things' which are so indicated have this everyday, domestic quality to them. Portia is saying: there's a house and some servants, who've somehow now all assembled on the stage, and there's me and there's you.

Little common everyday words, pointing to extraordinary happenings.

The wonder, the magic, the charm of the speech do not, though, lie simply in these simple words, but also in the way that Portia shapes the expression of them; and the shaping of them is indicated by the form of the verse on the page. There is a 'raggedness' about this speech, which is my way of saying that many of the lines have no punctuation at the end of them. The more 'ragged', the more thrilling the lines are to play. The more 'ragged', the higher the emotional stakes.

Now it's time to sound this whole speech out again.

I wonder if you felt, this second time through, that what Portia is saying is not all that romantic? That it's all a bit business-like? Well if you did, I agree with you, for *The Merchant of Venice* is a complex play. Even in these moments of two people declaring love for each other, the language is filled with the vocabulary of economics (*rich*, *account*, *sum* and *term in gross*). Soon it will be revealed to Portia that Bassanio has borrowed a small fortune in order to deck himself out for this adventure of trying to win the lottery and with it Portia herself. And one of the reasons Bassanio has given Antonio, to persuade him to lend him yet *more* money, is that by winning Portia, he could clear himself of all his *past* debts…

And now, just as all the assembled characters are celebrating the fact that Portia and Bassanio are to be married and that their futures are assured, a letter arrives for Bassanio from Antonio. It informs him that Antonio's latest enterprise has foundered, and he now can't pay Shylock back the money he had borrowed from him to finance Bassanio's expedition to Belmont. Because of the bond that Antonio signed with Shylock, failure to pay the money back means that Shylock, his great adversary, now has the legal right to kill Antonio in open court by demanding a pound of his flesh – for such is the agreement that Antonio has made with him.

Portia watches Bassanio silently reading the letter. She realises it's bringing shockingly bad news and asks him to tell her what has happened. Here again divided into 'thought-units' is what he says:

BASSANIO.   O sweet Portia,
    Here are a few of the unpleasant'st words
    That ever blotted paper.

                   Gentle lady
    When I did first impart my love to you,
    I freely told you all the wealth I had
    Ran in my veins: I was a gentleman,
    And then I told you true: and yet dear lady,
    Rating my self at nothing, you shall see
    How much I was a braggart,

                 when I told you
    My state was nothing, I should then have told you
    That I was worse than nothing:

                 for indeed
    I have engag'd my self to a dear friend,
    Engag'd my friend to his mere enemy
    To feed my means.

            Here is a letter lady,
    The paper as the body of my friend,
    And every word in it a gaping wound
    Issuing life blood.
             The Merchant of Venice: Act 3, Scene 2

The 'form' of the speech is identical to Portia's. Here all the thoughts begin mid-line. And here, even more than in Portia's speech, many lines are without any punctuation at the end of them.

Let's look at some of them:

                 when I told you
    My state was nothing, I should then have told you
    That I was worse than nothing:

Here are two connected thoughts: 'When I told you my state was nothing,' and 'I should then have told you that I was worse than nothing:'. But, as with Portia's phrases, each thought is shaped by the lines, into two parts: the first one, of two stresses, followed by another two stresses:

when I *told* you / My *state* was *noth*ing,

The second of three and three stresses:

I should *then* have *told* you / That *I* was *worse* than *noth*ing:

57

Put it all together and we hear two connected thoughts, though they are each shaped into two parts, because of Bassanio's desire to speak to Portia with as much clarity and sensitivity as he possibly can. But they are also so shaped because of the emotional strain that Bassanio is under. It is hard for him to say these things.

Shakespeare also links these connected thoughts by letting them come together in the middle line –

> My state was nothing, I should then have told you

– the second half of the line overwhelming the first.

Variety of pace of delivery must also be a part of our repertoire on the stage, as it is in life. I'll leave you now to sound it out.

I'm hoping that the 'raggedness' of the speech revealed to you the emotional turmoil that Bassanio was experiencing: how he was doing all he could to shape the expression of his thoughts with care, but that the outcome was inextricably bound up with how he was feeling, and therefore how he was *breathing*.

Shakespeare 'writes in' the breathing for us.

If you are still unsure about this this, I'm hoping to convince you by another line of argument. Shakespeare shows us that there are certain 'speech patterns' that we tend to say *before* we top up our breath. And this speech of Bassanio's that we've just been looking at is filled with such examples.

Shared lines and 'heralding phrases'

Bassanio's speech begins with a half-line because he is answering Portia, and the final part of *her* speech ends with an incomplete line.

What happens here is called a 'shared line' and it is among the first we have so far come across:

> PORTIA. With leave Bassanio I am half your self,
> And I must freely have the half of any thing
> That this same paper brings you.
> BASSANIO.   O sweet Portia,

We will look at shared lines in more detail later (see below, Chapter 6, pages 92–4). There are few of them in Shakespeare's early plays, but in the later plays they become the normal way that Shakespeare captures the sound of the seamless flow of conversation from one speaker to another.

And so here Bassanio completes the metrical line. Portia's longer part has three stresses in it and Bassanio's line makes up the other two. His initial three words are very much like what we ourselves would probably say in a similarly horrendous situation, when we have some terrible news to break. 'Oh darling…' we might say, or, 'Now listen for a moment…'

But what *sort of phrases* are these, and his 'O sweet Portia', perched there at the end of that line?

If we look a couple of lines further down we'll find 'Gentle lady' similarly sitting at the end of the line. Go another four lines and we have 'And yet dear lady' in the same place. Look further still and you'll find maybe five more such phrases including 'Here is a letter lady'. All these phrases are at the end of a line. But what else do they have in common? Aren't they all phrases that we say *before* we say something else? They signal that more is to come; and they *prepare us* for what is to come next.

The end of the line is the appropriate place for such phrases because the function of the end of the line, if it is not the end of the thought, is to prepare us and take us into the line to come.

I call such phrases 'heralding phrases' because they prepare everyone for something that's *about* to be delivered. And to capture the 'sound' of such phrases, Shakespeare places them purposefully at the line's end, *before* whatever is to follow. And he does this because that is how he has heard Bassanio speaking. Furthermore, by placing Bassanio's phrases where he does in the line, he can indicate to the actor exactly what he heard, which would include 'hearing' that noiseless 'topped-up' breath Bassanio took, before he said the new line that was to follow.

Think of how we begin to say anything new. We commonly use words like 'So' or 'Well' to announce to our audience that we are about to say something of importance. 'So,' we'll say, 'what we have to consider…'; or we might say, 'Well – yesterday went really badly…'

And what will we have done after that initial word? Yes, we'll have taken a breath, in order to make what is said next sound like *the start of something new*. So it is with all Bassanio's heralding phrases.

To take just one example from this speech:

> That ever blotted paper. Gentle lady
> When I did first impart my love to you,
> I freely told you all the wealth I had
> Ran in my veins:

The first line here contains the end of one thought and the beginning of the next.

You have a choice: do you breathe before 'Gentle lady' or not? Either is possible, but whichever you choose, the line is directing you (two thoughts in one line) to signal with the words 'Gentle lady' that what is to follow will be of more importance than what has preceded it. Whether you take a quick breath there or not, there should be no real gap in the line. Either way, once you have said 'Gentle lady' with the appropriate indication to make it clear to Portia that more is to follow, you'll want a new breath with which to begin the next part of the story.

These 'heralding phrases' are a device speakers use to gain their listeners' attention. For the actor who's sensitive to the way line follows line, as breath follows breath, the gains will be in terms of clarity of expression, and a revelation of the emotions that underlie those thoughts that are being expressed.

'Heralding phrases' alert us to the importance of what is to follow.

Before we end this chapter I'd like to 'mark up' Bassanio's speech so as to point to all those things we have been discussing. I have used <u>underlining</u> here to mark those 'heralding phrases'; ˇ to mark where I'd like you to try to remember to top up your breath; and *italics* to mark the gentle stresses.

But all should be easy and natural, albeit emotions are running high:

ˇ <u>*O sweet Por*tia,</u>

ˇ *Here* are a *few* of *the* un*plea*sant'st *words*
ˇ That *ever blot*ted *pa*per.

ˇ <u>*Gentle la*dy</u>

ˇ When *I* did *first* im*part* my *love* to *you,*
ˇ I *freely told* you *all* the *wealth* I *had*
ˇ *Ran* in my *veins*: I *was* a *gentle*man,
ˇ And *then* I told you *true*: <u>and yet dear lady,</u>
ˇ *Rat*ing my *self* at *noth*ing, <u>you shall see</u>
ˇ How *much* I *was* a *bragg*art,

ˇ <u>*when* I *told* you</u>

ˇ My *state* was *noth*ing, <u>I should then have told you</u>
ˇ That *I* was *worse* than *noth*ing:

ˇ <u>*for in*deed</u>

ˇ I *have* en*gag'd* my *self* to a dear *friend,*
ˇ En*gag'd* my *friend* to *his* mere *enemy*
ˇ To *feed* my *means.*

˘ *Here* is a *letter la*dy,
˘ The *paper as* the *body of* my *friend,*
˘ And *every word* in *it* a *gaping wound*
˘ *Issu*ing life *blood.*

Remember too that the breaks between all these new thought-units are *not pauses*. Maybe they are the opposite of pauses: maybe you'll find some of them work as acceleration points. Notice the varied rhythms I've suggested by the italics: five feminine endings; four trochaic beginnings. One line – 'I *have* en*gag'd* my *self to* a dear *friend*,' seems to me to have two stresses coming together – a *trochee* at the beginning of the fourth foot, which is very common in Shakespeare's writing.

In this chapter we have been dealing with new verse forms and new patterns of speech, and Bassanio's 'heralding phrases' are one such pattern. But it's important to see that it is the 'patterns of speech' that are creating this new verse form.

It's not that Shakespeare's writing has simply become haphazard – with lines breaking just anywhere – and we have to find a way to make them 'work'. On the contrary, his writing reveals exactly what he has heard: that something is affecting the way his characters are *expressing* their thoughts, and that 'something' is how they are *feeling*.

Our job is not to find a way to make Shakespeare's lines 'work', but to work out what is happening to the characters we are playing.

The characters are not interested in the story: they don't speak to keep the story moving forwards: they speak because they need to express what they are feeling. It is what they are feeling that creates the story.

One of the directors working at the Globe was tempted on one occasion to remove from the script all the capitals from the beginning of the verse lines unless they also began a new sentence. The point behind it was to make the verse seem, to this director, less artificial and therefore more 'real'. For me Shakespeare's verse absolutely captures what is 'real'. Maybe we should feel from now on that the capitals are simply there to remind us of the place to breathe new life into the new line – the place where Shakespeare heard his characters doing just that.

This is probably the most important thing to have learnt about Shakespeare's verse, but it is not, as you will realise, the end of this book. Our next leap forward takes us to the end of the sixteenth century and the writing of *Hamlet*: another 'breakthrough' play.

Five

Hamlet

A Play of 'Highways' and 'Pop-ups'

And then sir does he this?
He does: what was I about to say?
I was about to say something: where did I leave?

Hamlet: Act 2, Scene 1

The above lines are spoken by Polonius, the King's chief counsellor. He is a great talker; he loves the sound of his own voice and sometimes, as here, comes unstuck.

Everyone in *Hamlet* talks at great length – except the Ghost, who remains silent on his first two appearances, though he makes up for that when he meets Hamlet, his son. We are in a world of talkers. Many of the characters in this play are students, and we know that students are always good for some lengthy conversations. But here, students and soldiers, rulers, counsellors and gravediggers, all seem to have so much to say. If you were to read through all Shakespeare's plays in order of composition, when you came to *Hamlet* you would be struck by the sheer amount of talking that goes on; not action but *talking*. In fact surprisingly little happens in *Hamlet*. The drama lies in what is said and not said. Sometimes, through soliloquies and asides, the characters tell us what is going on inside their heads. And the characters also tell other characters what they think about yet further characters. *Hamlet* is a play in which people can't stop *talking*.

Like *The Merchant of Venice*, this is another of Shakespeare's 'break-through' plays, but to a different degree. The breakthrough we saw in *The Merchant of Venice* – Shakespeare's ability to capture a more intimate, personal way of speaking – was huge, and from now on becomes the way Shakespeare's verse works. *Hamlet*'s breakthrough is to dissect the very act of *talking*. How speech can unconsciously reveal things; how speech can consciously attempt to conceal things. How good speakers use certain techniques to maintain interest and achieve clarity, and how poor ones confuse.

In Chapter 2 I said that we could call one of Lucilius's lines from *Julius Caesar* a 'pop-up' thought, because it interrupts the main thought-line with a sort of interjection, the main thought continuing after the 'pop-up' is over. *Hamlet,* written shortly after *Julius Caesar,* is full of such 'pop-ups'. And 'pop-ups' are yet another kind of 'speech-pattern' – such as we saw in the previous chapter.

For most people the character of Hamlet probably expands and deepens what it is possible for a 'character' to be in a play; we could similarly say that 'pops-ups' can expand and deepen the work we have been doing with 'thought-units': because 'pop-ups' are really no more than thoughts within thoughts. The characters in *Hamlet* use them both consciously and unconsciously, sometimes to good effect, though sometimes they reveal to us more than they intend.

To use them well we must first identify them. I want us now to take a careful look at the way these 'pop-ups' are used by Horatio, Polonius, Claudius, Gertrude and Hamlet.

Horatio

Even more so than *The Merchant of Venice, Hamlet* begins with doubt. In fact it is the most doubtful beginning of any of Shakespeare's plays.[1]

> *Enter* BARNARDO *and* FRANCISCO, *two sentinels.*
> BARNARDO. Who's there?
> FRANCISCO. Nay answer me: Stand and unfold your self.
>
> *Hamlet*: Act 1, Scene 1

Two sentries come across each other in the dark. Barnardo, who's entered to relieve Francisco, shouldn't be the one to call out 'Who's there?' That's the job of Francisco, the man still on duty. But why doesn't Barnardo realise the figure he half makes out in the dark has to be his colleague

Francisco? It's because for two nights now, Barnardo has seen a ghost walking these battlements. Barnardo fears that the figure standing in front of him might be that ghost: the ghost of old King Hamlet, young Hamlet's father. It's a wonderfully dramatic and jittery opening to this great play.

Shortly after Barnardo relieves Francisco, he is joined on his watch by Marcellus, a fellow soldier, and by Horatio, Hamlet's fellow student. Horatio has come to Elsinore to attend Old Hamlet's funeral. Barnardo and Marcellus, feeling they have to tell someone about having seen the ghost of the dead King, have brought Horatio to watch with them that night in case the ghost should appear again – which it does. Trying to find some possible reason behind the ghost's appearances, Marcellus asks whether there is anything in the fact that Denmark seems to be preparing for war. Can either of his companions tell him?

Here's Horatio's reply. It's a typically (for *Hamlet*) lengthy speech. It is also full of 'pop-up' thoughts – though they will become more obvious once we have divided the speech up into 'thought-units' and printed it out again with the original First Folio punctuation.

But here is how we are used to seeing the beginning of the speech as printed in a modern version:

HORATIO.   That can I;
 At least, the whisper goes so. Our last King,
 Whose image even but now appeared to us,
 Was, as you know, by Fortinbras of Norway,
 Thereto pricked on by a most emulate pride,
 Dared to the combat; in which our valiant Hamlet –
 For so this side of our known world esteemed him –
 Did slay this Fortinbras; who, by a sealed compact,
 Well ratified by law, and heraldry,
 Did forfeit, with his life, all those his lands
 Which he stood seized on, to the conqueror;

Let's now investigate the 'form' of the whole of Horatio's speech, with the Folio punctuation, and see if once again we can find anything new in it. I'm going to divide it up into thought-units as I've done before, but I'm also going to *italicise* all my so called 'pop-up' thoughts.

HORATIO.   That can I,
 At least the whisper goes so:

        Our last King,
 Whose image even but now appear'd to us,
 Was (*as you know*) by Fortinbras of Norway,
 (*Thereto prick'd on by a most emulate pride*)

Dar'd to the combat.

In which, our valiant Hamlet,

(For so this side of our known world esteem'd him)

Did slay this Fortinbras: who by a seal'd compact,
Well ratified by law, and heraldry,
Did forfeit (*with his life*) all those his lands
Which he stood seiz'd on, to the conqueror:

Against the which, a moiety competent
Was gaged by our King: which had return'd
To the inheritance of Fortinbras,
Had he been vanquisher, as by the same cov'nant
And carriage of the article design,
His fell to Hamlet.

Now sir, young Fortinbras,
Of unimproved mettle, hot and full,
Hath in the skirts of Norway, *here and there,*
Shark'd up a list of landless resolutes,
For food and diet, to some enterprise
That hath a stomach in't: which is no other
(*And it doth well appear unto our state*)
But to recover of us by strong hand
And terms compulsative, those foresaid lands
So by his father lost:

and this (*I take it*)
Is the main motive of our preparations,
The source of this our watch, and the chief head
Of this post-haste, and rummage in the land.

Hamlet: Act 1, Scene 1

The first thing we gain from identifying these 'pop-ups' is to map out the 'highways' and the 'byways' of such a speech. The 'byways' are the 'pop-ups': some of them might be cut from a production – and some of them frequently are. But what we'd lose by cutting a large proportion of them is that 'something' that is so engaging about a tale well told. After all, good speakers enliven what they have to say by adding this and adding that, the main story becoming all the more palatable on account of the added detail.

Good speakers will differentiate between the two; they have multiple voices. One voice will let their listeners know that they are now mapping out the main thrust of their tale (the 'highway') and another voice will indicate that now they are making a little detour to fill in some background information, or to throw in a little witticism.

It's something we all do all the time. Describe an incident which has just happened to you and you will achieve clarity by having one voice for your 'highway' and another for all your 'byways'. The 'byways', or 'pop-ups', give us a moment's relaxation. A 'byway voice' signals that, though this might be interesting, we don't need to concentrate on it to the same extent as for the 'highway'. We have a moment's 'let-off', which can be refreshing and give us more appetite for what is yet to come. Indeed, when an actor is hard to listen to, it may well be because they have not realised that their speech achieves life and clarity from the interplay of the 'highways' and 'pop-ups'.

One voice for the 'highway' another for a 'pop-up'.

Hamlet is filled with such interplay.

You should now try sounding the speech twice. First, play it all, trying to differentiate between the 'highways' and 'pop-ups'. Then play only the main thrust of the story – just those lines and phrases that are *not* in my italics.

Did you feel after the second reading that you'd 'cut' nothing that would be missed? Or was your main impression that without all the detail the 'highway' had become heavy and less easy to digest? I'm sure if we cut it all we'd lose most of what makes Horatio, Horatio: a story-teller with an acute and witty mind that can inform but also engage us at the same time.

I hope you also saw how the line endings could be useful to you in setting out the story clearly. Shakespeare likes to get his characters' names prominently standing at the ends of lines: just watch the technique by which he achieves that at the start of this speech.

> That can I,
>
> *At least the whisper goes so:*
>
> Our last **King**,
> *Whose image even but now appear'd to us,*
> Was (*as you know*) by **Fortinbras of Norway**,
> (*Thereto prick'd on by a most emulate pride*)
> Dar'd to the combat.

Horatio takes control of the moment with his answer to Marcellus's question, 'Who is't that can inform me?': 'That can I'. We feel sure he's going to tell us something now, but instead of launching straight into 'our last King', he slips in that little filler, 'At least the whisper goes so', which suggests that what follows will not be just a dry history lesson. It also gives his listeners a further moment to prepare themselves for the main thrust of the tale to begin. Our appetite is whetted.

And when the first character is named, 'our last King', the naming of him makes more impact on account of the prominence the phrase receives by coming at the end of the line. The prominence is enhanced because the whole of the next line is another 'pop-up', though different in tone. This one reminds us of the ghost we've all just seen and increases our desire to hear what Horatio has to tell us, because although it has already sounded from his opening words as if he might be able to tell us why Denmark could be going to war, now it seems as if he might be able to connect this with the ghost's appearance. So these 'pop-ups' can be quite seductive; they hook us in.

The next one, '(*as you know*)', makes us feel we are all in this thing together, but this little filler also allows the next character's name to find its place at the end of the line, 'Fortinbras of Norway'. And the next 'pop-up', '(*Thereto prick'd on by a most emulate pride*)', adds a touch of humour and probably appeals to the Danes' patriotic fervour. After we are introduced to the King, and 'Norway', the names 'Hamlet', 'Fortinbras' and 'young Fortinbras' follow prominently at subsequent line endings.

The later 'pop-ups' continue to interest and inform, but the longest one of five and a half lines –

> *Against the which, a moiety competent*
> *Was gaged by our King: which had return'd*
> *To the inheritance of Fortinbras,*
> *Had he been vanquisher, as by the same cov'nant*
> *And carriage of the article design,*
> *His fell to Hamlet.*

– might suggest to us, not to worry too much if we don't get this next bit, because it won't spoil our understanding of the main story that is being told.

'Byways', or 'pop-ups', are entertaining: they can pull us into a story, they keep us engaged, they can by contrast give more prominence to the 'highways', and they can also say to us, 'You can take or leave this bit.' Being able to play them well will enliven your performance considerably.

Polonius

Perhaps we deserve a moment of relaxation now, so let's take a look at one of Polonius's scenes. It comes from Act 2, Scene 2 where he tells the King and Queen that he thinks that Hamlet's madness has been brought about by his thwarted love for Polonius's daughter Ophelia.

Here are the thought-units and the 'highways' and the 'pop-ups' as I find them. As you will see, there's very little in the way of 'highways'! I think you should sound this one out right away.

POLONIUS. My liege, and madam,

to expostulate

What majesty should be, what duty is,
Why day is day; night, night; and time is time,
Were nothing but to waste night, day, and time.

Therefore, since brevity is the soul of wit,
And tediousness, the limbs and outward flourishes,
I will be brief.

Your noble son is mad:

Mad call I it; for to define true madness,
What is't, but to be nothing else but mad.

But let that go.

GERTRUDE.   More matter, with less art.
POLONIUS. Madam, I swear I use no art at all:

That he is mad, 'tis true:

'Tis true 'tis pity,

And pity it is true:

A foolish figure,

But farewell it: for I will use no art.

Mad let us grant him then: and now remains
That we find out the cause of this effect,

Or rather say, the cause of this defect;
For this effect defective, comes by cause,
Thus it remains, and the remainder thus.

Perpend,

I have a daughter: *have, whilst she is mine,*
Who in her duty and obedience, mark,
Hath given me this: now gather, and surmise.

Hamlet: Act 2, Scene 2

His 'pop-ups' lighten the tone of the tragedy, give delight and frequently, even in less than brilliant productions of *Hamlet*, the Polonius gives audiences huge pleasure. We would not be without them: they are his defining characteristic.

Claudius

Claudius is another matter; he is a controller. So his 'pop-ups' are instruments of control. Here he is manipulating Laertes into agreeing to assassinate Hamlet as a way of revenging his father's, Polonius's, death:

CLAUDIUS. Now must your conscience my acquittance seal,

And you must put me in your heart for friend,

Sith you have heard, *and with a knowing ear,*
That he *which hath your noble father slain,*
Pursued my life.

LAERTES.   It well appears.

                         But tell me,
Why you proceeded not against these feats,
So crimeful, and so capital in nature,
As by your safety, wisdom, *all things else,*
You mainly were stirr'd up?

CLAUDIUS.   O for two special reasons,
Which may to you (perhaps) seem much unsinewed,
And yet to me they're strong.

                    The Queen *his mother,*
Lives almost by his looks: and for my self,
My virtue or my plague, be it either which,
She's so conjunctive to my life and soul;
That as the star moves not but in his sphere,
I could not but by her.

               The other motive,
Why to a public count I might not go,
Is the great love the general gender bear him,

Who *dipping all his faults in their affection,*
Would *like the spring that turneth wood to stone,*
Convert his gyves* to graces. So that my arrows

gyves – shackles

Too slightly timber'd for so loud a wind,
Would have reverted to my bow again,
And not where I had aim'd them.

Hamlet: Act 4, Scene 7

Please sound out these two Claudius voices: what is the nature of that voice that's revealed by his 'pop-up' thoughts which I've put in italics? It's certainly different from Horatio's and Polonius's.

One interesting difference between Claudius's 'pop-ups' and Horatio's is that most of Horatio's occur early in the line, leaving the more prominent place at the ends of the lines to be filled with the key points of the story he has to tell. Claudius's 'pop-ups' all appear at the end of the lines, *in* those most prominent places. It is his 'pop-ups' that are given pride of place as it were; and why? Because Claudius is not really dealing in facts at all as Horatio was. His energies are all focused on the spin he can put on them.

It is worth remembering too that our 'pop-up' or 'byway' voices can be of two contrasting sorts. They can be either something of a witty throw-away, or they can be made more colourful and assertive than the 'highway' they depart from. Claudius's are undoubtedly of this second kind. Shakespeare, in capturing the 'sound' of his speech on the framework of his verse lines, directs the actor playing him, by placing these 'pop-ups' at the lines' ends, and thereby showing that for Claudius these are the phrases that need to strike home and lodge themselves in Laertes's grieving ears.

Claudius's 'pop-ups' are those of a manipulator. We hear him managing Laertes, flattering him by taking him into his confidence and by admitting to him some of his own shortcomings. He is urbane, pleased with himself; he's a man who expects to be agreed with. He's brave, but he works hard to be convincing. He is in control. We've all met people like him.

Gertrude

Later in this same scene Gertrude has a speech that on the face of it should reveal a lack of control, but curiously it seems not to do so. It would not be surprising to find here a very 'ragged' verse form, as she has apparently just seen Ophelia drowning and is telling Laertes what has happened to his sister.

Not many 'pop-ups' here I think. Sound this one out now. Laertes's line is, 'Drown'd! O where?', to which Gertrude replies,

> There is a willow grows aslant a brook,
> That shows his hoar* leaves in the glassy stream:

> There with fantastic garlands did she come,
> Of crow-flowers, nettles, daisies, and long purples,
> *That liberal shepherds give a grosser name;*
> *But our cold maids do dead men's fingers call them:*

> There on the pendent boughs, her crownet weeds
> Clamb'ring to hang; an envious sliver broke,
> When down the weedy trophies, and her self,
> Fell in the weeping brook,

>   her clothes spread wide,
> And mermaid-like, a while they bore her up,
> Which time she chanted snatches of old tunes,
> As one incapable of her own distress,

> *Or like a creature native, and endued**
> *Unto that element:*

>   but long it could not be,
> Till that her garments, heavy with their drink,
> Pull'd the poor wretch from her melodious lay,
> To muddy death.

Hamlet: Act 4, Scene 7

The whole speech is odd. The form of it seems to yield little. I have found and marked only two 'byways'. The second one sounds so arch:

> *Or like a creature native, and endued*
> *Unto that element:*

What odd words to describe a girl drowning in a brook. The word 'endued' is only used about five times in the whole of Shakespeare and 'element' only about a dozen. When Shakespeare does use the word 'element' it usually means the 'sky', not the element of water. In *Twelfth Night*, written just after *Hamlet*, the word is even described by Feste as being 'overworn'.

The first 'byway', the *'liberal shepherds... dead men's fingers call them'* bit – is even odder. What possesses her to think of saying such a thing in this situation? Maybe these 'pop-ups' hold a greater clue for us than might at first appear.

hoar – pale grey
endued unto – equipped for

She has to say something in answer to Laertes's question, 'Drown'd? O where?', but she barely answers that at all. 'There is a brook' is all she says; not where this brook is, which has been his question. She seems to be at pains to explain that it was all a terrible accident, and Ophelia just didn't know what was happening to her. But was Gertrude actually near by, or was she seeing all this from afar? The detail suggests that she saw clearly everything that was happening: she names the different flowers that Ophelia had gathered for her garland. But if she was so close why did she not call for help or run herself to save her? I wonder if she is making it all up.

Perhaps she saw nothing. Perhaps she has simply been informed that Ophelia has drowned herself. Laertes has to be told, and she decides she must be the one to tell him. Given her position, she will be able to make her version the official one. Listening to her, it sounds like a tragic accident and that Ophelia's death was somehow peaceful, even somehow *beautiful*. 'A brook' sounds as if it would not be a danger to anyone other than a child. And this brook is already 'weeping' in sympathy, it seems, as is presumably the 'willow' too.

So, if I am right, Gertrude saw none of this and is improvising the whole speech. In order to convince Laertes that she has seen all these things and is *not* making it up, she has to keep talking, and she finds herself, maybe to her horror, saying this completely inappropriate thing about the rude name shepherds give to 'long purples', and in trying to smooth over that she finds herself then unfortunately talking about 'dead men's fingers'.

Why is she behaving in this way? She is desperate, but is trying to hide all that desperation. If it gets out that Ophelia has committed suicide, she will not be given a Christian burial. So Ophelia's death has to be an accident. Laertes is already up in arms about his father's hurried interring.

Gertrude has also undoubtedly heard that Hamlet is on his way home. So her story of the accidental death is also to try to save Hamlet from being seen as guilty for Ophelia's death as well as Polonius's. She also does not want to stoke up Laertes's rage any further; he has already threatened to kill Claudius. If all this is so, then the effort involved in passing this off as the truth will have been enormous. And so it seems: at the end of the scene, after Laertes has exited, she is left speechless.

Instead of Gertrude saying something to Claudius as he winds up the scene, the next voice we hear is that of the Gravedigger, entering for the next scene, who asks his assistant,

> Is she to be buried in Christian burial, that wilfully seeks her own salvation?
>
> *Hamlet*: Act 5, Scene 1, line 1

Gertrude's charade has only had a limited effect. The word from the grave-yard is that it was suicide.

The oddness of Gertrude's vocabulary in both her 'pop-ups' might be opening a window onto her duplicity. But the first one may have revealed even more about her. Why should some bawdy word for 'long purples' have popped into her mind in the middle of her improvisation? The ghost had spoken of her lustfulness when he first speaks to Hamlet.

> GHOST. But virtue, as it never will be moved,
> Though lewdness court it in a shape of heaven:
> So lust, though to a radiant angel link'd,
> Will sate itself in a celestial bed,
> And prey on garbage.
>
> *Hamlet*: Act 1, Scene 5

Maybe this 'pop-up' has found her out.

Hamlet

In Hamlet's first soliloquy (Act 1, Scene 2) the 'pop-ups' work in a com-pletely different way.

Here is the full speech as printed in a modern edition. Hamlet is in despair and suicidal:

> HAMLET. O, that this too too solid flesh, would melt,
> Thaw, and resolve itself into a dew!
> Or that the Everlasting had not fixed
> His canon 'gainst self-slaughter! O God! God!
> How weary, stale, flat, and unprofitable,
> Seems to me all the uses of this world!
> Fie on't? Ah, fie! 'tis an unweeded garden,
> That grows to seed; things rank and gross in nature
> Possess it merely. That it should come to this!
> But two months dead! Nay, not so much, not two.
> So excellent a king that was to this
> Hyperion to a satyr; so loving to my mother,
> That he might not beteem the winds of heaven
> Visit her face too roughly. Heaven and earth!
> Must I remember? Why she would hang on him
> As if increase of appetite had grown
> By what it fed on; and yet, within a month –
> Let me not think on't. Frailty, thy name is woman! –

A little month, or ere those shoes were old
With which she followed my poor father's body,
Like Niobe, all tears – why she, even she –
O God! a beast that wants discourse of reason
Would have mourned longer – married with mine uncle,
My father's brother; but no more like my father
Than I to Hercules. Within a month,
Ere yet the salt of most unrighteous tears
Had left the flushing of her gallèd eyes,
She married. O, most wicked speed, to post
With such dexterity to incestuous sheets!
It is not, nor it cannot come to good.
But break, my heart, for I must hold my tongue.

If we divide it into 'thought-units', the speech looks radically different. Different from any other speech we have so far looked at. If we were all to do this exercise, I know we would come up with many different versions. The speech is in 'free-fall'.

In my version below, I have again put what I consider to be the 'pop-ups' into italics. But I have also put in bold those self-interruptions of his which in another speech would probably be thought of as 'pop-ups' as well. (Maybe we should call these 'double pop-ups'!) The 'highway' here is only five lines long. And below, as opposed to the speech as printed above, the punctuation is, once again, that of the First Folio.[2]

HAMLET. O that this too too solid flesh, would melt,
Thaw, and resolve itself into a dew:
Or that the Everlasting had not fix'd
His canon 'gainst self-slaughter.

O God, O God!

How weary, stale, flat, and unprofitable
Seems to me all the uses of this world?

Fie on't? Oh fie, fie,

'tis an unweeded garden
That grows to seed: Things rank, and gross in nature,
Possess it merely.

That it should come to this:

But two months dead:

Nay, not so much; not two,

So excellent a King, that was to this

Hyperion* to a satyr:*

                so loving to my mother,
That he might not beteem* the winds of heaven
Visit her face too roughly.

                   Heaven and earth
Must I remember:

              why she would hang on him,
As if increase of appetite had grown
By what it fed on;

            and yet within a month?

Let me not think on't:

           Frailty, thy name is woman.

A little month,

        or ere those shoes were old,
With which she followed my poor father's body
Like Niobe, all tears.
          Why she, even she.

(O God!

       A beast that wants discourse of reason
Would have mourn'd longer)

            married with mine uncle,

My father's brother:

        but no more like my father,
Than I to Hercules.

        Within a month?

Ere yet the salt of most unrighteous tears
Had left the flushing of her galled eyes,
She married.

       O most wicked speed, to post*

With such dexterity to incestuous sheets:

It is not, nor it cannot come to good.

But break my heart, for I must hold my tongue.

            Hamlet: Act 1, Scene 2

Hyperion – god of the sun
satyr – half-man, half-goat
beteem – allow
post – hurry

This soliloquy has no ending: it's interrupted by the arrival of Horatio, Marcellus, and Bernardo who've come to tell Hamlet that his father's ghost has been seen.

What are we to think of this speech? There is something headlong about the course of it and yet it is composed of fragments. Yet the fragments are jammed together. It is certainly not full of gaps. If ever we needed convincing that a speech is made of many little phrases, like a mosaic, this is the one to do it.

The 'pop-ups' in the speech are the memories that surface unbidden from Hamlet's mind and the realisations that imprint themselves into his consciousness. On the one hand, the memories are of his mum and dad: Dad shielding Mum from the wind; her clinging to him, as if the more she touched him the more she wanted him; the shoes she wore for his funeral; how red her eyes were from weeping. On the other hand, the realisations are that the world no longer holds for him anything of value; what's happened defies belief; the difference between his uncle and his father is laughable; women are what is wrong with the world; no animal would have behaved as his mother has; what's happened is wicked, and no good can come of it.

Then there are the five cries of pain saying: stop these thoughts from coming!

Finally the 'highway' is left saying almost nothing at all: 'If only I could die, or kill myself… but I have to shut up'.

If you look at the 'form' on the page, once we've divided it up into our 'thought-units' – however roughly done, however much we feel unsure that we've really caught all its twists and turns – the shape we are left with is one of fragmentation: a soul in pieces.

There are a number of 'ragged' lines, which help to capture his disturbed state, but the line endings themselves still usefully map out differences and antitheses. Many of the line endings again refer to the characters in Hamlet's drama; his mother, his father and his uncle, and, though not always named, we can tell that the 'this' at the end of the eleventh line is his hated uncle and the 'him' at the end of the fifteenth line is his beloved father.

The fractures in the lines are so numerous that there are as many broken lines as there are lines that play through to the line's end unbroken.

Given this incredible shake-up of the form of the verse we need to ask ourselves questions again as to how this might affect our breathing and hence our delivery of the whole speech. You will remember, in the last chapter, my contention that the new line needs a new breath in order to play it creatively. You may also have noticed that at the same time I was suggesting that some 'mid-line' phrases might also benefit from the breath being 'topped up' before them.

Now it used to be said that it was an acting sin to break one of Shakespeare's lines in the middle, and to take a new breath 'mid-line', but if I ever thought that myself, I no longer do. If your instincts tell you to breathe mid-line, do so. But I must be clear: it's still best *not* to break a line *if you don't have to.*

Look at these four lines (I've marked the breaths in again for you to try):

> ˇ *Ere yet the salt of most unrighteous tears*
> ˇ *Had left the flushing of her galled eyes,*
> ˇ *She married.*
>   ˇ *O most wicked speed, to post*
> ˇ *With such dexterity to incestuous sheets:*

I'd say that there seems little reason to break the flow of the first two or the last of these lines. But I think everyone would want to breathe again in the third line after the full stop and before the onset of that 'O'. Especially as that 'O' is the sound that follows the taking in of such a deep breath!

> ˇ *O most wicked speed,* ˇ *to **post***

And *now* you'll notice I have added another possible breath point before '*to post*', which I've put there just in case you've used up much of the breath you took in order to say that '*O most wicked speed*', and that you no longer have enough left to give full emotional vent to that '*to post*'. But remember that you still need another breath before the next line,

> ˇ *O most wicked speed,* ˇ *to **post***
> ˇ *With **such dexterity** to incestuous sheets:*

or you won't have enough air in the lungs to play that line with the right degree of emotional discovery. And if you were ever tempted instead to take in an abnormally deep breath to cope with these emotional gymnastics that the lines call for, the results would not sound natural.

To sum up: a single breath is sufficient to express many lines with clarity and feeling. But Shakespeare also realises that just as frequently we take additional breaths so as to *shape* certain phrases, or even single words *within* the line. In other words, we take the 'extra' breaths in order to be more expressive.

And these places should always include some mark of punctuation. For instance in '˓ˇ*O most wicked speed,* ˇ *to post*', it is the comma before 'to post' which directs us to the possibility of breathing before it. So I'm now suggesting you may sometimes want to take breaths in quick succession.

Look at these earlier lines of Hamlet's:

> *How weary, stale, flat, and unprofitable*
> *Seems to me all the uses of this world?*

Although this first line could play through without a break, those three commas, giving emphasis to each of those bitter words, might mean that *your* Hamlet needs to snatch a breath between some or all of them.

> ˇ *How weary,* ˇ *stale,* ˇ *flat,* ˇ *and unprofitable*
> ˇ *Seems to me all the uses of this world?*

Mid-line breaths like these will be of the lightest and shortest duration. Even when you choose to take one, you yourself may wonder whether you actually did or not, they will be so fleeting and imperceptible.

So there we have it. You are free to follow your instincts. If your instinct tells you to play through a line, then do so. If you need to breathe within the line, do that. However, if you don't breathe *before* the new line, something will have been lost creatively.

The irony in all this is that actors usually breathe within a line exactly when and where they wish, but generally they fail to top up their breath before the new line when a thought is running on from one line to the next. In doing so they miss the sound of how Shakespeare's character is phrasing that particular thought.

So to sum up: don't break up lines needlessly. If we can 'master' the whole line and play it through on one breath, there is a joy released in being able to do so. And when the thoughts 'straddle' the lines and you find the way to express that thought in two parts, another joy will come your way as you recreate again the sounds that Shakespeare first heard.

Now we have added this third category when, within the line, some words and phrases (marked by some Folio punctuation) ask for some individual shaping, and it will be by the taking of these fleetingly snatched additional breaths that you will have achieved this. And remember this is all so as to achieve a greater level of naturalism, clarity and spontaneity. And to make *you* more creative.

But as I've said earlier, paying attention to where you breathe is what you should do as you are working on a part, just as a musician would do: learning to hear how your character *phrases* the expression of their thoughts. In other words this is a *rehearsal* technique so that, by the time you come to *performance,* you are free to play your part without having to think about where you breathe, yet knowing that you will have become at one with the phrasing as Shakespeare heard it and wrote it. It's now time for you to turn back to this soliloquy and sound it out.

To return to Hamlet: why is this fractured soliloquy, composed of 'pop-ups' so riveting? It's because it captures reality. We listen to it and we know that that is how our own minds work; images, like Hercules, suddenly rushing into consciousness. In the theatre the workings of a mind is what great soliloquies give us.

Never, before Hamlet, had a mind so intimately and nakedly revealed itself to an audience's view. It is totally engrossing; hearing it we may well understand things from it that even Hamlet, caught in the confusion of this torrent of words breaking from him, doesn't understand himself.

How can she have behaved in this way? I think if we had never seen this play before, we might well be able to listen to him and realise the answer to his question. Hamlet has to wait for his meeting with the Ghost in order to have it explained it to him. It is then that he is told that Gertrude and Claudius had been lovers for some time, long before their sudden marriage.[3] Maybe he gets close to knowing this during the soliloquy and that if he hadn't been interrupted by the arrival of Horatio and Marcellus…

When Jonathan Pryce played Hamlet in 1980 there was no Ghost: Pryce spoke the Ghost's words himself as if he'd been possessed by the spirit of his father.[4] It was a thrilling theatrical coup. And so although not the play as written, it made perfect sense for him to experience that moment when he suddenly knew what had gone on. And that all the actions he had witnessed between his father's death and the marriage, which before had seemed totally inexplicable and had driven him to thoughts of suicide, now were clear; now all those same actions made horrifying, but explicable, sense. For us, drawn in, watching and listening to him, either way, it is a totally involving relationship. Soliloquies have this power.

Soliloquy

Soliloquies happen when a character, alone, held by whatever moment of the drama they are caught in, *shares* with us, the audience, their predicament. Soliloquies demand our attention, and seem to ask us for solutions. If we are spoken to like this, we can't help but be involved, and while we may never shout out possible courses of action to those characters on the stage, we know from our own lives, it is sometimes simply by talking things over to a sympathetic and silent listener, that ideas and solutions come to us. So with soliloquies: it can be as if the audience's involvement prompts those who are soliloquising.

Soliloquies are not characters on their own, speaking to themselves.

While actors may occasionally find addressing the audience an unnatural thing to do, at the Globe, where actor and audience are both in the same light, it becomes a most natural way of proceeding. Audiences find these interactions an intensely personal experience, and most 'real'; partly because the pace of the character's unfolding thoughts reflects the speed with which their minds are working too. The result can be mesmerising.

In *Othello* soliloquies draw us into the perverted world of Iago. Soliloquies will draw us inside the murderously ambitious minds of the Macbeths. So we see things through their eyes with the result that for a while *we are on their side* and hope the Macbeths get away with the murder of poor old, innocent Duncan.

But it's worth asking a question with regards to any soliloquy: who does the character believe he or she is speaking to?

Audiences, when addressed, become different characters at different times. We can be an army, or a mob. We can be the witnesses at a trial. We can become the friends of the protagonists, as when Benedick in *Much Ado About Nothing* wittily shares his thoughts with us. Often we can become several different people within the same play. In *Richard III* we become opposing armies as we are appealed to and harangued by both Richmond and Richard within a couple of minutes. Some characters might be selective in who they choose to share their feelings with. Hamlet, though, shares his thoughts freely with all; it's as if he takes all of us to be his fellows. And his openness is what makes his character so universally appealing.

Later when we come to look at *Macbeth* we'll find that Lady Macbeth's first soliloquy is not so much to us as to her absent husband. In his turn, Macbeth may ask us,

> Is this a dagger, which I see before me,
> The handle toward my hand?
>
> *Macbeth*: Act 2, Scene 1

but most of the rest of the speech is towards the invisible dagger itself. Soliloquies can be prayers; once or twice it seems to me that, in the mind of the actor/character, some of the audience might have become that character's own forebears.[5]

But whoever we are, we will be drawn into the drama, and we will understand so much more than if we had remained simply observers. By being invited inside their minds, we feel the emotional pains of the hero's predicament, the joys and trials of the heroine; we also understand the awful excitement of temptation, and the daringness of these perverted plotters; and it is only later in these plays that we want those fascinating, but evil, characters stopped.

So this extraordinary soliloquy of Hamlet's draws us into his mind which is where we will stay until he comes to the last of his 1,422 lines; at which point we'll hear him say – and I think it's meant to make us smile, even if our hearts are breaking at the same time –

the rest is silence.

Hamlet: Act 5, Scene 2

Our interest in *Hamlet* is in what Hamlet thinks. His 'pop-ups' are where we catch the rawest minting of those thoughts.

The 'pop-ups' of Horatio and Hamlet serve different purposes: one gives us some moments of comparative relaxation, the other transfixes us more deeply. Polonius's 'pop-ups' reveal what is most characteristically amusing about him; those of Claudius define him very differently. Gertrude's reveal more than she meant us to see.

Identifying the 'pop-ups' helps us understand the character and what is happening to them in these passages. Playing the 'pop-ups' encourages us to capture the varying way people actually speak, all around us, every day. From now on we must be on the lookout for them.

So far in this book we have been dividing up the verse into thought-units, and now in this chapter we have taken this a stage further by dividing the thought-units into 'highways' and 'pop-ups'. Eventually, as our work moves towards performance, we should become less conscious of these divisions and discover something about the overall shape and flow of any particular speech. However, our thoughts should still remain *active* as we negotiate these divisions, and we should continue to focus on achieving a constant *variety of tone*.

The smoothness of the verse needs to be constantly ruffled.

Shakespeare's verse itself is pitted with deliberate *irregularities*, which further 'ruffle' his lines, as he captures the raw minting of speech, with its hesitations and pauses, together with odd emphases that temporarily throw the iambic beat off course, drawing our attention to some arresting and needful emphasis. These 'irregularities' – non-iambic beats, together with 'short lines', 'shared lines' and lines with extra syllables, should all be seen as exciting clues, that will further help us to understand the emotional life of these characters that we are trying to play.

'Short lines' – when the pulse of the play continues in silence – will reveal important actions or dramatic hesitations. 'Shared lines' – when two speakers form a complete line between them – will show us how characters relate to each other. And fluctuations *within* relationships are revealed by changes in the *forms of address*.

You'll have noticed already that characters in Shakespeare's plays sometimes call each other 'thou', and sometimes 'you'. And sometimes they can be saying 'you' to a character one minute and 'thou' the next. Whenever this happens, the feelings those characters have for each other will have changed too.

The next chapter will take a close look at these purposeful anomalies and irregularities. How, as we immerse ourselves in these texts, it is this 'ruffling' of the lines that finally convinces us of the *authenticity* of those voices that demand to be heard. We'll start this investigation by looking at the way the words 'you' and 'thou' can sometimes switch places and why.

Six

Forms of Address, Verse Irregularities
– and What They Tell Us

HORATIO. Now cracks a noble heart: Goodnight sweet
    prince,
And flights of angels sing thee to thy rest,

                    Hamlet: Act 5, Scene 2

The way Shakespeare uses 'you' and 'thou'

The lines quoted above are Horatio's final words to Hamlet at the moment of Hamlet's death. It is the only time in the play that he addresses Hamlet as 'thee'. At all other times he says 'you' to him. Hamlet sometimes says 'you' to Horatio, but more often calls him 'thou', or 'thee'. What lies behind these apparent irregularities, and what can we learn from them?

In David and Ben Crystal's excellent book *Shakespeare's Words*, they tell us very succinctly that 'in Old English, *thou* was singular and *you* was plural; but during the thirteenth century, *you* started to be used as a polite form of the singular – probably because people copied the French way of talking, where *vous* was used in that way. English then became like French, which had *tu* and *vous* both possible for singulars, giving speakers a choice.'

You will probably have been aware yourselves while reading out aloud from all the passages in this book how 'you' is more common that 'thou' or 'thee', and 'your' more common than 'thy' or 'thine'. But you may not have stopped to think why these different forms are used.

The basic rules are very simple. Most commonly, and especially when the speakers are of equal status, they say 'you' to each other. But frequently those of higher status (like kings to subjects, parents to children, masters to servants) will use 'thou' and in return those of lower status will deferentially use 'you' by way of reply. 'Thou', however, can also be used by those in a fond or intimate relationship. And frequently by parents to children, the 'status' use of 'thou' is probably overlaid with the love that the parent feels for their offspring.

Between lovers 'thou' is common, though especially by men to women; the women may continue to use 'you' in response. That might be because they are more cautious about using the 'thou' form to their lovers and so revealing too clearly the depth of their feelings, or because of the perceived 'status' difference between men and woman. But Romeo and Juliet use 'thou' to each other almost without exception. Here's Juliet calling down to Romeo from her balcony, with virtually the first words they say alone to each other:

Art **thou** not Romeo and a Montague?

And he answers,

Neither fair maid, if either **thee** dislike.

However, and this is the rather surprising thing we have to remember, 'thou' can also be used as an insult if it's said to someone to whom you should show respect, or to someone whom you would normally feel on equal terms with and would therefore each be expecting to use the 'you' form to the other. To an enemy you would 'thou' them. In fact the very first line of Shakespeare's that we looked at in this book was that of the Soldier who captured Lucilius in *Julius Caesar*, calling out as he did so,

Yield, or **thou** diest.

If we are speaking to God however, for instance in The Lord's Prayer, we say 'Thou', acknowledging the intimate and loving relationship we have with him.

These are the general rules about the use of 'you' and 'thou', but there is one other general category that we should take on board now, and that is when we are speaking to those who can't hear us, or are absent, asleep or dead. To all these the 'thou' form is used. One interesting example of this can be found in *The Winter's Tale*.

Hermione, Queen of Sicilia, only uses the 'thou' form in reference to her husband Leontes on one occasion, and it occurs while she is talking to their guest, Polixenes, King of Bohemia, who is Leontes's childhood friend. She is trying to persuade Polixenes, who has been staying with them for nine months already, to stay a little longer, which she knows would please Leontes. She tries to make a bargain with Polixenes: when her husband visits him in Bohemia she'll let him stay a month longer than was planned. Sound out her lines and try to work out why she says 'I love **thee**' to Leontes on this occasion:

> When at Bohemia
> You take my lord, I'll give him my commission,
> To let him there a month, behind the gest*
> Prefix'd for's parting:
>
>   yet (good deed)* Leontes,
> I love **thee** not a jar o'th'clock, behind
> What lady she her lord.
>
>   You'll stay?

The Winter's Tale: Act 1, Scene 2

The first and third thought-units are clearly spoken to, and heard by, Polixenes, but not so the middle one. Yet neither does she intend this to be heard by her husband – he has left Hermione and Polixenes together, and is probably watching his wife and his best friend from a distance. So this middle thought-unit is an 'aside' to her husband, only heard by the audience, and she uses the 'thou' form to him, partly because that is how you address those who can't hear you, but also because, in this instance, 'thou' is the appropriate language of someone expressing her unconditional love for her husband. Shortly afterwards Leontes will accuse his wife of having an affair with Polixenes, so, having heard Hermione's aside, we will realise that Leontes is gravely mistaken.

Characters in Shakespeare may lie to each other but never to the audience.

Hermione's use of 'thou' here is an interesting clue for both actors and directors alike, but even more interesting is how Shakespeare can chart the fluctuations *within* a relationship by the way that characters switch between the 'you' and 'thou' forms, revealing a change in their feelings towards each other. At the beginning of *The Winter's Tale* we hear Leontes using the loving 'thou' form to his wife as he reminds her of their courtship days:

gest – time or date
good deed – to tell the truth

LEONTES.   Why, that was when
Three crabbed months had sour'd themselves to death,
Ere I could make **thee** open **thy** white hand:
And clap **thy** self my love; then didst **thou** utter,
I am yours for ever.

The Winter's Tale: Act 1, Scene 2

But in the very next scene, Leontes, now falsely convinced of his wife's adultery, moves within two speeches, from the cooler use of 'you' to her, to the abusive use of 'thou', as he forbids his pregnant wife to have any more contact with their son Mamillius:

LEONTES. Give me the boy, I am glad **you** did not nurse him:
Though he does bear some signs of me, yet **you**
Have too much blood in him.

HERMIONE.   What is this? Sport?

LEONTES. Bear the boy hence, he shall not come about her,
Away with him, and let her sport her self
With that she's big-with, for 'tis Polixenes
Has made **thee** swell thus.

The Winter's Tale: Act 2, Scene 1

Another example of 'you' and 'thou' uses: Hamlet and Horatio

We'll return now to *Hamlet* to see how the relationship between Hamlet and Horatio finds different modes of expression with these alternating 'forms of address'. Usually, as I mentioned at the beginning of this chapter, Hamlet addresses Horatio as 'thou' while Horatio says 'you' by way of response.

Immediately we have to decide why Hamlet uses the 'thou' form, because we could interpret this in either of two ways. It could be that Hamlet is stressing his superior princely status over Horatio; however, a few lines from Act 3, Scene 2 should convince us otherwise. Here before the 'play scene' Hamlet calls for Horatio:

HAMLET. What ho, Horatio?

HORATIO. Here sweet lord, at **your** service.

HAMLET. Horatio, **thou** art e'en as just a man
As e'er my conversation cop'd withal.

Hamlet's use of 'thou' denotes his affection for Horatio, and if we are in any doubt about this we can look to a few lines later in this same speech, where he says:

> Dost **thou** hear,
> Since my dear soul was mistress of my choice,
> And could of men distinguish, her election
> Hath seal'd **thee** for her self.

Hamlet's relationships with the other major characters in the play are fraught with difficulty, but his relationship with Horatio remains constant. But then why does Hamlet use the 'you' form to Horatio at their *first* encounter in Act 1, Scene 2?

> HORATIO. Hail to **your** lordship.
>
> HAMLET.   I am glad to see **you** well:
>   Horatio, or I do forget my self.
>
> HORATIO. The same my lord, and **your** poor servant ever.

The answer here is fairly clear to see: Hamlet has just been interrupted during his first soliloquy, by the unexpected arrival of Horatio, Marcellus and Bernardo (see above, Chapter 5, pages 75–6), and doesn't realise that it's Horatio who has just spoken to him. 'I am glad to see you well', is simply Hamlet's polite response to some unknown well-wisher. Then immediately he realises it is Horatio, whom he hasn't seen for some several weeks.

However, he *continues* to use the 'you' form as the scene develops, Hamlet now taking issue with Horatio's description of himself as Hamlet's servant, and the reason he does so is that while the relationship between the two men remains constant, the full *expression* of that relationship is only apparent when they are alone together:

> HAMLET. Sir my good friend, I'll change that name with **you**:
>   And what make **you** from Wittenberg Horatio?
>   Marcellus.
>
> MARCELLUS. My good lord.
>
> HAMLET. I am very glad to see you: good even sir.
>   But what in faith make **you** from Wittenberg?

Hamlet continues to use the 'you' form to Horatio because of the presence of the two soldiers, whom he now greets; to start using 'thou' to Horatio would be too intimate a way of speaking in the presence of others. However, he switches to 'thou' just once, as the scene deepens emotionally:

HAMLET. But what is **your** affair in Elsinore?
We'll teach **you** to drink deep, ere you depart.
HORATIO. My lord, I came to see **your** father's funeral.
HAMLET. I pray **thee** do not mock me (fellow student)
I think it was to see my mother's wedding.

Horatio's mention of Hamlet's father's funeral reawakens the pain of that soliloquy Hamlet has just delivered, and for a moment we get a glimpse of the strong bond he feels for Horatio. Maybe this suggests that Hamlet takes Horatio aside for these few lines. But immediately afterwards the scene becomes a public one again: everything Hamlet says during the rest of the scene is addressed not only to Horatio, but to the soldiers as well – and so of course when speaking to the three of them, he naturally says 'you'.

But when they are alone together, Hamlet uses the intimate 'thou' form to his friend. And finally, he uses it again when he is dying,– even though others are now present – as he makes to Horatio one final request:

HAMLET. If **thou** didst ever hold me in **thy** heart,
Absent **thee** from felicity awhile,
And in this harsh world draw **thy** breath in pain,
To tell my story.

Hamlet: Act 5, Scene 2

It's not a relationship of equals as Horatio's continuing use of the 'you' form to Hamlet makes clear. However, at the end, just a few lines later, Horatio says:

HORATIO.   Goodnight sweet prince,
And flights of angels sing **thee** to thy rest,

Why the switch now? Well you may have guessed – it's because Hamlet is now dead. And to the dead, or any that can't hear us, the 'thou' form is used. And yet, beyond that accepted usage, we'd have to say that Horatio's 'thee', is also expressing the love he felt for Hamlet, which he could never speak of while Hamlet was alive.

These changes have been subtler than the ones we saw in *A Winter's Tale* – others that we'll come across later will also be more obvious and dramatic. But here in *Hamlet* we see Shakespeare responding sensitively to how someone speaks to a dear friend in private as opposed to when they are in company, and how these considerations can be put aside in moments of extremity, as when Hamlet is in pain or dying.

From now on, many of the scenes we will be looking at will give us further examples as to how the relationships between characters, by these alternating 'forms of address', are seen to be in a state of flux: all are important clues for the actors playing those roles. Such effects are miniature, but they are also substantial, and I now want to focus our attention on the skill with which Shakespeare handles details, not of vocabulary, but of poetic metre.

Throwing the rhythm in Hamlet

Earlier in this book we have talked about how Shakespeare purposefully varies the iambic rhythm by introducing trochaic beats into the lines, and how the reason behind this is to capture the way characters need to arrest our attention to some particular words they are using and in so doing to release and express some pent-up emotion. The most common place for these trochaic beats to occur is at the beginning of the line and these lines from Gertrude's speech, which we looked at (see above, Chapter 5, page 71) contain three such trochaic first feet:

> **There** on the pendent boughs, her crownet weeds
> **Clamb'ring** to hang; an envious sliver broke,
> When down the weedy trophies, and her self,
> **Fell** in the weeping brook,

> *Hamlet*: Act 4, Scene 7

These trochees add an emotional intensity to her account of Ophelia's death. However, we also find Shakespeare frequently employing this rhythm at the beginning of the third or fourth foot – on the fifth or seventh syllable in the line. The result is we then get two stresses coming together in the same line.

After the 'play scene' which has revealed to Hamlet Claudius's guilt, Hamlet is anxious and emotionally charged about the confrontation that he's about to have with his mother:

> How in my words somever she be shent,*
> To give them **seals, never** my soul consent.

> *Hamlet*: Act 3, Scene 2

Immediately on his way to his mother's closet he comes across Claudius at prayer and thinks about killing him there and then:

> Now might I do it **pat, now** he is praying,

> *Hamlet*: Act 3, Scene 3

shent – blamed

And then after he has mistakenly killed the concealed Polonius, thinking it was Claudius hiding behind the curtain, he's desperately trying to calm his distraught mother:

> Leave wringing of your **hands**, **peace**, sit you down,
>
> *Hamlet*: Act 3, Scene 4

And later in the same scene as he asks her how she could have left his father for Claudius:

> Could you on this fair mountain leave to feed,
> And batten on this **moor**? **Ha**? Have you eyes?

All these deliberate disturbances to the iambic rhythm allow the emotional weight of these varying situations to find authentic release. It's worth noting that all these double stresses are separated by a mark of punctuation, and, by looking out for such constructions this will help you to find more such lines for yourselves. Otherwise you should do what I'm always suggesting you do with any line of verse: look at it to understand it, and then simply say it as you feel it should be said, and for the most part, these dramatic double stresses will reveal themselves to you as you say the line out loud.

Purposeful irregularities in the lines

Hamlet also has its fair share of 'purposeful irregularities' within the lines. Sometimes one or two syllables are missing from the middle of a line, and these can show us places where Shakespeare imagines a pause within the flow of a speech. When Hamlet debates, in that most famous of all speeches, whether it is 'nobler in the mind to suffer' or whether he should act and 'take arms', he has his moment of doubt, sounding as a moment of thought-filled silence in the rhythm of the text:

> For in that sleep of death, what dreams may come,
> When we have shuffled off this mortal coil,
> Must give us pause.   There's the respect
> That makes calamity of so long life:
>
> *Hamlet*: Act 3, Scene 1

That third line is short – there are only eight syllables, or four stresses in the line rather than the five needed to make up a full pentameter. I've printed the line with a gap in it to show how it is – appropriately after the word 'pause' – that the two syllables are missing, during which Hamlet comes face to face with the fear of death. During this 'hesitation' he begins to realise that this is why we all cling on to life, rather than taking action and putting our lives at risk; putting up with hardship, rather than doing away with ourselves. But this pause is 'written in'. The rhythm of the line, and the drama, moves forward through a moment of stillness and silence.

A *short* Hamlet *line*

We'll frequently discover 'moments of silence' indicated in an even simpler way: this is not to do with gaps *within* the lines, they are simply lines that are short of a full length, and in Shakespeare these always point to some necessary silence, or some piece of stage-business taking the place of the missing syllables. Here's one dramatic example from *Hamlet* – the death of Polonius, stabbed by Hamlet as he hides behind a curtain, though Gertrude is frightened that Hamlet might be about to attack *her*.

(Because I want us to be aware of these 'forms of address' throughout this chapter, I have italicised Gertrude's use of '*thou*' to Hamlet. Later in the scene she switches between the intimate 'thou' form and the cooler 'you' form four times.)

> GERTRUDE. What wilt *thou* do? *thou* wilt not murder me?
>   Help, help, ho.
> POLONIUS.   What ho, help, help, help.
> HAMLET. How now, a rat? dead for a ducat, dead.
> POLONIUS. O I am slain.
> GERTRUDE.   O me, what hast *thou* done?
> HAMLET. Nay I know not, is it the King?
> GERTRUDE. O what a rash, and bloody deed is this?
>
>   *Hamlet*: Act 3, Scene 4

The line that is short is Hamlet's second line, 'Nay I know not, is it the King?' The line is missing two syllables, and thus missing the final stress in the line. Can you imagine what happens here? The final stress in the line is supplied by Polonius's body thudding through the curtain onto the floor. While Gertrude's line before this tells us she doesn't know what's happened behind the curtain, her next line makes clear that the evidence of what has happened is now lying at her feet. In the Folio there is no stage direction to tell us when Polonius's body is discovered or falls, but Hamlet's short line, and the lines of Gertrude's that surround it, give us all the clues we need.

Shakespeare's 'irregularities' are purposeful.

Before we leave this short passage, let's just notice this example of a shared line, because we are about to look at 'shared lines' in more detail. Here the iambic pentameter (with a trochaic first foot) is created by the two speakers – Gertrude comes in on cue (as you would naturally do when you hear someone cry out) with the result that the sound runs unbroken through the two parts of the line:

POLONIUS. O I am slain.

GERTRUDE.   O me, what hast thou done?

The development of the 'shared line' in Shakespeare's plays

So a shared line is one in which two speakers create a full pentameter line between them. As a pentameter contains five stresses, it will almost always be the case that one speaker's part-line will contain three stresses, and the other two. In the earliest of Shakespeare's plays there are very few of these 'shared lines'. As I mentioned briefly in Chapter 2, characters in those early dramas spoke past each other, rarely influenced by anything anyone else was saying. They waited till someone had finished, and then they had *their* say, and you can see this reflected in the texts by the way the characters finish their speeches at the end of a line and the next speaker's speech begins on a *new* line.

Then 'shared lines' begin to become more common, as Shakespeare begins to hear more acutely the rhythms of conversation – and 'shared lines' occur quite frequently in *Hamlet* – but within a couple of years after *Hamlet*, Shakespeare is writing a group of plays – often referred to as his 'problem plays' – and it is clear that by then 'shared lines' have become Shakespeare's chosen way of indicating the to and fro of conversation.

Shakespeare's 'problem plays'

The three plays that are usually so called are *Troilus and Cressida*, *Measure for Measure* and *All's Well that Ends Well*. They were all written in those first years of the seventeenth century during which Queen Elizabeth's life was ebbing away and when anxieties about her successor were rife, anxieties which were only settled in 1603 by the eventual crowning of James VI of Scotland as James I of England.

These three plays are fascinating, but not easy; it is as if Shakespeare, infected by the uncertainty of the times, couldn't write easy comedies any more. Instead he was drawn to tales of a darker nature that were more morally ambiguous. It is all relative, of course, because he was always drawn to problems that offer no easy solutions. It's just that these three plays are murkier than most; we are talking as much about lust as love. And with these plays we find more irregularities in the verse, more 'ruffling' of the lines, and more 'shared lines'.

The characters in these plays are intimately connected with, and dependent on, every word that is being spoken to them. So they respond 'on cue', at the *mid-line* point, right on the heels of the previous speaker's words. This mimics our own conversations, in which people frequently want to respond to what is being said before the other has finished talking – so much so that they might even overlap the previous speaker.[1] And in the plays, when one speaker completes the rhythm of a line which another has begun, and so creates a 'shared line', a similar effect is achieved. In listening intently to each other they fall into each other's rhythm. The speakers are breathing as one.

Just watch how people frequently nod in time to another speaker's words, signalling their readiness or impatience to have their turn. The nodding is a way of getting into the rhythm of the other speaker and being ready to take over, just as in a relay race the new runner gets up to speed before receiving the baton from their team-mate.

But just as the second half of a shared line captures the sound of someone eager to join the conversation, so the first half of a shared line captures the sound of how frequently we finish the expression of our thoughts with a phrase… of short duration. Shortly we will look at some 'shared lines' from *All's Well that Ends Well* which will clearly show you how they work. But first I will outline the story of that play for you.

All's Well that Ends Well

Helena is the daughter of a famous doctor, and when he died she was adopted by the Countess of Rossillion. The Countess has a son, Bertram, with whom Helena fell in love. Bertram has apparently been completely unaware of her feelings for him and certainly never felt any such feeling for her. He probably, at that stage of his life, thought only about himself.

Bertram's father also dies. Because Bertram is still not of age and comes from a noble family, he is ordered to go to Paris, where the King of

France is holding court, to become the King's ward. The King himself is suffering from an incurable disease and is close to death. Helena is distraught when Bertram leaves, but then remembers that her own father, the doctor, had left behind a special remedy which could cure the dying King. And a plan forms in her young brain. If she could cure the King maybe Bertram would feel differently about her…

In Act 1, Scene 3 the Countess has begun to suspect that Helena has fallen in love with her son and is demanding that Helena confess it. The dialogue is urgent and these four shared lines – marked in bold – are directing us to see how Helena comes in on cue; and in the first and last example, how the Countess also finishes her longer thought with one of these short concluding phrases.

(Again I italicise the 'forms of address' – the Countess here moving away from the intimate 'thee' form to the cooler 'you' form, while, quite properly, Helena address the Countess with (what we would describe for her as) the respectful 'you' form.)

> COUNTESS.   I charge *thee*,
>   As heaven shall work in me for *thine* avail
>   **To tell me truly.**
> HELENA.   **Good madam pardon me.**[2]
> COUNTESS. **Do *you* love my son?**
> HELENA.   *Your* **pardon noble mistress.**
> COUNTESS. **Love *you* my son?**
> HELENA.   **Do *you* love him madam?**
> COUNTESS. Go not about; my love hath in't a bond
>   Whereof the world takes note: Come, come, disclose:
>   The state of *your* affection, for *your* passions
>   **Have to the full appeach'd.**
> HELENA.   **Then I confess**
>   Here on my knee, before high heaven and *you*,
>   That before *you*, and next unto high heaven,
>   I love *your* son:
>
>   *All's Well that Ends Well*: Act 1, Scene 3

Shakespeare's 'shared lines' capture the rhythms of conversation.

At the end of this scene, the Countess, realising the depth of Helena's feelings for Bertram, decides to support Helena in her plan. (And if you read the end of this scene for yourself you'll see that the Countess reverts to the use of the loving and intimate 'thou' form to Helena in those final lines.)

The King is persuaded to undergo her 'cure' and as a reward agrees to give her Bertram in marriage.

Bertram is appalled by the thought of having to marry Helena, whom he considers completely beneath him and strenuously resists; but the King forces the marriage through, against Bertram's wishes. Bertram then flees, sending Helena a letter saying that unless she can get a ring from his finger (which he has no intention of taking off) and get him to father a child by her (which he has also no intention of doing) he will never acknowledge her as his wife. It's a very strange plot indeed.

Later in the play Helena will discover that Bertram, now a soldier in Italy, is lusting after a maid called Diana. So Helena befriends Diana and persuades her to seem prepared to sleep with Bertram. But Helena's plan is to take Diana's place in the bed. The strength of Bertram's desire for Diana forces him to agree to two things: that he'll give Diana his ring and that their love-making will take place in total darkness.

Before this, Helena needs to persuade Diana's mother that neither she nor her daughter have anything to fear…

Short lines within All's Well that Ends Well

Here, as Helena speaks to Diana's mother, is another 'moment of silence', similar to that which we found in *Hamlet*, but I won't mark out the gap for you this time, so see if you can find it.

> HELENA. You see it lawful then, it is no more,
> But that your daughter ere she seems as won,
> Desires this ring; appoints him an encounter;
> In fine, delivers me to fill the time,
> Her self most chastely absent: after
> To marry her, I'll add three thousand crowns
> To what is pass'd already.
>
> *All's Well that Ends Well*: Act 3, Scene 7

Did you find the short line? The gap in the text comes after 'chastely absent', at the colon, and before the word 'after'. Again it's a line with only four stresses (though this one has nine syllables as the word 'after' gives the line a 'feminine ending').

Isn't that such a sweetly subtle moment of silence? Helena contemplates, for a second or so, the nature of the encounter she is setting up for herself, before she moves on with the rest of her plans. Maybe she can put right all the wrong she did when she forced Bertram to marry her… ?

It is considerations like these that lead people to the opinion that the ambivalences in these 'problem' plays make them difficult to admire. I'd rather say they should lead us to consider what strange creatures we all are: in this play, for instance, it is the irresistible force of sexual desire that in time becomes one of the play's solutions. After all, it is because Bertram lusts after Diana that Helena is able to fulfil the conditions set by Bertram: namely that she obtain his ring and get herself pregnant by him. It is lust that allows her, under cover of darkness, to slip into the bed where Bertram believes Diana to be waiting for him.

Lines with extra syllables in All's Well that Ends Well

A further type of irregular line is one which contains an extra unstressed syllable mid-line. The following speech of Helena's has three such lines. In it Helena is persuading Diana's mother to let her daughter go ahead with her 'bed trick' scheme. See if by sounding this speech out you can find them:

> Take this purse of gold,
> And let me buy your friendly help thus far,
> Which I will over-pay, and pay again
> When I have found it.
>
> > The Count he woos your daughter,
> Lays down his wanton siege before her beauty,
> Resolves to carry her:
>
> > let her in fine consent
> As we'll direct her how 'tis best to bear it:
>
> Now his important blood will naught deny,
> That she'll demand:
>
> > a ring the County wears,
> That downward hath succeeded in his house
> From son to son, some four or five descents,
> Since the first father wore it.
>
> > This ring he holds
> In most rich choice: yet in his idle fire,
> To buy his will, it would not seem too dear,
> Howe'er repented after.

All's Well that Ends Well: Act 3, Scene 7

Did you find them? If not these are the three lines – with the two unstressed mid-line syllables marked in italics:

> When I have found *it. The* Count he woos your daughter,
> Resolves to carry *her: let* her in fine consent
> Since the first father wore *it. This* ring he holds

Such lines are called 'epic caesuras' and they are found in greatest number in these so called 'problem plays', and in *Othello*, which was written about the same time. It is as if Shakespeare was particularly attracted to this rhythm during these years. His lines often contain a 'caesura' (which simply means a break in a line of verse, such as when there is a thought change) but during this period it seems he frequently wanted to mark such moments by this extra syllable. And this gives us this short moment of silence, after which it's as if the line begins again with a new iambic beat.

However, it doesn't suit him to mark the thought break in this line with an extra unstressed syllable:

> That she'll demand: a ring the County wears,

which suggests here that the second half of this line – the new thought – overwhelms the first half of the line and that here he heard no moment of silence as Helena spoke it, rather he heard the thought break acting as an acceleration point.

The epic caesura in Measure for Measure

Measure for Measure, like *All's Well that Ends Well*, similarly deals with matters sexual, and it is also one of the plays in which these epic caesuras most frequently appear.

Here is a speech by Angelo, who early in the play seems, like his name, quite 'angelic', but later becomes most devilish. Angelo, temporarily in charge of the government of Vienna, has ordered a crackdown on promiscuity. The brothels have been closed, and fornication is punishable by death. But what Angelo is worried about in this speech is that while he was driving this policy through he did a terrible thing. It concerned a young brother and sister, Claudio and Isabella, whose parents, since we never hear about them, we have to assume are dead.

Claudio, though not yet married, is in a sexual relationship with Juliet though they intend to get married in the near future. Isabella, on the other hand, is applying to enter a convent and is actively seeking out an order of nuns who live by the strictest of rules. Juliet becomes pregnant by Claudio, and when the authorities learn of this, Angelo condemns Claudio to death. A friend of Claudio's, Lucio, goes to Isabella, just before she can take her final vows, and asks her to go to Angelo and plead for her brother's life.

Interestingly, Claudio feels she might prove to be successful because he's aware that men find Isabella most attractive. Indeed, he has already admitted to Lucio that:

> in her youth
> There is a prone and speechless dialect,
> Such as move men:
>
> *Measure for Measure*: Act 1, Scene 2

More enigmatic words from another enigmatic play! But the gist of what he is saying is the suggestion that men are attracted to her vulnerability ('prone') and that she doesn't even have to speak to have an effect on them.

We will discover that she's actually a brilliant speaker, but these signals that men seem to receive from her might explain *why* she wants to shut herself away in a convent. Isabella goes to the 'strict deputy', Angelo, and pleads with him for her brother's life. Angelo, to begin with, simply counters all her arguments, and then, like Lucifer, the brightest of all the 'angels', he falls from grace: to his horror and surprise he discovers he desires her sexually.

At their second interview he gives Isabella an ultimatum: he will spare her brother's life *if* she agrees to sleep with him. She is understandably outraged. Later Angelo will be led to believe that she will do as he demands; but as in *All's Well that Ends Well,* unknown to him, a substitute bedfellow will be found. Her name is Mariana, a woman once betrothed to Angelo, until rejected by him, but who still loves him and now agrees to take Isabella's place.

However, after their encounter Angelo goes back on his side of the bargain and orders the execution of Claudio to go ahead. This is the terrible thing he's done, and when Angelo learns that the Duke, who only left him in temporary control, is returning to Vienna and wants to look into all that has been going on in his absence, Angelo realises that his sins are catching up with him.

Angelo's speech from Act 4 contains four epic caesuras, which I've marked in italics. Sound it out and see how the extra mid-line syllables, suggest a 'moment of hesitation':

> This deed unshapes me quite, makes me unpregnant
> And dull to all proceed*ings*.

> *A* deflower'd maid,
> And by an eminent body, that enforc'd
> The law against *it*?

> *But* that her tender shame
> Will not proclaim against her maiden loss,
> How might she tongue *me*?

> *yet* reason dares her no,
> For my authority bears of a credent bulk,
> That no particular scandal once can touch
> But it confounds the breath*er*.

> *He* should have liv'd,
> Save that his riotous youth with dangerous sense
> Might in the times to come have ta'en revenge
> By so receiving a dishonour'd life
> With ransom of such shame:

> would yet he had liv'd.

> Alack, when once our grace we have forgot,
> Nothing goes right, we would, and we would not.

Measure for Measure: Act 4, Scene 4

Epic caesuras are quite easy to identify because the line will have one extra syllable in it. These four epic caesuras each occur in lines that have eleven syllables, but they are not to be confused with 'feminine endings', because the extra syllable is found, not at the end of the line, but mid-line. Of course you can find lines that have feminine endings *and* contain an epic caesura and then that line would have *twelve* syllables in it. Angelo has an example of one of these in Act 2, Scene 4 as he contemplates his growing desire for Isabella:

> And in my heart the strong and swelling evil
> Of my concep*tion: the* state whereon I studied...

This second line 'hesitates' in the middle of it with its epic caesura, but because the line ends with the word 'studied' it also has a feminine ending, as 'studied' is stressed on the first of its two syllables.

With Shakespeare's verse, the smallest differences make all the difference.

As an actor, once you become aware of these epic caesuras it will help you to play the texts with even more skill. It's as if the line begins again halfway through, enabling you to discover those tiny 'moments of silence' that give you the space you need to move through from one thought to the next.[3]

You might have wondered whether the following line from the speech above was another epic caesura, and that I had forgotten to mark it, because it also has eleven syllables and seems to have a clear break in the middle of it:

> With ransom of such shame: would yet he had liv'd.

But in fact this line has eleven syllables because it *has* a feminine ending – though it's a bit hard to spot. But its purpose is to 'sound out' a *contrast* with another line that has come just before it. Here we have them both and notice how the last two stresses in each of these lines are different. And remember, as always, you must sound them out:

> But it confounds the breath*er*.
>
> *He* **should** have **liv'd**,
> Save that his riotous youth with dangerous sense
> Might in the times to come have ta'en revenge
> By so receiving a dishonour'd life
> With ransom of such shame:
>
> would **yet** he **had** liv'd.

Once again I am struck by the subtlety of Shakespeare's writing: that just by the placing of these words accurately, within the rhythm of his verse, he can capture these nuances of speech that 'nail' the thoughts with astounding clarity. The second of these phrases capturing the remorse of the so desperately guilty man.

In *Measure for Measure* epic caesuras occur about once every fourteen lines of verse; in Shakespeare's early plays they are very much rarer. If you'd like to give yourself another little exercise on detecting these epic caesuras, turn back to Chapter 5, pages 74–5 and see how many you can find in Hamlet's speech 'O that this too too solid flesh would melt'.[4]

'Mirroring'

There is another characteristic rhythm, found in Shakespeare's plays, which is also followed by one of these 'moments of silence', yet usually of the very shortest duration.

I call it 'mirroring' and it is when one speaker mimics the rhythm of another in lines of just three stresses each.

In *Measure for Measure* we have this exchange between Angelo and the Provost, who is the keeper of the prison where Claudio is being held. (The bold typeface marks these moments of 'mirroring', and I'm again marking the 'forms of address', with italics.)

> ANGELO. Now, what's the matter Provost?
>
> PROVOST. Is it *your* will Claudio shall die to morrow?
>
> ANGELO. Did not I tell *thee* yea? hadst *thou* not order?
> **Why dost *thou* ask again?**
>
> PROVOST. **Lest I might be too rash:**
> Under *your* good correction, I have seen
> When after execution, judgement hath
> **Repented o'er his doom.**
>
> ANGELO. **Go to; let that be mine,**
> Do *you your* office, or give up *your* place,
> **And *you* shall well be spar'd.**
>
> PROVOST. **I crave *your* honour's pardon:**
>
> *Measure for Measure*: Act 2, Scene 2

These are not 'shared lines' where the speaker takes up and completes the other's pentameter. Put together, these pairs of short lines have six stresses in them rather than five. In fact the *purpose* of these 'mirroring' lines is a technique on the second speaker's part to *avoid* a shared line, which would have sounded more conciliatory.[5]

'Mirroring' is the sound of disagreement.

These men, clearly in disagreement about Claudio's imminent execution, are not 'breathing as one', and answer each other by a mimicking rhythm that seems to comment adversely on what the other has said. It's a way of speaking that we'll all recognise in ourselves and others.

You should also note that Angelo's shift from the use of 'thou' to 'you' in this passage probably indicates that he felt he was losing his 'cool' with the Provost and should address him as he would more normally do, without 'pulling rank', though he remains fairly aggressive. But maybe his becoming slightly more polite, at least on the surface, is in part, a result of the Provost's use of this assertive 'mirroring' technique.

In *Richard III*, one of Shakespeare's earliest plays, 'mirroring' forms part of a famous scene between Richard and Lady Anne, whom he is trying to seduce.

Richard has killed both Anne's husband and her father-in-law, the last Lancastrian king, Henry VI, in *Henry VI, Part Three* (see above, Chapter 2, page 33). Richard finally admits this to Lady Anne and says that he killed them both because he was in love with *her*. Anne's initial fury towards Richard begins to ebb away, especially when Richard threatens to kill himself if she won't accept the love he says he bears her. As she begins to fall for him their pentameters shift into a 'mirroring' exchange. And watch out also for variations in the forms of address, as we found in that passage from *Measure for Measure*. They are again marked by italics.

> ANNE. Arise dissembler, though I wish *thy* death,
>   I will not be *thy* executioner.
> RICHARD. Then bid me kill my self, and I will do it.
> ANNE. I have already.
> RICHARD.   That was in *thy* rage:
>   Speak it again, and even with the word,
>   This hand, which for *thy* love, did kill *thy* love,
>   Shall for *thy* love, kill a far truer love
>   To both their deaths shalt *thou* be accessary.
> ANNE. **I would I knew *thy* heart.**
> RICHARD. 'Tis figured in my tongue.
> ANNE. **I fear me, both are false.**
> RICHARD. **Then never man was true.**
> ANNE. **Well, well, put up *your* sword.**
> RICHARD. **Say then my peace is made.**
> ANNE. **That shalt *thou* know hereafter.**[6]
> RICHARD. **But shall I live in hope.**
> ANNE. **All men I hope live so.**
> RICHARD. **Vouchsafe to wear this ring.**
> ANNE. **To take is not to give.**
> RICHARD. Look how my ring encompasseth *thy* finger…
>
>   *Richard III*: Act 1, Scene 2

It is Richard who begins by 'mirroring' Anne's lines. Anne's lines are short, tentative appeals, and probably inviting a real dialogue, which would mean continuing an exchange in full pentameters. This is not what Richard wants and his 'mirroring' technique gives her no time to think, countering her attempts to understand him, and ends with her capitulating to the force of his seduction. 'Mirroring' can be a powerfully persuasive way of talking. Though it could be argued that halfway through this exchange, Anne starts to 'mirror' Richard's lines, as this new-found attraction she feels for him gives her a new-found confidence.

The forms of address are interesting too. Richard, as male wooer, uses 'thou' to Anne throughout the scene. Anne's use of 'thou' to Richard has been as to an enemy. But as she begins to fall for him, her stance softens and she switches to the politer 'you' form when she says to him 'put up your sword'. But then she goes further still and with her next line, 'That shalt thou know hereafter', she is using the intimate 'thou' form to him, no longer as a term of abuse, but as Richard's future lover.

There's probably only the shortest of pauses, or moments of silence, after each of these pairs of lines, until, that is, we get to the final pair when Anne accepts the ring that Richard offers her. Then the next silence coincides with the 'business' of him putting it on her finger, and only as he does it, does Richard speak again – now back in pentameters.

> Look how my ring encompasseth *thy* finger,

As the scene ends and Richard's wooing has been successfully accomplished, their 'forms of address' both settle for the politer 'you' form – after all this is a public street scene! Richard uses 'you' to her three times before she exits, and when he asks Anne to bid him farewell, she in her turn says:

> 'Tis more than *you* deserve:
> But since *you* teach me how to flatter *you*,
> Imagine I have said farewell already.

(It's worth remembering the obvious: although I've italicised fourteen 'you's and 'thou's in this passage not many of them are in stressed places – only three are.)

This chapter has been about small matters, delicate moments, subtle rhythmic variations. All of which, though certainly in no way showy or drawing attention to themselves, have a cumulative effect: which is to make these scenes and these characters come to life with a greater adherence to truth and reality. Modern audiences will not immediately understand the implications of those 'you / thou' shifts, but if *you* know what they mean, you can 'play' those shifts, and then our audiences will feel *and* understand what has just happened before their eyes.

It is almost time for us to move on and consider why Shakespeare frequently writes in prose, and then to examine his use of rhymed verse. Towards the end of this book we will return to blank verse and look at some examples of Shakespeare's late plays. But now, in order to test all we've been doing so far, I want you to work on a remarkable scene from *Measure for Measure*. It is the central part of Act 3, Scene 1 in which Isabella visits her condemned brother Claudio in prison. The scene is filled with 'shared lines' so it would be helpful if you could find someone to work on it with you. There will be lots of things for you to remember, and inevitably you won't remember everything at once. So be prepared to go over this scene many times, thinking about the advice I've given you regarding breathing, and stresses, and lines that are short or long, and so on. I haven't divided up the verse into thought-units, because that is the first thing *you* should now be doing with any new piece of text.

Seven

Measure for Measure
A Duologue to Work On

ISABELLA. Then Isabel live chaste, and brother die;
  "More than our brother, is our chastity.[1]
                        Measure for Measure: Act 2, Scene 4

By Act 3, Scene 1 of *Measure for Measure* the story has moved on. After
Angelo makes his ultimatum to Isabella – sleep with me, or your brother
dies – Isabella is left alone contemplating her predicament in a soliloquy
which culminates with her saying the lines quoted above, in which she
decides that Claudio has to die, and she has to live chaste, thus saving her
eternal soul. After which, she adds before exiting:

> I'll tell him yet of Angelo's request,
> And fit his mind to death, for his soul's rest.

She is confident that her brother holds 'such a mind of honour' that he
would die twenty deaths rather than permit her to submit to this 'abhorr'd
pollution'. So with a clear mind she goes to the prison to tell Claudio all
that has happened, confident that he will be prepared to die for her. What
happens is very, very different.

So here is this piece of text for you to work on. I've suggested that the
first thing you do is to spend some time reading it through so as to decide
how to divide it up into thought-units. I've found about thirty places
where I'd want to split a speech up into separate thought-units, and if I add

105

those to all the speeches that I *wouldn't* want to divide up, I think I've found sixty-seven thoughts in all. But there is no absolute right and wrong about this exercise, the important thing is to make your own judgements as to where *within* a speech a new thought presses into consciousness.

(You will find though in the Appendix that I have divided up the speeches – but try not to look there now!)

I have changed one word from the Folio. About forty lines into this duologue you'll come across Claudio's line, 'The precise Angelo?' The Folio has 'The prenzie, Angelo?' and repeats the word again three lines below. Most editors, and I agree, believe it is a misreading of 'precise' – here meaning 'puritanical'.

Isabella enters the prison and is taken to speak to the condemned Claudio, as she thinks, privately. Claudio is the first to speak:

> CLAUDIO. Now sister, what's the comfort?
>
> ISABELLA.   Why,
>   As all comforts are: most good, most good indeed,
>   Lord Angelo having affairs to heaven
>   Intends you for his swift ambassador,
>   Where you shall be an everlasting lieger;*
>   Therefore your best appointment make with speed,
>   Tomorrow you set on.
>
> CLAUDIO.   Is there no remedy?
>
> ISABELLA. None, but such remedy, as to save a head
>   To cleave a heart in twain:
>
> CLAUDIO.   But is there any?
>
> ISABELLA. Yes brother, you may live;
>   There is a devilish mercy in the judge,
>   If you'll implore it, that will free your life,
>   But fetter you till death.
>
> CLAUDIO.   Perpetual durance?
>
> ISABELLA. Aye just, perpetual durance, a restraint
>   Though all the world's vastidity you had
>   To a determin'd scope.
>
> CLAUDIO.   But in what nature?
>
> ISABELLA. In such a one, as you consenting to't,
>   Would bark your honour from that trunk you bear,
>   And leave you naked.

lieger – representative

CLAUDIO.   Let me know the point.

ISABELLA. Oh, I do fear thee Claudio, and I quake,
    Lest thou a feverous life shouldst entertain,
    And six or seven winters more respect
    Than a perpetual honour. Dar'st thou die?
    The sense of death is most in apprehension,
    And the poor beetle that we tread upon
    In corporal sufferance, finds a pang as great,
    As when a giant dies.

CLAUDIO. Why give you me this shame?
    Think you I can a resolution fetch
    From flow'ry tenderness? If I must die,
    I will encounter darkness as a bride,
    And hug it in mine arms.

ISABELLA.   There spake my brother:
    There my father's grave
    Did utter forth a voice. Yes, thou must die:
    Thou art too noble, to conserve a life
    In base appliances. This outward sainted Deputy,
    Whose settled visage, and deliberate word
    Nips youth i'th'head, and follies doth enew*
    As falcon doth the fowl, is yet a devil:
    His filth within being cast, he would appear
    A pond, as deep as hell.

CLAUDIO.   The precise* Angelo?

ISABELLA. Oh 'tis the cunning livery of hell,
    The damnest body to invest, and cover
    In precise guards;* dost thou think Claudio,
    If I would yield him my virginity
    Thou might'st be freed?

CLAUDIO.   Oh heavens, it cannot be.

ISABELLA. Yes, he would give't thee; from this rank offence
    So to offend him still. This night's the time
    That I should do what I abhor to name,
    Or else thou diest tomorrow.

CLAUDIO. Thou shalt not do't.

ISABELLA.   O, were it but my life,
    I'd throw it down for your deliverance
    As frankly as a pin.

enew – drive into the water
precise – puritanical
guards – trimmings on clothes

CLAUDIO.   Thanks dear Isabel.

ISABELLA. Be ready Claudio, for your death tomorrow.

CLAUDIO. Yes. Has he affections in him,
    That thus can make him bite the Law by th'nose,
    When he would force it? Sure it is no sin,
    Or of the deadly seven it is the least.

ISABELLA. Which is the least?

CLAUDIO. If it were damnable, he being so wise,
    Why would he for the momentary trick
    Be perdurably fin'd?* Oh Isabel.

ISABELLA. What says my brother?

CLAUDIO. Death is a fearful thing.

ISABELLA. And shamed life, a hateful.

CLAUDIO. Aye, but to die, and go we know not where,
    To lie in cold obstruction, and to rot,
    This sensible warm motion, to become
    A kneaded clod; And the delighted spirit
    To bathe in fiery floods, or to reside
    In thrilling region of thick-ribbed ice,
    To be imprison'd in the viewless winds
    And blown with restless violence round about
    The pendant world: or to be worse than worst
    Of those, that lawless and incertain thought,
    Imagine howling, 'tis too horrible.
    The weariest, and most loathed worldly life
    That age, ache, penury, and imprisonment
    Can lay on nature, is a paradise
    To what we fear of death.

ISABELLA.   Alas, alas.

CLAUDIO. Sweet sister, let me live.
    What sin you do, to save a brother's life,
    Nature dispenses with the deed so far,
    That it becomes a virtue.

ISABELLA.   Oh you beast,
    Oh faithless coward, oh dishonest wretch,
    Wilt thou be made a man, out of my vice?
    Is't not a kind of incest, to take life
    From thine own sister's shame? What should I think,
    Heaven shield my mother play'd my father fair:
    For such a warped slip of wilderness

perdurably fin'd – eternally damned

Ne'er issu'd from his blood. Take my defiance,
Die, perish: Might but my bending down
Reprieve thee from thy fate, it should proceed.
I'll pray a thousand prayers for thy death,
No word to save thee.

CLAUDIO.   Nay hear me Isabel.

ISABELLA. Oh fie, fie, fie:
Thy sin's not accidental, but a trade;
Mercy to thee would prove it self a bawd,
'Tis best that thou diest quickly.

CLAUDIO.   Oh hear me Isabella.

Measure for Measure: Act 3, Scene 1, lines 53–150

At this point Isabella begins to walk out on her brother, but in fact it's not the end of the scene because they have not been alone. The Duke, who has left Angelo in charge of the state, and apparently left the country for a while, has not gone away at all. He has disguised himself as a friar and has overheard all that Isabella and Claudio have been saying. He now calls out to the departing Isabella,

Vouchsafe a word, young sister, but one word.

And she, hearing his voice, replies,

What is your will.

And with that she stays to talk with the disguised Duke, who subsequently reveals to her the idea of the 'bed trick' – of Mariana taking her place in Angelo's bed.

I wonder how many of the textual clues you picked up as you were sounding the scene out. When you go through it again you should certainly become aware of some changes in the 'forms of address'. Also I'm hoping that you will begin to notice some gaps, or 'hesitations' in the text – maybe you'll find as many as ten of these. The way to spot these points of 'hesitation' amid the flow of the 'shared lines' is to discover where one or more syllables are missing. But try to resist counting them: rather try to be aware, as you play the characters, that maybe here, or there, there is a line that looks or *sounds* short – or even one that seems extra long. You should find places too where the rhythm becomes deliberately un-iambic. There is some 'mirroring'. And as you become aware of these anomalies within the regular run of the blank verse, as well as the way the characters move from using the 'you' form of address to using the 'thou' form – begin to work out *why*.

And once you've tried to work all this out for yourself, go to the Appendix, where I will share my thoughts with you about this remarkable scene.

It's the magic of Shakespeare's verse that he can capture, within its form, not only these magnificent scenes, which give rise to the brilliance of the language, but also all these hesitations, interruptions, and these most telling of touches that the language contains.

Verse is speech – though not all speech is verse. And it's not only Shakespeare's verse that can achieve such extraordinary nuances – his prose does too, as we will begin to explore in the following chapter.

Eight

Why Prose?

VIOLA. Art not thou the Lady Olivia's fool?

CLOWN. No indeed sir, the Lady Olivia has no folly, she will keep no fool sir, till she be married, and fools are as like husbands, as pilchards are to herrings, the husband's the bigger, I am indeed not her fool, but her corrupter of words.

Twelfth Night: Act 3, Scene 1

In Shakespeare everything that is not verse we call prose. It is unlike verse in that its rhythms are not regular but haphazard, and it has no line endings: on the page it simply fills up all the space available between the margins. There are a couple of plays by Shakespeare that contain no prose at all, but four of his plays, and *Twelfth Night* is one of them, contain more prose than verse.

You might expect that the question, 'Why prose?' could be answered easily. You might be tempted to say that prose is 'everyday' speech; it's ordinary and it's how we all talk when we are just saying ordinary, everyday things. But in saying this you'd only be right with regard to about one per cent of Shakespeare's prose. He does indeed write a few scenes where we see characters going about their 'everyday' tasks: preparing to serve up a meal, or conducting some piece of business in a court room, or managing a boat in bad weather, and it's true that some of these characters speak in a simple language that is certainly not verse. But that's because the situations they are in, the giving and taking of orders, etc., reveal nothing about their inner lives, or how they are *feeling*. Verse, we should remember, is thought which carries with it the emotion that the thought contains.

Sometime ago on BBC Radio 4 in a discussion about Shakespeare I heard Germaine Greer saying categorically that Shakespeare's prose has little connection with ordinary speech. What I think she meant was that, in the main, Shakespeare's prose is not an 'everyday language', that it is much more consciously shaped than casual speech is, neither does it capture the sounds of *heartfelt* spontaneous utterances as verse does.

So if our everyday speech bears little relation to Shakespeare's prose, why is there so much of it in his plays: a quarter of all his dramatic output is prose? The answer is that there are times when we don't *want* to be heartfelt; indeed times when we want to try and hide what our heart is feeling. And prose is a strategic way of speaking that achieves this goal. Cracking a joke might be one example. Some characters, we will discover, want to hide their hearts all the time.

Prose v. verse

I want to look at a part of Act 2, Scene 2 from *Antony and Cleopatra*. A top-level meeting is underway between Caesar and Antony where they are trying to sort out their differences. The stakes are high. Lepidus is acting as intermediary. Caesar is supported by Maecenas, Antony by Enobarbus.

Continue to sound these passages out – they are all good to practise on – and doing so in this next passage should make clearer to you the difference between the sound of Enobarbus's prose, and the verse spoken by all the others.

ANTONY.   Truth is, that Fulvia,
To have me out of Egypt, made wars here,
For which my self, the ignorant motive, do
So far ask pardon, as befits mine honour
To stoop in such a case.

LEPIDUS.   'Tis noble spoken.

MAECENAS. If it might please you, to enforce no further
The griefs between ye: to forget them quite,
Were to remember: that the present need,
Speaks to atone you.

LEPIDUS.   Worthily spoken Maecenas.

ENOBARBUS. Or if you borrow one another's love for the instant,
you may when you hear no more words of Pompey return

it again: you shall have time to wrangle in, when you have
nothing else to do.

ANTONY. Thou art a soldier only, speak no more.

ENOBARBUS. That truth should be silent, I had almost forgot.

ANTONY. You wrong this presence, therefore speak no more.

ENOBARBUS. Go to then: your considerate stone.

CAESAR. I do not much dislike the matter, but
    The manner of his speech: for't cannot be,
    We shall remain in friendship, our conditions
    So diff'ring in their acts.
                  Yet if I knew,
    What hoop should hold us staunch from edge to edge
    O'th'world: I would pursue it.

Antony and Cleopatra: Act 2, Scene 2

It doesn't matter if we don't follow all the political details in this passage for now. What is interesting is that Enobarbus is not speaking verse like all the others. Caesar's comment about 'the manner', not 'the matter' of Enobarbus's speech suggests that he feels that Enobarbus is somehow speaking inappropriately for such an important meeting. In other parts of the play Enobarbus speaks verse, so what's up with him here?

He might be feeling many conflicting emotions. He might be worried, or angered by how these negotiations are progressing and frustrated that in this exalted company he has no voice. So what does he do? He deliberately makes an inappropriate remark, both to give vent to his feelings and yet somehow to hide the true nature of them at the same time: maybe he's trying to make the assembled company laugh.

Jokes by their very nature are subversive: they undermine what is serious, and they always contain an element of surprise. Frequently it's the rhythm of a joke that gives us the surprise, and hence the laugh. The *iambic* rhythm is death to jokes, but it's the nature of prose's rhythms to be haphazard; to be therefore surprising.

Prose is a rhythm fit for jokes.

This was brought home to me all the more vividly during rehearsals of *Titus Andronicus* at the Globe in 2006. I was helping with the text, trying to be, as Mark Rylance used to describe my role there, the 'ear on the play'.[1]

It was a most exciting production by Lucy Bailey, memorably designed by Bill Dudley, with Douglas Hodge in the leading role of Titus giving a thrilling performance.

One day we were rehearsing Act 3, Scene 2. In this scene, Titus, his brother Marcus, his daughter Lavinia and his grandson Lucius have assembled for a meal. It is a scene of extreme family grief. Not only has Lavinia just been raped and had her tongue cut out and her hands cut off, but in the previous scene, in which Titus first saw Lavinia in this mutilated state, he has had to chop his own left hand off, in a vain attempt to save the lives of two of his sons, who are about to be executed for a murder they didn't commit. In his grief Titus suggests that Lavinia, to cure her own heartache and suffering, should take a knife between her teeth and make a hole near her heart for all her tears to run into. Her tears would then take the pain from her heart by drowning it.

Marcus is horrified by this and says to his brother:

> Fie brother fie, teach her not thus to lay
> Such violent *hands* upon her tender life.

To which Titus responds:

> How now! Has sorrow made thee dote already?
> Why Marcus, no man should be mad but I:
> *What* violent *hands* can she lay on her life:
>
> Ah, wherefore dost thou urge the name of *hands*...
>
> O *handle* not the theme, to talk of *hands*,
> Lest we remember still that we have none...

> *Titus Andronicus*: Act 3, Scene 2

(The italics are mine.)

Douglas Hodge was playing this speech with great strength and feeling, but when he came to that last line,

> Lest we remember still that we have none

he was throwing the iambic beat off at the end of the line and instead of it sounding like this,

> Lest we remember still that we have **none**

he was sounding it like this,

> Lest we remember still that we **have** none

At the end of the rehearsal I asked him why he was doing that and he said to me, 'Oh, I thought I might be able to get a laugh here!'

Titus Andronicus is the most gruesome play imaginable, but it is also sometimes blackly funny in its gruesomeness. As an actor, Douglas's instincts were that the horror needed puncturing at this point with a sudden flash of ghoulish humour, and he sensed the way to do that was by 'throwing' the rhythm.

In order to get a laugh, as indeed he did when he played the scene in performance, he knew that he would have to surprise his audience with something out of the normal run of the lines. The iambic rhythm, the 'sound of sincerity', would not have got the laugh. But by ditching the rhythm, the verse line now had this 'prose-like' ending, and became funny. And that's what I learnt from Douglas that day.

So occasional jokers, like Enobarbus, and like Douglas's Titus for this brief moment, sometimes speak prose, while the professional clowns in Shakespeare, those who make their living by being, as Feste, the Clown says in *Twelfth Night*, a 'corrupter of words', always do.[2]

Clowns sometimes speak through a literal mask, but whether they have a painted face or not, we always sense there's a distance between what they say and what they *might* be feeling. And it is this 'double take' that prose achieves: saying one thing in such a way that we feel there must be some other meaning lying beneath it.

Prose, though, is *not* reserved solely for those of humble stock, as we might all have been told in school or elsewhere. Just as verse is not some 'heightened language' reserved for the highly educated.

Falstaff

There is one character in Shakespeare who has a larger part even than Hamlet, and that is Falstaff; though admittedly his part stretches over three plays.[3]

Sir John Falstaff, who certainly did not lack for a good education, always speaks in prose and therefore has more of it than any other character in Shakespeare.

Here he is in a scene towards the end of *Henry IV, Part One*. The climactic battle between Prince Hal and Hotspur will take place on the morrow: Hal is bidding Falstaff goodnight.

Read the scene out loud: perhaps you are going to have your first taste of Shakespeare's incomparable prose:

> FALSTAFF. Hal, if thou see me down in the battle, and bestride
> me, so; 'tis a point of friendship.
>
> PRINCE. Nothing but a colossus can do thee that friendship. Say
> thy prayers, and farewell.

FALSTAFF. I would it were bed-time Hal, and all well.

PRINCE. Why, thou ow'st God a death.

[*Exit.*]

FALSTAFF. 'Tis not due yet: I would be loath to pay him before his day. What need I be so forward with him, that calls not on me? Well, 'tis no matter, Honour pricks me on. But how if Honour prick me off when I come on? How then? Can Honour set to a leg? No: or an arm? No: Or take away the grief of a wound? No. Honour hath no skill in surgery, then? No. What is Honour? A word. What is in that word Honour? Air: A trim reckoning.* Who hath it? He that died o' Wednesday. Doth he feel it? No. Doth he hear it? No. Is it insensible then? yea, to the dead. But will it not live with the living? No. Why? Detraction will not suffer it, therefore I'll none of it. Honour is a mere scutcheon,* and so ends my catechism.

Henry IV, Part One: Act 5, Scene 1

We will investigate the prose just as we did our verse passages. Let us see what we can discover about the 'form' of the prose by dividing this last speech up into 'thought-units'. Falstaff's first 'thought-unit' here will be said to the exiting Prince; the rest, to the audience.

FALSTAFF. 'Tis not due yet: I would be loath to pay him before his day.

What need I be so forward with him, that calls not on me?

Well, 'tis no matter, Honour pricks me on.

But how if Honour prick me off when I come on? How then?

Can Honour set to a leg? No: or an arm? No: Or take away the grief of a wound? No.

Honour hath no skill in surgery, then? No.

What is Honour? A word.

What is in that word Honour? Air: A trim reckoning.

Who hath it? He that died o'Wednesday.

Doth he feel it? No.

Doth he hear it? No.

trim reckoning – an ironic way of saying 'a fine ending'
scutcheon – coat of arms on a shield, often hung up at a funeral

Is it insensible then? yea, to the dead.

But will it not live with the living? No.

Why? Detraction will not suffer it, therefore I'll none of it.

Honour is a mere scutcheon, and so ends my catechism.

Look at how *strongly* all those 'thought-units' end: 'catechism', 'none of it', 'No', 'dead'. Prose, is similar to verse in this respect. Just as the last stress in any line of verse is always of importance, so the 'punch' in any line of prose, will always come at the end. (But remember, as there are no 'line-endings' in prose, where a line ends in any particular edition, is simply determined by the space available on that page.)

Dividing up Falstaff's speech has revealed something of its 'form': the variety of the thought lengths. On the other hand, many of the phrases balance other phrases, or they get progressively longer in a patterned way. Notice also the large amount of repetition: 'Honour' is mentioned sixteen times, (and I retain the Folio's capitalisation it gives to this word) though after the eighth time the word becomes simply 'it', until the final 'Honour' in the last line. Variety of thought lengths, and consciously balanced thought lengths, are typical of prose. Repetitions are typical of prose, as is Falstaff's list of 'leg', 'arm' and 'wound'. So far from being an 'everyday' language, prose is already beginning to reveal a fine concern with 'structure'.

Dividing the speech up also throws light on Falstaff's last word 'catechism', because the overall 'form' of the passage now reveals itself to be a series of questions and answers. The actual catechism, as used in the Christian Church to lay out the basic articles of faith, is just such a series. Falstaff's, though, proves to be in its conclusion a kind of anti-catechism.

Falstaff as a 'prose entertainer'

Falstaff, although he is a character playing a part in the unfolding of the drama, also takes 'time out' to become what I'd call a 'prose entertainer'. Polonius, who we will meet again in the next chapter, is another. Both of them like to share with the audience something that they hope we might find amusing. The list of these 'prose entertainers' is quite long, and later we shall come across some like the Shepherd and his Son, when we look at *The Winter's Tale*, and there are others like Launce in *The Two Gentlemen of Verona* and the Gobbos in *The Merchant of Venice* who are there for you to discover at a later date, but who will not otherwise find a place in this book.

Falstaff always wants to make us laugh. He wants us to laugh with him about the absurdity of concepts like honour, because if we do, he'll be safe. If everyone agrees with him he will not be called to account for his lack of bravery.

So, unlike a verse speaker, Falstaff uses words, not to reveal something he feels deeply about, but to get himself out of situations that he has no relish for. Like Feste, though for less admirable reasons, he is another 'corrupter of words'. And just as when Douglas Hodge as Titus threw the rhythm of his line, so these lines, unlike lines of verse, surprise us by their varying rhythms and different thought lengths – by their unpredictability.

Let's look at the rhythms and counter play of the varying thoughts:

> Doth he **feel** it? **No.**
>
> Doth he **hear** it? **No.**
>
> Is it in**sens**ible then? **yea,** to the **dead.**
>
> But will it not **live** with the **living**? **No.**
>
> **Why?** Detraction will not **suffer** it, **therefore** I'll **none** of it.
>
> **Honour** is a mere **scutcheon**, and so **ends** my **catechism**.

Although I'm pointing out where I feel the stresses *might* fall here, all actors would need to find how the rhythms work for them. In performance it should all sound very easy, very colloquial. However, we do have to 'listen' attentively to the prose and coax it to reveal its rhythms. While it may seem to be artless, it is in fact very consciously structured.

The first of these two lines above seem to me to have two stresses each and deliberately repeat each other, in that four of the five words in these two lines are identical, which makes for amusement and might even encourage some audiences to chime in with the second 'No'.

The second pair of lines each have three stresses; the first line is full of 'e' sounds (there can be something mocking about an 'e' sound), whereas the second is full of 'i' sounds (more picky and pedantic), and 'playing' those 'sounds' could give some amusing character to that second pair of lines. But again you don't have to do too much.

The next line –

> **Why?** Detraction will not **suffer** it, **therefore** I'll **none** of it.

– has a wonderful run to it. After that initial 'Why' the rhythm of one half mimics the other, while the 'suffer it'/ 'none of it' makes a kind of rhyme. The 'f's of 'suffer' and the 'f' of 'therefore' seem deliberate. All these devices give the line some status, more than it probably deserves. But we are more likely to feel that Falstaff has made a good point because the line has this witty ring to it and so will linger longer in our memory. To speak memorably is to speak effectively.

The final line before the old rogue exits chimes those two words 'scutcheon' and 'catechism' with their similar letters sounding similar yet both disparaging the other. The 'c'/'k' sound, sounding 'cutting' and somewhat aggressive.

Prose and 'humorous' characters

Our 'prose entertainers', although they take part in scenes interacting with other characters, also tend, like Falstaff, to be marked out as those that speak directly to the audience in prose soliloquies. However, there are another group of prose speaking comics whose humorous qualities arise from their idiosyncratic vocabulary, but they tend not to address the audience directly. Quite a number of these characters can be found in the comic scenes of *Henry V*, and none is funnier that the Welsh Captain, Fluellen. Here he is in a short scene with the English Captain, Gower, on the night before the battle of Agincourt. Gower is speaking rather loudly:

> GOWER. Captain Fluellen.
>
> FLUELLEN. 'So, in the name of Jesu Christ, speak fewer: it is the greatest admiration in the universal world, when the true and ancient prerogatives and laws of the wars is not kept: if you would take the pains but to examine the wars of Pompey the Great, you shall find, I warrant you, that there is no tiddle taddle nor pibble babble in Pompey's camp: I warrant you, you shall find the ceremonies of the wars, and the cares of it, and the forms of it, and the sobriety of it, and the modesty of it, to be otherwise.
>
> GOWER. Why the enemy is loud, you hear him all night.
>
> FLUELLEN. If the enemy is an ass and a fool, and a prating coxcomb; is it meet, think you, that we should also, look you, be an ass and a fool, and a prating coxcomb, in your own conscience now?
>
> GOWER. I will speak lower.
>
> FLUELLEN. I pray you, and beseech you, that you will.
>
> *Exit.*
>
> *Henry V*: Act 4, Scene 1

Characters like Fluellen and his bête noire MacMorris, the Irish Captain, or like Nym and Bardolph, two of Falstaff's old cronies who also turn up in *Henry V*, all have this in common: that they seem not to be in control of the words that come out of their mouths. They all seem to be in thrall to some particular and partial view of the world, which as soon as they open their mouths engulfs them. It is almost as if they are mad, and while it will become clear later that prose is the way that Shakespeare captures the voices of the truly mad, this set of 'humorous' characters remain delightfully on the side of the sane: they are not certifiable, and we delight in their oddity.[4]

A scene in which prose becomes verse

The passage we looked at from *Antony and Cleopatra* mixed verse and prose together: Enobarbus joked in prose, while everyone else spoke verse. This is quite common in Shakespeare's plays, but much more common is having a scene completely written in *either* verse or prose. But we can learn most from those scenes where one rhythm takes over from the other; where verse becomes prose, or prose becomes verse. Looking at one of these scenes will show us more clearly *why* Shakespeare uses these two different rhythms.

The passage we are going to look at is long, but it is my favourite example of a scene that begins in prose only to become verse at a crucially dramatic point. It is Act 1, Scene 2 from *As You Like It,* and we join it about 150 lines in from the beginning.

The situation at the beginning of the play is that Frederick has taken the dukedom from his brother by force and banished him. The banished Duke's daughter, Rosalind, has not been sent away with her father but has been allowed to remain at court because of the close friendship between her and her cousin, Frederick's daughter Celia. Orlando, whose father, when alive, was a strong supporter of Rosalind's father, has arrived at court, where he is a stranger, to wrestle Duke Frederick's champion, Charles. Charles has already killed three men that day in the ring, but now Frederick seems strangely unsure as to whether he wants this further bout to go ahead.

Although the passage is long, read it through, still out loud if you can, and despite the fact that you'll have many characters to give voice to, see if you can work out why it begins in prose and why the prose gives way to verse when it does. (I will continue to divide up the speeches, both verse and prose, into possible thought-units, though, as you will see from now on, I am indicating my divisions in the prose 'thought-units' by an oblique slash.)

> *Flourish. Enter Duke Frederick, Lords, Orlando, Charles, and Attendants.*

DUKE F. Come on, since the youth will not be entreated, his own peril on his forwardness.

ROSALIND. Is yonder the man?

LE BEAU. Even he, madam.

CELIA. Alas, he is too young: yet he looks successfully.

DUKE F. How now daughter, and cousin: Are you crept hither to see the wrestling?

ROSALIND. Ay my liege, so please you give us leave.

DUKE F. You will take little delight in it, I can tell you there is such odds in the man: / In pity of the challenger's youth, I would fain dissuade him, but he will not be entreated. / Speak to him ladies, see if you can move him.

CELIA. Call him hither good Monsieur Le Beau.

DUKE F. Do so: I'll not be by.

LE BEAU. Monsieur the challenger, the Princess calls for you.

ORLANDO. I attend them with all respect and duty.

ROSALIND. Young man, have you challenged Charles the wrestler?

ORLANDO. No fair Princess: he is the general challenger, I come but in as others do, to try with him the strength of my youth.

CELIA. Young gentleman, your spirits are too bold for your years: / you have seen cruel proof of this man's strength, if you saw your self with your eyes, or knew your self with your judgement, the fear of your adventure would counsel you to a more equal enterprise. / We pray you for your own sake to embrace your own safety, and give over this attempt.

ROSALIND. Do young sir, your reputation shall not therefore be misprised: / we will make it our suit to the Duke, that the wrestling might not go forward.

ORLANDO. I beseech you, punish me not with your hard thoughts, wherein I confess me much guilty to deny so fair and excellent ladies any thing. / But let your fair eyes, and gentle wishes go with me to my trial; wherein if I be foiled, there is but one shamed that was never gracious: if killed, but one dead that is willing to be so: I shall do my friends no wrong, for I have none to lament me: the world no injury, for in it I have nothing: only in the world I fill up a place, which may be better supplied, when I have made it empty.

ROSALIND. The little strength that I have, I would it were with you.

CELIA. And mine to eke out hers.

ROSALIND. Fare you well: pray heaven I be deceiv'd in you.

CELIA. Your heart's desires be with you.

CHARLES. Come, where is this young gallant, that is so desirous to lie with his mother earth?

ORLANDO. Ready sir, but his will hath in it a more modest working.

DUKE F. You shall try but one fall.

CHARLES. No, I warrant your Grace you shall not entreat him to a second, that have so mightily persuaded him from a first.

ORLANDO. You mean to mock me after: you should not have mocked me before: but come your ways.

ROSALIND. Now Hercules, be thy speed young man.

CELIA. I would I were invisible, to catch the strong fellow by the leg.

Wrestle.

ROSALIND. O excellent young man.

CELIA. If I had a thunderbolt in mine eye, I can tell who should down.

Shout. [Charles is thrown.]

DUKE F. No more, no more.

ORLANDO.   Yes I beseech your Grace, I am not yet well breath'd.

DUKE F.   How dost thou Charles?

LE BEAU. He cannot speak my lord.

DUKE F.   Bear him away: What is thy name young man?

ORLANDO.   Orlando my liege, The youngest son of Sir Rowland de Boys.

DUKE F. I would thou hadst been son to some man else, The world esteem'd thy father honourable,

But I did find him still mine enemy:

Thou shouldst have better pleas'd me with this deed,
Hadst thou descended from another house:

But fare thee well, thou art a gallant youth,
I would thou hadst told me of another father.

Exit Duke.

CELIA. Were I my father (coz) would I do this?

ORLANDO. I am more proud to be Sir Rowland's son,
His youngest son, and would not change that calling
To be adopted heir to Frederick.

ROSALIND. My father lov'd Sir Rowland as his soul,
And all the world was of my father's mind,
Had I before known this young man his son,
I should have given him tears unto entreaties,
Ere he should thus have ventur'd.

CELIA.   Gentle cousin,
Let us go thank him, and encourage him:

My father's rough and envious disposition
Sticks me at heart:

                      Sir, you have well deserv'd,
If you do keep your promises in love;
But justly as you have exceeded all promise,
Your mistress shall be happy.

ROSALIND.   Gentleman,
Wear this for me:

              one out of suits with fortune
That could give more, but that her hand lacks means.

Shall we go coz?

CELIA.   Ay: fare you well fair gentleman.

ORLANDO. Can I not say, I thank you? My better parts
Are all thrown down, and that which here stands up
Is but a quintain, a mere lifeless block.

ROSALIND. He calls us back:

                 my pride fell with my fortunes,
I'll ask him what he would:

                 Did you call sir?

Sir, you have wrestled well, and overthrown
More than your enemies.

CELIA. Will you go coz?

ROSALIND. Have with you: fare you well.

Exit.

ORLANDO. What passion hangs these weights upon my tongue?
I cannot speak to her, yet she urg'd conference.
O poor Orlando! thou art overthrown
Or Charles, or something weaker masters thee.

As You Like It: Act 1, Scene 2

So what are the things we might have noticed? Something about the nature of prose perhaps, what its qualities are? Something about the different atmosphere that is created when we hear the verse take over?

Note that all the characters in this scene, except for Charles who only speaks in mocking prose, speak in both these rhythms. This should convince us once and for all, that speaking in verse and prose is nothing to do with status, but that it's all to do with differing situations. Crucially, what happens here is that the prose is overwhelmed by the verse when Orlando defeats Charles and triumphs against all the odds.

Let us look in more detail at the nature of the prose and then consider why the characters are speaking like this.

CELIA. Young gentleman, your spirits are too bold for your years: / you have seen cruel proof of this man's strength, if you saw your self with your eyes, or knew your self with your judgement, the fear of your adventure would counsel you to a more equal enterprise. / We pray you for your own sake to embrace your own safety, and give over this attempt.

ROSALIND. Do young sir, your reputation shall not therefore be misprised: / we will make it our suit to the Duke, that the wrestling might not go forward.

ORLANDO. I beseech you, punish me not with your hard thoughts, wherein I confess me much guilty to deny so fair and excellent ladies any thing. / But let your fair eyes, and gentle wishes go with me to my trial; wherein if I be foiled, there is but one shamed that was never gracious: if killed, but one dead that is willing to be so: I shall do my friends no wrong, for I have none to lament me: the world no injury, for in it I have nothing: only in the world I fill up a place, which may be better supplied, when I have made it empty.

We noticed in Falstaff's speeches how balanced his phrases were and how varied the thought lengths. Here in Orlando's last thought-unit we see something similar:

> wherein if I be foiled, there is but one shamed that was never gracious:
>
> if killed, but one dead that is willing to be so:
>
> I shall do my friends no wrong, for I have none to lament me:
>
> the world no injury, for in it I have nothing:
>
> only in the world I fill up a place, which may be better supplied, when I have made it empty.

Five phrases: the first four are in two parts; the final one in three. This is not an 'everyday' language. Remember how we talked about Falstaff's list? Well, this is Orlando's. And although Orlando's 'repetitions' are not as obvious as Falstaff's, nevertheless we have: 'but one shamed', 'but one dead'; 'the world no injury', 'only in the world'.

Look at Celia's speech: how deft it is, how neat. I have divided it up further now to show more clearly the balance of her phrases:

> Young Gentleman, your spirits are too bold for your years:
>
> you have seen cruel proof of this man's strength, if you saw your self with your eyes, or knew your self with your judgement, the fear of your adventure would counsel you to a more equal enterprise.
>
> We pray you for your own sake to embrace your own safety, and give over this attempt.

Celia seems to be making a special effort to phrase her thoughts with care; speaking cautiously, politely and being sensitive to the way Orlando might be feeling before he steps into the ring. At the same time both she and Orlando sound as if they are slightly self-conscious of the way they are speaking; as if they are censoring themselves, as if they are not speaking freely.

How carefully Celia phrases this line:

> the fear of your adventure would counsel you to a more equal enterprise.

The delightful understatement at the end of it, 'a more equal enterprise' (Orlando's encounter with Charles plainly *not* being a meeting of equals!) always makes me smile.

But what does this careful talk conceal? What are they trying to achieve?

Clearly the two women want to dissuade this nice young man, whom they've only just clapped eyes on, from pitting himself against a professional wrestler who has just killed a trio of challengers. And we in the audience also know, though Orlando and the girls don't, that Orlando's brother Oliver has *asked* Charles the wrestler to make sure his brother *is* killed in the contest.

So the stakes are high; but how do you dissuade a young man whom you've never met before from doing something so dangerous when he seems so bent on doing it? You do it subtly; you try to ascertain gently whether there is any chance of his giving up on this crazy idea and *if there isn't*, then the last thing you want to do is to take away any confidence that he might have. So you *hide* your fears as you talk to him. And in a nutshell this is it. All this clever, careful talk is an attempt to hide something else. Prose acts like a mask. Instead of revealing all, as verse does, prose puts up a smoke screen. The women don't want Orlando to fight, but the situation is such that they can't show him how much they don't want him to.

Prose is a language which says one thing to hide another.

As soon as you censor any of your thoughts, you have to put some other words out there in their place, so it seems as if nothing is missing. Sometimes this accounts for the fact that in prose, characters 'go on and on' speaking at length, adding more and more details, more and more examples, in an effort to persuade us that *nothing is being hidden*, which an awkward silence might give the lie to. Sometimes the difficulty of this task is such that the prose speaker seems to be losing control of their mental processes as they pile one thing on top of another. And indeed Shakespeare uses prose to capture the sounds of those minds that have lost all control – the minds of those we call mad.

Orlando, though, displays such ease and self-control in response to the speeches of the two girls that it is as if it matters little to him what the outcome of the fight might be and that he has no great attachment to life. What happens here is his so carefully balanced phrases are his deliberate attempts to sound calm, nonchalant even, helping him to hide any nervousness he might be feeling. In fact the forthcoming fight means everything to him. It's the only way he has to prove his worth and who he is, and to tell the world who his father was.

So the brilliance of prose is that it invites us to look behind the words. The words give us a surface, usually witty in some way, and this surface covers, or tries to cover over, what is really going on beneath. And prose is brilliant for audiences as well, because the audience, who see your thoughts at the same time as they hear your words, will, if you act well, *see* what your character is trying to hide.

But Orlando doesn't get killed: he knocks Charles unconscious, and everyone on stage, with the probable exception of Duke Frederick and his nearest advisors, breathes more than a sigh of relief, more like a gasp of delight. And *in that moment* verse pours into the play. It's as if the characters have been freed and are now able to express themselves without any concealment.

At this point we also have a lot of shared lines which help capture the excitement and exhilaration of the moment. These characters are eager to speak as soon as possible and the shared lines direct them to come in right on the heels of the previous speaker's words.

> DUKE F. No more, no more.
>
> ORLANDO.   Yes I beseech your Grace,[5]
>   I am not yet well breath'd.
>
> DUKE F.   How dost thou Charles?
>
> LE BEAU. He cannot speak my lord.
>
> DUKE F.   Bear him away:
>   What is thy name young man?
>
> ORLANDO.   Orlando my liege,
>   The youngest son of Sir Rowland de Boys.
>
> DUKE F. I would thou hadst been son to some man else,
>   The world esteem'd thy father honourable,
>   But I did find him still mine enemy:
>
>   Thou shouldst have better pleas'd me with this deed,
>   Hadst thou descended from another house:
>
>   But fare thee well, thou art a gallant youth,
>   I would thou hadst told me of another father.
>
>   *Exit Duke.*

At last Orlando can say who he is. The more important line of course is when he says who his father was, because he was not only the banished Duke's friend, but Frederick's enemy.

Sound this line out and you'll find it has only four stresses – the fifth stress is missing:

The **youngest son** of Sir **Rowland** de **Boys**.

(I know the line has ten syllables, but you wouldn't want to say it as if it were a regular pentameter, because that would give a false stress to the second syllable of Rowland's name. At all others times in the play when Rowland's name is mentioned, it is stressed on the first syllable. What actually happens here is the, 'of Sir' sounds as one syllable rather than two.

Sound it out again as if it were a regular verse line and you'll see what I mean:

> The **youngest son** of **Sir Rowland** de **Boys.**

Stressed like this the line doesn't work. The missing fifth stress is deliberate; Shakespeare gives us here a *moment of silence*. Or maybe a silence filled with a gasp.

And in that moment the whole court realises what has happened: Frederick's enemy has returned in the shape of his son. And then Frederick has to speak.

The difference between verse and the prose that preceded it is beautifully illustrated in the lines that follow Frederick's exit.

> CELIA. Were I my father (coz) would I do this?
>
> ORLANDO. I am more proud to be Sir Rowland's son,
> His youngest son, and would not change that calling
> To be adopted heir to Frederick.
>
> ROSALIND. My father lov'd Sir Rowland as his soul,
> And all the world was of my father's mind,
> Had I before known this young man his son,
> I should have given him tears unto entreaties,
> Ere he should thus have ventur'd.
>
> CELIA.   Gentle cousin,
> Let us go thank him, and encourage him:

All three characters are now speaking their minds freely – in verse; saying what would have been forbidden before. But it's Rosalind's speech that I want to focus on.

She is the most emotional of the three. She says that had she known *before* who this young man was – the son of her banished father's dearest friend – she would have added tears to her imploring him not to fight. But if she *had* known, and if she *had* wept, she would no longer have been able to censor her thoughts. Her tears would have given her away. Her true feelings would have come to the surface and, had she spoken then, it would have been in verse.

Maybe Shakespeare mentions her tears in *this* speech because in Shakespeare's mind she *is* now crying; crying with relief at the outcome of the fight and that this beautiful young man is still alive. And probably she is also crying for her banished father; and crying with sorrow for the deceased Rowland. And that's why Celia says what she does, the 'gentle' of 'gentle cousin' acknowledging how moved Rosalind is; so she suggests to her cousin that maybe they should both go and say something to this wonderful, brave young man.

It would be wrong to say that 'verse' is 'truth' and that prose is 'the sound of lying'. Verse, let us remember, is only 'the *sound* of sincerity', while prose could be said to be the 'sound of speaking artfully'. What we can say is that the purpose of prose is to hide something else. And, except in the mouths of villains who, as a rule, will have already revealed to the audience their true motives, verse releases feelings that are genuine.

But have you realised that we have reached a surprising conclusion? Namely, that prose, or at least ninety-nine per cent of it, is a more artificial language than verse is. Prose watches itself, conscious of the effect that it is trying to create. The verse says it like it is, spontaneous and uncensored.

Finally we should notice that with prose there are more unstressed syllables than stressed ones. In verse of course the number of stressed and unstressed syllables is basically equal. Look at this line of Falstaff's:

Why? detraction will not suffer it, therefore I'll none of it.

Five stresses in fifteen syllables. Or take a look at this line of Celia's:

the fear of your adventure would counsel you to a more equal enterprise.

How many stresses would you give it? I'd only give it five again and there are nineteen syllables here.

So prose runs more quickly. It's not the rhythm of our heartbeat any longer. The speed of it reflects the workings of our imaginations; the nimbleness of it reflects how our brains are continually making instant connections. So prose is a cerebral activity, and it is full of new ideas, lists, repetitions; full of antitheses; consciously creating shapes with words and playing with rhythms. All are signs of 'cleverness', of wit, of a mind working overtime. And the reason for all these brilliant *inventions* is to hide something else that you don't wish others to see.

Though of course, if the over-working mind ever spirals out of control, then we enter the realms of madness, and as the next chapter will show, prose is also the language that Shakespeare uses in these extreme situations.

I'd like to end this chapter with Harold Pinter's description of what lies behind the speeches he wrote for *his* actors; it is also a description that brilliantly characterises for me the *prose* in Shakespeare's plays:

SPEAKING THE SPEECH

The speech we hear is an indication of that which we don't hear. It is a necessary avoidance, a violent, sly, anguished or mocking smoke screen which keeps the other in its true place.

Harold Pinter to the National Student Drama Festival,
Bristol 1962

Nine

Sounding Prose
Reason and Madness

Speak the speech I pray you, as I pronounc'd it to
you trippingly on the tongue: But if you mouth it, as
many of your players do, I had as lief* the town-crier
had spoke my lines...

Hamlet: Act 3, Scene 2

By the time Hamlet is giving these instructions to the actors (who have
arrived at Elsinore to play before the court) many of the courtiers themselves are convinced that Hamlet is mad. But as we'll discover, Hamlet is
only pretending to be mad, his pretence mainly relying on a wild way of
talking – which, as we'll see, means speaking in prose, rather than in verse.
Later in this chapter we will look at the ways Shakespeare uses prose to
capture the voices of those, like King Lear and Ophelia, whose madness is
no pretence, but seemingly beyond their control. But before that we must
consider *how* we should go about sounding the prose.

as lief – just as soon

Actors and prose

Actors generally need less help with prose than with verse; after all, it's what they are used to dealing with. Less than half a century after Shakespeare's death in 1616, most plays were being written not in verse, but in prose. And so it has remained ever since. However, Shakespeare's prose still needs work; its haphazard rhythms have to be sought out, and you must learn to respond to the way it flows and where it changes directions. It won't sustain you in the same way that verse does with its underlying emotional rhythms, and the prose is always harder to learn accurately.

Also, prose needs energy. Remember, apart from when something is being read out (prose letters, proclamations, and such like) prose is performing two functions simultaneously. One is to cope with your character's underlying situation; the other is to keep that underlying situation from being exposed. If ever I am talking to people about the difference between verse and prose, I find I have to stand to talk about prose. I just seem to need that extra energy I get from being on my feet!

To begin with, let's return to *Hamlet*. The famous quote at the beginning of this chapter comes close to the halfway point in the play. Hamlet is rehearsing *The Murder of Gonzago*, the play that he hopes is going to trap Claudius into revealing that he killed Hamlet's father. Hamlet needs the actors to perform convincingly because he knows that theatre at its best has such power over audiences that they can sometimes forget that they are actually watching a play.

A couplet written in 1647 ran:

> Frozen with grief we could not stir away
> Until the Epilogue told us 'twas a play.[1]

Earlier Hamlet has told us his whole plan.

> I have heard, that guilty creatures sitting at a play,
> Have by the very cunning of the scene,
> Been struck so to the soul, that presently*
> They have proclaim'd their malefactions.*
> For murder, though it have no tongue, will speak
> With most miraculous organ.
>
> I'll have these Players,
> Play something like the murder of my father,
> Before mine uncle. I'll observe his looks,

presently – immediately
malefactions – wrongdoings

I'll tent him to the quick: If he but blench
I know my course.

Hamlet: Act 2, Scene 2

When we are speaking verse the iambic rhythm and the run of the lines guides us as to how we should speak it. The rhythm keeps us on track and the line both *runs* and *breaks*, and divides the expression of our thoughts into *parts*. With prose, the rhythms are irregular, and there are no line endings to guide us either. So we have to do more of the work for ourselves. There is, however, one helpful indicator, if we choose to use it, and that is the punctuation as printed in the First Folio.

The First Folio of 1623 and its punctuation

As I mentioned in my Author's Note, great care was taken over its publication, but it is in no way faultless, and we owe much to the numerous editors of Shakespeare, who over the years, have attempted to sort out some of the tangles and misprints that are found in the First Folio. I believe that care was taken over the punctuation too, but it has been felt, and still is in many quarters, that the 'original' First Folio punctuation is 'beneath serious notice'.[2] I want to convince you otherwise.

Later in this book, in Chapter 14, I advance the idea that the 'original First Folio' punctuation can also be of help to us in our verse-speaking, by way of indicating certain points of emphasis and meaning in the lines, that would otherwise, possibly, escape us. For now, though, I want to concentrate on how this 'original punctuation' can be of initial assistance as we navigate our way through passages of prose. I warn you, using the 'original punctuation' might seem like cheating – it virtually tells you *how to say it!*

Original punctuation

The great difference between the punctuation in the Folio and in most modern editions is that this 'original punctuation' is designed more for the *speaker* than the *reader*. In the Folio, a word or phrase that needs some emphasis, so as to make clear what is being said, will be *followed* by a punctuation mark. By contrast modern punctuation concerns itself with grammatical structure. The meanings attached to the different punctuation marks have altered somewhat as well. In the seventeenth century the question mark was used not only for questions, but also for exclamations – of surprise, say; more like a modern exclamation mark – while in the original texts the exclamation mark is used only rarely. The colon, by contrast, was used very frequently in Shakespeare's time, sometimes taking the place of what would be represented by a full stop today; but frequently the colon could be used to mark a point of *strong emphasis* as well.

The word 'emphasis' is our key to understanding the way in which this 'original punctuation' can be of help to us in the speaking of prose, and no punctuation mark is of more help than the humble comma. Follow the commas: give just the right degree of *emphasis* to the word or phrase that occurs *before* each comma, and the pattern of the speeches will be revealed to you.

Putting the punctuation to work

Continue to sound out Hamlet's words, as his advice to the players continues, and let the punctuation guide you. I have added slash-marks to indicate the thought-units.

> HAMLET. Be not too tame neither: but let your own discretion
>   be your tutor. / Suit the action to the word, the word to
>   the action, with this special observance: That you o'er-step
>   not the modesty of nature; for any thing so over-done, is
>   from the purpose of playing, whose end both at the first
>   and now, was and is, to hold as 'twere the mirror up to
>   nature; to show virtue her own feature, scorn her own
>   image, and the very age and body of the time, his form
>   and pressure. / Now, this over-done, or come tardy off,
>   though it make the unskilful laugh, cannot but make the
>   judicious grieve; The censure of the which one, must in
>   your allowance o'erweigh a whole theatre of others. / O,
>   there be players that I have seen play, and heard others
>   praise, and that highly (not to speak it profanely) that
>   neither having the accent of Christians, nor the gait of
>   Christian, pagan, nor man, have so strutted and bellowed,
>   that I have thought some of nature's journey-men had
>   made men, and not made them well, they imitated
>   humanity so abominably.
>
> *Hamlet*: Act 3, Scene 2

The speech as punctuated here in the First Folio has just four full stops, two colons, three semi-colons, a pair of brackets and twenty-four commas; but how beautifully the commas set out the argument and the structure.

We will look at the middle of this speech in more detail to see how the stresses fall with the punctuation, light though they all are.

(Basically to make this as clear as possible I have put the word before the commas in bold, though I have felt the need to put in bold some additional words as well.)

> for any thing so over-**done**, is **from** the purpose of **playing**,
> whose end both at the **first** and **now**, **was** and **is**, to hold as
> 'twere the **mirror** up to **nature**; to show **virtue** her own **feature**,
> **scorn** her own **image**, and the very **age** and **body** of the **time**,
> his **form** and **pressure**.

Wasn't that easy? Didn't all this fall from your lips, as if there could be no problem at all with speaking lines such as these? And after the initial run of commas, the semi-colon marking the end of the phrase 'the mirror up to nature' gave you that slightly heavier break, helping you to 'set up' those three examples that followed it. The only problem is that editors generally no longer trust the punctuation. They certainly make sure that all the words that the characters say are faithfully recorded, but the punctuation has become something of a free-for-all.

Sound out the same passage as punctuated by one modern copy:

> for anything so o'erdone is **from** the purpose of **playing**, whose
> **end**, both at the **first** and **now**, **was** and is to **hold**, as 'twere, the
> **mirror** up to **nature**; to show **virtue** her own **feature**, **scorn** her
> own **image**, and the very **age** and **body** of the time his **form**
> and **pressure**.[3]

It's harder, isn't it? The flow of ideas has been interrupted and the meaning no longer springs off the page. I miss the emphasis that was given to 'overdone', and the importance given to the word 'time'. Also this modern edition gets bogged down around 'was and is to hold, as 'twere, the mirror up to nature;' – an unnecessary complication that breaks the clear flow of the thought. Most important of all, I miss the strong comparison given to 'was and is' by the comma after 'is'.

Most modern editors understandably feel the need to use punctuation that adheres to the rules of grammar, whereas the punctuation in the Folio uses a more 'acoustic' system, one which is concerned with the sound of a phrase, and the clear release of the thought in the mouth of a skilled speaker. The punctuation in the First Folio certainly includes some errors, but any punctuation which deviates wildly from it, will inevitably suggest to the actors rhythms other than those that Shakespeare and his contemporaries heard.

The Folio punctuation helps us to hear the sounds that Shakespeare heard.

Antithesis

Antithesis, or the comparing of opposites, is one of Shakespeare's most frequently used devices: it brings clarity and meaning to his writing. The continuation of Hamlet's speech gives you three further examples of antithesis. Keep sounding it out.

> Now, this **over-done**, or come **tardy off**, though it make the
> unskilful **laugh**, cannot but make the judicious **grieve**; The
> censure of the which **one**, must in your allowance o'erweigh a
> whole **theatre** of others.

Antithesis is one of the lynch-pins of all Shakespeare's writing: we always need to be looking out for it. I sometimes think it's what we have two hands for – so that they are always ready to help illustrate any antithetical statements we want to make.

Notice how often Shakespeare makes his points by these antitheses. These last lines are constructed around it. 'Over-done' against 'tardy off'; 'unskilful laugh' against 'judicious grieve'; 'which one' against 'a whole theatre of others'.

Sound out how this passage as it is punctuated in another modern edition:

> Now this overdone or come **tardy off**, though it makes the
> unskilful **laugh**, cannot but make the judicious **grieve**, the
> censure of the which one must in your allowance o'erweigh a
> whole **theatre** of others.

Immediately two commas are missing: the first after 'Now' had usefully pulled our attention to what was about to be said; the second after 'over-done' had indicated that important antithesis between 'over-done' and 'tardy off'. Then, in lightening the punctuation after 'grieve', and omitting the comma after 'one', we have not only lost that further antithesis – 'one' and 'others' – but have also been hurried through to the end of the sentence. In so doing, our understanding that the 'which **one**' referred back to the 'judicious' has been jeopardised, which the weightier semi-colon after 'grieve' and the (admittedly unusual) capital letter given to the following 'The', had helped to make clear.

But didn't your initial reading of this passage with the 'original punc-tuation' simply go without a hitch? It's not that I think that actors wouldn't find for themselves the importance of the word 'overdone'; or the play of 'one' as against 'others', but we shouldn't turn our backs on the clues that the punctuation of the First Folio can give us.

Wit and madness: Hamlet and King Lear

Both *Hamlet* and *King Lear* are rich in prose: a quarter of all the lines in *King Lear* are in prose and the percentage of prose lines in *Hamlet* is even slightly greater. These two plays also deal in similar matters – Hamlet, and Edgar in *King Lear*, both pretend to be mad, and a fair proportion of the prose in these plays can be accounted for by their masquerades. But Ophe-lia and King Lear also speak prose, or 'non-verse', as they go mad and lose their ability to cope with what is going on around them. To pretend to be something you are not is a dangerous thing to attempt, but it is a clever thing to bring off: it's a display of wit. So prose could be said to be holding 'wit' in its grasp, at one end of its reach, and with its opposite outstretched hand holding 'madness'.

For the rest of this chapter we will look at the voices of 'wit' and 'mad-ness' in these two plays and take special care to look at those places where verse gives way to prose and vice-versa. Remember how emotionally uplifting was that scene in *As You Like It* when Orlando defeated the wrestler Charles and verse flooded into that play for the first time. In the two plays we are looking at now the prose/verse junctures will be much more frequent, but also subtler and on a smaller scale, and therefore eas-ier to overlook. But overlook them we shouldn't, for these 'junctures' will help us to define accurately what is happening in the minds of our pro-tagonists, and if we observe them properly they will enliven, enrich and make more specific our playing of these scenes.

Hamlet's 'antic disposition'

The first verse/prose juncture that indisputably occurs in *Hamlet* happens, not before our eyes on stage, but *between* scenes. In Act 1, Scene 5, after Hamlet has met the Ghost, he swears Horatio and Marcellus to secrecy, and tells them that he might, sometime in the future, start acting strangely – 'To put an antic disposition on'. His scheme, we will learn, is to pretend to be mad to try and hide from Claudius his true intentions while he goes about planning how he might be able to revenge his father's murder. The scene ends with these three lines of verse:

> The time is out of joint: Oh cursed spite,
> That ever I was born to set it right.
> Nay, come let's go together.

When we next see Hamlet in Act 2, Scene 2 with Polonius our verse/prose juncture has already happened offstage: Hamlet is now speaking in prose and pretending to be mad. Polonius is taken in by Hamlet's performance, and decides he's the one best placed to get to the bottom of Hamlet's madness. He believes that it's his thwarted love for Ophelia that has made him mad.

POLONIUS. How does my good lord Hamlet?

HAMLET. Well, God-a-mercy.

POLONIUS. Do you know me, my lord?

HAMLET. Excellent, excellent well: you're a fishmonger.

POLONIUS. Not I my lord.

HAMLET. Then I would you were so honest a man.

POLONIUS. Honest, my lord?

HAMLET. Ay sir, to be honest as this world goes, is to be one man picked out of two thousand.

POLONIUS. That's very true, my lord.

HAMLET. For if the sun breed maggots in a dead dog, being a good kissing carrion—— / Have you a daughter?

POLONIUS. I have my lord.

HAMLET. Let her not walk i'th'sun: / Conception is a blessing, but not as your daughter may conceive. / Friend look to't.

POLONIUS. How say you by that? Still harping on my daughter: / yet he knew me not at first; he said I was a fishmonger: / he is far gone, far gone: / and truly in my youth, I suffered much extremity for love: very near this. / I'll speak to him again.

Hamlet: Act 2, Scene 2

We should pause to consider why Polonius is speaking in prose here too. And the reason is that he is playing a game with Hamlet; he's trying to outwit him. He is very conscious of how he is shaping his questions. He is also showing off to us in the audience, delighted with his own performance and his own cleverness. This is the way those many characters in Shakespeare who want us to think they are witty fellows sound, and this sound cannot be captured by the sincere rhythms of verse. Polonius is another of our prose entertainers, though rather like an amateur – he only *intends* to be funny on occasions.

A prose/verse juncture followed by a verse/prose juncture

These next two junctures happen in quick succession before our eyes. Polonius tells Hamlet he will take his leave of him, to which Hamlet replies:

> You cannot sir take from me any thing, that I will more
> willingly part withal, except my life, my life.

And in virtually the next moment Rosencrantz and Guildenstern, two old school friends of Hamlet's, are being shown into his presence and a prose/verse juncture takes place, only to be followed almost immediately by its opposite. Indeed the switch lasts for such a short time – just three lines – that the First Folio printers do not notice the change and continue to print this passage as if it were prose, not hearing the verse rhythm of the following three lines:

> GUILDENSTERN. Mine honour'd lord?
>
> ROSENCRANTZ.   My most dear lord?[4]
>
> HAMLET. My excellent good friends? How dost thou Guildenstern?
>   Oh, Rosencrantz; good lads: How do ye both?

And now comes the second juncture as the scene reverts to prose:

> ROSENCRANTZ. As the indifferent children of the earth.
>
> GUILDENSTERN. Happy, in that we are not over-happy: on
>   Fortune's cap, we are not the very button.
>
> HAMLET. Nor the soles of her shoe?
>
> ROSENCRANTZ. Neither my Lord.
>
> HAMLET. Then you live about her waist, or in the middle of her
>   favours?
>
> GUILDENSTERN. Faith, her privates, we.
>
> HAMLET. In the secret parts of Fortune? Oh, most true: she is a
>   strumpet. What's the news?

Hamlet: Act 2, Scene 2

Let's pause a while to discuss what we've just seen. The first greetings between the three old friends are in verse rhythm. It's no matter that they are not usually printed as verse – the First Folio printers frequently found it difficult to distinguish verse from prose in the manuscripts from which they were setting their type – but if it sounds like verse, then we hear our 'sound of sincerity' and that's all that matters. And what we hear is that Hamlet sounds genuinely happy about seeing his old school friends again. He asks them how they are. But their replies are immediately less direct; they begin to make some jokes, and a joke is so often our way of covering something else from view. They are censoring something and Hamlet senses it.

So these two sudden and short-lived junctures, that it would be so easy to overlook, are in fact very telling, and by observing them the scene will be greatly enriched, as will be our own satisfaction in the way we can play them. We move from Hamlet having successfully fooled Polonius with his 'crazy' talk, to Hamlet's genuine delight at seeing his two old school friends – after all, they might become, like Horatio, further allies to help him defeat Claudius – only for that delight to be replaced by a terrible sense of betrayal: his two old friends have been 'turned', and they are in the pay of the enemy.

But Hamlet uses prose for his own ends too. Behind its dancing surface he can hide what he is truly feeling. He seems to be taking his former school friends into his confidence, getting them to admit that the King and Queen have sent for them to come to Elsinore, and then, as if to help them, Hamlet tells them that he will explain why Claudius and his mother are so concerned about him. And he does so in this much quoted and 'poetic' piece of prose.

I want you to sound this out now and afterwards we'll discuss what Hamlet is up to. Remember to use the 'emphasis-pointing' commas, but also notice how the First Folio employs a variety of punctuation marks within this speech, suggesting that here, the speech flows faster, and here, less so. (Remember those 'oblique slashes' are my additions to the text: marking out the 'thought-units' as they occur in the prose.)

> HAMLET. I have of late, but wherefore I know not, lost all my
> mirth, forgone all custom of exercise; / and indeed, it goes
> so heavily with my disposition; that this goodly frame the
> earth, seems to me a sterile promontory; this most
> excellent canopy the air, look you, this brave o'er-hanging
> firmament, this majestical roof, fretted with golden fire:
> why, it appears no other thing to me, than a foul and
> pestilent congregation of vapours. / What a piece of work
> is a man! how noble in reason? how infinite in faculty? in

form and moving how express and admirable? in action, how like an angel? in apprehension, how like a god? the beauty of the world, the paragon of animals; and yet to me, what is this quintessence of dust? / Man delights not me; no, nor woman neither; though by your smiling you seem to say so.

Hamlet: Act 2, Scene 2

The speech has all the ingredients we've begun to expect from prose: the wonderful list of man's attributes – 'noble in reason', 'infinite in faculties' and so on – and before that those typically balanced phrases:

that this **goodly frame** the **earth,**
seems to **me** a sterile **prom**ontory;
this most **excellent canopy** the **air,**
look you,
this **brave** o'erhanging firmament,
this majestical **roof fretted** with **golden fire:**
why,
it ap**pears** no other **thing** to **me,** than a **foul** and **pestilent**
congregation of **vapours.**

Here we see a build to a climax. Four phrases with three stresses in each of them followed by a line with five stresses and then one with seven. Again we see these antitheses. The goodly earth has become a sterile promontory; the brave firmament appears like pestilent vapours. And we must learn how to enjoy playing them.

But what is really going on here? Hamlet seems to be explaining to old friends how he is feeling. But, like his speech to the players, it is in prose, and among prose's many qualities, we should remind ourselves, is its nature to conceal rather than reveal. The speech is a smoke screen. Some of it is not quite the truth. He *does* know why he's 'lost all his mirth', and later we'll learn that, instead of having 'foregone all custom of exercise', he has 'been in continual practice' with his fencing, as he tells Horatio in Act 5, Scene 2.

It is not a pack of lies though: he does say he is unhappy and the world has turned sour for him. But as to why, he keeps that to himself behind very *carefully* shaped prose. What he is hiding from everyone apart from Horatio is that he has met his father's ghost, who has told him that he was murdered by his own brother, Claudius. He reveals nothing of this to his spying old classmates.

Prose will hide a greater truth behind lesser ones.

A later verse/prose juncture

A similar move from verse into prose happens when Hamlet unexpect-
edly comes across Ophelia. He sees her as he is pursuing the thoughts
that began with that most famous line of all – 'To be or not to be, that is
the question'. It's her appearance that brings his ruminations to an abrupt
end.

> HAMLET. Thus conscience does make cowards of us all,
>
>> And thus the native hue of resolution
>> Is sicklied o'er, with the pale cast of thought,
>> And enterprises of great pith and moment,
>> With this regard their currents turn awry,
>> And lose the name of action.
>>
>>> Soft you now,
>> The fair Ophelia?
>>
>>> Nymph, in thy orisons
>> Be all my sins remember'd.
>
> OPHELIA. Good my lord,
>> How does your honour for this many a day?
>
> HAMLET. I humbly thank you: well, well, well.
>
> OPHELIA. My lord, I have remembrances of yours,
>> That I have longed long to re-deliver.
>> I pray you now, receive them.
>
> HAMLET. No, no, I never gave you aught.
>
> OPHELIA. My honour'd lord, I know right well you did,
>> And with them words of so sweet breath compos'd,
>> As made the things more rich,
>>
>>> their perfume lost:
>> Take these again, for to the noble mind
>> Rich gifts wax poor, when givers prove unkind.
>>
>> There my lord.
>
> HAMLET. Ha, ha: Are you honest?
>
> OPHELIA. My lord.
>
> HAMLET. Are you fair?
>
> OPHELIA. What means your lordship?
>
> HAMLET. That if you be honest and fair, your honesty should
>> admit no discourse to your beauty.

Hamlet: Act 3, Scene 1

As with Rosencrantz and Guildenstern, he begins speaking to her openly in verse and then almost immediately begins to suspect that this meeting with Ophelia is more than a chance encounter. Is she spying on him too?

Maybe it's while he is saying,

> I humbly thank you: well,   well,   well.

that suspicion strikes. This is still a line of verse, and you could think of it, as I've set it out, as having two gaps between its final *well*s, as if during these gaps he is thinking how to deal with Ophelia. His technique with Ophelia is different to the way he dealt with Rosencrantz and Guildenstern. The net of spies are closing in, and so he has to find a way of fooling anyone listening in on his conversation with Ophelia, while, at the same time, to try to warn her against getting involved.

After one more similarly halting line of verse he begins to appear to speak less rationally – and so in prose. Maybe he hopes that Ophelia will see through his mad performance and get his true message. His assumed madness is designed for the ears of Polonius and any others he suspects might be listening in:

> I have heard of your paintings too well enough. God has given you one face, and you make your self another: / you jig, you amble, and you lisp, and nickname God's creatures, and make your wantonness, your ignorance. / Go to, I'll no more on't, it hath made me mad. I say, we will have no more marriages. / Those that are married already, all but one shall live, the rest shall keep as they are. / To a nunnery, go.

The true message for Ophelia might be: 'Get away from here to where you can be safe; forget about marriage'. Sadly, she only sees the 'performance', as she reveals to us in the very next line after Hamlet's exit:

> O what a noble mind is here o'er-thrown?

Claudius, who has been listening with Polonius to this scene, is *not* however taken in by Hamlet's performance. He correctly thinks that there's something behind it all:

> Love? His affections do not that way tend,
> Nor what he spake, though it lack'd form a little,
> Was not like madness.

In fact earlier Rosencrantz and Guildenstern seem not to have been taken in by Hamlet either, and Guildenstern says with great accuracy, when reporting back to Claudius, that Hamlet:

> … with a crafty madness keeps aloof:
> When we would bring him on to some confession
> Of his true state.

However, in looking at Hamlet's scenes with Ophelia and Rosencrantz and Guildenstern we have begun to account for why over a quarter of the play is written in prose. It is in prose that Hamlet can try to hide those things from others that he doesn't want them to find out about. But it is a dangerous game: it deeply distresses Ophelia, whom he loves, and fails to fool his uncle Claudius, his only true enemy. We, who are watching all this, know these are just 'performances', and that he is in control of them: when he speaks to us in soliloquy, or to Horatio, or to his mother in private, he reverts to verse.

Prose and true madness in Ophelia

Later in *Hamlet* Ophelia can no longer keep control of her thoughts, or keep in touch with reality. Her 'verse/prose juncture' happens off stage, as Hamlet's first one did. While she has been upset by Hamlet's behaviour in the 'nunnery scene' and in the following 'play scene', it is only when we next see her in Act 4, after her father has been killed, that we realise that she is no longer speaking verse. Her speech has become a mixture of prose and songs, as if she has become the Fool in the play – like Feste in *Twelfth Night*, or the Fool in *King Lear* who similarly reveals what he wants to say via cryptic ballads. She, however, has become genuinely disturbed, but her language, being the genuine article, is simpler than some of Hamlet's pretended madness was, with his 'sun breed maggots in a dead dog'.

> OPHELIA. I hope all will be well. / We must be patient, but I cannot
> choose but weep, to think they should lay him i'th'cold
> ground: / My brother shall know of it, and so I thank you for
> your good counsel. / Come, my coach: / Goodnight ladies:
> Goodnight sweet ladies: Goodnight, goodnight.
>
> *Hamlet*: Act 4, Scene 5

She is almost certainly remembering her father's recent burial, but there has been no good counsel offered to her; there is no coach; there's probably only one lady on stage; and it's probably not night. But her mind is telling her otherwise.

The truly mad seem to see things that are not there. I said in the previous chapter that prose can be connected with a heightened mental state that the character is giving free rein to, in order to hide something else behind it. But in its extreme form, a hyperactive disturbed mental state becomes seemingly uncontrollable and reveals itself as an illness, hiding what those characters once were. Unless we were to believe that for these characters, to continue to be what they were, would be an even more unendurable state to be in, and that their 'madness' might therefore be a kind of willed refuge…

Prose and true madness in King Lear

The great scenes of madness in Shakespeare are found in *King Lear*. And here we will find the subtlest and most frequent occurrences of these 'prose/verse' junctures, as Lear's mind hovers between reason and madness. Lear is driven mad by the way his two elder daughters treat him and by others who support them. To begin with, Lear just *fears* that he might lose his reason.

> LEAR. I prithee daughter do not make me mad,
>
> *King Lear*: Act 2, Scene 4

As his daughters drive him out into the storm, he says to them and to the Fool who accompanies him,

> LEAR.   You think I'll weep,
>   No, I'll not weep,
>
> I have full cause of weeping, but this heart
> Shall break into a hundred thousand flaws
> Or ere I'll weep;
>
>   O Fool, I shall go mad.
>
> *King Lear*: Act 2, Scene 4

At his maddest he will speak in prose, or in a fluid mixture alternating between prose and verse. Edgar will later comment on this juxtaposition of the two rhythms:

> O matter, and impertinency* mix'd,
> Reason in madness.
>
> *King Lear*: Act 4, Scene 6

As Lear slips in and out of lucidity, it is as if 'matter' and 'reason' are captured in verse, 'impertinency' and 'madness' in prose. So in what follows we must be on the lookout for these verse/prose and prose/verse junctures, as they will be our guide to what is happening in Lear's mind.

Lear's descent into madness, and recovery from it, is brilliantly charted in the play. And you must now sound out the major stages of this journey as it unfolds in the following pages. To begin with, his actions only seem mad to others. He won't ask his daughters for shelter from the storm but facing it instead, encourages it to increase its ferocity and destroy ungrateful mankind.

> LEAR. Blow winds, and crack your cheeks; Rage, blow
> You cataracts, and hurricanoes spout,
> Till you have drench'd our steeples, drown'd the cocks.
>
> You sulph'rous and thought-executing fires,
> Vaunt-couriers of oak-cleaving thunder-bolts,
> Singe my white head.
> And thou all-shaking thunder,
> Strike flat the thick rotundity o'th'world,
> Crack nature's moulds, all germens spill at once
> That make ingrateful man.
>
> FOOL. O Nuncle, court holy-water in a dry house, is better than
> this rain-water out o'door. / Good Nuncle, in, and ask thy
> daughters' blessing, / here's a night pities neither wisemen,
> nor fools.
>
> *King Lear*: Act 3, Scene 2

Here Lear is still in verse, maybe acting 'madly', but we understand why. And to him too his actions make perfect sense. Here with him is the Fool, the professional clown, whose enigmatic remarks, like all the professional fools in Shakespeare, are always cloaked in prose or rhyme or song. And it is so because they are always, as it were, 'on duty', acting their part.

The next time we see Lear he is still trying to explain his 'mad' actions to his followers. He still won't take refuge in a hovel that has been found for him:

> LEAR. Thou think'st 'tis much that this contentious storm
> Invades us to the skin:

---

impertinency – nonsense

so 'tis to thee,
But where the greater malady is fix'd,
The lesser is scarce felt.

Thou'ldst shun a bear,
But if thy flight lay toward the roaring sea,
Thou'ldst meet the bear i'th'mouth,

King Lear: Act 3, Scene 4

And then out of the hovel bursts Edgar. Edgar, innocent of all wrong doing, who to escape the death warrant that is out for him, has disguised himself as Poor Tom, a deranged beggar. Crucial to his disguise is his beggar's mad patter; it's what has kept him safe and out of the reach of the law. And now in this scene he comes face to face with Lear, his own godfather, and he can't allow himself to be recognised. But Edgar's 'mad' act is enough to tip Lear over the edge.

Keep reading all these glorious passages out loud. But I want you to notice in particular the headlong run of commas in Edgar's second speech, and how only commas separate some of the cluster of thought-units which bring it to its conclusion. Most modern editions can't refrain from slowing the whole speech up. But the lack of heavier punctuation marks will release the sounds of his assumed madness. And we shouldn't feel that all of it needs to be clearly articulated or understood, or even clearly heard – it's dramatic gabble, not literature:

EDGAR. Away, the foul fiend follows me, / through the sharp hawthorn blows the cold winds. / Humh, go to thy bed and warm thee.

LEAR. Didst thou give all to thy daughters? And art thou come to this?

EDGAR. Who gives any thing to poor Tom? Whom the foul fiend hath led through fire, and through flame, through ford, and whirl-pool, o're bog, and quagmire, that hath laid knives under his pillow, and halters in his pew, set rats-bane by his porridge, made him proud of heart, to ride on a bay trotting horse, over four inched bridges, to course his own shadow for a traitor. / Bless thy five wits, / Tom's a cold. O do, de, do de, do de, / bless thee from whirl-winds, star-blasting, and taking, / do poor Tom some charity, whom the foul fiend vexes. / There could I have him now, and there, and there again, and there.

Storm still.

LEAR. Has his daughters brought him to this pass? / Couldst thou save nothing? Would'st thou give 'em all?

FOOL. Nay, he reserved a blanket, else we had been all sham'd.

LEAR. Now all the plagues that in the pendulous air
Hang fated o'er men's faults, light on thy daughters.

KENT. He hath no daughters sir.

LEAR. Death traitor, nothing could have subdued nature
To such a lowness, but his unkind daughters.

Is it the fashion, that discarded fathers,
Should have thus little mercy on their flesh:

Judicious punishment, 'twas this flesh begot
Those pelican daughters.

EDGAR. Pillicock sat on Pillicock hill, alow: alow, loo, loo.

FOOL. This cold night will turn us all to fools, and madmen.

King Lear: Act 3, Scene 4

With Lear's first question to Edgar –

Didst thou give all to thy daughters? And art thou come to
this?

– we sense that he has made an irrational jump. A juncture has been
arrived at. And although it's almost still verse, it's now not quite a regular
verse line, and nor is his next speech. But then it's as if Lear sees the 'sense'
behind what Edgar is saying and doing, and his speeches then revert to
verse.

But what a scene! Lear beginning to lose control of his mind and slip-
ping into prose; Edgar maintaining his mad disguise with his garbled
prose speeches; the Fool with his jokes and gnomic comments; and the
banished Kent, also in disguise, also under threat of death if he's discovered to be still in the country, the lone voice of sanity. Although all he says
here is the short line:

He **hath** no **daugh**ters **sir**.

But though it's a short line it is still in verse rhythm: the voice of reason.

Later Lear crosses over into prose again as he begins to hallucinate.
They have reached a refuge in some lowly building, and Lear imagines he
sees his two elder daughters there. He decides that he is going to put them
on trial. But the Fool's second line tells us that, as Lear thinks he is pointing out Goneril to them all, he is actually only staring at a stool.

LEAR. Arraign her first 'tis Goneril, / I here take my oath before
this honourable assembly [she] kicked the poor king her
father.

148

FOOL. Come hither mistress is your name Goneril?

LEAR. She cannot deny it.

FOOL. Cry you mercy I took you for a joint stool.

LEAR. And here's another whose warp'd looks proclaim,
    What store her heart is made on,

                                    stop her there,
    Arms, arms, sword, fire, corruption in the place,
    False justicer why hast thou let her 'scape.

EDGAR. Bless thy five wits.

KENT. O pity: Sir, where is the patience now
    That you so oft have boasted to retain?

EDGAR. My tears begin to take his part so much,
    They mar my counterfeiting.

LEAR.   The little dogs, and all;
    Trey, Blanch, and Sweet-heart: see, they bark at me.

Lear's prose, with which this passage began, switches back into verse, and later again back into prose. As the scene comes towards the end, Kent finally manages to get the King to rest for a while:

KENT. Now good my lord, lie here, and rest awhile.

LEAR. Make no noise, make no noise, draw the curtains: so, so, /
    we'll go to supper i'th'morning.

FOOL. And I'll go to bed at noon.

King Lear: Act 3, Scene 6[5]

An extraordinary scene in which Lear hallucinates further, seeing dogs barking at him, and finally imagining he is being put into a four-poster bed with curtains around it. And throughout the Fool continues with his enigmatic comments. The final line in this passage is his final line in the play. Later we hear he is dead.

Edgar is so moved by Lear's condition that he slips out of his mad vocal disguise, to tell us what he is feeling:

My tears begin to take his part so much,
They mar my counterfeiting.

and like Rosalind, whose tears only came once she began to speak in verse, so it is with Edgar. And meanwhile, Kent continues in rational heartfelt verse to try and look after his old King.

In Act 4, Scene 6, Lear's hallucinations grow more pronounced. Sometimes they are expressed in verse which frequently seems to be on the

verge of disintegration, sometimes in prose. He enters, talking to himself
in prose, imagining himself giving a soldier some money and watching an
unskilled archer drawing his bow. He imagines seeing a mouse and tempts
it with a piece of imaginary toasted cheese. He takes Edgar to be another
soldier, but seeing Gloucester, who has recently had his eyes put out, Lear
wonders whether he is his daughter Goneril 'with a white beard'. Gloucester, though he can no longer see, recognises Lear's voice and asks 'Is't not
the King?' To which Lear replies with some cogency, and he's temporarily
back into verse:

> Aye, every inch a King.
> When I do stare, see how the subject quakes.
> I pardon that man's life. What was thy cause?
> Adultery? thou shalt not die: die for adultery?
> No, the wren goes to't, and the small gilded fly
> Does lecher in my sight.

The junctures are coming thick and fast and soon we are back in prose:

> LEAR. See how yond justice rails upon yond simple thief. / Hark
> in thine ear: Change places, and handy-dandy, which is
> the justice, which is the thief: / Thou hast seen a farmer's
> dog bark at a beggar?
>
> GLOUCESTER. Ay sir.
>
> LEAR. And the creature run from the cur: there thou mightst
> behold the great image of authority, a dog's obeyed in
> office.
>
> Thou rascal beadle, hold thy bloody hand:
> Why dost thou lash that whore? Strip thy own back,
> Thou hotly lusts to use her in that kind,
> For which thou whipp'st her.
>
> *King Lear*: Act 4, Scene 6

And it is to a similar jumble of lines that Edgar, who is watching all, says
those lines quoted earlier,

> O matter, and impertinency mix'd,
> Reason in madness.

What Shakespeare is drawing our attention to, through Edgar, is the way
true madness hovers between these two states of lucidity and confusion.
And these 'junctures' we have been seeking out in this chapter should be
a great guide for us as to what is happening inside Lear's troubled brain.

Not that everything is clear cut even so. Hallucinations are sometimes expressed in prose, but as above, also in verse, as Lear seems to 'see' the beadle whipping a prostitute in front of him.

And then Lear recovers. His youngest daughter, Cordelia, returns from France and finds him. Doctors attend him, and when he wakes after a long sleep, he is confused, but he now knows he's confused, though as yet he is unaware of his daughter's presence. But when he speaks he is speaking simply in verse. Now as you reach one of the later stages of Lear's journey, and you sound out this beautiful passage, be aware of just how simple the words he uses are – so many monosyllabic words:

> LEAR.   Pray do not mock me:
> I am a very foolish fond old man,
> Fourscore and upward, not an hour more, nor less;
>
> And to deal plainly,
> I fear I am not in my perfect mind.
> Me thinks I should know you, and know this man,
> Yet I am doubtful: For I am mainly ignorant
> What place this is:
>
>   and all the skill I have
> Remembers not these garments:
>
>   nor I know not
> Where I did lodge last night.
>
>   Do not laugh at me,
> For (as I am a man) I think this lady
> To be my child Cordelia.
>
> CORDELIA.   And so I am: I am.
>
> *King Lear*: Act 4, Scene 7

It is an emotional moment of reunion and restoration. We are back in verse, though somewhat halting, and with that pause after the short line, 'And to deal plainly'. Some lines have extra syllables in them, but in all of them you'll feel the five stresses that are a better guide to discovering how to say a line than counting the syllables, because as often as not these extra syllables get swallowed up in the speaking of them. We are back with our 'sound of sincerity'.

The alternation of verse and prose has been subtly used to map out Lear's collapse into unreason and his recovery; but these two different rhythms, the regular and the haphazard, are invaluable guides for actors.

Hamlet's non-mad prose

We began this chapter with Hamlet talking to those actors who had pitched up at Elsinore. Everything he says to them in the couple of scenes he has with them is in prose; all slightly hyper and manic. And the advice he gives to them on playing – is that manic as well? It's hard to say; of course one could interpret it in many ways. What I find hard to believe is that Shakespeare would have simply slipped all his own ideas about the art of acting into the middle of this play. What we have to remember about the mask-like face of prose is that it will frequently hide one truth behind another.

Hamlet's purpose is clear: he will use the players to trap Claudius. But he's got to get Claudius and his mother to come and watch the play. So he lets it be known that he has suddenly become enthusiastic about 'theatre'; that he is even writing some lines for the play; and that he's anxious that his mother and stepfather should come and watch it. And so they do. His new-found enthusiasm is another smoke screen.

And maybe the advice to the players is meant to be somewhat funny as well: a prince telling the foremost actors of his generation how to act and to 'speak the speech as *I* pronounced it to you'!

To Horatio he calmly reveals all,

> HAMLET. There is a play tonight before the King,
> One scene of it comes near the circumstance
> That I have told thee, of my father's death.
>
> *Hamlet*: Act 3, Scene 2

speaking in verse to him as he always does – except on a couple of occasions that is.

The first is on his return from England, when he and Horatio have wandered together into a graveyard, where they find the Gravedigger preparing Ophelia's grave, though as yet neither Hamlet nor Horatio know of her death. Hamlet speaks lightly and wittily – in prose – about the Gravedigger singing as he digs, and about the careless way he tosses the bones about that he come across while digging. So why is this scene in prose? Once again I'd say that it is hiding something, and here I'd say it's hiding the very reason why Hamlet has wandered this way into a graveyard in the first place. I think it's because he now senses his own death is near; that he's now drawn to this place of death, and that he needs to see it and understand it, to look into its face, and as he says to Horatio, to see 'to what base uses we may return'.

Then later there is another point in the play when he can no longer take Horatio completely into his confidence, and that is right towards the end, when he senses correctly that another trap is being laid for his life. The court fop, Osric, has brought him an invitation from the King to come and fence with Laertes. Both Hamlet and Horatio have been running witty rings round Osric – in prose, of course – but Hamlet continues to speak in prose after Osric has exited.

> HORATIO. You will lose this wager, my lord.
>
> HAMLET. I do not think so, since he went into France, I have been in continual practice; I shall win at the odds: / but thou wouldst not think how ill all's here about my heart: / but it is no matter.
>
> HORATIO. Nay, good my lord.
>
> HAMLET. It is but foolery; but it is such a kind of gain-giving as would perhaps trouble a woman.
>
> HORATIO. If your mind dislike any thing, obey it. / I will forestall their repair hither, and say you are not fit.
>
> HAMLET. Not a whit, we defy augury; there's a special providence in the fall of a sparrow. / If it be now, 'tis not to come: if it be not to come, it will be now: if it be not now; yet it will come; the readiness is all, since no man has aught of what he leaves. / What is't to leave betimes?
>
> *Hamlet*: Act 5, Scene 2

The last speech, recalling a passage in the New Testament,[6] is beautiful and remarkable for its simplicity and yet it is redolent with meaning: the wisdom behind the phrase 'the readiness is all'. Earlier in the play Hamlet was not 'ready', now he is. It is also so typical of much of the prose we have been studying with its balanced antithetical phrases.

In a sense Hamlet does tell Horatio that maybe the end is near, but through the prose he does so obliquely, coolly, fittingly. It reminds me of Orlando's careful, carefree prose before he went into the wrestling ring with Charles the Duke's champion.

What we have learnt in this chapter is how the fluctuations between verse and prose can happen so swiftly and so delicately, and for so many different reasons. Prose always wants to hide something from view, though if we play it well our audiences will hear the surface run of words and 'see' what is being hidden at the same time. So becoming aware of these 'junctures' and actively seeking them out will much enrich your ability to play these deep and glorious plays with greater understanding and sensibility.

Four of Shakespeare's plays have more prose than verse in them. *As You Like It* we have already looked at. The others are *Twelfth Night*, *Much Ado About Nothing* and *The Merry Wives of Windsor*. But the great prose play is *Much Ado About Nothing* and to that we should now turn. However, just before we do, I want you to have a copy of the play to hand, because at a certain point in the following chapter I'm going to ask you to read the whole of Act 4, Scene 1, before we examine together one of the most famous duologues from this brilliant play.

Ten

Much Ado About Nothing

The Play of Verse-shy Characters

I learn in this letter, that Don Pedro of Aragon, comes this night to Messina.
Much Ado About Nothing: Act 1, Scene 1

There are many letters in Shakespeare's plays. The letter with which *Much Ado About Nothing* begins, though we are told its contents, is never read out verbatim. If it had been we would have heard that it was written in prose as letters generally are, and as are almost all the letters that Shakespeare includes in his plays. Some of them, like the letter that Macbeth sends to his wife, are of crucial importance to the way those stories unfold. But *Much Ado About Nothing* is worlds away from *Macbeth* and as its title suggests we are in for a comedy, and so in the end it'll prove. The play ends with a dance celebrating a double wedding – though the happy outcome is achieved only after a well-intentioned bit of plotting has succeeded and a slanderous one has been foiled.

Much Ado About Nothing has this in common with those other prose-filled plays, *Twelfth Night* and *The Merry Wives of Windsor*: the characters spend considerable amounts of their time plotting against each other – notably the plots laid against Falstaff in *The Merry Wives of Windsor*, and against Malvolio in *Twelfth Night*. The very act of plotting against others involves actions that are hidden, requiring the cloak of prose in order to carry them out. Although the plots against Falstaff and Malvolio cause them some pain, they are neither as well or evilly intentioned as the various plots in *Much Ado About Nothing*

More than seven out of every ten lines in *Much Ado About Nothing* are prose. Some of it simply reflects light-hearted behaviour; characters are having a good time, wanting to appear witty, and entertaining each other with games and dances. The prose that most catches our attention to begin with, however, is that which fuels the main story-line: the relationship between Beatrice and Benedick.

The play begins with good news. The letter at the head of this chapter, and the play, tells Leonato, the Governor of Messina, of the imminent arrival of some of his old friends: soldiers, who are planning to stay with him and his family. The soldiers are returning from a successful campaign, and Beatrice, Leonato's niece, enquires of the messenger who brought the letter, whether one Signior Mountanto is amongst them. 'Mountanto' is her own mocking name for Benedick, as Leonato explains to the messenger:

> LEONATO. You must not (sir) mistake my niece, there is a kind
> of merry war betwixt Signior Benedick, and her: they
> never meet, but there's a skirmish of wit between them.

Much Ado About Nothing: Act 1, Scene 1

'A skirmish of wit between them': a perfect description of an amusing, but competitive exchange of opinions. And shortly after, once Benedick arrives, such a skirmish indeed breaks out between them – in prose of course. Benedick has made a witty remark to Leonato, and Beatrice pounces.

What follows is another duologue, and as with the one in Chapter 7, try to find someone else to work on it with you: the scenes will come alive more vividly if you do and you will learn so much by listening to each other. With this passage, to remind you of the helpfulness of the 'original punctuation', I am again going to put in bold those words that are followed by a mark of punctuation – but you'll notice I make one or two minor exceptions.

> BEATRICE. I wonder that you will still be **talking**, Signior
> **Benedick**, no body **marks** you.
>
> BENEDICK. What my dear Lady **Disdain!** are you yet **living?**
>
> BEATRICE. Is it possible disdain should **die**, while she hath such
> meet food to **feed it**, as Signior **Benedick?** / Courtesy it
> self must convert to **disdain**, if you come in her **presence.**
>
> BENEDICK. Then is courtesy a **turn-coat**, / but it is certain I am
> loved of **all ladies**, only you **excepted:** and I would I could
> find in my heart that I had not a **hard heart**, for truly I
> **love none.**

BEATRICE. A dear happiness to **women,** they would else have
been troubled with a **pernicious suitor,** / I thank God and
my **cold blood,** I am of your humour for **that,** I had rather
hear my dog bark at a **crow,** than a man swear he **loves me.**

BENEDICK. God keep your ladyship still in that **mind,** so some
gentleman or other shall 'scape a predestinate **scratched face.**

BEATRICE. Scratching could not make it **worse,** an 'twere such a
face as **yours** were.

BENEDICK. **Well,** you are a rare **parrot teacher.**

BEATRICE. A bird of **my** tongue, is better than a beast of **yours.**

BENEDICK. I would my horse had the **speed** of your **tongue,** and
so good a **continuer,** / but keep your way i' **God's name,** I
have **done.**

BEATRICE. You always end with a **jade's trick,** I know you of **old.**

Much Ado About Nothing: Act 1, Scene 1

I'm sure having the words in bold helped you to play the scene with the
clarity it requires in order to bring out all of the wit it contains. But just
remember you don't need those words to be put in bold because the Folio
punctuation is already indicating to you the very same thing.

I've marked one of the lines above in a different way:

BEATRICE. A bird of **my** tongue, is better than a beast of **yours.**

And that's because the antithesis between '**my**' and '**yours**' has to be the
main thrust of that line, even though 'bird' still has to be played off against
'beast'. But then you'll notice how the word '**tongue**' is picked up, empha-
sised, and wittily used by Benedick. Notice too how Beatrice's line has
three words beginning with 'b'. There's some mockery there in the sound
of those 'b's – and making the 'b' sound also draws Benedick's attention
to her lips:

BEATRICE. A **b**ird of **my** tongue, is **b**etter than a **b**east of **yours.**

Round One to Beatrice, I think, as Benedick calls a halt to the contest. It's
certainly a spirited conversation, and we certainly don't mind how long it
goes on for, because it's fun, and part of its fun is in seeing just how long
these two can keep it going for. But we might also be asking ourselves, since
it is so early on in the play, *why* these two have this effect on each other.
There must be something between them, surely, or something has happened between them in the past. And so it seems to be. Before Benedick
arrives on stage, Beatrice has made these enigmatic remarks about him.

> He set up his bills here in Messina, and challeng'd Cupid at the
> flight: and my uncle's fool reading the challenge, subscrib'd for
> Cupid, and challeng'd him at the bird-bolt.
>
> *Much Ado About Nothing*: Act 1, Scene 1

(By which she means that, on a previous visit, Benedick had made it known that Cupid would never be able to make him fall in love with anybody, but Beatrice, describing herself as her 'uncle's fool', decided she would sign up on Cupid's behalf and challenge Benedick with an absurd version of Cupid's bow: a 'bird-bolt' being an arrow with a blunt point for shooting birds. And maybe it was on that occasion that Beatrice 'won' the contest and Benedick – for a while – fell for her.)

And later when Don Pedro says to her, 'you have lost the heart of Signior Benedick', she replies,

> Indeed my lord, he lent it me awhile, and I gave him use for it,
> a double heart for his single one, / marry once before he won it
> of me, with false dice, therefore your grace may well say I have
> lost it.
>
> *Much Ado About Nothing*: Act 2, Scene 1

Whatever she is hinting at here, she does so with wit and discretion; so she uses prose, of course.

Interestingly, in the play's opening scene, when Benedick's friend Claudio has declared his love for Leonato's daughter Hero –

> In mine eye, she is the sweetest lady that ever I looked on.

– Benedick has responded by comparing her with her cousin Beatrice:

> I can see yet without spectacles, and I see no such matter: /
> there's her cousin, an she were not possessed with a fury,
> exceeds her as much in beauty, as the first of May doth the last
> of December:
>
> *Much Ado About Nothing*: Act 1, Scene 1

So Beatrice's speeches seem to be referring to some romantic attachment that she and Benedick had for each other sometime before the play begins, and Benedick's comments about her beauty seem to reveal some desire for her that lingers on in some way or other.

But on the surface it seems they can't stand one another, and indeed later on, Beatrice's arrival on stage is enough to drive Benedick away. Don Pedro, Benedick's commanding officer, sees her approaching, at which point Benedick immediately begs to be sent on some errand so he can escape.

> DON PEDRO. Look here she comes.
>
> *Enter Claudio, and Beatrice, Leonato, Hero.*
>
> BENEDICK. Will your grace command me any service to the
> world's end? / I will go on the slightest errand now to the
> Antipodes that you can devise to send me on: I will fetch
> you a tooth-picker now from the furthest inch of Asia:
> bring you the length of Prester John's foot: fetch you a hair
> off the great Cham's beard: do you any embassage to the
> Pigmies, rather than hold three words' conference, with
> this harpy: / you have no employment for me?
>
> DON PEDRO. None, but to desire your good company.
>
> BENEDICK. O God sir, here's a dish I love not, I cannot endure
> this Lady tongue.
>
> *Much Ado About Nothing*: Act 2, Scene 1

And with that, and the second mention of Beatrice's 'tongue', he exits.

Now Benedick's speech to Don Pedro is funny, and yet its humour can't quite hide his desperation. The speech certainly has some of those ingredients that we have noticed before in Shakespeare's prose – here an imaginatively invented list of crazy tasks. But when Don Pedro simply asks him to stay, Benedick finds he cannot and leaves the stage.

So what are he and Beatrice hiding? We might have been tempted to say that they are hiding their love for each other, because we might also have guessed (correctly) that they will eventually end up together. But I don't think that is quite the whole story. I think their prose skirmishes are their attempts to hide how 'vulnerable' each makes the other feel. They each think that the other *doesn't* love them, and so their witty sparring is a way of both punishing the other and keeping the other at bay. But all this is primarily designed to *hide their vulnerability at the same time*.

If only they could be told by a third party that they are loved by the other one, and if only they could believe it, then everything would be different. And of course that's exactly what happens, and it is this, the well-intentioned plot that the others cook up, which finally and amusingly brings them together.

d Benedick and other verse-shy speakers

rice and Benedick are the most conspicuous characters in the
play for their use of prose, many others too are notable for the amount of
prose they speak. As a group, soldiers frequently like to hide their feelings
behind the banter of prose and as in *All's Well that Ends Well*, as in *Henry
V*, *Much Ado About Nothing* is rich in prose-speaking soldiers, along with
other urbane and witty characters who spend time in their company –
Beatrice being one. She and Benedick generally reveal little about their
true selves; they enjoy appearing not to take things too seriously, and so
the way of speaking that comes naturally to them is to carry on conversations in witty, barbed prose. However, they do speak verse together on a
couple of occasions. The second is before their own marriage; the first during Hero's aborted first marriage ceremony.[1]

Hero is Leonato's daughter and Beatrice's younger cousin. She and the
dashing young soldier Claudio have fallen in love, and Claudio is also
Benedick's best friend.

Hero's wedding is terminated when Claudio refuses to marry her
because he believes she has been having a sexual relationship with Borachio. The villainous Borachio has concocted this, the 'slanderous plot', to
aid Don John's schemes to undermine both his brother, Don Pedro, and
Claudio. The villainous Don John is yet another of those 'rival brothers'
that abound in Shakespeare's plays. We have already met some of them:
Duke Frederick and his brother, the banished Duke from *As You Like It*,
and Oliver and Orlando, from the same play; and Claudius and his brother,
Old Hamlet, whom he murdered. All of these stories would have reminded
Shakespeare's audience of that first 'rival brother' story: Cain and Abel.

The wedding begins light-heartedly enough, in prose. A few jokes to
set things off:

> LEONATO. Come Friar Francis, be brief, only to the plain form
> of marriage, and you shall recount their particular duties
> afterwards.
> FRIAR. You come hither, my lord, to marry this lady.
> CLAUDIO. No.
> LEONATO. To be married to her: Friar, you come to marry her.
>
> *Much Ado About Nothing*: Act 4, Scene 1

But soon it's clear that Claudio's 'No' meant what it said. After about a
dozen lines he takes over the service and the sound has changed. He is
speaking in verse and everyone else follows.

CLAUDIO. Stand thee by Friar,

> father, by your leave,
> Will you with free and unconstrained soul
> Give me this maid your daughter?

LEONATO. As freely son as God did give her me.

CLAUDIO. And what have I to give you back, whose worth
> May counterpoise this rich and precious gift?

DON PEDRO. Nothing, unless you render her again.

CLAUDIO. Sweet Prince, you learn me noble thankfulness:

> There Leonato, take her back again,
> Give not this rotten orange to your friend,
> She's but the sign and semblance of her honour:

And not long after this Claudio, Don Pedro and Don John walk out of the church leaving everyone aghast and leaving Hero in a dead faint on the floor. Her father, Leonato, believing her to be guilty, prays she'll never open her eyes again.

In this part of the scene Beatrice and Benedick have only a little to say, but like the others, here they speak in verse. Once the Friar has said that he believes that Hero has been wronged, and that somehow the princes must have been mistaken in their accusations, Benedick has a suggestion to make:

> Two of them have the very bent of honour,
> And if their wisdoms be misled in this:
> The practice of it lives in John the bastard,
> Whose spirits toil in frame of villainies.

And later, once the Friar tries to convince Leonato and the others that the way to proceed is to let it be known that Hero has actually died, Benedick urges them to take the Friar's advice and says he will keep this a secret:

> Signior Leonato, let the friar advise you,
> And though you know my inwardness and love
> Is very much unto the prince and Claudio.[2]
> Yet, by mine honour, I will deal in this,
> As secretly and justly, as your soul
> Should with your body.

So here when things have got really serious, so has Benedick, his voice and his verse now sounding out a new note of 'sincerity'.

An ultimate return to prose

But it's probably true to say of them that being of a serious frame of mind is not where either Beatrice or Benedick feel most comfortable. Their minds are so lively, so imaginative, that unless they have to deal with events as serious as those that have just happened in church, they enjoy being light of heart. And when they are not hiding their 'vulnerable' inner selves, they enjoy being merry.

We can see something of this in the final scene when Benedick is arranging his marriage to Beatrice. The scene begins in verse, and Benedick speaks here in verse like all the others. Sound this out loud (again with a partner if possible) and see if you can discover *why* the verse gives way to prose where and when it does. The women all enter masked and so Benedick needs to find out which of them is Beatrice:

BENEDICK. Soft and fair Friar, which is Beatrice?

BEATRICE. I answer to that name, what is your will?

BENEDICK. Do not you love me?

BEATRICE.   Why no, no more than reason.

BENEDICK. Why then your uncle, and the Prince, and Claudio,
    have been deceived, they swore you did.[3]

BEATRICE. Do not you love me?

BENEDICK.   Troth no, no more than reason.

BEATRICE. Why then my cousin Margaret and Ursula
    Are much deceiv'd, for they did swear you did.

BENEDICK. They swore that you were almost sick for me.

BEATRICE. They swore that you were well-nigh dead for me.

BENEDICK. 'Tis no such matter, then you do not love me?

BEATRICE. No truly, but in friendly recompense.

LEONATO. Come Cousin, I am sure you love the gentleman.

CLAUDIO. And I'll be sworn upon't, that he loves her,
    For here's a paper written in his hand,
    A halting sonnet of his own pure brain,
    Fashioned to Beatrice.

HERO.   And here's another,
    Writ in my cousin's hand, stol'n from her pocket,
    Containing her affection unto Benedick.

BENEDICK. A miracle, here's our own hands against our hearts:
    / come I will have thee, but by this light I take thee for
    pity.

> BEATRICE. I would not deny you, but by this good day, I yield
> upon great persuasion, and partly to save your life, for I
> was told, you were in a consumption.
> BENEDICK. Peace I will stop your mouth.[4]
>
> *Much Ado About Nothing*: Act 5, Scene 4

And with that he kisses her; and as you can see for the past couple of speeches they have been firmly back in prose, which is, I suspect, where they will prefer to spend most of their lives together.

But why? Did you work that out too? It seemed from their last lines of verse, before Claudio and Hero produce the sonnets that Benedick and Beatrice have written, but not delivered to each other, as if their marriage might not go ahead after all. And I think the breakdown between them happened *because they were speaking verse*.

The 'sound of sincerity' left them feeling too vulnerable; it's not that they can't cope with genuine feelings, but to express these feelings in public seems beyond them. As earlier in the play, it was their friends who brought them together, so once again these same friends come to their present aid, and happily what their hearts can't declare, their pens have already written to each other, and thus with a laugh and a kiss their contract is sealed.

Their return to prose is by mutual agreement. Beatrice and Benedick know what they know, which is how much they love each other, but it's not something they feel able to declare in the presence of others. So the prose hides what they don't want to say, but all of us, audience and characters alike, 'see' what they are hiding. For much of the play their prose has been a way of camouflaging the vulnerability they feel in the other's company. But beyond that, the wit they display is a vital ingredient of who they are, and it is fitting that it is in this mode that they should finish the play. Somehow, typically for Shakespeare, having created these two brilliant characters, he never tries to create another pair like them again.

Shared prose can indicate a mutually understood evasion of true feelings.

Before we leave them, though, there is one hugely important duologue between the two of them which we must look at. We might have expected it to be in verse, because it's a highly emotional scene, but surprisingly it is in prose. It comes at the end of Act 4, Scene 1 – the scene in the church after Hero had been denounced by Claudio – it's a scene that had been virtually all in verse, and in this middle section Beatrice and Benedick are verse speakers as well.

Now this is the point where I want you to put this book aside for a while and for you to pick up your Complete Works, or your copy of *Much Ado*, and read the whole of Act 4, Scene 1, but try and work out, as you do so why, after the stage clears leaving Beatrice and Benedick together, the scene reverts to prose.

Now you've read one of the longest scenes in the play I hope you felt it was thrilling. And it ends with this emotional scene between Beatrice and Benedick – but it is in prose. Doesn't this contradict all I have been saying? Can anything remain to be hidden here? Maybe as you read it you came up with some ideas of your own.

The first thing we might notice is that the nature of their habitual brittle 'give and take' is markedly different here from their earlier encounters in the play. Beatrice is responding, but not engaging with Benedick's lines as we might expect her to do. She speaks, *but her mind seems to be elsewhere*. There is something within her which is either being censored or has not yet come to light. What Claudio has done in the church has such profound implications for her and her family that she cannot articulate any of this yet – and especially to Benedick, whom she loves, but whose close friendship with Claudio makes this impossible situation all the more catastrophic.

Beatrice is in shock; later, when the words tumble out of her, she will be close to distraction, speaking uncontrollably. The language that can capture the stillness of shock, that wants to hide that shock, and the dislocated thoughts of a brainstorm is prose and not verse. Certainly the emotions are running high, but more importantly, so much more is being concealed.

Now as we look at this scene together I also want you to be aware of those places where Benedick uses the 'thou' form of address to Beatrice, and where he switches back again to using the less intimate 'you' form. I will indicate these 'thou' form uses by marking them in italics, and I'll also mark those places where he switches back to the 'you' form. So far in the play he has only addressed her as 'you', as he continues to do in these opening lines:

> BENEDICK. Lady Beatrice, have you wept all this while?
>
> BEATRICE. Yea, and I will weep a while longer.
>
> BENEDICK. I will not desire that.

BEATRICE. You have no reason, I do it freely.

BENEDICK. Surely I do believe your fair cousin is wrong'd.

BEATRICE. Ah, how much might the man deserve of me that
would right her!

BENEDICK. Is there any way to show such friendship?

BEATRICE. A very even way, but no such friend.

BENEDICK. May a man do it?

BEATRICE. It is a man's office, but not yours.

Benedick, we should note, and we may understand why, is speaking with care and caution. For her part, Beatrice is not really *engaging* with Benedick. Everything that Benedick has said has been brushed aside by her, so now Benedick changes the subject.

BENEDICK. I do love nothing in the world so well as you, is not
that strange?

The impasse they have reached reveals the first thing that has been buried in the scene and that is Benedick's friendship with Claudio. Claudio has destroyed Hero's love and left her, as if dead, on the church floor. And because of this friendship Beatrice has said to him, 'It is a man's office, but not yours.'

But it's more than that. Claudio has not only cruelly rejected Hero on her wedding day, he has at the same time created a gulf between Beatrice and Benedick on what promised to be the day of *their* betrothal.

So far they have not spoken of their love for each other. Since they both discovered how they are each apparently loved by the other, they have had no time to be alone together.[5] So now rather awkwardly Benedick declares his love for Beatrice, and the awkwardness arises because Claudio's shadow stands between them.

Benedick uses two negatives in this next speech to her, and Beatrice gives and withholds in equal measure:

BENEDICK. I do love nothing in the world so well as you, is not
that strange?

BEATRICE. As strange as the thing I know not. / It were as
possible for me to say, I loved nothing so well as you, but
believe me not, and yet I lie not, I confess nothing, nor I
deny nothing, / I am sorry for my cousin.

Benedick presses her further but she continues to parry everything he says; and though now there is a greater degree of engagement with *what*

Benedick is saying, something still remains hidden, withheld, waiting to come to light. Here too comes the first of our switches in Benedick's forms of address:

> BENEDICK. By my sword Beatrice *thou* lov'st me.
>
> BEATRICE. Do not swear by it and eat it.
>
> BENEDICK. I will swear by it that *you* love me, and I will make him eat it that says I love not you.
>
> BEATRICE. Will you not eat your word?
>
> BENEDICK. With no sauce that can be devised to it, I protest I love *thee*.
>
> BEATRICE. Why then God forgive me.
>
> BENEDICK. What offence sweet Beatrice?
>
> BEATRICE. You have stayed me in a happy hour, I was about to protest I loved you.
>
> BENEDICK. And do it with all *thy* heart.

And even when she does declare her love, still something is withheld:

> BEATRICE. I love you with so much of my heart, that none is left to protest.
>
> BENEDICK. Come, bid me do any thing for *thee*.

And then we get there. We have built to this point and as Beatrice says her next line, we find out what has been hidden all this time:

> BEATRICE. Kill Claudio.

And probably the actuality of wanting Claudio dead has even been hidden from Beatrice herself until the moment before she says it.

Prose can sometimes conceal something even from the one who's about to speak it.

When Benedick asked her at the beginning of this scene whether she has been 'weeping all this while' we might assume she was simply weeping for Hero. She says 'I am sorry for my cousin', but her tears must also be for herself, sensing as she does the very real possibility that her blossoming relationship with Benedick might not survive this catastrophe. And now what we find emerging from a yet deeper place is a yet more deeply buried desire, which is that she wants Claudio dead.

Benedick instinctively rejects this call to 'kill Claudio', and she equally instinctively rejects him:

BENEDICK. Ha, not for the wide world.

BEATRICE. You kill me to deny it, farewell.[6]

But Benedick prevents her from leaving:

BENEDICK. Tarry sweet Beatrice.

BEATRICE. I am gone, though I am here, there is no love in you,
/ nay I pray you let me go.

BENEDICK. Beatrice.

BEATRICE. In faith I will go.

BENEDICK. We'll be friends first.

BEATRICE. You dare easier be friends with me, than fight with
mine enemy.

BENEDICK. Is Claudio *thine* enemy?

and then even more is revealed that has been hidden all this while, hidden deep in Beatrice's character.

BEATRICE. Is he not approved in the height a villain, that hath
slandered, scorned, dishonoured my kinswoman? / O that
I were a man! / what, bear her in hand until they come to
take hands, and then with public accusation uncovered
slander, unmitigated rancour? / O God that I were a man!
/ I would eat his heart in the market-place.[7]

BENEDICK. Hear me Beatrice.

BEATRICE. Talk with a man out at a window, a proper saying.

BENEDICK. Nay but Beatrice.

BEATRICE. Sweet Hero, she is wronged, she is slandered, she is
undone.

BENEDICK. Beat?*

Those tears are born not only out of grief for the loss of love, and out of rage against Claudio, but they are also tears of *frustration* that, as a woman in this man's world, she is powerless to act in this situation.

And then she is unstoppable. A magnificent tirade against men follows, full of angered invention and wit and lists, revealing a mind so close to the edge that she is close to losing all control completely.

BEATRICE. Princes and counties! surely a princely testimony, a
goodly count, Count Comfect, a sweet gallant surely, / O
that I were a man for his sake! or that I had any friend

Beat – she interrupts him as he says her name

167

would be a man for my sake! / But manhood is melted into courtesies, valour into compliment, and men are only turned into tongue, and trim ones too: he is now as valiant as Hercules, that only tells a lie, and swears it: / I cannot be a man with wishing, therefore I will die a woman with grieving.

All of which are finally brought to a halt by Benedick's

Tarry good Beatrice, by this hand I love *thee*.

And do we notice anything about this line? Yes, it's in verse! No doubt a fact that's usually hidden by all the prose surrounding it; but no matter, because if it is sounded out in performance as instinctively you'd want to say it, it will ring out resoundingly and sincerely, and from there there's no going back. And her response:

<u>Use</u> it for my <u>love</u> some <u>other</u> <u>way</u> than <u>swear</u>ing by it.

is just as strong: although not a line of verse, it seems to me to have five stresses, as Benedick's verse line had. Then come two more lines before the final speech. Interestingly you'll see the first of these has fourteen syllables in it as had Beatrice's previous line. But notice how the strength of Beatrice's line makes Benedick drop the lover's 'thou' and prepare for what he now suspects he has to do:

Think *you* in your soul the Count Claudio hath wronged Hero?

Notice too the number of 'o' sounds in these lines – 'o's' and 'a's' fill the mouth with more emotional sounds than the other vowels do. Beatrice replies –

Yea, as sure as I have a thought, or a soul.

– and we are into the final moments of the scene as Benedick says:

Enough, I am engaged, I will challenge him, / I will kiss your hand, and so I leave you: / by this hand Claudio shall render me a dear account: / as you hear of me, so think of me: / go comfort your cousin, I must say she is dead, and so farewell.

Much Ado About Nothing: Act 4, Scene 1

So spare; so understated; so much still unexpressed; so much between them still buried in the prose. The outcome still unsure: would their love for each other survive a duel between Benedick and Claudio?

But having things buried, just as Beatrice's grief, rage and frustration are, is meat and drink to actors and so exciting to play. Equally for the audience it is exciting to watch such a scene. Because when a prose scene like this is played well, the audience get intimations of what is being hidden behind the words (even if what is hidden is also temporarily hidden from the characters – though not of course from the actors), those words, which try to keep what cannot be expressed out of sight.

And if we look back at the shifts in the form of address, what do we find in this scene that we could usefully use when we come to playing it? Well, the shifts are all Benedick's, since Beatrice always uses the 'you' form when she is speaking directly to him.[8] But I have to admit Benedick's switches are not so clear-cut as we saw in the earlier examples we looked at.

He first uses 'thou' when he says, 'By my sword, Beatrice, thou lovest me,' and also a few lines later when he says, 'I protest I love thee.' However, in between these two lines he switches back to using the 'you' form. One might have thought by his use of 'thou' that he was definitely moving towards the expected vocabulary of the male lover. But as Penelope Freedman has pointed out in her book *Power and Passion in Shakespeare's Pronouns*, there are certain 'speech acts', like 'swearing', or 'charging' someone to do something, or 'blessing' someone, that attracts 'thou' usages. So Benedick's 'swearing by his sword', and his 'protesting' might well give rise to these 'thou' uses – though such 'speech acts' as swearing, clearly 'up the emotional temperature' as well. But his line of verse, 'Tarry good Beatrice, by this hand I love thee,' despite its 'swearing' character is indisputably the voice of the male wooer, though Beatrice's response to it makes it clear to him that his lover's language is no longer appropriate, and the scene ends with the restraint that the formal use of the 'you' form brings to it.

Now you should return to your copy of the play and sound out this last duologue – hopefully with a partner – and run it though without all my interruptions and suggestions and see how you get on.

Prose and 'the lower orders'

Much Ado About Nothing is full of clever people, characters who pride themselves on their wit and their light-hearted attitude to life. However, ironically, the play is rescued from disaster by a group of people who are far from clever. They are the Watch, the local constabulary, whose foolishness is a source of much delight. They are certainly not clever like Feste in *Twelfth Night*, or Touchstone in *As You Like It*, or the Fool in *King Lear*.

To differentiate them from the professional fools, they are sometimes called 'natural fools'. Like the clever fools they too speak in prose, but for different reasons.

Here follows the first part of their opening scene. Some new members of the Watch are being instructed. It's quite a long passage, but amusing. Some of the jokes arise because the characters frequently use a word incorrectly: I have put these incorrect words in italics. See if you can work out what they meant to say, as you read it out.

> *Enter* DOGBERRY *with his compartner and the Watch.*
>
> DOGBERRY. Are you good men and true?
>
> VERGES. Yea, or else it were pity but they should suffer *salvation* body and soul.
>
> DOGBERRY. Nay, that were a punishment too good for them, if they should have any *allegiance* in them, being chosen for the Prince's watch.
>
> VERGES. Well, give them their charge, neighbour Dogberry.
>
> DOGBERRY. First, who think you the most *desertless* man to be constable?
>
> WATCH 1. Hugh Oat-cake sir, or George Sea-coale, for they can write and read.
>
> DOGBERRY. Come hither neighbour Sea-coale, / God hath blessed you with a good name: to be a well-favoured man, is the *gift of fortune*, but to write and read, comes *by nature*.
>
> WATCH 2. Both which Master Constable ⁹
>
> DOGBERRY. You have: I knew it would be your answer: / well, for your favour sir, why give God thanks, and make no boast of it, and for your writing and reading, let that appear when there is no need of such vanity, / you are thought here to be the most *senseless* and fit man for the constable of the watch: therefore bear you the lantern: / this is your charge: You shall *comprehend* all vagrom* men, you are to bid any man stand in the Prince's name.
>
> WATCH 2. How if a* will not stand?

vagrom – vagrant
a – a colloquial way of saying 'he'

> DOGBERRY. Why then take no note of him, but let him go, and
> presently call the rest of the watch together, and thank
> God you are rid of a knave.
>
> VERGES. If he will not stand when he is bidden, he is none of the
> Prince's subjects.
>
> DOGBERRY. True, and they are to meddle with none but the
> Prince's subjects: / you shall also make no noise in the
> streets: for, for the watch to babble and to talk, is most
> *tolerable,* and not to be endured.
>
> *Much Ado About Nothing:* Act 3, Scene 3

What we might first notice are the words that Dogberry and Verges mistake. They will continue to do so throughout their four delightful scenes. This is a comic trait that they share with other characters in Shakespeare: Bottom the Weaver in *A Midsummer Night's Dream*, Mistress Quickly, who appears in the two parts of *Henry IV*, *Henry V* and *The Merry Wives of Windsor*, and Elbow, another comic constable in *Measure for Measure*, amongst others. What all these characters have in common is a desire to appear to be smarter than they actually are. So they use grand words, hoping that will make their fellows look up to them more, as being somehow wittier or better educated. But they slip up because the words they want to use somehow escape them and these other words, usually meaning the very opposite of what they intend to say, take their place.

Prose can be the language of those who pretend to be something they are not.

It's also true that most of the least educated characters in Shakespeare are clowns of this sort, so it's probably for this reason that prose has come to be associated with their lack of education, rather than their clownishness. But the folly of this particular group consists of their trying to hide who they truly are. They shouldn't bother: Corin doesn't.

Corin is a shepherd in *As You Like It* who speaks in both verse and prose. He speaks prose when he is wittily engaging Touchstone, the play's professional fool, but when we first meet him, as he first meets Rosalind, now disguised as a boy, he speaks in simple unassuming verse.

> ROSALIND. I prithee shepherd, if that love or gold
> Can in this desert place buy entertainment,
> Bring us where we may rest our selves, and feed:
> Here's a young maid with travel much oppressed,
> And faints for succour.

CORIN.   Fair sir, I pity her,
And wish for her sake more than for mine own,
My fortunes were more able to relieve her:
But I am shepherd to another man,
And do not shear the fleeces that I graze:

My master is of churlish disposition,
And little recks to find the way to heaven
By doing deeds of hospitality.

Besides his cote, his flocks, and bounds of feed
Are now on sale, and at our sheep-cote now
By reason of his absence there is nothing
That you will feed on:

                         but what is, come see,
And in my voice most welcome shall you be.

As You Like It: Act 2, Scene 4

Corin is in no way more educated than Dogberry and the Watch. He is, though, absolutely himself and content to be just who he is. He's not especially funny, but he represents something genuine and a contrast to the world of the court that Rosalind and Celia have left behind. His verse is simple, direct and the genuine article, too.

In that scene from *Much Ado About Nothing* with Dogberry and the Watch, it only appears that it's Dogberry and Verges who have this affliction for getting their words wrong. By contrast the questions of the Watch themselves sound almost intelligent. But later, when the Watch overhear Borachio and Conrade, we'll discover that the members of the Watch also fall victim to this desire to sound more learned than they really are.

On the night before Hero's wedding, Don John and Borachio stage a slanderous charade, in which Borachio gets Margaret, his girlfriend, to talk to him amorously from out of Hero's window, so that Claudio, who'll be watching from a distance with Don Pedro and Don John, will believe Margaret is Hero and therefore that he's seen his bride to be with another man.

But later the same night the Watch, who have given no indication that they could ever catch and arrest anyone, overhear Borachio spilling the beans to another of Don John's cronies, Conrade. The Watch arrest them – but they do so for the wrong reason! They arrest them because they believe they hear them talking about a thief, who goes by the unlikely name of 'Deformed'. Borachio, who is drunk and therefore rather hard to follow, is actually trying to explain how fashions rob folk of their money –

but seest thou not what a deformed thief this fashion is?

– at which one of the Watch pricks up his ears,

> I know that Deformed, a* has been a vile thief, this seven years,
> a* goes up and down like a gentle man: I remember his name.

And as they move in for the arrest, watch out for more italics below.

> WATCH 1. We charge you, in the Prince's name stand.
>
> WATCH 2. Call up the right master constable, we have here
> *recovered* the most dangerous piece of *lechery,* that ever
> was known in the Common-wealth.
>
> WATCH 1. And one Deformed is one of them, I know him, a
> wears a lock.
>
> CONRADE. Masters, masters.
>
> WATCH 2. You'll be made bring Deformed forth I warrant you,
>
> CONRADE. Masters.
>
> WATCH 1. Never speak, we charge you, let us *obey you* to go
> with us.

Much Ado About Nothing: Act 3, Scene 3

So they arrest the pair because they think that they are in cahoots with this imaginary thief. In so doing they reveal that they have picked up the bad vocal habits of Dogberry and Verges. In their efforts to mouth correct but important-sounding words, the Second Watchman attempts to say 'uncovered' and 'treachery', yet *'recovered'* and *'lechery'* come out of his mouth.[10] And the First Watchman gets into a bit of a mess with his 'let us *obey you* to go with us'.

And why do they get in such a muddle with their words in this scene? It's precisely because arresting these ne'er-do-wells is probably the most important and exciting thing they have ever done. And understandably they get somewhat carried away, and want to appear as being cleverer and wittier and more articulate than they really are – and in trying to achieve that, they slip up.

However, we mustn't forget their arrest does finally lead to the uncovering of the plot against Hero and Claudio – and the eventual happy outcome of the comedy.

Finally let's look at Dogberry's best remembered speech. It comes at the end of the scene in which Borachio and Conrade have been examined by the Watch, now with the help of the Sexton. Conrade has had the temerity to call Dogberry an ass. Dogberry is mortified, but especially

a – for 'he'

because the Sexton has left and won't be able to add this insult to the written record of the hearing.

> DOGBERRY. Dost thou not *suspect* my place? dost thou not
> *suspect* my years? / O that he were here to write me down
> an ass! / but masters, remember that I am an ass: though
> it be not written down, yet forget not that I am an ass: /
> No thou villain, thou art full of *piety* as shall be proved
> upon thee by good witness, / I am a wise fellow, and
> which is more, an officer, and which is more, a
> householder, and which is more, as pretty a piece of flesh
> as any in Messina, and one that knows the law, go to, and
> a rich fellow enough, go to, and a fellow that hath had
> losses, and one that hath two gowns, and every thing
> handsome about him: / bring him away: / O that I had
> been writ down an ass!
>
> *Much Ado About Nothing*: Act 4, Scene 2

The amusement we get from his misplaced words has to take second place in this speech, to the delight with which we hear his own description of himself, and to the huge laughs that usually greet his forlorn cries that he might have missed the opportunity to be remembered as an ass!

Later Dogberry will be generously thanked by Leonato; with few exceptions Shakespeare seems to find the best in everyone. Certainly that is true of his clowns. At the end of *All's Well that Ends Well*, for instance, the braggart Parolles is found out for what he is and disgraced; but the old courtier Lafew, who was the first to have suspicions about him, decides to take him on and give him a position, saying,

> though you are a fool and a knave, you shall eat, go to, follow.
>
> *All's Well that Ends Well*: Act 5, Scene 2

Dogberry is no knave, though he is a bit of a fool.

Prose is the language of those who want to hide their feelings. It is the language of all those who want to appear witty. It is the language of the clown and the madman. When serious events strike and reason returns to the mad, prose gives way to verse. So whenever you come across any prose, always ask yourself what may lie hidden behind its surface.

Nine of Shakespeare's plays begin in prose, but only one indisputably ends in prose and that is *Much Ado About Nothing*.[11] With its large quantities of prose you won't be surprised to hear that it has a smaller amount of *rhymed verse* in it than any other of Shakespeare's comic plays. The comedies with the most rhyme are *Love's Labour's Lost* and *A Midsummer Night's Dream*, in both of which almost half the lines rhyme. The play of Shakespeare's which has the third largest number of rhyming lines is a history play, *Richard II*, while the fourth is a tragedy, *Romeo and Juliet*. In the next chapter we will consider why, like the prose, *rhymed verse* is so unevenly distributed through his plays.[12]

Eleven

Rhyming Verse

O she doth teach the torches to burn bright:
It seems she hangs upon the cheek of night,
As a rich jewel in an Ethiop's ear:
Beauty too rich for use, for earth too dear:
Romeo and Juliet: Act 1, Scene 5

At different times and on different occasions, Shakespeare uses rhymed verse, blank verse and prose. And the oldest of the three forms is rhymed verse. Before Shakespeare's time it was the way most plays were usually written. It is the most mysterious of the three forms, but proportionally in Shakespeare's writing it figures the least. For every twenty lines he wrote, thirteen are in blank verse, five in prose, but only two rhyme. For Shakespeare, rhyme can be the language of lovers; of magical spells; of encapsulated wisdom; of discoveries. Or rhyme can simply be the way someone comes up with a quick rejoinder with which to outsmart others.

Actors don't always find rhyme easy to deal with. And one thing that actors have sometimes asked me is whether the *characters* they are playing are aware that they are trying to rhyme? The answer is that some are; but most are not. And in this chapter, while I want to focus on characters who I believe are *not* trying to rhyme, we'll start off with some who clearly are.

Intentional rhyming

In *Love's Labour's Lost*, which has more rhymed lines than any other of Shakespeare's plays, Berowne frequently outsmarts his three friends, who are often trying to gang up on him. His way of winning many an argument is, as illustrated in the lines below, by 'out-rhyming' them.

> KING. How well he's read, to reason against reading.
>
> DUMAINE. Proceeded well, to stop all good proceeding.
>
> LONGAVILLE. He weeds the corn, and still lets grow the weeding.
>
> BEROWNE. The spring is near when green geese are a-breeding.
>
> DUMAINE. How follows that?
>
> BEROWNE.   Fit in his place and time.
>
> DUMAINE. In reason nothing.
>
> BEROWNE.   Something then in rhyme.
>
> *Love's Labour's Lost*: Act 1, Scene 1

Berowne and his friends are clearly aware that they are playing a rhyming game, as Berowne's last line tells us.

The boys in *Love's Labour's Lost* are brimming over with the excitement of being young and clever and being together, but we won't be surprised to learn that pretty soon they will come across four young women. Then it's not long before the young men begin writing love poems to them – in rhyme of course. Being in love makes us want to rhyme, because rhymes are harmonious and mysterious; and rhymes unite words just as the lovers wish to be united with the object of their desires.

But as of now these boys are still just flexing their muscles, playing verbal games with each other; preparing themselves for these more serious games to come.

If you haven't already sounded out those few lines from *Love's Labour's Lost* you should do so now.

Now you've tasted for yourself the fun of that particular game – for that is what it is – a game, seeing who can come up with the final and best rhyme, because the one who does will know that victory is theirs. Something similar can be seen in the opening scenes from *Romeo and Juliet* – which is the play which has more rhymed lines than any other of Shakespeare's tragedies.

Playing the intentional rhyming in Romeo and Juliet

When we first meet Romeo we hear him falling into rhyme as he reveals to his cousin Benvolio his love for – not Juliet, whom he hasn't yet met – but Rosaline. Here follows a more extended passage for you to sound out and begin to see how to make the rhymes work for you. And you mustn't be afraid of the rhymes! Actors frequently have reservations about rhyming which go beyond the question of whether the characters they are playing are conscious of their rhyming or not. They can find it's simply unnatural, too artificial, a worn-out convention; sometimes directors feel the same. Actors also ask whether they need to 'play up' the rhyme, or will it just take care of itself? Technically you need to make sure that the word you are going to rhyme *with* has been 'set up' in such a way that when the rhyme happens, everyone gets it. Though as almost all rhymes happen at the ends of the lines, this should cause you no real problems, as being aware of the importance of the last stress in the verse line should by now be second nature to you all. Here's Romeo sighing for his – Rosaline:

ROMEO.   and she's fair I love.

BENVOLIO. A right fair mark, fair coz, is soonest hit.

ROMEO. Well in that hit you miss, she'll *not* be **hit**[1]
With Cupid's arrow, she hath Dian's **wit**:

And in strong proof of chastity well **arm'd**:
From love's weak childish bow, she lives un**charm'd**.

She will not stay the siege of loving terms,

Nor bide th'encounter of assailing eyes.

Nor open her lap to saint-seducing gold:

O she is rich in beauty, only **poor**,
That when she dies, with beauty dies her **store**.

BENVOLIO. Then she hath sworn, that she will still* live **chaste?**

ROMEO. She hath, and in that sparing makes huge **waste?**

For beauty starv'd with her se**verity**,
Cuts beauty off from all pos**terity**.

She is too fair, too wise: wisely too **fair**,
To merit bliss by making me des**pair**:

She hath forsworn to love, and in that **vow**
Do I live dead, that live to tell it **now**.

Romeo and Juliet: Act 1, Scene 1

still – always

This is a passage, as you can see, that is not *all* in rhyme. Most of the rhymes are couplets of Romeo's invention – and a couplet simply means a pair of lines that end with a rhyme – but one, when Romeo makes use of Benvolio's 'chaste' and rhymes it with 'waste', sounds out differently.

What effect does that have when we hear it?

It's one of the most common uses of rhyme in Shakespeare, and we saw it briefly in action with Berowne and his friends in *Love Labour's Lost* at the beginning of this chapter. As used here by Romeo, it is an exuberant 'capping' of Benvolio's word, rhyming with it to make a witty exclamation of his own about how frustrating it is to be in love with Rosaline – the Folio's question mark after 'waste' acting as a modern exclamation mark would do. For his pursuit of Rosaline is sexually exciting and sexually frustrating in equal measure. Because she is so cold and seemingly uninterested in Romeo, Romeo swings wildly from a depression which begins to worry his family and friends, to passages like these, fun-filled and high-spirited as he dances in and out of rhyme.

Romeo, like Berowne, is aware that he is rhyming. That is what these would-be lovers do. So filled with feelings is he, that his need to give vent to these feelings, and the need to express them, calls out for rhymes, the language of love, where everything is harmony thanks to rhyming words that seem to kiss each other just as the lovers themselves wish to do. Romeo's rhymes are a way of dealing with the excess of feelings that are overwhelming him.

Unrequited feelings in Shakespeare are frequently expressed in rhyme.

You should now have another 'go' at that passage, and this time you should try to become aware of how it is the rhymes themselves that are helping you to cope with those indescribable feelings within you, that the rhymes are even a way to mock the very frustrations you are burdened with: they might even be a way of mocking Rosaline as well, whom you are, nevertheless, obsessed by.

How did you get on? If you were able to feel that by *playing* those rhymes you were able to get rid of, at least temporarily, the excessive weight of feelings that Romeo is bearing, that the *finding* of those rhymes gave you delight, even if that delight was somewhat manic, then you will have mastered this first rhyming lesson, and will be ready to move on to encounter the yet more fascinating faces that rhyme can reveal to us.

Alternating rhyme

In the very next scene Benvolio suggests that Romeo should go to the Capulets' party because he might meet some other girls there, and Benvolio's six-line speech, with its rhyming couplet at the end of it, throws Romeo a challenge. And it's a challenge because rhymes are clever, and because they're clever – who knows, this one might turn out to be true as well. So can Romeo find a way to 'cap' this bit of cleverness? Romeo proves himself up to the task by outsmarting his friend, by improvising a more complex rhyming game: can you see what it is?

> BENVOLIO. At this same ancient feast of Capulet's
> Sups the fair Rosaline, whom thou so loves:
> With all the admired beauties of Verona,
> Go thither and with unattainted eye,
> Compare her face with some that I shall **show**,
> And I will make thee think thy swan a **crow**.
>
> ROMEO. When the devout religion of mine **eye**
> Maintains such falsehood, then turn tears to **fire**:
> And these who often drown'd could never **die**,
> Transparent heretics be burnt for **liars**.
> One fairer than my love: the all-seeing **sun**
> Ne'er saw her match, since first the world **begun**.
>
> *Romeo and Juliet*: Act 1, Scene 2

Only the last two lines in Romeo's speech are a couplet, such as we've been dealing with till now; the first four are made up of *alternating* rhyming lines. Such a rhyme scheme is sometimes described by the letters '*ababcc*', signifying which words rhyme with which. Shakespeare's poem *Venus and Adonis* is written in this form. It's clearly harder to improvise such a sequence and will take more skill to act it, because you are now dealing not with a two-line, but a four-line, passage. It's a harder juggling act to keep all those words in the air for double the length of time. Go back over Romeo's six lines again and be conscious of the need to keep the word 'eye' in your mind, so it is there, ready to be rhymed with 'die', while at the same time you are throwing up the word 'fire' to be rhymed with 'liars' a moment later.[2] And remember as you say those four lines, we must feel that you are *improvising* them – but with grace and ease.

Romeo 'outsmarts' Benvolio with his more complex improvisation – which happens to be identical in form to the last six lines of a sonnet, such as he'll improvise with Juliet after they first meet at the party – which he now declares he has no appetite for.

While it is great fun to juggle with all these intentional rhyming passages – capturing the excitement and frustrations of these young, would-be lovers – those occasions when these same characters are *not conscious* of trying to rhyme should be for the actor even more rewarding.

Rhyme and revelations: Romeo's 'bolt from the blue'

Sometimes in life realisations come to us 'out of the blue'. These moments are rare of course, but when they happen it's as if a thought has somehow taken possession of *us*, rather than that we've actually had the thought for ourselves. At times like these some instinct tells us that 'that's it', that we've found the truth, the answer we were looking for, or maybe the answer to what was worrying us. Whichever, it's a 'eureka moment': we've made a discovery. And in Shakespeare these rare moments frequently come to us in rhyme.

In his first two scenes, Romeo is having fun, composing snatches of love poems: he knows exactly what he is doing. However, something totally different happens to Romeo when he first sees Juliet at the Capulet's feast, which he and his friends gatecrash. Interestingly, Romeo's Rosaline is also among the invited guests somewhere; but the audience get no glimpse of her because Romeo never seems to see her either. Once Juliet appears, he only has eyes for her. He asks a passing servant who the girl is, but the servant professes not to know. The words Romeo then uses are some of the most beautiful, I think, that Shakespeare ever wrote and here they are for you to sound out now:

> O she doth teach the torches to burn bright:
>
> It seems she hangs upon the cheek of night,
> Like a rich jewel in an Ethiop's ear:
>
> Beauty too rich for use, for earth too dear:
>
> So shows a snowy dove trooping with crows,
> As yonder lady o'er her fellows shows;
>
> The measure done, I'll watch her place of stand,
> And touching hers, make blessed my rude hand.
>
> Did my heart love till now, forswear it sight,
> For I never saw true beauty till this night.
>
> *Romeo and Juliet*: Act 1, Scene 4[5]

The final couplet reveals that he now knows what true love is; but the first four lines are even more remarkable. They are remarkable because they are so odd. Maybe the pleasure we get from those simple rhymes slightly obscures the oddness of what he's actually saying. He's aware that Juliet's presence in the room changes everything. Her presence gives life even to inanimate objects. The torches come alive and 'learn' from Juliet's beauty that they have a duty to illuminate that beauty more brilliantly. Night 'enters' the room with a human face and hovers around Juliet in order for Juliet to become for a while the night's most precious possession. Juliet seems to be not a girl to fall in love with, but an immortal, a goddess. But a moment later Romeo realises that all these revelations are telling him that he's in love for the first time and that she is the one that he loves and that he must go to her and take her hand.

It's one of Shakespeare's greatest gifts, this instinct he has to animate the inanimate: the torches; the night. He writes with the eye of a painter, in that everything within the scene contributes to it, and in this scene he lends that eye to Romeo.

Romeo has been assailed by a vision; he's been taken out of himself, as if the words that came to him had been spoken by another. Only when the words have been said does Romeo realise how they rhymed and how that now, once the rhymes have been heard, nothing can change that. But it is the magic of these unbidden rhymes that have assured him that what he's found was the 'answer' to everything that he had been looking for.

Unbidden rhymes are the sound of receiving an answer.

Rhyme sounding like the truth

But why should it seem that rhyme is the form in which truths might come to us?

Partly it's because rhyme is so often the form in which old wise sayings and insights have been packaged up. So we still hear people saying things like 'An apple a day keeps the doctor away', or – and this is one that I myself find difficult to ignore – 'See a pin and pick it up, all the day you'll have good luck'. Rhyme brings together two unconnected words, but once a rhyme is heard, it's as if these words have always secretly belonged to each other and that some truth has now been revealed to us. Once the rhyme has sounded we can't forget it – the words become super-glued together. Rhyme is also the language of spells and thus associated with magic. Rhyme is dangerous and in many parts of the world if you rhyme inadvertently during a conversation you may have to say some special word, or perform an action like spitting, to nullify the possible bad effects that the rhyme might bring.[4] Rhyme seals up a meaning. Rhyme can seduce us by its teasing delightfulness. It sounds like the way a god or goddess might speak and deliver some message to us.

In Shakespeare's day much that was taught in schools or to apprentices was taught in rhyme. Peter Ackroyd in his book *Albion* tells us that, because verse was a more direct and easier form of communication than prose, 'Sermons were turned into rhyme and moral homilies also acquired the natural dimensions of verse'.[5]

In *Othello* when the Duke is trying to make peace between Othello and Brabantio, after Brabantio's daughter, Desdemona, has eloped with Othello, he makes a speech filled with good advice in rhyming couplets:

> When remedies are past, the griefs are ended
> By seeing the worst, which late on hopes depended.
>
> To mourn a mischief that is past and gone,
> Is the next way to draw new mischief on.
>
> What cannot be preserv'd, when Fortune takes:
> Patience, her injury a mock'ry makes.
>
> The robb'd that smiles, steals something from the thief,
> He robs himself, that spends a bootless grief.

> *Othello*: Act 1, Scene 3

The Duke is hoping that these words of his will give comfort to the distraught father. They rhyme just like countless sayings rhyme, and because they rhyme we are predisposed to feel that they ought to be true. The Duke knows he is rhyming: he'll have said these lines on many similar occasions. But while rhymes predispose us to feel that they contain some truth, if the same 'truths' are trotted out too often, they can lose their power to convince us, becoming merely the repository of old and tired 'received opinions'. Brabantio is not assuaged by the Duke's words and he mocks them with some immediately improvised rhymes of his own:

> BRABANTIO. So let the Turk of Cyprus us beguile,
> We lose it not so long as we can smile...
>
> These sentences, to sugar, or to gall,
> Being strong on both sides, are equivocal.
>
> But words are words, I never yet did hear:
> That the bruised heart was pierc'd through the ears.

So we have to differentiate between rhyming words that are just 'used' to win some argument, and those that come 'unbidden' to us by direct revelation. And yet in both cases we prick up our ears to the magic of the rhyme, only to dismiss the first when its magic doesn't work for us, and we 'see through' the trick of it.

However, as Brabantio leaves the scene, a deeply disappointed man, he rhymes once more, and this time his rhyme will linger in the memory, seeming to cast a shadow over the course of the play, as he says to Othello:

> Look to her (Moor) if thou hast eyes to see:
> She has deceiv'd her father, and may thee.

These words of Brabantio's have the power to sound as if they may very well contain some truth. Later when we come to look at *Macbeth* we shall see how the rhymes of the Witches similarly infiltrate and poison the very fabric of that play. Rhymes are not always welcomed.

Though Romeo's 'bolt from the blue' when he first saw Juliet had been rapturously received, by contrast, later in that same scene, Juliet experiences similar moments of her own, but the rhymes she hears, while also being unbidden, frighten her.

Juliet's 'bolts from the blue'

Romeo and Juliet have not danced together; instead, in the few moments that they have had alone, they have improvised a sonnet (see below, pages 187–8), kissed, and fallen in love, only to have been parted as Juliet's mother calls for her. Now as Romeo is leaving, Juliet wants to find out Romeo's name without making her desires too obvious to her Nurse. As you sound out this passage, watch out for where the further rhymes occur.

> JULIET. Come hither nurse, what is yond gentleman:
> NURSE. The son and heir of old Tiberio.
> JULIET. What's he that now is going out of door?
> NURSE. Marry that I think be young Petruchio.
> JULIET. What's he that follows here that would not dance?
> NURSE. I know not.
> JULIET. Go ask his name: if he be married,
>   My grave is like to be my wedding bed.
> NURSE. His name is Romeo, and a Montague,
>   The only son of your great enemy.
> JULIET. My only love sprung from my only hate,
>   Too early seen, unknown, and known too late,

Prodigious* birth of love it is to me,
That I must love a loathed enemy.

NURSE. What's this? what's this?

JULIET.   A rhyme, I learnt even now
   Of one I danc'd withal.

                              One calls within, Juliet.[6]

NURSE.   Anon, anon:
   Come let's away, the strangers all are gone.

                                          Exeunt.

                       Romeo and Juliet: Act 1, Scene 4

Her most obvious lines of rhyme are these:

My only love sprung from my only hate,
Too early seen, unknown, and known too late,
Prodigious birth of love it is to me,
That I must love a loathed enemy.

The tragedy of the play is mapped out by these lines: Romeo and Juliet have fallen in love with each other, neither knowing that they belong to rival families, between whom there is a deadly and bloody feud. Now Juliet, sole child of the Capulet family, has just been told that the man she has fallen for is called Romeo, the Montagues' only son.

Immediately these four lines of rhyme are in her mouth; they possess her, take her over, as if the words are not really hers. It's as if some other voice has spoken out of her. In that moment she realises that her life has changed for ever. And once she has uttered those words, she senses that they are probably telling her a truth *because her words rhyme*. She is not trying to rhyme, she has been 'struck' by a thought. Once she has expressed it, she realises, no doubt to her horror, that it rhymed; and now that it's been spoken it can't be unspoken. And we *know* that she's heard herself rhyming because when her Nurse asks her what she said, Juliet replies:

A rhyme, I learnt even now
   Of one I danced withal.

Apart from the four lines we've just looked at, there are a couple of other rhymes here. One is Juliet's and you might not have spotted it.

Go ask his name: if he be married,
My grave is like to be my wedding bed

prodigious – unnatural

185

To complete the pentameter, in this line 'married' needs to be three syllables long, with a pronounced 'ed' as the third syllable, rhyming with 'bed'.

This is another 'bolt from the blue'. This thought: a sudden, unbidden fear that she might have fallen for a married man. Again she is not meaning to rhyme, but she'll be aware once the words are out that they do rhyme, and therefore sound so filled with the possibility that those fears could turn out to be true.

So twice, in this passage, Juliet has heard herself rhyme. Twice she has heard that 'sound' of being given an 'answer'. Her first fear however proves not to be true: Romeo isn't already married. But there is no escaping the truth she heard in those other four rhyming lines. And excitingly for us in the audience, we are there listening to her at the very moment when she realises things that we have known the answers to sometime before. Moments like these should be a gift for an actor to play.

Concluding rhymes

The Nurse's final lines are a couplet. She answers as someone calls out Juliet's name, saying that they are on their way; then she rhymes her 'anon' with 'gone'. This is a 'concluding' rhyme and is probably the most common type of rhyme that we will come across in Shakespeare's plays. It's very frequently found at the end of scenes, and it gives us a feeling that either something has been successfully tied up, or that the characters have agreed to bring some, as yet unfinished, business to a temporary halt. The right word, the rhyme, has slipped into place and we feel that on this occasion certainly nothing more needs to be said.

Shakespeare's sonnets always end on a rhyming couplet, and before we leave this famous pair of lovers, we have to experience the actual moment of their falling in love with each other as they improvise a sonnet together.

Shakespeare and the form of the sonnet

Improvising sonnets was quite a common pastime amongst would-be poets four hundred years ago. A full Shakespearian sonnet is a poem of fourteen lines. The rhyme scheme of a regular sonnet is *abab, cdcd, efef, gg*. Shakespeare occasionally includes a sonnet in one of his plays, as he does in *Romeo and Juliet*. But Shakespeare also wrote his own sequence of more than 150 sonnets. They were first published in 1609, but he had probably begun composing them by the mid-1590s, exactly at the same time as he was writing *Romeo and Juliet*.

Romeo and Juliet's sonnet

After Romeo's own 'bolt from the blue', he takes Juliet by the hand, speaking his excuses for being so bold in the form of a sonnet, which Juliet not only listens to, but becomes a joint improviser of with him.

Whether you are on your own, or reading with a partner, sound out this sonnet now and remember to consider *how* the fact that you are improvising this will affect your delivery of it. But that doesn't mean that hesitations creep in, because to hesitate would ruin the game, the magic, and the play. It is the fact that they *can* create a sonnet together – seemingly effortlessly – that proves their love for each other is unquestionably true: they are already speaking and thinking as one:

> ROMEO. If I profane with my unworthiest hand,
>   This holy shrine, the gentle sin is this,
>   My lips two blushing pilgrims did ready stand,
>   To smooth that rough touch, with a tender kiss.
>
> JULIET. Good pilgrim, you do wrong your hand too much,
>   Which mannerly devotion shows in this,
>   For saints have hands, that pilgrims' hands do touch,
>   And palm to palm, is holy palmers' kiss.
>
> ROMEO. Have not saints lips, and holy palmers too?
>
> JULIET. Ay pilgrim, lips that they must use in prayer.
>
> ROMEO. O then dear saint, let lips do what hands do,
>   They pray (grant thou) lest faith turn to despair.
>
> JULIET. Saints do not move, though grant for prayers' sake.
>
> ROMEO. Then move not while my prayer's effect I take:
>
> *Romeo and Juliet*: Act 1, Scene 4

And so at the conclusion of those fourteen lines Romeo kisses her. Romeo then begins another sonnet, but this time they kiss again after only three and a half lines, and this time it is Juliet who initiates this second kiss by saying that her lips now bear Romeo's sin:

> ROMEO. Thus from my lips, by thine my sin is purg'd.
>
> JULIET. Then have my lips the sin that they have took.

ROMEO. Sin from my lips? O trespass sweetly urg'd:
Give me my sin again.

[They kiss again.]

JULIET.   You kiss by'th'book.

Yes, the second kiss comes mid-line, which goes to show that if it's really important, you can break some lines in the middle! But that's as far as this second sonnet is allowed to develop because at this moment the Nurse comes up to them and whisks Juliet away.

NURSE. Madam your mother craves a word with you.

Often after a rhyme, or after a series of rhymes, there seems to hang a moment of suspension, filled with unspoken questions like 'What now?', 'Where do we go from here?' And in the long term rhyme in Shakespeare will always give place to blank verse as life takes over again.

So it is with Romeo and Juliet; when they next meet later that night, he in her orchard, she on her balcony, rhyme is not the language for planning the rest of their lives together. Rhyming tends to freeze the action, holding the moment in suspension; planning requires the onward surge of blank verse and we'll see this in operation in what could be the very next play that Shakespeare writes.

A Midsummer Night's Dream

Romeo and Juliet and *A Midsummer Night's Dream* were probably written in the same year: 1595. They share certain themes, but whereas the first of these is tragic, the other, as its title suggests, is full of confusions, but of the comic kind. And most commentators feel that the tragedy would have been written first.

The play is peopled by three groups of characters: first, the inhabitants of the kingdom of the Fairies; second, Theseus, Hippolyta and the four lovers who represent the top of Athenian society; and thirdly a group of labouring men, known (after their manual labour) as the Mechanicals.

Theseus is Duke of Athens and is about to marry Hippolyta, Queen of the Amazons, whom he has defeated in war and then concluded a peace with. Lysander, Demetrius, Hermia and Helena are the four lovers. Lysander loves Hermia and Demetrius used to love Helena, who still loves him. However, he now proclaims he loves Hermia and Hermia's father favours him over Lysander.

The Mechanicals are gathered together to put on a play which they hope will be chosen as part of Theseus's wedding celebrations.

Meanwhile in the Fairy kingdom, Oberon, King of the Fairies, is at odds with his wife Titania. They each accuse the other of infidelities, including suggestions that Oberon is over fond of Hippolyta and Titania of Theseus.

So there is much opportunity for conflict and confusion.

A Midsummer Night's Dream is the play of Shakespeare's which has the highest *proportion* of rhymed lines bar none.[7] Unsurprisingly, perhaps, the Fairies with their magical spells frequently speak in rhyme; also the old-fashioned play the Mechanicals rehearse and perform is all written in rhyme as plays before the time of Shakespeare normally were. So there is much rhyme we could look at, but I want to focus on the lovers.

Unintentional rhyming arising out of an excess of romantic excitement

Because Hermia's father is determined to stop her marrying Lysander, she and Lysander decide to run away from Athens in order to get married secretly elsewhere. It is the excitement generated by this plan to elope together that first releases rhyme into the play.

> LYSANDER.   If thou lov'st me, then
> Steal forth thy father's house tomorrow night:
> And in the wood, a league without the town,
> (Where I did meet thee once with Helena,
> To do observance to a morn of May)
> There will I stay for thee.
>
> HERMIA.   My good Lysander,
> I swear to thee, by Cupid's strongest bow,
> By his best arrow with the golden head,
> By the simplicity of Venus' **doves,**
> By that which knitteth souls, and prospers **loves,**
> And by that fire which burn'd the Carthage **Queen,**
> When the false Troyan under sail was **seen,**
> By all the vows that ever men have **broke,**
> (In number more than ever women **spoke)**
> In that same place thou hast appointed **me,**
> Tomorrow truly will I meet with **thee.**
>
> LYSANDER. Keep promise love: look here comes Helena.
>
> *A Midsummer Night's Dream*: Act 1, Scene 1

As you'll see, the rhyming doesn't happen immediately after Lysander has suggested that they should run away together, but it *grows* out of the desire and excitement that each feels for the other in this heady and romantic situation.

For the actress playing Hermia it's important for her to be aware of this moment when her blank verse yields to rhyme and so she will need to 'set up' the word 'doves' with care, so that the word 'loves' will then be able to bask in the rhyme it creates.

Their dialogue has been going on for some forty lines before this first rhymed line pops up between them. But from this moment onwards (apart from Lysander's last line as he sees Helena entering) Hermia and Lysander continue to speak in rhyme until they temporarily fall back into blank verse when everything gets fraught between the lovers in the confusions of Act 3.

Unintentional rhyming arising out of a desire for union that is still out of reach

Now their friend Helena enters; Helena, who has more rhymed lines than all the other mortals in the play. One thing we should now consider is that rhyme is frequently associated with desires that are as yet unfulfilled and Helena's desires are utterly unfulfilled. Dumped by Demetrius, she is like a ghost, a lost soul, all of whose thoughts are still focused on Demetrius: why did she lose him and how can she win him back? And all her lines in this, her first scene, rhyme.

> HERMIA. God speed fair Helena, whither away?
> HELENA. Call you me fair? that fair again unsay,
>
> Demetrius loves your fair: O happy fair!
> Your eyes are lode-stars, and your tongue's sweet air
> More tuneable than lark to shepherd's ear,
> When wheat is green, when hawthorn buds appear,
>
> Sickness is catching: O were favour so,
> Yours would I catch, fair Hermia ere I go,
> My ear should catch your voice, my eye, your <u>eye</u>,
> My tongue should catch your tongue's sweet <u>melody</u>,*
>
> Were the world mine, Demetrius being bated,*

You will see that '*eye*' and '*melody*' have been underlined, as many more pairs of words will be throughout this book, to signify that in Shakespeare's time these would have rhymed.
bated – excepted

The rest I'll give to be to you translated.

O teach me how you look, and with what art
You sway the motion of Demetrius' heart.

HERMIA. I frown upon him, yet he loves me still.

HELENA. O that your frowns would teach my smiles such skill.

HERMIA. I give him curses, yet he gives me <u>love</u>.

HELENA. O that my prayers could such affection <u>move</u>.

HERMIA. The more I hate, the more he follows me.

HELENA. The more I love, the more he hateth me.

HERMIA. His folly Helena is no fault of mine.

HELENA. None but your beauty, would that fault were mine.

Helena's incessant rhyming is surely meant to make us smile a little, but in fact what she is actually saying – and we must always take literally what characters are actually saying – is somewhat crazy. And it's her love for Demetrius that has brought her to this state. She is saying what a pity it is that Hermia's beauty was not like some sort of illness, because if it were, then it might be possible to 'catch' her beauty from her and in that way Demetrius would possibly fall for her all over again.

Helena's lovesick state means she is desperate to find 'answers' to everything that has gone wrong between her and Demetrius, even if they sound somewhat deranged. But the fact that her 'answers' fall into rhyme encourages her to feel that she might be on to something, because positive thoughts that fall into rhyme are always the ones that *sound* most convincing and therefore most comforting.

But how does it *happen* that all her answers to Hermia's lines rhyme and her own thoughts are shaped by couplets? She isn't consciously trying to rhyme, as those characters engaged in some sort of 'rhyming game' are. She's just wanting to come up with the best answers; and those words of Hermia's that she rhymes with, together with her own, inspire her to answers and conclusions which sound so fitting and right and – yes – happily they rhyme too and therefore sound so *reasonable*. In the end her rhyming is an unconscious by-product of her determination that she will never give up on her quest to be at one again with Demetrius. For her it is a matter of life and death.

Now read the scene again and discover how it *feels* to be Helena, not needing to be *able* to rhyme, but needing those 'perfect' answers which attain perfection *because* they rhyme.

Once our Helena is left alone on stage she has the following rhyming soliloquy, commenting first on the happy couple who have just left her:

> How happy some, o'er other some can be?
> Through Athens I am thought as fair as she.
>
> But what of that? Demetrius thinks not so:
> He will not know, what all, but he do know,
> And as he errs, doting on Hermia's <u>eyes</u>;
> So I, admiring of his <u>qualities</u>:
>
> Things base and vile, holding no quantity,
> Love can transpose to form and dignity,
>
> Love looks not with the eyes, but with the mind,
> And therefore is wing'd Cupid painted blind.
>
> Nor hath Love's mind of any judgement taste:
> Wings and no eyes, figure, unheedy haste.
>
> And therefore is Love said to be a child,
> Because in choice he is so oft beguil'd,
>
> As waggish boys in game themselves forswear;
> So the boy Love is perjur'd every where.
>
> For ere Demetrius look'd on Hermia's eyne,*
> He hail'd down oaths that he was only mine.
>
> And when this hail some heat from Hermia felt,
> So he dissolv'd, and showers of oaths did melt,

Obsessed as she is by Demetrius, it is all she can talk about. To her friends; to the audience; to anyone who will listen. Talking things through, even if those we are talking to make no response, often leads us to encouraging solutions, and the rhymes that continue to come instinctively to her encourage her as well. They lead her to feel she is making great sense and discovering truths about her situation. So each rhyme, especially if you play them with a proper sense of 'discovery', which means making sure to 'set up' the word you are going to rhyme with, and then feeling some satisfaction once the rhyme has sounded, allows you to lead Helena with confidence to the next such moment and so her sense of being on top of the situation she is in, grows.

eyne – eyes

192

And in this speech Helena discovers, to her own delight, that it's not so much that Demetrius is at fault, it is more the fault of the boy Cupid, who's blind and hasty and completely immature. Though, maybe, Hermia's eyes are a bit to blame too.

As the speech, which she has shared with the audience, comes to an end, her rhymes have not only given her some solace, a feeling that she is making progress, but they have also led her to the point where she gets her great idea – as sharing problems with friends, and she no doubt regards us in the audience as her friends, frequently does. And her idea is certainly a partial 'answer' to her problems:

> I will go tell him of fair Hermia's flight:
> Then to the wood will he, tomorrow night
> Pursue her; and for this intelligence,
> If I have thanks, it is a dear expense:

It's an answer that satisfies her, because it's a way of spending some time with Demetrius, even if it probably won't please Hermia over much.

> But herein mean I to enrich my pain,
> To have his sight thither, and back again.

But of course seeing him, being in his company for a while, might solve everything. The rhymes have carried her moment by moment through the speech from a possibly tearful start to a delighted, positive conclusion. You should now go back over the speech again and feel how the rhymes are what are giving you the strength you need to go on and win Demetrius back.

Do you see how Helena will do anything to try to win him back? She'll betray her best friend for him; offer to be his dog; eventually she'll stay all night in the woods with him, even though he and the others just seem bent on mocking her. But it's her constancy – the strength of her love, which is revealed by her rhyming – that will finally win the day and thereby solve the play's problems. She is our heroine.

So Demetrius follows the elopers into the woods, and Helena follows him. Once in his company, you'll notice that she feels no need to keep up the rhyming. Rhyming gives her consolation when she's out of his company; being with him is all she wants. So for a short scene, the 'sound of sincerity' returns with their blank verse. Though Demetrius's 'sound of sincerity', at this stage of the play, is that he can't stand the sight of her!

In the woods Oberon overhears Helena's failed attempts to rekindle Demetrius's love for her and decides to intervene. He gets his mischievous sidekick, Puck, to give Demetrius a drug which will cause him to fall in love with Helena all over again. But Puck gives the drug to Lysander instead. So when Lysander wakes up and sees Helena alone in the woods *he* then declares he has fallen in love with her.

Because *A Midsummer Night's Dream* is a comedy, we are clearly invited to find the behaviour of these characters amusing. But it is an interesting fact that Shakespeare's comedies frequently start from a dark place (Hermia is threatened with death if she refuses to marry Demetrius) and move towards a happy resolution, whereas tragedies often begin on a triumphant note, only to head towards death at the close. But in both genres Shakespeare loves to mingle joy and sorrow, laughter and tears.

One side effect of the drug that Puck administers, is that those under its influence find that they are inclined to rhyme. Interestingly therefore, they feel and behave identically to those who've fallen in love without the aid of any drug. Inevitably the effect of the drug is that those under its influence also feel absolutely certain about everything; as they rhyme, they discover they have all the 'answers' they need.

Unintentional rhyming as a consequence of intoxication

Here is Lysander as he's woken up by Helena. Now see how the rhymes fuel Lysander's absolute confidence as you play him:

HELENA. Lysander, if you live, good sir awake.

LYSANDER. And run through fire I will for thy sweet sake.

Transparent Helena, nature here shows art,
That through thy bosom makes me see thy heart.

Where is Demetrius? oh how fit a <u>word</u>
Is that vile name, to perish on my <u>sword</u>!

HELENA. Do not say so Lysander, say not so:
What though he love your Hermia? Lord, what though?
Yet Hermia still loves you; then be content.

LYSANDER. Content with Hermia? No, I do repent
The tedious minutes I with her have spent.

Not Hermia, but Helena now I love;
Who will not change a raven for a dove?

> The will of man is by his reason sway'd:
> And reason says you are the worthier maid.
>
> Things growing are not ripe until their season;
> So I being young, till now ripe not to reason,
>
> And touching now the point of human skill,
> Reason becomes the marshal to my will,
>
> And leads me to your eyes, where I o'erlook
> Love's stories, written in love's richest book.

A Midsummer Night's Dream: Act 2, Scene 2

Lysander is delighted with himself. He feels that he has never before in his life made such sense. Everything is so clear to him that he goes so far as to say that his totally irrational drug-induced behaviour is all based on 'reason'. He now feels that Helena is the most divine of creatures, though before he fell asleep he was utterly devoted to Hermia, who is still asleep only a few yards away. Of course this is exactly what had happened to Demetrius when he fell out of love with Helena, though in his case no drug had been administered.

Lysander has been hypnotised with the result that is he is not fazed by anything. Any discrepancy there is between how he was and how he now is can be *explained*, and because it's – to him – oh so simple, he probably finds it really amusing too that he never realised all this before. And his amusement probably accounts for Helena's next lines, which also continue to rhyme and therefore reveal that she now has the 'answer' to this particular situation. For her the answer is that this is all some distasteful *joke* on Lysander's part.

> Wherefore was I to this keen mockery born?
> When at you hands did I deserve this scorn?

and when her speech ends with

> O, that a lady of one man refus'd,
> Should of another therefore be abus'd.

– she storms off.

Their rhymes lead them to feel that they both have the 'answer', but in fact neither of them has the real 'answer', because neither knows what we know, which is that one of them has been hypnotised. Rhyme is here pinpointing those moments when understanding *seems* to strike.

Now we are not dealing with the discoveries of a single character, but of two different characters who both believe two different things. They are at cross-purposes with one another, which is what almost all comedy is based on.

Oberon then sets about 'correcting' Puck's error by anointing Demetrius's eyes, and so he too declares his love for Helena. However, Helena, having just been threatened by Demetrius that he might assault her if she continues to follow him, doesn't believe him. She thinks he is just joking too.

Rhyme giving way to blank verse

Towards the end of the play when the lovers wake up, and find Theseus and Hippolyta and Egeus, Hermia's father, gazing down on them, the time for rhyme is finally over. Everything has been sorted out, and now they need to make sense of all that has happened to them and to begin to plan the rest of their lives together as well. Once they revert to blank verse it's as if they've suddenly grown up; they begin to say really interesting things. Lysander has had the antidote put into his eyes so he no longer yearns for Helena. Demetrius, though, has received no antidote, but it seems he is no longer afflicted by the compulsion to rhyme any more either.

Demetrius has been the 'problem' in the play. His desertion of Helena, his mad pursuit of Hermia and his rage against Lysander, turned him into a not very likeable character. But on waking he gives his account of what happened to him, and everything changes.

> My lord, fair Helen told me of their stealth,
> Of this their purpose hither, to this wood,
> And I in fury hither followed them;
> Fair Helena, in fancy followed me.
>
> But my good lord, I wot not by what power,
> (But by some power it is) my love to Hermia
> (Melted as the snow) seems to me now
> As the remembrance of an idle gaud,
> Which in my childhood I did dote upon:
>
> And all the faith, the virtue of my heart,
> The object and the pleasure of mine eye,
> Is only Helena.
>
> To her, my lord,
> Was I betroth'd, ere I saw Hermia,
> But like a sickness did I loathe this food,
> But as in health, come to my natural taste,

Now do I wish it, love it, long for it,
And will for evermore be true to it.

A Midsummer Night's D

The 'sound of sincerity' is back. Is there any expla.
Not really: he became obsessed by Hermia, and there
except to say, as Helena did, that Cupid was to blame.

But should we feel worried that he is only saying what he is sa
because he's still drugged? Is he going to be drugged for the rest of his life?

Oberon had told Puck that the spell would mean that anybody under
its influence would fall in love with 'the next live creature that it sees'. Puck
mistook Lysander for Demetrius and put the spell in Lysander's eyes with
these words: words which, because they are a spell, rhyme of course,

Churl, upon thy eyes I throw
All the power this charm doth owe:
When thou wak'st, let love forbid
Sleep his seat on thy eye-lid.

A Midsummer Night's Dream: Act 2, Scene 2

So Lysander would have fallen for the first person he clapped eyes on and
it just happened to be Helena that came his way.

But when Oberon anoints Demetrius's eyes his spell is more carefully
worded.

Flower of this purple <u>dye</u>,
Hit with Cupid's <u>archery</u>,
Sink in apple of his eye,
When his love he doth espy,
Let her shine as <u>gloriously</u>
As the Venus of the <u>sky</u>.

When thou wak'st if she be <u>by</u>,
Beg of her for <u>remedy</u>.

A Midsummer Night's Dream: Act 3, Scene 2

Oberon's spell is specifically directed towards being effective only if
Helena, 'his love', 'be by'. And then the spell doesn't direct Demetrius to
fall for her all over again. Rather it directs him to see *her* as she really is: as
glorious 'As the Venus of the sky'. And when he wakes to see her, he calls
her 'perfect' and 'divine'; everything about her, her eyes, her lips, her hand,
all blow him away by their beauty. The only trouble is that at that point in
the play Helena believes that Demetrius is, like Lysander, mocking her too.

rd II: a third play written in 1595?

chard II might also have been written during 1595. It would be appropriate if it was, since this is the *history* play of Shakespeare's which has more rhyme (*much* more rhyme) than any of the others. I want to focus on one particular use that Shakespeare makes of rhyme in it, which is when characters are *falsely trying to convince others of their sincerity*. To do this we will just look at how the play begins and how it ends.

Rhymes can also be instruments of deception.

In the opening scene a great quarrel breaks out between Henry Bullingbrook, the future Henry IV, and Thomas Mowbray, a committed supporter of King Richard. The quarrel is over the murder of the Duke of Gloucester, possibly on Richard's orders. Bullingbrook, who can't accuse the King directly, accuses Mowbray of being complicit in the crime.[8] Both men have challenged each other to trial by combat, but it's in Richard's interests to bring this row to an end. He commands the two men to pick up the gages (or gloves) they have flung at each other's feet.

I've marked in bold the four occasions in this rhyming extract when one character 'caps' another by rhyming with the last word they have said. We noticed this was done by both Berowne and Romeo to 'outsmart' whomever they were talking to. Here, where the stakes are higher, it is done in an attempt to negate what the previous speaker has just said.

> KING. Norfolk, throw down, we bid; there is no **boot**.*
>
> MOWBRAY. My self I throw (dread sovereign) at thy **foot**.
>
> > My life thou shalt command, but not my shame,
> > The one my duty owes, but my fair name
> > Despite of death, that lives upon my <u>grave</u>
> > To dark dishonour's use, thou shalt not <u>have</u>.
> >
> > I am disgrac'd, impeach'd, and baffled* here,
> > Pierc'd to the soul with slander's venom'd spear:
> > The which no balm can cure, but his heart **blood**
> > Which breath'd this poison.
> >
> > > KING.   Rage must be with**stood**:
> > Give me his gage: lions make leopards **tame**.
> >
> > MOWBRAY. Yea, but not change his spots: take but my **shame**,
> > And I resign my gage.

boot – alternative
baffled – publicly shamed

> My dear, dear lord,
> The purest treasure mortal times afford
> Is spotless reputation: that away,
> Men are but gilded loam, or painted clay.
>
> A jewel in a ten times barr'd up chest,
> Is a bold spirit, in a loyal breast.
> Mine honour is my life; both grow in one:
> Take honour from me, and my life is done.
>
> Then (dear my liege) mine honour let me try,
> In that I live; and for that will I die.

Richard II: Act 1, Scene 1

So we see something of a 'battle of rhymes' between the King and Mowbray, like two wrestlers each vying for the upper hand. But Mowbray's 'need' is greater than the King's – his very life is at stake – and so he maintains his advantage by 'capping' the King and then produces sixteen rhymed lines with which to proclaim his honour and 'innocence'.

Richard then tries to win over his cousin Bullingbrook, but Bullingbrook uses the same tactics to keep the floor and then follows that with eight rhyming lines of his own:

> KING. Cousin, throw down your gage, do you **begin**.
>
> BULLINGBROOK. O God defend my soul from such foul **sin**.
>
> Shall I seem crest-fall'n in my father's sight,
> Or with pale beggar-fear impeach my height
> Before this out-dar'd dastard?
>
> Ere my <u>tongue</u>
> Shall wound my honour with such feeble <u>wrong</u>;
> Or sound so base a parle: my teeth shall <u>tear</u>
> The slavish motive of recanting <u>fear</u>,
> And spit it bleeding in his high disgrace,
> Where shame doth harbour, even in Mowbray's face.

Richard's tactics have failed; the seriousness of the situation means that he has to switch back into four lines of blank verse, in which he proclaims his judgement:

> KING. We were not born to sue, but to command,
> Which since we cannot do to make you friends,
> Be ready, (as your lives shall answer it)
> At Coventry, upon Saint Lambert's day:

But Richard can't quite leave it like that. It would have been more dignified if he had omitted to say the next four lines and gone straight on to the scene's final 'concluding couplet'. But his extreme irritation by being out-manoeuvred by these two suggest to him that, if he could end the scene with some memorably scathing 'put-downs' then he would gain some sense of consolation. And rhymes will fit that bill and will punch home his final 'answer' to them.

> There shall your swords and lances arbitrate
> The swelling difference of your settled hate:
> Since we cannot atone you, we shall see
> Justice design the victor's chivalry.
>
> Lord Marshal, command our officers at arms,
> Be ready to direct these home alarms.
>
> *Exeunt.*

It would be wrong to say that Mowbray and Bullingbrook were conscious of *trying* to rhyme, but right to say that their extreme need to sound more genuine and more outraged than their rival produces these enclosed 'watertight' statements that rhyme can provide.

In a way you can't argue with a rhyme, because in situations like these it is designed to say *nothing*. It simply sounds impressive. It's designed not to advance any rational argument, but simply to maintain the expression of a feeling, and here that feeling is what we might call the 'voice of out-raged innocence'. It's a 'sound bite', a political ploy.

It's time for you to return to those speeches again, bearing the above in mind.

We saw in *Romeo and Juliet* and in *A Midsummer Night's Dream* that the lovers in these two plays, once they had found their life partners, no longer needed the comfort that rhyme had brought them and they began to speak in blank verse again. Here by contrast we'll see how in *Richard II* rhyme continues to be used as a political weapon, in an attempt to pull the wool over our eyes, and the eyes of some of the characters.

The play ends with a scene that is almost all written in rhyme, as Exton, Richard's murderer, comes to claim his reward from Bullingbrook, who has himself ordered Richard's death and has now become King Henry IV in his place. So the play that began with the row over Gloucester's mur-der ends with an attempt to excuse and move on from Richard's murder.

And the same rhyming techniques are used here: twice Bullingbrook
'caps' Exton (as I have shown again in bold) and then goes on to produce
sixteen lines of cynical rhymed verse of his own. They are lines which
sound good and which, because the rhymes seem to close off all possibility of argument and discussion, often seem to win the day.

> EXTON. Great king, within this coffin I present
> Thy buried fear.
>
> Herein all breathless <u>lies</u>
> The mightiest of thy greatest <u>enemies</u>
> Richard of Bordeaux, by me hither **brought.**
>
> BULLINGBROOK. Exton, I thank thee not, for thou hast **wrought**
> A deed of slaughter, with thy fatal hand,
> Upon my head, and all this famous land.
> EXTON. From your own mouth my lord, did I this **deed.**
> BULLINGBROOK. They love not poison, that do poison **need,**
> Nor do I thee: though I did wish him <u>dead,</u>
> I hate the murderer, love him <u>murdered.</u>
>
> The guilt of conscience take thou for thy labour,
> But neither my good word, nor princely favour.
>
> With Cain go wander through shade of night,
> And never show thy head by day, nor light.
>
> Lords, I protest my soul is full of woe,
> That blood should sprinkle me, to make me grow.
>
> Come mourn with me, for that I do lament,
> And put on sullen black incontinent:
>
> I'll make a voyage to the holy-land,
> To wash this blood off from my guilty hand.
>
> March sadly after, grace my mourning here,
> In weeping after this untimely bier.

Who really deserves to be called Cain? Exton who carried out Bullingbrook's orders, or Bullingbrook himself, who ordered the killing? Neither
in fact killed their own brother, as Cain did, but Richard *was* Bullingbrook's first cousin.

Listening to these lines in the theatre we may well feel that this cannot
be the end of a story. And indeed it isn't: rather it's the beginning of one.
Richard II is the first of the cycle of the eight history plays to which Shakespeare had *already* written the end some years before.[9] To hear the real end

of the story we have to look at the last lines from *Richard III*. The words are spoken by Richmond, now King Henry VII, and the first Tudor king:

> Abate the edge of traitors, gracious Lord,
> That would reduce these bloody days again,
> And make poor England weep in streams of blood;
> Let them not live to taste this land's increase,
> That would with treason, wound this fair land's peace.
> Now civil wounds are stopped, Peace lives again;
> That she may long live here, God say, Amen.

Richard III: Act 5, Scene 5

The last four lines rhyme conclusively and memorably, as in their way did the last lines of *Richard II*. But context is all, and however grief-struck Bullingbrook might be anxious to appear, we cannot forget that what he is apparently grieving about is the murder of his cousin, which he himself ordered.

Rhyme is mysterious, powerful, connected with magic and the magical force of words. At its most revealing it can bring us insights that seem to be coming from somewhere outside ourselves. At its most playful it can simply be a game.

Somewhere in between the two, we see it being used in many different ways: bringing episodes to conclusions; ridding oneself of excessive feelings; comforting with wise advice; and responding to the need characters have to find answers to their problems – whether those problems are honourable or, as we have seen in those passages from *Richard II*, merely a need to *sound* so.

Our next chapter will address the question as to why Shakespeare continues to value rhyme in his plays, while some of his contemporaries were beginning to feel that the time for rhyme was over.

Twelve

To Rhyme or Not to Rhyme

From jigging veins of rhyming mother-wits,
And such conceits as clownage keeps in pay,
We'll lead you to the stately tent of war,
Where you shall hear the Scythian Tamburlaine
Threat'ning the world with high astounding terms,
And scourging kingdoms with his conquering sword.
View but his picture in this tragic glass,
And then applaud his fortunes as you please.

Tamburlaine, Part One: Prologue

Shakespeare v. Marlowe

Not all of Shakespeare's contemporaries were fond of rhyme – Christopher Marlowe being one. And to discover why this was so we have to take a step back in time to see how blank (that is unrhymed verse) became the form that took the theatre by storm in the late 1580s and effectively ousted rhymed verse to the sidelines. So this chapter will give us an opportunity to experience both the seductive power of Marlowe's 'new' blank verse line, and to widen our understanding of why, and in what circumstances, Shakespeare continued to champion the use of rhyme – together with some rather old-fashioned rhythms, that were always associated with rhymed verse as well.

Marlowe and Shakespeare were both born in 1564; Marlowe, the elder by two months, in Canterbury in February, and Shakespeare in

Stratford-upon-Avon in April. Marlowe's first great success as a dramatist was with *Tamburlaine* in 1587 – maybe some two or three years before any of Shakespeare's plays were produced. The two men must have known each other but how well we don't know.

There are some people who believe a different story – that Shakespeare didn't write any plays at all, and that they were all written by Christopher Marlowe. And they point to the many similarities between Marlowe's writing and Shakespeare's early output to advance their case. They have to get round the fact that Marlowe was apparently killed during a private house party in Deptford in 1593, but their theory goes that he survived, went into hiding and lived to write all of Shakespeare's plays as well as his own.[1] However, if he did, he curiously failed to follow the mission statement that he advances in his own Prologue to *Tamburlaine* quoted above. Here he clearly states that from now on rhyme is out. He will occasionally end a play or speech with a rhyme, but that is about all. As we have already seen, Shakespeare uses rhyme much more liberally than that.

In John Southworth's fascinating book *Shakespeare the Player*, he suggests the possibility that Shakespeare was a member of the Admiral's Men in the late 1580s, the company for which Marlowe was writing. If so, Shakespeare would have acted in Marlowe's plays, inevitably would have been bowled over by his writing, and this might explain the similarities between the two playwrights in the late '80s and early '90s.

But in fact the two men were very different. Marlowe was breaking the mould. He wanted to create a new kind of popular drama that owed nothing to the insistently rhyming verse plays that were then in vogue. His plays would be subversive in theme, and based on a blank verse line that would energise those stories and avoid those rhymes that interrupt the onward adrenalin rush that he wanted to release. While rhyme will divide any speech up into couplets or quatrains, Marlowe wanted his speeches to go on rising line after line to dizzying heights where they astounded his audiences as his characters reached, almost literally, to pull down the stars and the heavens.

It's time for you to sound out some of Marlowe's lines for yourselves, and as you do so remember it is with his plays that blank verse first takes the stages of the public theatres by storm.[2]

At the beginning of *Tamburlaine, Part One*, Tamburlaine, who is of humble shepherd stock, is confronted by a Persian lord called Theridamas, who has been sent by Mycetes, King of Persia, to destroy both Tamburlaine and his hopelessly outnumbered band of followers. Tamburlaine, rather than fighting, calls for a parley and in a speech of close to fifty lines so impresses and overwhelms Theridamas that Theridamas decides to join Tamburlaine and abandon Mycetes.

Here is the beginning and the end of this speech. Give yourself a taste of the power of this 'new' and (probably) just pre-Shakespearian drama by sounding it out.

Tamburlaine is impressed by the commanding presence of Theridamas, as his opening line shows:

TAMBURLAINE. With what a majesty he rears his looks:—

> In thee (thou valiant man of Persia)
> I see the folly of thy emperor:
> Art thou but captain of a thousand horse,
> That by characters graven in thy brows,
> And by thy martial face and stout aspect,
> Deserv'st to have the leading of an host?

> Forsake thy king and do but join with me
> And we will triumph over all the world.
> I hold the Fates bound fast in iron chains,
> And with my hand turn Fortune's wheel about;
> And sooner shall the sun fall from his sphere,
> Than Tamburlaine be slain and overcome…
> And when my name and honour shall be spread,
> As far as Boreas* claps his brazen wings,
> Or fair Boötes* sends his cheerful light,
> Then shalt thou be competitor with me,
> And sit with Tamburlaine in all his majesty.

Tamburlaine: Act 1, Scene 2

Did you feel the surging strength of these lines? If not, go back and sound it out again and make sure you *release* each line and play it through to its line ending without a break. None of these lines has a mid-line comma, and the power of Marlowe's writing comes from the unhesitating confidence with which each line builds on its predecessor. This is much less than half the length of the full speech; in fact this play and its sequel, *Tamburlaine, Part Two*, are filled with numerous speeches of thirty, forty or fifty lines or more.

Notice how 'end-stopped' it is: how many lines end with a monosyllabic word and how many 'names' are included which become part of the characteristic texture of the whole. Maybe it reminded you of Queen Margaret's speech from *Henry VI* that we worked on earlier, which displayed

Boreas – the North Wind
Boötes – a northern constellation

something of the same surging confidence. Shakespeare probably learnt much from listening to, and maybe acting in, the plays of his exact contemporary.

Tamburlaine's speech is barely over before Theridamas decides to join up with him. Tamburlaine now possesses not just the band of five hundred foot soldiers that he had before making this speech, but has an army three times the size and, because the new recruits are all cavalry, also immeasurably more powerful. No wonder that Theridamas later says of Tamburlaine's eloquence (the italics are mine):

> You see, my lord, what *working* words he hath…
>
> *Tamburlaine*: Act 2, Scene 3

It is a fitting testimony to the power of speech when it is shaped into lines of this length and carried on the rhythm of the human heartbeat.

Marlowe's plays were designed to shock. His characters, often known since as 'over-reachers', would live outside the norms of society; they were not kings or gods: rather they were those who wanted to supplant their rulers and become kings and gods in their stead. And going to see these plays could be dangerous as well: at an early performance of *Tamburlaine* a live gun was fired on stage which killed a pregnant woman and a child in the audience and badly wounded yet another spectator. But Marlowe's vision worked. The heady combination of his lyrical yet powerful verse line, together with the outrageous characters he gave life to, created a theatrical revolution. Shakespeare cannot but have been impressed by Marlowe's daring, and the sheer beauty of some of his lines.

Here's Tamburlaine on kingship:

> Is it not passing* brave to be a King,
> And ride in triumph through Persepolis?
>
> *Tamburlaine, Part One*: Act 2, Scene 5

And somewhat earlier, looking on the woman he will later marry:

> Zenocrate, lovelier than the love of Jove,
> Brighter than is the silver Rhodope,
> Fairer than whitest snow on Scythian hills,
> Thy person is more worth to Tamburlaine,
> Than the possession of the Persian crown,
> Which gracious stars have promised at my birth.
>
> *Tamburlaine, Part One*: Act 1, Scene 2

passing – surpassing

See again Marlowe's love of names. Audiences flocked to these plays. Even then, most wouldn't have known (and nor did I) that Rhodope was a mountain in Thrace and the site of silver mines; my guess until I read the notes was that it might have been the name of some sparkling river. But no matter: audiences drank up the glorious sound of Marlowe's lines and of these exotic names. Other writers tried their best to imitate him; some of the audiences might even have been tempted to try to speak like the characters from his plays in their own daily lives.[3]

Shakespeare's attachment to the older dramatic forms

Shakespeare was different. While his early history plays probably do owe much to Marlowe, his instincts, though he embraced the new, never led him to turn his back on all older forms of writing.

As a boy in Stratford Shakespeare would have seen the various companies of players that visited the town. His father, John, who rose to be Bailiff of Stratford for a while, may well have been involved in the organising of these theatrical visits. William would have been in those audiences, seeing what went down well, what moved the assembled company, what made them roar with laughter.

Unlike Marlowe, he loves the effects that rhyme and traditional rhythms could bring about, and, especially in his early plays, he makes abundant use of them. While Marlowe seemed only interested in the new, Shakespeare seems to have wanted to fuse the new and the old together.

Love's Labour's Lost

Love's Labour's Lost, one of Shakespeare's earlier comedies, probably written around 1594, has an incredible freshness to it; it is romantic, racy, filled with the most exuberant language and packed with rhyme and examples of many of these older forms of writing. It has twice as much rhymed verse as blank and more than a third of the text is not verse at all but prose. Some of the rhythms, as we shall see, are also delightfully surprising.

The King of Navarre has gathered around him three friends; their aim is to set up an Academy for the purpose of studying life and how to live it better. But one of the three, Berowne, questions whether the harsh rules that they have to subscribe to are really necessary and so jeopardises the whole enterprise before it has even got off the ground. Now the King takes him to task for it.

> KING. Berowne is like an envious sneaping <u>frost</u>,
>   That bites the first-born infants of the spring.
> BEROWNE. Well, say I am, why should proud summer <u>boast</u>,
>   Before the birds have any cause to sing?
>   Why should I joy in any abortive birth?
>   At Christmas I no more desire a rose,
>   Than wish a snow in May's new fangled shows:
>   But like of each thing that in season grows.
>   So you to study now it is too late,
>   That were to climb o'er the house to unlock the gate.[4]
> KING. Well, sit you out: go home Berowne: <u>adieu</u>.
> BEROWNE. No my good lord, I have sworn to stay with <u>you</u>.
>   And though I have for barbarism spoke more,
>   Than for that angel knowledge you can say,
>   Yet confident I'll keep what I have swore,[5]
>   And bide the penance of each three years' day.
>   Give me the paper, let me read the same,
>   And to the strict'st decrees I'll write my name.
> KING. How well this yielding rescues thee from shame.

Love's Labour's Lost: Act 1, Scene 1

We must, I think, pause a while to admire the life and liveliness of this writing and the brilliance of Berowne. In particular it is his habitual ability to come up with the winning 'answer'; and in rhyming verse sequences the way to outdo anyone else's argument is to out-rhyme them. And when you were sounding it out, I hoped you realised that Berowne's second speech included four lines in an *abab* rhyme scheme.

At the beginning of this passage the King has two unrhymed lines, and immediately Berowne 'caps' them by rhyming with them *both*, turning them into another *abab* pattern:

> KING. Berowne is like an envious sneaping **frost**,
>   That bites the first-born infants of the **spring**.
> BEROWNE. Well, say I am, why should proud summer **boast**,
>   Before the birds have any cause to **sing**?

Again when the King bids him 'adieu', which would be anglicised in its pronunciation ('adyoo') Berowne outsmarts him by rhyming it with his 'you'.

Rhyme can be a way to outsmart others.

This 'capping' or 'trumping' your opponent is one of rhyme's delights. When used in this way it reveals itself as a game, a pastime: Berowne admits that he has been speaking 'for barbarism' against 'that angel knowledge' like any university debater. You can still say that rhyme is the 'sound of having the answer', but here it runs to no greater depths than coming up with the answer to a crossword puzzle.

Older dramatic rhythms surfacing in Love's Labour's Lost

Shakespeare is clearly not worried by Marlowe's suggestion that from now on these 'jigging veins of rhyming mother-wits' should be banished from the stage. Shakespeare is not going to give up on all this exuberant and witty rhyming. But notice also that Marlowe with his word 'jigging' is also referring to *rhythms* that he found equally displeasing. What is he taking a swipe at here? The answer is that the plays that preceded Marlowe and Shakespeare were not only written in rhyme, they were also frequently written in lines that were not pentameters and in rhythms that were decidedly non-iambic.

Here are a few lines from *Ralph Roister Doister*, a comedy which was probably written about the middle of the sixteenth century, shortly before the time that Marlowe and Shakespeare were born. Ralph is in love and he is asking Mathew to help him win the lady of his dreams. The rhymes will cause you no problems, but as you sound it out, the rhythms might surprise you.

> RALPH. I am utterly dead unless I have my desire.
> MATHEW. Where be the bellows that blew this sudden fire?
> RALPH. I hear she is worth a thousand pound and more.
> MATHEW. Yea, but learn this one lesson of me afore:
>   An hundred pound of marriage-money, doubtless,
>   Is ever thirty pound sterling, or somewhat less;
>   So that her thousand pound, if she be thrifty,
>   Is much near about two hundred and fifty.

Rhythms like these are to be found in some of Shakespeare's plays – *Love's Labour's Lost* for one – and so we should work out how to deal with them.

In fact the variety of rhythms, and the lengths of verse lines found in this comedy, might well lead us to the conclusion that Shakespeare is defiantly and happily ignoring Marlowe's likes and dislikes, and wanting to show the world just what he can do with rhyme. For besides the *iambic* pentameter rhyming verse of Berowne's we have been looking at, you can find in *Love's Labour's Lost* examples of *Doggerel Verse*, *Trochaic Verse*, the delightfully named *Poulter's Measure*, *Fourteeners*, *Sixteeners*, and several more varieties as well. None of these will cause you much trouble, though the 140 or so lines that are in a rhythm similar to those lines from *Ralph Roister Doister* may take a little time to master – but once you have, you'll discover a rhythm emerging that delivers joy and delight.

Anapests in Love's Labour's Lost

As soon as Berowne has signed up to the King's decrees for the Academy, he points out to the other three that somehow they have forgotten that the Princess of France, and three of her ladies, are coming to visit on an embassy from the King of France, her father. But Berowne and the others have just signed up to having nothing to do with women for the next three years. So immediately they have to forgo one of their vows and the young men and women are obliged to meet, at the end of which meeting it is clear that the men, at least, have become quite enamoured of the women. And it is the Princess's attendant lord, Boyet, who points out to her that the King of Navarre, Ferdinand, has fallen for her.

Boyet does so in an extended passage of rhyming verse, but you'll soon realise that the underlying rhythm here is not iambic. See if you can discover the rhythm for yourself – basically it is the same rhythm as those eight lines from *Ralph Roister Doister*. Just look at the lines – say them instinctively as you feel they should be said and this delightful rhythm should just reveal itself to you.

> BOYET. If my observation (which very seldom lies
>   By the heart's still rhetoric, disclosed with eyes)
>   Deceive me not now, Navarre is infected.
> PRINCESS. With what?
> BOYET. With that which we lovers entitle affected.
> PRINCESS. Your reason?
> BOYET. Why all his behaviours did make their retire,
>   To the court of his eye, peeping thorough desire.
>   His heart like an agate with your print impress'd,
>   Proud with his form, in his eye pride express'd.
>   His tongue all impatient to speak and not see,

Did stumble with haste in his eye-sight to be,
All senses to that sense did make their repair,
To feel only looking on fairest of fair:
Me thought all his senses were lock'd in his eye,
As jewels in crystal for some prince to buy.
Who tend'ring their own worth from where they were glass'd,
Did point you to buy them along as you pass'd.
His face's own margent did quote such amazes,
That all eyes saw his eyes enchanted with gazes.
I'll give you Aquitaine, and all that is his,
An you give him for my sake, but one loving kiss.

Love's Labour's Lost: Act 2, Scene 1

Did you get it? Each line has four rather than five stresses, and it is not iambic, as the rhythm running through each line is made up of three beats rather than two: two short or unstressed syllables are followed by one long or stressed syllable. These are called *anapests*. There is some slight variation from line to line, but the last line has its full quota of twelve syllables and four stresses.

An you **give** him for **my** sake, but **one** loving **kiss**.

– which is almost identical to the rhythm of that first line taken from *Ralph Roister Doister*:

I am **utterly dead** unless I **have** my **desire**.

(except that this has a thirteenth syllable – the second 'I' – which in saying it, gets swallowed up by the 'unless'). On the other hand, some of the other lines from *Love's Labour's Lost* have *less* than twelve syllables, in which case, if there are only eleven syllables, the first stress in the line will fall on the second rather than the third syllable, as in this line:

Did **point** you to **buy** them along as you **pass'd**.

But the line still has the same effect: it dances in the same way, and the four stresses remain constant. Now you see what the rhythm is, you might need to go back and sound it all out again.

We certainly can't dignify this by calling it 'the sound of having the answer'. It's certainly the sound of being very clever; also it sounds funny – it's a comic rhythm. I'd like to call it 'the sound of having a laugh'. We instantly realise that the speaker is being light-hearted; that his aim is to amuse, even if the Princess's own reaction is somewhat more ambiguous. As she exits, she says, maintaining the same jokey rhyming rhythm:

> PRINCESS. Come **to** our pavilion, Bo**yet** is dis**pos**'d.
>
> BOYET. But to speak that in words, which his eye hath disclos'd.
> I only have made a mouth of his eye,
> By adding a tongue, which I know will not l**ie**.
>
> ROSALINE. Thou art an old love-monger, and speakest skilfull**y**.
>
> MARIA. He is Cupid's grandfather, and learns news of him.
>
> ROSALINE. Then was Venus like her mother, for her father is but grim.
>
> BOYET. Do you hear, my mad wenches?
>
> MARIA.   No.
> BOYET.   What then, do you see?
>
> ROSALINE. Aye, our way to be gone.
> BOYET.   You are too hard for me.
>   *Exeunt.*

So the girls continue this gleeful banter, proving in their own rhyming and quick-wittedness that they are quite a match for Boyet. Here of course the rhyming is a game, and all the participants know that they have to make a conscious effort to find fitting rhymes and rhythms to keep the game going.

But why is the rhythm intrinsically funny? I think it's similar to the way we somehow find penguins delightful and funny all at once. It's the way they walk. It's like us, but not like us. In the same way, we recognise these anapests as a regular rhythm, but it's not the way we normally talk: it's certainly not the rhythm of our own heartbeats. Shakespeare must have heard these rhythms in the plays he watched when he was growing up and realised from the audiences' reactions that here was a comic rhythm that was infectious and made people feel happy.

Actually we came across a line written in this rhythm back in Chapter 8. At the time I let it pass as prose. It was a line of Enobarbus's when he was trying to undermine the seriousness of the meeting between Antony and Caesar. At one point he said,

> That **truth** should be silent, I had **al**most for**got**.

It's the same rhythm and it's just deliciously cheeky: 'He's having a laugh.'

While anapests are mostly found in Shakespeare's early plays like *Love's Labour's Lost*, *The Comedy of Errors* or *The Taming of the Shrew*, there are two such lines right at the end of *King Lear*, written a decade later.

King Lear: *the final lines*

Besides giving you something specific to be on the lookout for, this exercise will give us an excuse to look at the last twenty-odd lines of this giant of a play: the play that some consider to be the greatest that Shakespeare wrote. And as you search for these two anapestic lines, I want you to notice, at the same time, how this vast, panoramic play ends with a passage that is *almost all made up of monosyllabic, simple words.* Monosyllabic lines, such as many of these are, are found throughout all Shakespeare's writing, and monosyllabic lines must never be rushed. So remember this as you sound this scene out.[6]

We have briefly met Lear, Edgar, Kent and Cordelia in Chapter 9. But much has happened since then. Edgar has killed his half-brother, the wicked Edmund, in a duel, and Edgar has also reported that Kent, who has been in disguise for most of the play, is close to death. Goneril, Lear's eldest daughter, has just committed suicide shortly after she fatally poisoned her own sister, Regan. Albany, husband to Goneril and one of the few honourable people in the play, is also on stage at the end. Now Lear carries in the body of his dead daughter, Cordelia, telling those on stage how she has been hanged after their army has been defeated.

> KING LEAR. And my poor fool is hang'd: no, no, no life?
>
> Why should a dog, a horse, a rat, have life,
> And thou no breath at all?
>
>   Thou'lt come no more,
> Never, never, never, never, never.
>
> Pray you undo this button.
>
>   Thank you sir,
>
> Do you see this? Look on her? Look her lips,
> Look there, look there.
>
>   *He dies.*
>
> EDGAR.   He faints, my lord, my lord.
>
> KENT. Break heart, I prithee break.
>
> EDGAR.   Look up my lord.
>
> KENT. Vex not his ghost, O let him pass, he hates him,
> That would upon the rack of this tough world
> Stretch him out longer.
>
> EDGAR.   He is gone indeed.
>
> KENT. The wonder is, he hath endur'd so long,
> He but usurp'd his life.[7]

ALBANY. Bear them from hence, our present business
    Is general woe:

               Friends of my soul, you twain,
    Rule in this realm, and the gor'd state sustain.

KENT. I have a journey sir, shortly to go,
    My master calls me, I must not say no.

EDGAR. The weight of this sad time we must obey,
    Speak what we feel, not what we ought to say:
    The oldest hath borne most, we that are young,
    Shall never see so much, nor live so long.

The play ends with eight lines of rhyme – four couplets in which Albany, Kent and Edgar bring their parts to a conclusive summing up of their respective positions. Albany renounces any power he might command by handing over the reins of government to Kent and Edgar, but Kent is dying and so Edgar is left to bear 'the weight of this sad time'. And in so doing he brings the play to its conclusion with his final and 'conclusive' rhyme. I hope you found the simplicity and clarity of the writing absolutely at one with the trauma with which the play ends and were never tempted to rush through any of these monosyllabically filled lines. I'm also hoping that you found the anapestic lines. Here they are and here's that rhythm:

    I have a **journey** sir, **shortly** to **go**,
    My master **calls** me, I **must** not say **no**.[8]

    I'm not going to suggest that this couplet is all about 'having a laugh'. This is unlike *Love's Labour's Lost*, though the rhythm of one of Boyet's lines, that we were looking at earlier, is identical,

    Proud with his **form**, in his eye pride **express'd**.

The 'sound' of Kent's lines differ from *most* anapestic lines because they both begin with a stressed syllable (as does this line of Boyet's) which immediately makes for a more *arresting* statement. Kent's lines command our attention because of their *oddness* in this situation; the lines have a cryptic sound to them. Kent is dying, speaking in words redolent of some ancient understanding. But the anapestic rhythm might also suggest to us that he is jesting at death's approach, which maybe is what the truly wise man does.

    Anapests were a well-loved rhythm written for the comics earlier in the sixteenth century. The play *Cambyses* was first published about 1569 when Shakespeare and Marlowe were just five years old. It may have been written even earlier. In it the comic character Ambidexter speaks to the audience in much this same rhythm. Here he's just witnessed Meretrix, a prostitute, beating up three soldiers.

> AMBIDEXTER. O the passion of God! be they **here** still or **no**?
> I **durst** not **abide** to see **her** beat them **so**!
> I **may** say to **you** I was **in** such a **fright**,
> Body of **me**, I see the **hair** of my **head** stand up**right**.

Making a contrast with Ambidexter's speedy, comic dialogue, the non-comic plot of the play is written in iambic lines but not in iambic pentameters. Instead we have rhyming iambic lines of fourteen syllables, with seven stresses, and are simply called 'fourteeners'. In the days before Marlowe and Shakespeare this was a rhythm that many plays were written in.

Fourteeners in Cambyses

The play tells the story of the sixth-century BC Persian tyrant Cambyses. In the play he kills his own brother, and his wife, and cruelly shoots to death the young son of a courtier whose father had offended him by telling him that he drank too much. Here is the tyrant having killed the courtier's young son in full view of the audience; and if that is not enough, Cambyses then has the boy's heart cut out of his body. The stage management will have been busy!

Now have a go at these 'fourteeners' for yourself.

> CAMBYSES. Behold Praxaspes, thy son's own heart. O how well
> the same was hit!
> After this wine to do this deed I thought it very fit.
> Esteem thou mayst right well thereby no drunkard is the king,
> That in the midst of all his cups could do this valiant thing.
>
> My lord and knight, on me attend, to palace we will go
> And leave him here to take his son when we are gone him fro.*

We are a long way away here from the sound of the plays of Shakespeare. But it's interesting to see what difference another four syllables makes to the sound of the lines. Though still iambic they completely change the feel of the line, though of course the rhyme makes a huge difference as well. I think they sound 'theatrical' rather than 'natural'; and my guess is that the audiences felt that they sounded both outrageously grand and somewhat

fro – from

'tongue-in-cheek' at the same time. The boastful rhymes of the tyrant no doubt invited the audience to hiss the villain for all his wicked ways. Listening to this I think you'd always be very conscious of the 'theatricality' of the play and maybe aware that the actors were taking especially deep breaths in order to master the longer lines, as I think you might have had to do when you sounded them out.

These older rhythms, line-lengths and incessant rhymes had been around for some time and would have been around longer but for the arrival of blank pentameter verse and the growing sophistication of the audiences. They had survived because they made for 'easy listening'. You knew where you were with them and the rhymes made it easier to follow what was being said.

Fourteeners in Love's Labour's Lost

However, even these old fourteeners get used by Shakespeare on a couple of occasions in *Love's Labour's Lost*. One of these is towards the end of the play when the comic characters present a pageant called 'The Nine Worthies' before the French Princess and the young ladies and gentlemen. The pageant never makes it through to its intended end, because a fight breaks out between two of the performers. So we in the audience only get to see five of the nine Worthies and most of them are not allowed to finish their parts because of the raucous behaviour of Berowne and the rest of the on-stage audience.

Costard the clown presents the opening Worthy, Pompey the Great. His lines are written in fourteeners with seven stresses. He is then followed by Sir Nathanial, the curate, who presents Alexander, whose form is appropriately an '*alexandrine*', or a line of six stresses. The lines of the last two Worthies to make it to the stage are reduced to five and four stresses respectively.

It's perhaps no wonder that the show fails to be completed. But here at least is Pompey as played by Costard. He gets his first line wrong, however:

> I Pompey am, Pompey surnam'd the Big.

The on-stage audience tells him he should have said 'the Great' (which indeed supplies the word for his first rhyme), and then he continues, now with his three 'jigging' fourteeners:

That oft in field, with targe and shield, did make my foe to sweat:
And travelling along this coast, I here am come by chance,
And lay my arms before the legs of this sweet lass of France.

Love's Labour's Lost: Act 5, Scene 2

So in Shakespeare's *Love's Labour's Lost* many of these older forms of rhyming verse appear again to delight and amuse; to mock the past in both subject matter and poetic form, but to honour it as well. We are given a colourful display of wit, a gorgeous celebration of being young and lively: almost the opposite to that 'sound of sincerity' that we know *blank* verse to be. Doesn't this make rhymed verse of this kind more like prose – its witty mask hiding true feelings? Well, yes, it does.

Rhymed verse sometimes has a similar effect to prose.

To demonstrate this, in Shakespeare's early play *The Two Gentlemen of Verona* he writes a scene in rhyme, while in *The Merchant of Venice*, written a few years later, he writes a very similar scene in prose. In both of them a young woman discusses with her female companion which of her many suitors she should show favour to. First we meet Julia from *The Two Gentlemen of Verona*, then we catch up with Portia again, whom we've met before.

JULIA. What think'st thou of the fair Sir Eglamour?

LUCETTA. As of a knight, well-spoken, neat, and fine;
But were I you, he never should be mine.

JULIA. What think'st thou of the rich Mercatio?

LUCETTA. Well of his wealth; but of himself, so, so.

JULIA. What think'st thou of the gentle Proteus?

LUCETTA. Lord, Lord: to see what folly reigns in us.

JULIA. How now? what means this passion at his name?

LUCETTA. Pardon dear madam, 'tis a passing shame,
That I (unworthy body as I am)
Should censure thus on lovely gentlemen.

The Two Gentlemen of Verona: Act 1, Scene 2

In the scene from *The Merchant of Venice* it is the maid, Nerissa, at the same point in the story, who lists Portia's suitors and Portia who wittily describes them; now, however, not in rhymed verse but in prose.

PORTIA. I pray thee over-name them, and as thou namest them,
I will describe them, and according to my description
level at my affection.

NERISSA. First there is the Neapolitan prince.

PORTIA. Ay that's a colt indeed, for he doth nothing but talk of
his horse, and he makes it a great appropriation to his own
good parts that he can shoe him himself: I am much afraid
my lady his mother play'd false with a smith [...]

NERISSA. What say you then to Falconbridge, the young baron
of England?

PORTIA. You know I say nothing to him, for he understands not
me, nor I him: he hath neither Latin, French, nor Italian,
and you will come into the court and swear that I have a
poor penny-worth in the English: he is a proper man's
picture, but alas who can converse with a dumb show?

The Merchant of Venice: Act 1, Scene 2

Both Julia and Portia initiate this 'naming of the suitors' because they
really want to find a way, without making it too obvious, to talk about the
men they are desperate to talk about, Proteus and Bassanio.

Portia's witty prose, I would suggest, is hiding much uncertainty and
heart-ache beneath her jokes. And she has another problem: that Bassanio
has not yet arrived in Belmont to declare himself a suitor, though she has
met him on a previous visit. So she is dependent on Nerissa to bring up
his name, which later in the scene she obligingly does.

Lucetta's rhymed verse similarly mocks these suitors, but mocks her
young lady even more as she so clearly sees through Julia's ploys to bring
up Proteus's name. The ability to rhyme on the spot, as Lucetta does, is a
sign of her cleverness; and the way Lucetta pounces on Julia's words, and
rhymes with them, has the effect of outsmarting Julia, and points up Julia's
naivety in contrast to her, Lucetta's, knowingness. She 'caps' her. But it's
clear that both the rhymed verse and the prose are ways to release the wit
in these so similar scenes, as well as what lies behind them.

The differences between Marlowe and Shakespeare

For Shakespeare rhyme and different rhythms can happily recall fond
times past. As of course he does to great effect in the play about Pyramus
and Thisbe that the Mechanicals present at the end of *A Midsummer
Night's Dream*.

But Marlowe always wanted to stress the 'now' rather than the past. He
had a remarkable vision of what theatre could achieve and he both realised
that in his own plays and showed others the way forward. Yet in some ways

he is more of a poet than Shakespeare, insofar as he seems always to be searching for the perfect line.

In *Dr Faustus*, when Faustus sees Helen of Troy, whom he has magically conjured up, he says:

> Was this the face that launch'd a thousand ships?
> And burnt the topless towers of Ilium?
> Sweet Helen, make me immortal with a kiss…
>
> I will be Paris, and for love of thee,
> Instead of Troy shall Wittenberg be sack'd,
> And I will combat with weak Menelaus,
> And wear thy colours on my plumed crest:
> Yea I will wound Achilles in the heel,
> And then return to Helen for a kiss.
>
> Oh thou art fairer than the evening's air,
> Clad in the beauty of a thousand stars.

These are beautiful blank verse lines indeed.

But when writing poetry rather than plays, Marlowe rhymes as others do. I'm going to quote two lines from his epic poem *Hero and Leander* because Shakespeare quotes the second of these, no doubt by way of homage to his murdered contemporary, in *As You Like It*.

> Where both deliberate, the love is slight;
> Whoever lov'd that lov'd not at first sight?[9]

In Marlowe's plays, however, there are very few rhymes; so fewer seductive moments, such as Shakespeare weaves into *A Midsummer Night's Dream*, *Macbeth* and *The Tempest*. And this despite the fact that in *Dr Faustus* he wrote a play about a character who sells his soul to the devil so that he can study magic. It is Faustus who conjures up Helen and does all sorts of magic tricks during the course of the play, but we feel in watching the play that Helen is just a stage illusion, if we compare her, say, to the ghosts and magical spirits who walk in Shakespeare's plays.

Marlowe wanted to see what Man could achieve without the aid of magical forces; without resorting to the seductive power of rhyme. He takes our breath away with the daring of his characters and the power of his blank verse, but he always wants us to be watching critically, rather than being lulled into a reverie by rhyme. So he wins our admiration, but maybe not our love.

By contrast Shakespeare always wants to delight us as well as to shock and move us, and rhymes and cheeky rhythms are some of the ways he achieves that. But look again at the closing lines of our chapter heading. Speaking of Tamburlaine in that Prologue Marlowe writes:

> View but his picture in this tragic glass,
> And then applaud his fortunes as you please.

There seems something deliberate about how resolutely those words 'glass' and 'please' stubbornly refuse to rhyme, then as now. Marlowe wants us to make up our own minds about his protagonist; there is something about rhyme which wants to tell us what to think and undermines our critical judgements. Can our rhymes always be trusted? That is the question my next chapter seeks to address.

Thirteen

Trusting Rhyme
Twelfth Night and All's Well that Ends Well

Prove true imagination, oh prove true,
That I dear brother, be now ta'en for you.
Twelfth Night: Act 3, Scene 4

Then shalt thou give me with thy kingly hand
What husband in thy power I will command:
All's Well that End's Well: Act 2, Scene 1

Shakespeare always found a place for rhyme. It was too delightful, too powerful a force – so why banish it from his plays? It is true that the plays of his that contain the most rhyme were written around those early years between 1594–6. And quite a number of the rhymed lines that occur in the later plays are accounted for by the increasing number of songs that appear in them, notably in *As You Like It*, *Twelfth Night*, *The Winter's Tale* and *The Tempest*.[1]

However, important passages of rhyme occur in some of the later plays too. And while we'll find rhymes bringing with them more 'bolts from the blue', or arising out of intense feelings of unrequited love, or other unful-filled desires, we will find in *Twelfth Night*, in *All's Well that Ends Well*, and in a later chapter, *Macbeth*, rhymes that bring with them a sense of ambivalence, as if rhymes might be a trap into which we could be misled, fooled, even destroyed.

While Christopher Marlowe largely shunned the beguiling magic that rhyme brings in its wake, because it undermined the audience's judgements, Shakespeare now discovers a new dramatic situation to exploit, in leaving his characters unsure whether the rhymes they hear are truly insights or deceptions.

Twelfth Night: *Viola's 'bolt from the blue'*

Twelfth Night probably dates from 1601: it might well be the very next play that Shakespeare wrote after *Hamlet*. And though it's a bit soon to be talking about another 'breakthrough' play, the special atmosphere that surrounds *Twelfth Night* means that it has to be credited as such.

The story focuses on a pair of twins, Viola and Sebastian. Their father has probably recently died, and they are on a voyage, to where we don't know, but the first thing we do know about them is that their ship is wrecked. Viola survives the shipwreck, but she fears Sebastian, her brother, must have drowned. Coming ashore in a strange country Viola decides to dress as a young man, partly so that she might get employment for herself with the local ruler, Count Orsino, of whom she remembers her father talking. Orsino agrees to take the 'boy' on, and almost immediately he is sending Viola to woo the Countess Olivia on his behalf. Viola makes some initial objections: that she'll not be admitted, or if she is, she won't be listened to. But eventually she agrees to go and says to him,

> I'll do my best
> To woo your lady:

but then as Orsino leaves her alone on stage a thought strikes her:

> yet a barful* strife,
> Whoe'er I woo, my self would be his wife.

Twelfth Night: Act 1, Scene 4

Her couplet ends the scene, but to call it simply a 'concluding couplet' would be to undervalue what happens here. To me it seems that, like Romeo, like Juliet, Viola experiences here a 'bolt from the blue'. And I'm describing it in this way because I believe she has not been aware of her true feelings towards Orsino – until now.

For the last three days (that's how long she's been at Orsino's court) she'll have been getting used to her new environment: learning the ropes;

barful – full of obstacles

convincing everyone of her maleness; pretending in a way to be her own dear lost brother. Now at the moment of setting out on her first assignment she senses that it couldn't be a more difficult one. 'A barful strife' indicates that she's going to be subjected to two contrary forces. What are they, she might still be wondering, even as the thought strikes her? On the one hand, as she has said, she is going to do her 'best' to win Olivia's hand in marriage for Orsino; on the other she realises as she rhymes 'wife' with 'strife' that she wants to marry him herself!

Now of course these lines, as with most lines, could be played, and have been played, many ways, so it doesn't have to be this 'bolt from the blue' as I call it: Viola might have realised what was happening to her sometime earlier and is now just wanting to let us know the secret that's in her heart. But there's something about the *brevity of her utterance* which make me feel she's been taken unawares.

So while this may be the shortest passage I'm ever going to ask you to sound out, try these lines of Viola's both ways: first try it as simply a bit of delicious information to share with the audience; then, as if the knowledge of what you feel for Orsino only hits you *as you say* that second line.

Which did you prefer? I hope the second, as the first of these options seems to me to strike a rather jaunty note, as if Viola might even wink at us as she says it. That is not Viola as I see her, and so I vote for option two. I feel this rhyme hits her with the force of a shock. But she has no time to consider the matter further, as four or five attendants are already waiting, on Orsino's orders, to escort her to Olivia's. But it's the brevity of the moment that is so arresting: overwhelming for *you* playing the part; and exciting, delightful and amusing for *us*, because we are there with Viola *as she experiences it*. And I would go further still, and say that playing it in this way is what the rhyme is directing us to do.

In these plays rhyme pinpoints the exact moment when a thought strikes us. In Shakespeare most rhymes are monosyllabic. The time it takes to say one of these monosyllabic words is a fraction of a second. It is the same with any moment of discovery. The moment between not knowing something and knowing it is incalculably small. So these rhymes are like the proverbial light bulb being switched on. The rhyme chimes at the exact moment of discovery, which is when the second word is sounded.

As the rhyme sounds out, the discovery is made.

Despite the fact that she now knows she's in love with Orsino, Viola, being the remarkable character that she is, goes to Olivia's and indeed tries her 'best' to woo her on Orsino's behalf.

The ambivalence of Olivia's rhyming in Twelfth Night

Olivia and Viola have much in common – even their names are created out of the same five letters – both are probably of an age, and Olivia has recently had to contend with the deaths of both her father and her brother; though, unlike Viola, she has been suddenly left responsible for the management of a large estate.[2] She wants nothing to do with Orsino and his attempts to woo her. She has declared to the world that she is in mourning and intends to remain so for the foreseeable future. Olivia therefore rebuffs all Viola's attempts to interest her in Orsino's love for her; however, in the exchanges between them, the disguised Viola speaks so eloquently about love and so fulsomely and honestly about Olivia's beauty, that Olivia falls in love with Viola – or rather with Cesario, the name Viola has assumed in her male disguise.

By the end of the interview Olivia, who possibly only allowed the 'boy' admittance to her house to relieve the boredom of her morning, to her utter amazement can't conceive of a life without him. She ends the scene with these two couplets, and you must now sound them out:

> I do I know not what, and fear to find
> Mine eye too great a flatterer for my mind:

> Fate, show thy force, ourselves we do not owe,*
> What is decreed, must be: and be this so.

> *Twelfth Night*: Act 1, Scene 5

Just like Viola's lines at the end of the previous scene, these also give us much more than a conventional rhyming conclusion; they are lines that assail Olivia with the force of a visitation: they make her question whether she knows what is happening to her or not; and they conclude with a wish that Fate can do with her as Fate wishes, so long as she ends up with this beautiful young man. But no doubt as she hears the two couplets rhyming, she too senses that the words are revealing to her some truth.

But while we in the audience are in no doubt that Viola loves Orsino and that therefore the rhyme that ended her scene with him was telling

owe – own

her a truth, we are also in no doubt that Olivia has been mistaken, because we know that she has fallen for a girl in boy's clothes. Olivia has, with her rhyming, been given an 'answer', but it is ambivalent. It's one that will turn out to be partly true and partly false, because, as you may have known, at the end of the play Olivia will marry Viola's lost twin brother, Sebastian. So we could consider the 'answer' she has received to be 'ambivalent'. She is somewhat mistaken, and being 'somewhat mistaken' is what a comedy – which this play is – is all about.

Olivia v. Juliet

Six or seven years separate the writing of *Romeo and Juliet* and *Twelfth Night* and if we compare Juliet's earlier 'bolts from the blue' with Olivia's, you will see how by 1601 Shakespeare's characters have become more multi-layered, more complex. Here to remind us are Juliet's four lines of rhyming verse:

> My only love sprung from my only hate,
> Too early seen, unknown, and known too late,
> Prodigious birth of love it is to me,
> That I must love a loathed enemy.

Juliet's lines are so clear-sighted: no doubts creep in here. Whereas Olivia's four lines are riddled with doubt:

> I do I know not what, and fear to find
> Mine eye too great a flatterer for my mind:
> Fate, show thy force, ourselves we do not owe,
> What is decreed, must be: and be this so.

Of course the situation and the tone of the two scenes are very different, and one is in no way 'better' than the other; nevertheless, it shows us that Shakespeare is now drawn to explore more complex characters who are more aware of their own vulnerability. Let's consider what happens after these lines of Olivia's.

The way scene follows scene in Shakespeare

Frequently something hangs in the balance after such a rhymed conclusion; holding you there as you weigh up the implications of the 'answer' which has brought your character to this new state of awareness. For the audience it's as if a 'snapshot' has been taken of the character in that moment when their world has changed from how it was before. And for the actors such moments are not to be rushed.

Concluding rhymes momentarily freeze the action.

The first thing that happens *is* such a moment of suspended animation – Olivia contemplating her new future and we in the audience wondering what will happen next. But at the same time the actors for the next scene are *already* making their entrance.

In Shakespeare's day there were no lighting cues as we have now; and certainly no falling curtains or blackouts to separate one scene from another and facilitate a scene change hidden from the eyes of the audience. Everything was – and still is at the Globe, where I work – out in the open. So Shakespeare's texts are written in such a way that the action is continuous and one scene not only follows another, but overlaps the other. In order to maintain the energy of the play, as one scene ends and the last line sounds, the first line of the next scene receives its cue.[3] So as actors are leaving the stage after one scene, others are already entering, already speaking. Characters in Shakespeare are usually in mid-dialogue as a scene begins.

So it is here: after Olivia's couplet, two actors enter. The one following behind is the speaker and his line is,

> Will you stay no longer: nor will you not that I go with you.

Who is the character that is being spoken to? Is it Viola? Viola, who only exited some twenty lines earlier and is now making a re-entrance? It looks like Viola, but then we realise it's not Viola, but rather her twin brother Sebastian, who is dressed identically, and who until now we have not seen.

Olivia has been somewhat mistaken. She has fallen in love with Cesario, but actually it's Viola's performance *as* Sebastian she has fallen for. Which way it will turn out still hangs in the balance, though it seems, by the way that Sebastian enters at just this point, as if 'Fate' has responded to Olivia's final words, and is about to show its 'force'.

> Fate, show thy force, ourselves we do not owe,
> What is decreed, must be: and be this so.

While Olivia and Sebastian will have to wait another three acts before they are actually playing a scene together, for a moment, as she turns to make her exit *after* he has entered, *we* are able to see them sharing the stage together and ponder what is to come. Such is the magic of theatre.

Viola and Olivia: the confusions deepen

Before Olivia and Sebastian finally meet in Act 4, Viola and Olivia meet twice more in Act 3. Towards the end of the first of these meetings their blank verse gives way to rhyme as their feelings become more intense. This is another of those scenes in which the changing 'forms of address' gives us valuable clues as to the way Olivia tries and fails to control her unrequited love for Cesario – and I will again mark these key changes with italics. (Viola uses the deferential 'you' form throughout) We join the scene about halfway through:

> OLIVIA. Be not afraid good youth, I will not have *you*,
>   And yet when wit and youth is come to harvest,
>   *Your* wife is like to reap a proper man:
>   There lies *your* way, due west.
>
> VIOLA.   Then westward ho:
>   Grace and good disposition attend your ladyship:
>   You'll nothing madam to my lord, by me:
>
> OLIVIA. Stay: I pri*thee* tell me what *thou* think'st of me?
>
> VIOLA. That you do think you are not what you are.
>
> OLIVIA. If I think so, I think the same of *you*.

The scene begins with Olivia using 'you' to Viola, but then, when Viola is about to leave and Olivia asks her to stay, we have her first switch into using 'thou'. You could interpret this switch as Olivia now 'pulling rank' on Orsino's servant, commanding him to stay and answer her. But I don't think it can be that. It sounds like a cry from the heart as she sees 'him' leaving, declaring her love for him as she does so. If so this is a rather desperate gamble on Olivia's part. And Viola's cool reply has the effect of moving Olivia back to the formal, more reserved 'you' form and in this way the scene continues for a while:

> VIOLA. Then think you right: I am not what I am.
>
> OLIVIA. I would you were, as I would have you be.
>
> VIOLA. Would it be better madam, than I am?
>   I wish it might, for now I am your fool.

OLIVIA. O what a deal of scorn, looks beautiful?
In the contempt and anger of his lip,

And then as Olivia's speech continues we move into rhyme, and shortly after she switches back to using the intimate 'thou' form again:

A murd'rous guilt shows not it self more soon,
Than love that would seem hid: Love's night, is noon.

Cesario, by the roses of the spring,
By maid-hood, honour, truth, and everything,
I love *thee* so, that maugre* all *thy* pride,
Nor wit, nor reason, can my passion hide:

Do not extort *thy* reasons from this clause,
For that I woo, *thou* therefore hast no cause:
But rather reason thus, with reason fetter;*
Love sought, is good: but given unsought, is better.

VIOLA. By innocence I swear, and by my youth,
I have one heart, one bosom, and one truth,
And that no woman has, nor never <u>none</u>
Shall mistress be of it, save I a<u>lone</u>.

And so adieu good madam, never more,
Will I my master's tears to you deplore.

OLIVIA. Yet come again: for *thou* perhaps mayst <u>move</u>
That heart which now abhors, to like his <u>love</u>.

Twelfth Night: Act 3, Scene 1

The first couplet is one of those 'bolts from the blue', played by Olivia as an 'aside' to the audience:

A murd'rous guilt shows not itself more soon,
Than love that would seem hid: Love's night, is noon.

Olivia has had another of those eureka moments: as she gazes on Viola's angry 'lip', she knows that she is looking at someone who is in love. Olivia is right; but again the moment is filled with ambivalence, because unfortunately, it's not with her that Viola is in love, but Orsino. But this false insight now encourages her to make a (rhymed) declaration of her love, shifting again into the 'thou' form as she turns to Viola, saying:

Cesario, by the roses of the spring,
By maid-hood, honour, truth, and everything,

maugre – in spite of
fetter – bind yourself

> I love *thee* so, that maugre all *thy* pride,
> Nor wit, nor reason, can my passion hide:

As we saw with Helena in *A Midsummer Night's Dream*, these rhymes, unlike the rarer 'bolts from the blue', come from an unrequited *inner* desire. She is desperate that her feelings should be reciprocated, and Olivia now believes she has seen in Cesario's face that 'he' loves her, but she suspects that, because he's a servant, he dares not *acknowledge* his love for her. So she creates, with her rhyming speech that follows the lines quoted above, an 'answer' to this problem, and her rhymes make everything sound so positive and so simple.

Such a nakedly unconditional speech as Olivia's has to be answered as fulsomely, and so Viola's rhymed speech follows. Neither are 'trying' to rhyme, but their 'need' to respond to the emotional intensity of their situation organises the shaping of their thoughts into rhymed sequences.

Playing these characters you should feel this physically, as if you are carrying a weighty burden close to your heart that you want to be freed from. Feel this within you and the rhymes will help you to reach the pitch of intensity required.[4] And if you 'play' these rhymes well, they will repay you tenfold. They will give to Olivia's words of love a desperate hopefulness, and an innocence of expression. To Viola, the rhymes will give her words a more heart-heavy sound revealing her impossible situation. Not 'by the roses of the spring' for her, but 'my master's tears to you deplore'.

Now is your moment to sound this scene out, and if you have a partner to play it with, so much the better. You can then swap roles and play it through twice.

Olivia meets Viola twice more, and in both scenes she switches between the 'you' and 'thou' forms as she tries to control her feelings and gives way to them in turn. Olivia also, of course, finally meets Sebastian, Viola's twin brother, stopping a duel between him and her uncle, Sir Toby Belch – though at this stage in the play Viola doesn't know that her brother has survived the shipwreck.

Olivia's very first words to Sebastian, using the 'thou' form, are such as might be said to a long-lost lover, because of course Olivia falsely (and amusingly) *believes* she has spoken to him many times before.

OLIVIA.   I pri**thee** gentle friend,
     Let **thy** fair wisdom, not **thy** passion sway

> In this uncivil, and unjust extent
> Against **thy** peace. Go with me to my house,
>
> *Twelfth Night*: Act 4, Scene 1

No wonder that Sebastian, who has never seen this beautiful woman till now, and hearing her speak like this, thinks that he might be dreaming.

Viola's impossible situation

Viola's position is 'impossible' because she can't afford to drop the male disguise which has made Olivia fall in love with her, and has by now had the same effect on Orsino too – though for him there is the added confusion that he believes he has fallen in love with a young boy. In the scene you've just sounded out, Viola comes close in her rhyming sequence to telling Olivia that she is a woman:

> I have one heart, one bosom, and one truth,
> And that no woman has, nor never none
> Shall mistress be of it, save I alone.

And in Act 2, Scene 4, which we will focus on in the next chapter, Viola has already made a similarly veiled suggestion to Orsino, saying to him, among other enigmatic statements:

> I am all the daughters of my father's house,
> And all the brothers too:

Just as Olivia seems lost in the ambivalences of her own situation, so too is Viola, and the reason Viola is so spell-bound is because she has virtually become her lost brother.

Now taking leave of Olivia after a further meeting between the two of them, Viola learns something that gives her hope that her twin brother Sebastian might not have drowned after all. On the way back to Orsino's, she gets involved in a duel with Sir Andrew Aguecheek. He's a cowardly fool, but Viola has been told he's an expert duellist. She still never contemplates dropping her disguise, and though terrified, she squares up to Sir Andrew. In the nick of time (though she is not actually in much danger) she is rescued by Antonio, who has three months earlier saved her twin brother Sebastian from the sea and now understandably takes Viola to be Sebastian. When she denies that she is in possession of a purse Antonio has lent Sebastian, he reacts angrily, calling her Sebastian to her face, before he is promptly taken away by officers who've come to arrest him for piracy. Viola has now heard her brother's name spoken and it produces five pairs of rhymed lines, or couplets, from her. The first is another moment of sudden understanding, the rhyme pinpointing that the 'answer' fully comes to her on that so single of words, 'I'.

> Me thinks his words do from such passion fly
> That he believes himself, so do not I:

The 'answer' of course is that Antonio has mistaken her for her brother, and so the second couplet, developing immediately out of the first, becomes her heartfelt wish that her instincts are not now fooling her with any false promises; rhymes after all always sound so true and comforting, that she prays that she is not now being deceived:

> Prove true imagination, O prove true,
> That I dear brother, be now ta'en for you.

So now she goes over the evidence again, sharing with the audience why Antonio might have mistaken her for Sebastian. And the evidence she produces seems to support her first instinctive response, not only because of the good reasons she advances, but also because her words still fall into rhyme, sounding to her as if she has to be in possession of the solution to this puzzle.

> He nam'd Sebastian: I my brother know
> Yet living in my glass:* even such, and so
> In favour was my brother, and he went
> Still in this fashion, colour, ornament,
> For him I imitate: O if it <u>prove</u>,
> Tempests are kind, and salt waves fresh in <u>love</u>.

Twelfth Night: Act 3, Scene 4

She is not trying to rhyme, though she may be half aware that her words once uttered are falling into couplets. She's certainly conscious that her thoughts sound so reassuring. So each of those little rhymes, as they fall from her lips, *know / so* and *went / ornament* seem to be saying to her: '*It's all true, he is alive.*'

Now put those five couplets together yourself and sound them out, discovering how the rhymes help to *release* and *shape* the expression of her joy, though it's a joy tempered by her fear that she might be jumping to a false conclusion.

---

glass – mirror

I hope you enjoyed playing those rhymes because it is one of the emotional high points of the play, especially because Viola's rhymes come accompanied by this degree of ambivalent uncertainty, while we in the audience know that her hopes for her brother's survival will eventually be realised. But there's another reason why her words rhyme and that is because Viola has been dealing in magic and what she has just revealed to us is what her 'spell' consists of.

Rhyme is the language of magic.

Her spell begins each day with her getting dressed in copies of her brother's clothes and as she does so seeing *his* reflection 'living' in her mirror. No doubt she then greets him, calling him Sebastian; but she must never mention his name to anyone else. For how could she? During the day she *is* him, walking and talking like him, despite her new name; as she says, she has been imitating him. And in pretending to be Sebastian she has made Olivia fall in love with him. The reason why she won't drop her disguise to avoid fighting the duel with Sir Andrew is because she knows that Sebastian would never run away from any challenge made to him, and so neither can she. So long as she is imitating him it is as if he is still alive, yet while she does so, her own life is on hold.

This also explains why in the final scene she endures (almost silently) all the reproaches that are heaped upon her, and why she has to risk losing Orsino's love, even her very life, because the magic (that now seems to be working) demands that she can only stop being Sebastian once he walks onto the stage and is reunited with her.

How moving all this is for us watching the play, but also what an interesting detail it is for any actor playing the part to consider; that she has been *imitating* Sebastian, living for him, keeping him alive. Viola has proved such a convincing man because she has been watching her twin brother growing up beside her all their short lives.

Sebastian was on the point of death after the shipwreck. It has taken Antonio three months to nurse him back to health, and maybe Viola's magic has helped as well. Once he is fully recovered, some instinct tells him, he must leave Antonio – in order to seek out Orsino, he says, but it's Viola he wants to find, and senses it will be at Orsino's court that he'll learn what has happened to her.[5] Rather wonderfully, once Sebastian arrives, he'll find Viola has created for him a world replete with a woman who already loves him, and a group of wastrels, Sir Andrew and his companions, who need to be sorted out by him.

If you grasp the opportunities that these rhymes give you, they open up for you those moments that are always the most thrilling to watch: magical moments, when a revelation, a change of direction, happens in front of us and in the twinkling of an eye. But now, in these later plays they come with this added ingredient: while actors should always enjoy playing these rhymes, the characters in the plays have to treat them with caution. Wholeheartedly believing that they have the 'answer' might be leading them astray.

Actors should welcome rhymes… but characters need to treat them with caution.

Rhyme is so comforting, but what if the assurances that rhymes seem to be giving us are leading us astray? They are for Helena, the central character in *All's Well that Ends Well.*

Rhyme in All's Well that Ends Well

We last met Helena in Chapter 6. There I outlined her story as to how she had fallen in love with Bertram, who certainly at that time had no similar feelings towards her. However, by saving the life of the dying King of France, she is allowed to choose Bertram as her husband. Once the marriage has been solemnised, Bertram, outraged by being forced into this wedding, deserts her. And it is only after many trials and tribulations that Helena becomes pregnant by Bertram, without him knowing he has ever slept with her, and thus saves her marriage.

The part of the story that we have not so far looked at is how Helena, a young girl of humble origins, manages to convince the dying King that she might be able to save his life. And she does it by harnessing the power of rhyme.

But while we are watching how Helena uses rhyme to gain her objectives, we must also look out for changes in the 'forms of address' – because in this scene they are as extraordinary as any we have seen so far. The first thing to notice is that when she finally comes into the King's presence (Act 2, Scene 1), his initial greeting to her is rather informal, because he uses the 'you' form to her, rather than the 'thou' form which kings frequently use to their subjects to assert their status:

KING. Now fair one, does **your** business follow us?

And once he's heard what she's come about and is about to decline her offer of help, he again uses same form, saying,

KING. We thank **you** maiden,

Helena then asks him, as he won't accept her help, at least to say something more to her before she leaves – in so doing she keeps the conversation between them alive. Immediately the King changes the form in which he is addressing her and starts to use the 'thou' form. This is where we have to use our judgements about what lies behind this change. It could be that the 'thou' form is an indication that he's now using his status and his power and telling her categorically that the interview is over. However, I think his move to 'thou' suggests the opposite: a growing fondness for this brave young girl, which, as with his initial use of the 'you' form, is also unusual.

> KING. I cannot give **thee** less to be call'd grateful:
> **Thou** thought'st to help me, and such thanks I give,
> As one near death to those that wish him live:
> But what at full I know, **thou** know'st no part,
> I knowing all my peril, **thou** no art.

The King's four rhyming lines of 'conclusion' are designed to indicate that there is nothing more to be said. But now comes the moment when Helena falls into rhyme to persuade him that isn't the case. With all the certainty of adolescence Helena now initiates a sequence of seventy or so lines of rhyming couplets. Her rhyming suggesting that she has 'the answer'. As we would expect, she is, as of now, using the polite 'you' form to the King:

> HELENA. What I can do, can do no hurt to <u>try</u>,
> Since **you** set up **your** rest 'gainst <u>remedy</u>:
>
> He that of greatest works is finisher,
> Oft does them by the weakest minister:
>
> So holy writ, in babes hath judgement shown,
> When judges have been babes; great floods have flown
> From simple sources: and great seas have dried
> When miracles have by the great'st been denied.
>
> Oft expectation fails, and most oft there[6]
> Where most it promises: and oft it hits,
> Where hope is coldest, and despair most fits.

(Once again I have underlined those words that would have been heard as rhymes in Shakespeare's day, but no longer to us.)

The King again says farewell with another 'concluding couplet' of his own. And, as you'll see, he continues to use the intimate 'thou' form to her – as in fact he'll do for the rest of the scene:

KING. I must not hear thee, fare thee well kind maid,
  Thy pains not us'd, must by thy self be paid,
  Proffers not took, reap thanks for their **reward**.

But if he was going to find a rhyme to go with 'reward' he is prevented by
Helena's own rhyming interruption. She 'caps' his word, and as we've seen
with other characters who use this 'capping' technique, in doing so gains
the upper hand.

HELENA. Inspired merit so by breath is **barr'd**,

  It is not so with him that all things knows
  As 'tis with us, that square our guess by shows:

  But most it is presumption in us, when
  The help of heaven we count the act of men.[7]

  Dear sir, to my endeavours give consent,
  Of heaven, not me, make an experiment.

  I am not an impostor, that proclaim
  My self against the level of mine aim,

  But know I think, and think I know most sure,
  My art is not past power, nor you past cure.

KING. Art thou so confident? Within what **space**
  Hop'st thou my cure?

HELENA. The greatest grace lending **grace**,
  Ere twice the horses of the sun shall bring
  Their fiery coacher his diurnal ring [...]
  What is infirm, from your sound parts shall fly,
  Health shall live free, and sickness freely die.

KING. Upon thy certainty and **confidence**,
  What dar'st thou venture?

HELENA.   Tax of **impudence**,

So as the bold highlighting makes clear she 'caps' him twice more, never at
a loss for a further rhymed word to maintain her ongoing momentum.

  A strumpet's boldness, a divulged shame
  Traduc'd by odious ballads: my maiden's name

  Sear'd otherwise, nay worse of worst extended
  With vilest torture, let my life be ended.

And then we see in the King's reply that his resolve is weakening, and his
long rhyming speech, no longer 'rhymes of conclusion', is now the sound
of his conviction that she has 'the answer':

KING. Methinks in thee some blessed spirit doth speak,
His powerful sound, within an organ weak:

And what impossibility would slay
In common sense, sense saves another way:

Thy life is dear, for all that life can rate
Worth name of life, in thee hath estimate:

Youth, beauty, wisdom, courage, all
That happiness and prime, can happy call:

Thou this to hazard, needs must intimate
Skill infinite, or monstrous desperate,

Sweet practiser, thy physic I will try,
That ministers thine own death if I die.

And now she makes her bargain with the King, but something almost unheard of happens: as Helena reaches her ultimate goal, she changes her form of address and begins to use 'thou' to the King![8]

HELENA. If I break time, or flinch in proper<u>ty</u>
Of what I spoke, unpitied let me <u>die</u>,

And well deserv'd: not helping, death's my fee,
But if I help, what do you promise me.

KING. Make thy demand.

HELENA.   But will you make it even?

KING. Aye by my sceptre and my hopes of heaven.

HELENA. Then shalt **thou** give me with **thy** kingly hand
What husband in **thy** power I will command:
Exempted be from me the arrogance
To choose from forth the royal blood of France…

But such a one **thy** vassal, whom I know,
Is free for me to ask, **thee** to bestow.

KING. Here is my hand, the premises observ'd,
Thy will by my performance shall be serv'd:

All's Well that Ends Well: Act 2, Scene 1

The King immediately agrees and after a few more lines the scene comes to an end.

In fact, as we know, it all goes horribly wrong. The King is cured, but Bertram is horrified by the forced marriage, so it seems that Helena has lost everything that she had risked her life on – she had agreed that if she failed to cure the King she would have to die as well as him.

Just as we noticed with some of the ambivalent rhyme we found in *Twelfth Night*, Helena's rhymes have persuaded the King that she has the 'answer' he needs, yet they come at a great price: Bertram deserts her and it takes all her perseverance, courage and wiles to win him back, three acts later.

Like other characters we have looked at earlier, Helena is not *trying* to rhyme or *aware* that she is rhyming. Instead, she is so determined to strike her bargain – which may result in Bertram loving her – that she harnesses all that power that young adolescents are occasionally capable of; it's as if she wills herself into some sort of trance: she taps into a way of speaking that we'd have to liken to 'speaking in tongues'. She is also, like Viola, dealing in magic: her rhymes are an hypnotic spell under which the King falls. Yet for her to move from the respectful and proper use of 'you' to the King, and adopt the 'thou' form, could only have happened if she was in some way possessed. Certainly you could argue that in that moment when she starts to 'thou' the King in her efforts to make sure she wins Bertram – I cure you and you give me Bertram – she oversteps the mark, and while her rhymes still ring out, fuelling her confidence, she has been led into error.

When I heard this change of speech 'forms' in the rehearsal room at the Globe in 2011, the hair on the back of my neck stood up. It was partly brought about by the long rhyming sequence before it, but with the 'thou's' issuing from the mouth of the actress playing the part, the whole atmosphere in the room literally changed and the actress's stature grew. Helena was suddenly in control and the King became, as it were, *her* ward, to do with as she would.[9]

Never underestimate the power of words.

Now finally go back and sound out this great scene, making use of all the rhymes and being alert to those two key moments when the forms of address change. I haven't given you quite the full text of this scene, so if you want to play it out in full you'll need to refer to your Collected Works.

Rhyme today

We have now come to the end of our examination of the three different forms that Shakespeare writes in – blank verse, prose, and rhymed verse.

Looking back I find it easy to assert that the underlying rhythm of blank verse, our heartbeat, carries the emotion of the speaker along with the sentiments that are being expressed; also that the length of this blank verse line relates to the way we naturally breathe when speaking; we certainly don't speak in 'fourteeners'!

And I have no problem with the notion that the haphazard rhythms of prose parallel the quick firings of our brains and therefore capture those moments when 'head' rules and masks the 'heart'.

I'm happy about both these because we use prose every day – even if it's not usually as consciously patterned as the sort that Shakespeare writes – and often still speak in blank verse without knowing it. But we rarely speak in rhyme, unless by accident. We no longer consciously use rhyme as a teaching tool, except to the very young, and may only think about rhyme at all when we are composing our annual Valentine card. And *yet* rhyme is still all around us, touching our lives on a daily basis.

When I consider those lines of Romeo's –

> O she doth teach the torches to burn bright:
> It seems she hangs upon the cheek of night,
> Like a rich jewel in an Ethiop's ear:
> Beauty too rich for use, for earth too dear:

– I know that I am drawn to them in a special way *because* of the rhymes. The rhymes hold the lines in an embrace; the rhyming words seem to be alive as they vibrate with each other; alive for ever, immortal. Hearing these lines I feel I can hold them in my hands just like I might hold an exquisite miniature.

Witness the way rhymes change the way we feel in thousands and thousands of popular songs, even though rhyme works its magic *because* we don't actually have to be 'over-conscious' of it. And the actual rhyming words are not in themselves important: it is rhyme itself that creeps into us, under our radar.

> Lights flicker from the opposite loft,
> In this room the heat pipes just cough,
> The country music station plays soft,
> But there's nothing really nothing to turn off,
> Just Louise and her lover so entwined,
> And these visions of Johanna that conquer my mind.

> Bob Dylan, 'Visions of Johanna', *Blonde on Blonde*, 1966

Hearing these lines changes the way I *feel*; they remind me how bitter-sweet love is. And I know that without the rhymes I would feel this much less strongly even though I'm aware how un-romantic some of these rhyming words are too. I mean – 'cough' and 'off'! But the words in themselves matter not at all: for it is rhyme itself that has the power to seduce us.

Shakespeare's words are incomparable, of course, and his words always matter, but when we expose ourselves to rhyme, the rhyme itself is also and always working on us independently of the words, working on us at a subliminal level, penetrating our senses, changing our moods.

Now we have come to the end of our basic examination of the three different 'forms' that Shakespeare writes in. So let's sum them up as to what they are:

Blank verse is the sound of sincerity – the emotional expression of thought.

Prose is a cerebral activity, the language of invention – saying one thing to hide another.

(But as for rhymed verse – which is the form *least* often found in Shakespeare's plays – I discover that I have the most to say...)

Rhymed verse is the sound of magic; of being filled with unrequited feelings; it can tell us things we never thought we knew; it can fool us with false promises; and we can, if we wish, use it to outsmart others.

Shortly, in Chapters 15 and 16, we are going to examine two of Shakespeare's greatest plays – *Macbeth* and *The Winter's Tale*. We will use them to review everything we have learnt so far. These two plays of Shakespeare's maturity are filled with some of the most remarkable lines of blank verse he ever wrote, so it's fitting that our very next chapter should focus on how the Folio's original punctuation can assist us with the playing of Shakespeare's verse, just as it did with his prose.

Fourteen

Folio Punctuation

I'll put a girdle round about the earth,
In forty minutes.
A Midsummer Night's Dream: Act 2, Scene 1[1]

In Chapter 9 I said it was always a good idea to use the punctuation found in the First Folio if you can, because it punctuates as much, or more, with the speaker in mind than with the reader. The First Folio is, as I expect you remember, the name given to the 1623 publication of thirty-six of Shakespeare's plays, half of which had not been printed before, and without this publication we would probably be forever without those eighteen plays. What I said there was that the original punctuation was especially useful in helping you to shape the prose, frequently pointing out for you more places of emphasis and antithesis than found in most modern editions. But it can also be of immeasurable help when you are dealing with the phrasing of verse as well.

There are, however, three difficulties to bear in mind. The first is that mistakes have inevitably crept into the Folio's punctuation, so at times it's just wrong. Secondly I am not an expert on the punctuation of this or any period. And thirdly there are many who believe that the punctuation has no 'theatrical authority' whatsoever and that the punctuation was ultimately the work of the typesetters in the printing house, or of the person we would call a 'copy editor', and if so how can it help us get closer to the phrasing that Shakespeare heard and his actors used?

240

About these first two difficulties I can do nothing, but I want to address the last one because I think that it's possible to make a case for the playhouse having a hand in punctuating these play-texts. If so, the punctuation might help us when we come to phrasing these texts for ourselves. And by 'phrasing' of course I mean simply how we'd want to say it.

We need to think for a moment about how any of these playscripts would have come into existence.

First, to state the obvious, Shakespeare writes his play.

This initial copy has become known as his 'foul papers'. It was probably the practice of authors at that time to read their finished play out loud to the company they were offering the play to, so as to ascertain whether they wanted to put this particular play on or not. If the play was given the green light, the author, or someone else, would then make a 'fair copy' of the play, which then became the property of the company planning to stage it. We can call this the 'prompt copy'. From this, scripts were made for all the actors, but each actor was only given his own lines, plus something like a three-word cue. These are called 'cue scripts'; and it was from these 'sides', as they were also sometimes called, that the players worked.

Shakespeare's punctuation in The Book of Sir Thomas More

We don't know how Shakespeare punctuated his first draft, or 'foul papers', of any of his printed plays, because none of these manuscripts have survived. But it seems that a few pages of a surviving play in manuscript, known as *The Book of Sir Thomas More*, do contain passages written in Shakespeare's hand. The rest of the manuscript is written by a number of different hands: it was quite common at the time for a group of playwrights to collaborate on a script. The play ran into trouble with the censors, was never put on and never came to be printed during Shakespeare's lifetime. But this manuscript has survived.

Here is one of the speeches that it is thought Shakespeare wrote for the character of Sir Thomas More, as he tries to prevent the London mob from rioting against the foreigners in the city. He is replying to the citizens' demands that these foreigners should be forcibly removed.

This is how the speech appears (now with modernised spelling) in these 'foul papers'. There are only three small crossings out, including where Shakespeare substitutes the word 'and' by 'with'. The beginnings of the lines are without capitals: I want you to sound it out now – but to begin with I have removed *all* of the punctuation. I want to see how you get on

241

without any and so whether the run of the lines themselves will be a sufficient guide for you to make sense of what you are reading:

> MORE. grant them removed and grant that this your ~~y~~ noise
> hath Chid down all the majesty of England
> imagine that you see the wretched strangers
> their babies at their backs ~~and~~ *with* their poor luggage
> plodding to th' ports and coasts for transportation
> and that you sit as kings in your desires
> authority quite silenc'd by your brawl
> and you in ruff of your ~~yo~~ opinions cloth'd
> what had you got I'll tell you you had taught
> how insolence and strong hand should prevail
> how order should be quell'd and by this pattern
> not one of you should live an aged man
> for other ruffians as their fancies wrought
> with self same hand self reasons and self right
> would shark on you and men like ravenous fishes
> would feed on one another

How did you get on? My guess is you were not left feeling helpless by the absence of any punctuation. I also hope you felt, as I do, that there was something 'Shakespearian' about what you've just read.

We should keep in the forefront of our minds that Shakespeare was an actor writing for fellow actors, and to an actor *how* you phrase something is of paramount importance. It is inevitable that as he wrote his plays he 'heard' how the thoughts were being phrased *as* he was writing them; maybe it was even his practice to *speak it*, as he wrote it. And maybe he heard not only the character, but the voice of the actor for whom he was writing the part.[2]

Heminge and Condell, the two colleagues of Shakespeare's who were the guiding spirits of the publication of the First Folio, tell us in their introduction that Shakespeare's 'mind and hand went together: And what he thought, he uttered with that easiness, that we have scarce received from him a blot in his papers'. To write with so few crossings out, *as he does in this speech of More's*, suggests that once he puts pen to paper the 'voices' of the characters are already in his head. So all he has to do is to write out what he hears them saying. And they speak in lines, because that is how they sound to him, and that is how they sound because that is how he hears them breathing.

Now here is the speech again with all Shakespeare's punctuation restored – though as you may be surprised to see, it only amounts to *four commas* – which I've marked in bold:

MORE. grant them removed and grant that this your ~~y~~ noise
     hath Chid down all the majesty of England
     imagine that you see the wretched strangers
     their babies at their backs, ~~and~~ *with* their poor luggage
     plodding to th' ports and coasts for transportation
     and that you sit as kings in your desires
     authority quite silenc'd by your brawl
     and you in ruff of your ~~yo~~ opinions cloth'd
     what had you got, I'll tell you, you had taught
     how insolence and strong hand should prevail
     how order should be quell'd, and by this pattern
     not one of you should live an aged man
     for other ruffians as their fancies wrought
     with self same hand self reasons and self right
     would shark on you and men like ravenous fishes
     would feed on one another

Certainly you'd have to say that in this speech Shakespeare punctuates very lightly indeed![3] And you might have wondered why on earth did he bother to put in those four commas, when other, heavier punctuation marks are missing? But in fact the positioning of the third and fourth comma is most interesting, and points to something which, without their inclusion we would be likely, as actors, to overlook. These commas record something that Shakespeare heard: both seem to record a moment when Shakespeare hears More taking a *mid-line breath* as the rhythm of these lines become more dynamic: this is where More reaches the crux of his argument, which is that, if the citizens of London continue to target the foreigners, they run the risk of being treated in the same way themselves.

The third of these commas – 'I'll tell you, you had taught' – marks the moment when More ups the emotional stakes and makes his anger at what the mob is doing, clear to all. And he achieves this by the way the tone of his voice changes. He sounds a warning. This comma creates a moment of tension and its release. The first half of the phrase, 'I'll *tell* you,' is one of our 'heralding phrases' (see Chapter 4, pages 58–61); we know something else is to come and this one sounds, as it's meant to, somewhat threatening. This is where the tension is created. The second half – '*you* had *taught*' – begins the slow release of the tension: slow because we've now reached the end of the line, so the tension won't be fully released until the next line kicks off with its emotive word 'insolence', weighty with its two stresses. So the comma marks this little miracle when, as we listen, we become aware that the 'game' is changing. It also usefully separates the two 'you's'.

Similarly with the fourth comma, 'how order should be *quell'd,* and *by* this *pattern*', we now have the *consequence* of their actions spelled out and the comma records the sound of More's voice stressing those key words and creating another moment of tension and release. By this change of tempo and change of emotional weight he moves his logical argument onward towards its horrifying conclusion.

So these two commas that Shakespeare inserts are where he hears the pattern of More's voice changing gear, and the flicked commas are his way of marking it.

You might think a question mark was needed after More's 'what had you got,' and before 'I'll tell you,' rather than just a comma (if that is indeed what is there: the manuscript is unclear.) But the reason why there is only this faint comma is surely because More was never going to give the citizens even a chance to answer that question. So Shakespeare, by not adding any stronger punctuation, is recording *exactly* what he heard. He wanted More to leap from 'what had you got,' – the comma after it recording the breath he snatches here – and come in with his 'I'll tell you,' before the citizens can draw breath to answer him, and by so doing makes that first moment of tension all the more breathtaking.[4]

I have marked up these four lines to show clearly what I have been talking about and for you to sound them out again. The *italics* mark only the most important stresses in these lines:

> ˇ what had you *got,* ˇ I'll *tell* you, ˇ *you* had *taught*
> ˇ how *insolence* and strong hand should prevail
> ˇ how order should be quell'd, ˇ and by this *pattern*
> ˇ not *one* of you should live an aged man

These three commas cleverly lead the actor towards these moments of emotional release. They are also moments when I believe Shakespeare 'heard' how More was breathing mid-line.

It's only logical to believe, even if Shakespeare's original punctuation was frequently as sketchy as this, that the punctuation which he *has* included would have eventually found its way into any printed version.

If this play had ever gone into rehearsals it would certainly have acquired more punctuation (and Shakespeare would be aware too that further punctuation would be needed to record more of what he had originally 'heard' so that others might be able to 'see' it on the page).

What were rehearsals like?

About rehearsals we know next to nothing, but who knows whether it wasn't the practice, if Shakespeare's first script was light on punctuation, for the actors to write in some punctuation for themselves as they worked under Shakespeare's watchful eye, and listening ear. For while the concept of a director is still some way off, that is in fact the role Shakespeare would have played, besides the fact that he would, in all probability, also be appearing in his own play as one of the cast. Maybe the bookkeeper, the man in charge of the prompt copy, also took this opportunity to write the same punctuation into the promptbook at the same time.

If any of this is a possibility then there is a chance that some of the punctuation that ends up in the Folio derives not only from those 'foul papers', but also from what went on in the theatre *as* the play was being rehearsed.

All this is guesswork I know. And so we will approach this conundrum from the opposite direction as well, which is to see whether the Folio punctuation can give us some quantifiable benefits that modern editors fail to provide. If it were to do so, we might be more persuaded of its 'theatrical origin'.

Comparing the Folio's punctuation with modern versions

Most modern editions simply punctuate according to today's standards of punctuation, which clearly favours readers over those who want to perform these texts. Modern texts add more punctuation than is necessary, and that punctuation tends to be heavier as well. So we'll often find fewer commas and more semi-colons; we'll find fewer colons and more full stops: in other words there tends to be less flow to the lines.

To begin with let's go back to the very first speech we looked at in this book. Here it is, as before, with its Folio punctuation:

> Safe Antony, Brutus is safe enough:
> I dare assure thee, that no enemy
> Shall ever take alive the noble Brutus:
> The gods defend him from so great a shame,
> When you do find him, or alive, or dead,
> He will be found like Brutus, like himself.

And here it is in a modern version. I will mark the five additions or differences in bold. There are also two omissions and only three of the punctuation marks are the same in both:

> Safe, Antony; Brutus is safe enough.
> I dare assure thee that no enemy
> Shall ever take alive the noble Brutus.
> The gods defend him from so great a shame!
> When you do find him, or alive or dead,
> He will be found like Brutus, like himself.

Before we comment on what has been *added*, let's see what has been removed. Two commas from the original version don't make it into the modern one: the one in the middle of the second line and the comma after 'alive' in the fifth line have both been omitted. This is because modern punctuation doesn't put a comma before 'that' or normally before 'or' either.

The first lost comma takes away our awareness of the emotional weight that falls on the phrase 'I dare assure thee'. The unpunctuated line suggests that all we need to do is to move smoothly through to the end of it.

The second lost comma makes the phrase 'or **alive** or **dead**' somehow more ordinary; whereas that comma in the original makes us feel that Lucilius is clearly envisaging both possibilities with his 'or **alive,** or **dead**' and is contrasting the two.

Now to what has been added. The first line has been slowed up by the extra, and heavier punctuation. That added comma before 'Antony' is called a vocative comma, and the Folio almost always avoids them. (Commas like these are merely a matter of grammar and in no way reflect the way we speak – we say 'Hello William', but we write 'Hello, William'.) After the 'Antony' the heavier semi-colon takes some of the impetus out of the whole line and diminishes Lucilius's moment of triumph at the end of it.

The end of this line also comes to a full stop, while the original text (as happens so often) uses a colon instead. The colon is a wonderful, open-ended mark, which suggests not a moment of complete closure, but just a stage on a journey. If we see a full stop we are not inclined to make it sound alive with open-ended possibilities.

Similarly the colon at the end of the third line gives us another lively moment in the original which is dulled by the modern text's full stop.

Finally my modern text adds an exclamation mark at the end of the fourth line. Exclamation marks are the curse of modern editions. In the original texts they are used sparingly, if at all. In modern texts they are much overused. I dislike the exclamation marks because it is so hard for actors to ignore them. When they see an exclamation mark they feel they have to give the line some special emphasis. When we talked about this fourth line of Lucilius's at the beginning of this book, I suggested it might be treated in many different ways. One possibility would be for the actor to say the line as a heartfelt 'aside'. But adding an exclamation mark at the end of the line would discourage any actor from considering that possibility.

Re-punctuation may well direct us away from the line as Shakespeare heard it.

The fundamental difference between the original punctuation and modern punctuation is that while modern punctuation follows the rules of grammar, the punctuation marks in the Folio are used to give *emphasis* to the word or phrase that *precedes* them. The original punctuation is not directing us so much to the *sense*, as to the *feelings* that lie buried in the lines. The punctuation is connected to our emotions, and sometimes to our breathing as well – and thus to the way thoughts are phrased. Shakespeare may occasionally sound smooth and mellifluous, but more frequently he will sound jagged and fraught. And the punctuation will guide us. The more punctuation there is, the more agitation we will find.

We will now examine how the different marks of punctuation were used in Shakespeare's day.[5] But before that I want you to sound out these two lines from *Richard II*, as they are printed in a modern text. Mowbray is saying farewell to the assembled company before he goes off to fight a duel to the death:

> MOWBRAY. As gentle and as jocund as to jest
> Go I to fight. Truth hath a quiet breast.

Richard II: Act 1, Scene 3

Well, that was easy, wasn't it? The punctuation allowed the sense to come through, and it certainly didn't slow things up in a needless way. But might the original punctuation have given us more?

The emphasising comma

Do you remember, in Chapter 4, when I added a comma to one of Portia's speeches, and it completely changed its meaning? Now look at the Folio's punctuation here, because I want to draw your attention to the comma after 'Truth'. Its function here is to make the word stand out – to give it emphasis:

> MOWBRAY. As gentle, and as jocund, as to jest,
>   Go I to fight: Truth, hath a quiet breast.

So Shakespeare's 'emphasising comma' directs us to understand that the word 'Truth' is emotionally important. It is a dare, a boast, a challenge. Without the comma we might miss the importance of the word completely as it is *not* in what would normally be the stressed place. The comma makes clear too that what we have here is a *trochaic* foot with its attendant frisson of surprise. Going by my modern edition, without its emphasising comma, we might just give the line an unthinking 'iambic wash' and say it like this:

> Go *I* to *fight*. Truth *hath* a *quiet breast*.

But what a loss that would be. A loss for Mowbray's character, for whom these might be the last words he ever speaks, and a loss for Shakespeare too, who will have heard the surprising emphasis that Mowbray gives to the word 'Truth' as he was writing it, and wouldn't then want that emotional moment lost. He may have inserted this comma as he was writing his first draft of the play, but if he didn't feel the need to do so then, I feel that it's much more likely to have been added to the text in rehearsals, rather than something in the printing house added later on.

Also those first three commas in the first line (also not included in the modern edition) are a wonderful clue as to the phrasing of those three 'j' sounds. Those commas are *not* telling us to *pause* at those points in any way: they are just encouraging us to emphasise those clever 'j' sounds to bring out the spirited way Mowbray is speaking. A pause can simply be a moment filled with nothing. A moment of emphasis, or a breath that follows emphasis – these are moments filled with emotional life.

The semi-colon and the emphasising semi-colon

The *semi-colon* is more frequently used to give variety of pace within a line of tripping commas. But in this next example (lines that we looked at not long ago) we have a semi-colon being used to mark a point of emphasis *within* a thought that otherwise would only need a comma for clarity.

We are back with Helena in the first scene of *A Midsummer Night's Dream*. Here's the Folio:

> HELENA. But what of that? Demetrius thinks not so:
>   He will not know, what all, but he doth know,

And as he errs, doting on Hermia's eyes;
So I, admiring of his qualities:

Within the run of this thought, shaped by those commas – the workhorse among all the marks of punctuation – the *emphasising semi-colon* suggests to the actress playing Helena that she can vent a little of her jealousy towards Hermia's 'eyes;' before she has reached the conclusion of what she is saying.

My modern edition (and I am really not criticising them; I use them all the time. It's just we should use both new and original texts if we can) only gives me an unremarkable comma after 'eyes'. More damagingly, though, it doesn't see any need to keep the two internal commas in that second line. But those two commas suggest the importance of the stress on 'all', which is needed to get maximum fun out of the line. And the second is probably also directing us to a *trochaic* beat on the 'but'. I think the line sounded to Shakespeare like this:

> *He* will not *know*, what *all*, **but** he doth *know*,

The colon's many uses

The *colon*, although it has lots of uses, can be used for weightier moments of emphasis as well. Here from *Julius Caesar*, we have Antony left alone with the body of the assassinated Caesar (Folio again):

> ANTONY. O pardon me, thou bleeding piece of earth:
> That I am meek and gentle with these butchers.
>
> *Julius Caesar*: Act 3, Scene 1

Punctuating grammatically, my modern editions simply give a comma at the end of the first line, and one of them puts a dreaded exclamation mark at the end of the second.

The colon frequently suggests an action. We had one in a scene we looked at earlier from *As You Like It*. Here the colon points to the moment when Rosalind puts her necklace around Orlando's neck:

> ROSALIND.   Gentleman,
> Wear this for me: one out of suits with fortune
> That could give more, but that her hand lacks means.

My modern edition prints a semi-colon rather than a colon but, worse, leaves out the wonderful comma after 'more,' in the following line. Why wonderful? Well, Rosalind has just fallen in love with Orlando, but she doesn't know how to give him any indication of what she is feeling. If the line is played through without any emotional shaping, without the comma after 'more', it sounds somewhat like an excuse she's making:

That could give more but that her hand lacks means.

The phrase 'could give more,' (with its comma) suggests that she would like to give *herself* to him were she able to; so this little comma alerts us to consider why this phrase should be invested with more meaning than its place in an unpunctuated line would suggest. And that makes all the difference.

Do we really think that all this punctuation was done in the busy printing house? Or is it more likely that it happened as Shakespeare or Burbage coached the tall young boy who was rehearsing the part of Rosalind?[6]

Sound out the following short passage from *King Lear* (it's one we haven't encountered yet) and try to work out what the colon in doing in the first line of Lear's second speech. Lear's daughter Goneril has spitefully dismissed half of her father's followers:

LEAR. What fifty of my followers at a clap?
　　Within a fortnight?

ALBANY.　　　　　　　　What's the matter, sir?

LEAR. I'll tell thee: life and death, I am asham'd
　　That thou hast power to shake my manhood thus,
　　That these hot tears, which break from me perforce
　　Should make thee worth them.

King Lear: Act 1, Scene 4

What did you think? The answer is that colons also mark an interruption. And the colon after 'I'll tell thee' indicates the moment when Lear, overwhelmed by rage and hurt, can no longer continue speaking, and 'these hot tears… break from' him. Again I don't call this a pause; it's a moment filled with his attempts to control himself. My modern text has simply an unremarkable full stop there with a flurry of exclamation marks following in the lines to come.

The question mark

Those lines from *King Lear* begin with three question marks. But are they all questions? Albany, Goneril's husband, is certainly asking a question which he expects to be answered, but Lear's lines sound more like exclamations of incredulity. And probably that's what they are. The Folio uses question marks to punctuate both exclamations and genuine questions.

Here are some lines from *Hamlet* that we looked at earlier when Rosencrantz and Guildenstern first meet Hamlet in Act 2, Scene 2.

> GUILDENSTERN. Mine honoured lord?
>
> ROSENCRANTZ. My most dear lord?
>
> HAMLET. My excellent good friends? How do'st thou
> Guildenstern? Oh, Rosencrantz; good lads: How do ye
> both?

It's not that they are all uncertain whether they are seeing who they think they are seeing. The first three question marks here denote the 'sound' of delighted surprise.

Here are some lines from *The Winter's Tale* – a play that we have dipped into already, but one that we will be returning to in more detail in Chapter 16. They are from Act 1, Scene 2 at the moment when Leontes's disturbed behaviour is first noticed by his friend Polixenes, and his wife Hermione. Here we can see again, as with that passage from *King Lear*, question marks indicating genuine questions, and those pointing to exclamations:

> POLIXENES.   What means Sicilia?
>
> HERMIONE. He something seems unsettled.
>
> POLIXENES.   How? my lord?
>
> LEONTES. What cheer? how is't with you, best brother?
>
> HERMIONE. You look as if you held a brow of much distraction:
> Are you mov'd (my lord?)
>
> LEONTES.   No, in good earnest.
> How sometimes nature will betray its folly?
> Its tenderness? and make it self a pastime
> To harder bosoms? Looking on the lines
> Of my boy's face...

The first six question marks might all be taken to be genuine questions. But the three in Leontes's final speech are exclamations, as he attempts to cover the jealous suspicions he's harbouring about Polixenes and

Hermione, by telling them he's become rather foolishly emotional after chatting with his son Mamillius. These final three question marks clue us to the exclamatory nature of his protestations – he's saying, 'What a softy I am – and you two – you harder hearted couple – you're amusing yourselves at my expense.' My modern text can only offer me commas in place of the first two question marks, and an exclamation mark after the third.

But the important thing is how the text *looks* on the page, and thus how the look of it prompts the actor. Here are Leontes's lines in my modern edition:

> No, in good earnest.
> How sometimes nature will betray its folly,
> Its tenderness, and make itself a pastime
> To harder bosoms!

The modern text looks calm and reasoned – Leontes is in control. The Folio's three question marks break up the text, suggesting to the actor, that Leontes is striving to camouflage his deepest fears with some self-mockery, but that his charade is barely in control, close to hysteria:

> No, in good earnest.
> How sometimes nature will betray its folly?
> Its tenderness? and make it self a pastime
> To harder bosoms?

Abbreviations

You may have noticed the abbreviations that are found throughout the original texts; usually these find their way into modern editions too.

I quoted these lines of Caesar's from *Antony and Cleopatra* in Chapter 8.

> CAESAR. I do not much dislike the matter, but
> The manner of his speech: for't cannot be,
> We shall remain in friendship, our conditions
> So diff'ring in their acts. Yet if I knew,
> What hoop should hold us staunch from edge to edge
> O'th'world: I would pursue it.

Antony and Cleopatra: Act 2, Scene 2

While my modern text doesn't, unsurprisingly, follow the original punctuation (I especially miss the emphasis given by that Folio colon to the phrase 'O'th'world:'), it does faithfully follow all these abbreviations: the 'for't'; the 'diff'ring' and the 'O'th'world',. Both the Folio and modern texts do this to show that some syllables have been removed so their inclusion doesn't 'throw' the metrical movement of the line.

However, in most cases this should *not affect the way we say these words*. If we say them easily, colloquially, those extra syllables will simply not be heard. So we can say 'for it' and 'differing' as we normally speak, the first sounding as one syllable and the second as two (rather than three) syllables. The unpronounceable 'O'th'world' is just an indication in the texts that the 'O'th'' counts as one syllable and so the full phrase is iambic. So just say 'Of the world' as you would normally say it and we will hear it not as three syllables but as two.

With some words it's impossible to get rid of a missing syllable in this way. This happens later in this same scene where Enobarbus is talking about how Cleopatra appeared in her barge before her first meeting with Antony.

> ENOBARBUS.   she did lie
> In her pavilion, cloth of gold, of tissue,
> O'er-picturing that Venus, where we see
> The fancy out-work nature.

Here that 'O'er' is an accepted abbreviation for 'over' and for the sound of the line it's better to say the monosyllabic 'O'er' than to try and squeeze in an 'over'. (We will be returning to Enobarbus's speech in our final chapter.)

Expressive punctuation 1

Now I'd like us to experience a beautiful passage of verse, beautifully punctuated in the Folio, and to see how much you can get from following the indications that the line endings and the original punctuation can give you. The sequence in question, over the page, is from *Twelfth Night* (Act 2, Scene 4). In it Orsino, who is becoming increasingly fond of the disguised Viola, tries to tell him/her that the love that men can feel outweighs those that any woman is capable of. Viola disagrees:

VIOLA.   Aye but I know.

ORSINO.   What dost thou know?   1

VIOLA. Too well what love women to men may owe:

> In faith they are as true of heart, as we.   2
> My father had a daughter lov'd a man
> As it might be perhaps, were I a woman   3
> I should your lordship.

ORSINO.   And what's her history?

VIOLA. A blank my lord: she never told her love,   4
> But let concealment like a worm i'th' bud
> Feed on her damask cheek:

>   she pin'd in thought,   5
> And with a green and yellow melancholy,
> She sat like Patience on a monument,
> Smiling at grief.   6

>   Was not this love indeed?

> We men may say more, swear more, but indeed   7
> Our shows are more than will: for still we prove
> Much in our vows, but little in our love.

ORSINO. But died thy sister of her love my boy?

VIOLA. I am all the daughters of my father's house,
> And all the brothers too: and yet I know not.   8

> Sir, shall I to this lady?

ORSINO.   Aye that's the theme,
> To her in haste: give her this jewel: say,   9
> My love can give no place, bide no denay.

1. Viola is going on to say more, but Orsino cuts her off. In the Folio interrupted speech is sometimes marked by a full stop. Then there is a half-line pause after Orsino's interruption. Maybe Viola needs a moment to consider whether she should tell him what is in her mind.

2. Her midline comma is delightful. Viola could make the 'as we' that follows it into something of an afterthought, reminding herself that she has to keep pretending to be a boy.

3. The phrasing of the line '*As* it might *be* per*haps, were* I a *woman*' could be given this double stress either side of the comma, as I've indicated by the italics. If so the comma points to another trochee.

4. Viola has five colons in this scene, all filled with that open-ended sound. The statements hang there. How far dare she push them?

5. And as she talks about herself, though of course pretending not to, she no doubt finds *herself* 'smiling at grief' *as she says it.*

6. Then with the full stop after 'grief' it's as if the scene almost freezes and Orsino doesn't know what to say.

7. The three commas help the wit in her line 'We men... but indeed' and mark the antithesis in the last line.

8. Viola's colon after the phrase 'And all the brothers too:', with its open-ended sound, proves too much for Orsino. Rather than asking her what she means, he remains dumb and it's left to Viola to get him off the hook, by suggesting that maybe it's time she was going.

9. With the first colon Viola begins to exit; then Orsino thinks about the jewel, and the second colon probably represents the moment when he hands it over to her. Then, with them both in touching distance, he finds he has to say something else, to send some message, but his comma after 'say,' suggests to me that *as* he says 'say,' he doesn't immediately know *what* he's going to say!

And with that they exit their several ways.

There's nothing showy about the punctuation, but together with the line endings and the line beginnings it's a great guide.

My modern text doesn't have a full stop after Viola's first line and fails to give us the comma after 'heart' in the line 'In faith they are as true of heart, as we'. Also it re-punctuates the first line and a half of Orsino's final speech – ironically slowing up his 'Aye that's the theme, / To her in haste:' with a comma after 'Aye' and a full stop after 'theme', and then gives us semi-colons instead of the more interesting Folio colons: more interesting because the colons point to moves, actions and interruptions, and thus bring out more graphically how Orsino seems flustered and unsure. Nor do we have that lovely comma after his 'say,' in his penultimate line.

It also adds some unnecessary commas, but *otherwise* I have to tell you, my modern text retains *all the other original punctuation in this scene* and so here proves something of an exception to the rule.[7] Clearly sometimes some editors end up acknowledging that the phrasing of the Folio could *hardly* be bettered.

Now you must put all these suggestions to work and sound out the whole scene again.

Expressive punctuation 2

Punctuation can sometimes point to a particularly idiosyncratic way of speaking. Here in the scene from *Julius Caesar* that follows, the Folio's punctuation captures the sound of Casca's breathless terror on account of what he has seen that night. It is from Act 1, Scene 3. His breathlessness is captured by the excessive use of commas, which become more packed together as the scene continues. I have marked all this punctuation in bold.

Now see whether all these punctuation marks help you to discover the 'breathless' sound of Casca's voice:

> *Thunder, and Lightning. Enter* CASCA, *and* CICERO.
>
> CICERO. Good even, Casca: brought you Caesar home?
> Why are you breathless, and why stare you so?
>
> CASCA. Are not you mov'd**,** when all the sway of earth
> Shakes**,** like a thing unfirm**?**
>
>   O Cicero,
> I have seen tempests, when the scolding winds
> Have riv'd the knotty oaks**,** and I have seen
> Th'ambitious ocean swell**,** and rage**,** and foam**,**
> To be exalted with the threat'ning clouds:
> But never till tonight, never till now,
> Did I go through a tempest-dropping-fire.
> Either there is civil strife in heaven,
> Or else the world**,** too saucy with the gods,
> Incenses them to send destruction.
>
> CICERO. Why, saw you any thing more wonderful?

CASCA. A common slave, you know him well by sight,
    Held up his left hand, which did flame and burn
    Like twenty torches join'd; and yet his hand,
    Not sensible of fire, remain'd unscorch'd.

    Besides, I ha'not since put up my sword,
    Against the Capitol I met a lion,
    Who glaz'd upon me, and went surly by,
    Without annoying me.

                  And there were drawn
    Upon a heap, a hundred ghastly women,
    Transformed with their fear, who swore, they saw
    Men, all in fire, walk up and down the streets.

    And yesterday, the bird of night did sit,
    Even at noon-day, upon the market place,
    Hooting, and shrieking.

                 When these prodigies
    Do so conjointly meet, let not men say,
    These are their reasons, they are natural:
    For I believe, they are portentous things
    Unto the climate, that they point upon.

CICERO. Indeed, it is a strange disposed time:
    But men may construe things after their fashion,
    Clean from the purpose of the things themselves.

Notice also that Casca has eight 'ragged' lines here (with no punctuation at the lines' ends), which act like further marks of punctuation, as he takes a new breath with which to say the new line.

So the 'raggedness', the packed commas, the shortness of the phrases, are a brilliant example of how agitation can be written into the text via the punctuation and the line endings. Shakespeare shares Casca's breathlessness as he writes this scene and he marks it by flicking away with that sequence of expressive commas. And by contrast we can see in Cicero's lines a man unruffled and calm of speech despite the tempest that is storming around them.

My modern text omits five of Casca's breathless commas but gives an *extra one* for Cicero in the line –

    But men may construe things, after their fashion,

– and so robbing us of his excessive smoothness.

And finally...

It's time now to leave the evidence with you and for you to decide whether you feel that I have made a case for the value of the original punctuation or not and whether it could point to what went on in the playhouse. For myself I feel that once we've understood how these punctuation marks were used four hundred years ago, they can in some ways help us to feel we are gazing on the most contemporary of documents. And if you are interested in finding copies of the Folio, there are many today that are available to buy.[8]

We can look at Shakespeare's lines and hear those voices from long ago sounding as fresh now as they were then. We can take in the punctuation and see smoothness and agitation; we can hear moments of emotional tension and release; we can see when an action happens: when a necklace is given, or when an old king puts his hand up to his face to hide his tears.

Finally, on a lighter note, I want to comment on that line of Puck's which I quoted at the beginning of this chapter. It came as a response to Oberon's demand that he finds a magic herb, and that he wants him to be back again with it before 'the Leviathan can swim a league'. Puck replies:

> PUCK. I'll put a girdle round about the earth,
>   In forty minutes.

Well, it looks innocuous enough, but the fact is that I've never seen a modern copy which keeps that comma after the word 'earth'. In failing to do so they are partly responsible for changing the meaning of the line.

So because of this missing comma Puck's response *usually* sounds as if he's going to find the herb for sure, but that his route is going to have to take him right round the world first; even so, he assures Oberon that he'll be back again in forty minutes – which might suggest he'll be reappearing sometime in Act 4! But the comma after earth points to 'earth' being given some extra emphasis – it is already given prominence by being at the end of the line – which is why I say the editors who miss this comma are only assisting in the confusion so caused.

What Puck is saying to Oberon is that the task he has been given is just too *easy*. And easy it proves as he returns in about four minutes, rather than forty. With the comma in place and the resulting emphasis on 'earth' we should realise that he's *boasting* – that were he to be given leave to be away for *forty* minutes he could circumnavigate the whole globe:

> PUCK. I'll put a girdle round about the **earth,**
>   In **forty** minutes.

As I said at the end of the last chapter, the next two chapters will give us an opportunity to review everything we have studied so far. However, we will also use them to *deepen* our understanding of Shakespeare's working method – how Shakespeare constructs his plays – and to *refine* our techniques for performing them.

We now need to brace ourselves for the task we have in hand. *Macbeth* is certainly one of the greatest plays that he ever wrote. It is also one of the most challenging to undertake: its progress represents a descent into hell. Before you move on to the next chapter I want you to find a copy of the play and read it – you can certainly read it *all* if you like – but I want you to pay special attention to the first Act, and try to work out why, at the end of these seven short scenes, this much admired married couple have jointly undertaken to murder their King and guest while he is sleeping in their own house.

Fifteen

Macbeth

Deepening and Reviewing Our Work

> for now I am bent to know
> By the worst means, the worst, for mine own good,
> All causes shall give way. I am in blood
> Stepp'd in so far, that I should wade no more,
> Returning were as tedious as go o'er:
>
> *Macbeth*: Act 3, Scene 4

Macbeth was written some time around 1606 and, while it is one of Shakespeare's shortest plays, *The Oxford Dictionary of Quotations* includes a higher proportion of lines from it than from any other of his works. It is unquestionably one of his greatest achievements, remembered above all for its two leading characters: Macbeth, and Lady Macbeth, his wife. These are roles that many actors dream of playing, yet these parts are as challenging as any that Shakespeare wrote. But by the end of this chapter I hope you'll feel ready to take on these challenges, should you be amongst that number that desire to play them. However, playing any character will always involve more than simply knowing how to say the lines: you also have to be able to 'inhabit' them – to get under their skins.

Uncovering the motives behind a murder

Premeditated murders are not that common in Shakespeare's plays.[1] There are a few in the Histories, though even in those plays, most of the violent deaths occur in battle; while in the Tragedies, the multiple killings, which bring some of those plays to an end, all tend to happen in confusion and in the heat of the moment. Not so the series of murders in *Macbeth*: all are premeditated. Murder permeates every pore of this play, and gives it its atmosphere of intense foreboding. *Macbeth* simply *is* Shakespeare's 'murder mystery play', though the mystery is not a 'whodunnit': rather it's a 'why was it done?' The first to die is King Duncan, murdered in his sleep by Macbeth, with the connivance and aid of his wife. That much is clear – the mystery is 'why did they do it?' To be able to play Macbeth and Lady Macbeth convincingly you'll need to find answers to that question.

So, if you haven't done so already, now is the time to lay this book aside, and read those first seven scenes of *Macbeth*. Be on the lookout for anything out of the ordinary, or anything that simply surprises you in what the characters say or do – though sometimes you might be surprised by what they *don't* say or do. Moments such as these will take some searching out because Shakespeare knows that what leads Macbeth and his wife to commit murder lies deeply buried in their psyches, and were he to drag their motives into the light of day he would undermine the dark and mysterious story he has to tell. The Macbeths are challenging to play because so much about them is hidden, both from each other and even from themselves. Macbeth's words at the beginning of this chapter, 'I am in blood / Stepp'd in so far', might well serve as a warning that we must be prepared to step 'far' into the depths of this play as well.

Of course I'd be fascinated to hear what you discovered – what your impressions were of Act 1 – but I shall just have to make some guesses. If you've never read the play before you probably found the first scene somewhat surprising – and surprisingly short as well. Here it is in its entirety:

> *Thunder and Lightning. Enter three* WITCHES.
>
> WITCH 1. When shall we three meet again?
> In thunder, lightning, or in rain?
>
> WITCH 2. When the hurley-burley's done,
> When the battle's lost, and won.
>
> WITCH 3. That will be ere the set of sun.

WITCH 1. Where the place?

WITCH 2.   Upon the heath.

WITCH 3. There to meet with Macbeth.

WITCH 1. I come Gray-Malkin.

ALL. Paddock calls anon:
    Fair is foul, and foul is fair,
    Hover through the fog and filthy air.

Exeunt.

Immediately we hear the lines are rhyming and their rhythm is unusual. *Romeo and Juliet* apart, *Macbeth* has more rhyme in it than any other of Shakespeare's tragedies, and we will later need to account for why. As for the rhythm, it is certainly not iambic, and the lines are not pentameters. But we have encountered this rhythm before: it's identical to the way Puck occasionally speaks in *A Midsummer Night's Dream* – I quoted these lines of his in Chapter 11:

    Churl, upon thy eyes I throw
    All the power this charm doth owe:
    When thou wak'st, let love forbid
    Sleep his seat on thy eye-lid.

A Midsummer Night's Dream: Act 2, Scene 2

As with the Witches, these are trochaic four-beat lines, which sound trance-like, unearthly; but whereas Puck's lines seem mostly mischievous, we sense that the Witches' lines are malicious, as if Shakespeare deliberately wants to unsettle us, right at the start of this play, by this less-than-human sound.

The incident upon which the unfolding of the drama hinges

I obviously can't go on guessing what you felt especially noteworthy, but I'm very interested in what you made of these lines that Lady Macbeth says to her husband in the last of those seven scenes – I hope you found them surprising:

            What beast was't then
    That made you break this enterprise to me?
    When you durst do it, then you were a man:
    And to be more than what you were, you would
    Be so much more the man. Nor time, nor place
    Did then adhere, and yet you would make both:

They have made themselves, and that their fitness now
Does unmake you. I have given suck, and know
How tender 'tis to love the babe that milks me,
I would, while it was smiling in my face,
Have pluck'd my nipple from his boneless gums,
And dash'd the brains out, had I so sworn
As you have done to this.

Macbeth: Act 1, Scene 7

Macbeth, you may remember, has just told his wife that he wants to call a halt to their plans for killing Duncan. Forget for a moment about whose baby this is that Lady Macbeth has suckled – it's one of the most debated passages in the play – but simply focus on what it is that Lady Macbeth is reminding her husband about. Because in reminding him, we hear her say something so extraordinary, and yet so obvious that we might have already guessed it – or half-thought it to ourselves as we were reading the play – but which, now it's been said, we should realise has had a bearing on everything that we have read up until this point: Lady Macbeth's words reveal that she and her husband must have begun contemplating getting rid of Duncan – of murdering him – *before the play begins*.

Lady Macbeth is reminding Macbeth how he had sworn to her that he would kill Duncan; and while, when they made this pact there seemed no likely 'time, nor place' in which such an act might successfully be attempted, Macbeth had then assured her, which she also takes time to remind him of, that he would somehow contrive such an opportunity. And now, when such an occasion has fallen into their hands, and Duncan is a guest in their house, how can it be that Macbeth is saying to her 'No'?

So the full story of *Macbeth* started before, maybe long before those Witches gather on that war-torn, foggy stage. It started with a married couple, who one day, or maybe one night, vowed to murder their King – the blameless Duncan. Later we'll have to consider *why* Shakespeare has withheld this apparently vital piece of information until this moment – right at the end of Act 1.

Diving deeper into the details

Deepening your lines of enquiry, by trying to puzzle out what lies behind the words, will bring rewards to you whatever play of Shakespeare's you are working on – but for *Macbeth* it is an essential undertaking, for without doing so it's not easy to understand why things happen in the way they do. So never be content to think, 'Things like that happen in plays'; rather ask yourself, as a curious child might, '*Why* has this happened?'

In this chapter we will continue to follow the fortunes of Macbeth and his wife, using their words as a way of *reviewing* much of what we have touched upon so far in this book. We will look in detail at some of their greatest speeches, as well as two of the scenes they have together. But we must also take this opportunity to see what lies *behind* some of the words, in order to take ourselves *deeper* into the play's mysteries – the first of which is when Macbeth is thrown into panic almost as soon as he enters in Scene 3.

Macbeth's first terror-attack

As you'll have seen, the play is just over a hundred lines long when Macbeth and Banquo make their first appearance, but we are already in the third scene of the play.[2] They are not the first to enter: the three Witches, with whom the play began, are already back on stage waiting to meet them. Macbeth and Banquo are generals and, by their awe-inspiring prowess on the battlefield, they have just saved King Duncan from defeat at the hands of rebels (assisted by foreign invaders).

In the immediately preceding scene, Macbeth's courage and ability has been praised by everyone from the King down. Now Macbeth and Banquo enter, talking to each other as they do so:

MACBETH. So foul and fair a day I have not seen.

BANQUO. How far is't call'd to Forres?
         What are these,
So wither'd, and so wild in their attire,
That look not like th'inhabitants o'th'earth,
And yet are on't?
      Live you, or are you aught
That man may question?
        you seem to understand me,
By each at once her choppy finger laying
Upon her skinny lips: you should be women,
And yet your beards forbid me to interpret
That you are so.

MACBETH.   Speak if you can: what are you?

WITCH 1. All hail Macbeth, hail to thee Thane of Glamis.

WITCH 2. All hail Macbeth, hail to thee Thane of Cawdor.

WITCH 3. All hail Macbeth, that shalt be King hereafter.

BANQUO. Good sir, why do you start, and seem to fear
    Things that do sound so fair?

                          i'th'name of truth
    Are ye fantastical, or that indeed
    Which outwardly ye show?

                   My noble partner
    You greet with present grace, and great prediction
    Of noble having, and of royal hope,
    That he seems rapt withal:

Nothing is more surprising in this scene than the fact that Macbeth, our leading character, who has so far spoken only one and a half lines in the play (in fact just seventeen monosyllabic words), having heard what the three Witches have said to him, seizes up and seems terrified. This is the warrior who had killed countless of his country's enemies that very day, dispatching one (as you read in the play's second scene) by cutting him open from the navel to the jaws – 'unseam'd him from the nave to'th'chops' – before fixing his head upon their battlements. We are directed to focus on Macbeth's seemingly unaccountable reaction to what the Witches say because Banquo, that other battle-hardy warrior, comments on it in surprise:

    Good sir, why do you start, and seem to fear
    Things that do sound so fair?

Macbeth seems unable to answer Banquo's question, and we have to wait another twenty lines before he finds his voice again.

    What has happened to him? We know Macbeth has been fighting all day; the battle has swayed this way and that, but victory is finally his. Of course, the last thing he could have expected is to be accosted by three Witches telling him that he would one day be king. But, as we now realise, because of what Lady Macbeth will say to him four scenes later, for him to be king is a dream that he and his wife have harboured for some time. So, when the Witches say, 'All hail Macbeth, that shalt be King hereafter', rather than planting some new idea in his head, their words must have reminded him of other words – words that he and wife said to each other on that fateful day, or night, when their pact was made. And now, to his horror, he realises that the Witches know what's in his mind – and, worse still, that they always will. What had been intimately whispered in secret has now been declaimed on a windy heath – what had been private has been made public, because Banquo has heard it all. The genie is out of the bottle.

Macbeth now acts like a guilty thing, half hoping that Banquo won't remember, or won't take too seriously, what the Witches have said. Were you to re-read this third scene now, I think you'd find that everything that Macbeth says and does begins to take on a new significance in the light of what Shakespeare only chooses to state clearly in that seventh scene.

The implications of this murder-pact are hugely significant. Is it something husband and wife continually talk about, or never talk about? When Macbeth's away fighting in Scotland's defence, does Lady Macbeth constantly wonder if today will be the day when he does it? Or does she sometimes doubt that he'll ever be able to do it? At the moment he seems to be doing the opposite – saving Duncan's life by destroying his enemies. If Macbeth ever thinks about the oath he made to his wife, does he perhaps hope that she might have put it out of her mind? Has his phenomenal success made him happy with his present position? Even if we can't solve all these questions, they are still worth asking; and it's possible that a close examination of the text might, in the end, suggest to us some answers.

Macbeth and Banquo: friends or enemies?

Before we turn to Macbeth's first soliloquy, there are some curiosities, some details – some words – that we need to examine in the lines that lead up to it, that it might be so easy to overlook. I am going to point out these words by italicising them. We left the play with Macbeth struck dumb and terrified by what the Witches had said to him; though while he is lost for words, we'll later discover that he has heard the Witches saying to Banquo –

> Thou shalt get kings, though thou be none:

– and Banquo, as we'll also learn later, unlike Macbeth, already has a son, called Fleance. Once Macbeth finds his voice again, he asks the Witches to tell him more, and they promptly vanish:

> BANQUO. The earth hath bubbles, as the water has,
>   And these are of them: whither are they vanish'd?
> MACBETH. Into the air: and what seem'd corporal, melted,
>   As breath into the wind. Would they had stay'd.
> BANQUO. Were such things here, as we do speak about?
>   Or have we eaten on the insane root,
>   That takes the reason prisoner?

MACBETH. Your *children* shall be *kings*.

BANQUO.   *You* shall be *King*.

MACBETH. And *Thane* of *Cawdor too*: *went* it not *so*?

BANQUO. To th'*self*-same *tune*, and *words*:   who's here?

Enter ROSS *and* ANGUS.

(The gap I've inserted in Banquo's last line is to point out that the line is short, and it's in that gap that Ross and Angus enter, taking Macbeth and Banquo by surprise.)

Look at those last three lines before their entrance – they seem such simple innocuous lines, but they are exactly the sort that we could over-look. They are not some sort of 'filler' – especially not in a play as short as *Macbeth*. Shakespeare could easily have brought in Ross and Angus three lines earlier, but no, he waits intrigued, to see what will happen next, as Macbeth and Banquo – these brothers-in-arms – look at each other in silence. And the silence has been created because Banquo's line, 'That takes the reason prisoner?', as you might have noticed, is also short – short because it's a line that Macbeth chooses not to answer.

What does happen here? Why does Shakespeare bother with these lines? They tell us nothing new? Three lines and a pause – amounting to some thirteen seconds in all. But something *has* happened: and that is, that what Macbeth and Banquo feel towards each other has begun to change.

These lines could be played in any number of ways. After the disappearance of the Witches, the two men could become almost hysterical as they joke about what they have been promised. Alternatively they could still be caught in the wonder of it all, and in working on the scene you could come up with many more alternative interpretations as to how these lines might be delivered, depending on what you sensed these two characters were *feeling*. But common to all possible interpretations, the text gives us this pause in which Macbeth *changes the subject*, and Banquo's responses suggest that he finds both Macbeth's first statement and his subsequent question somewhat *odd*: sitting weirdly side by side, as they do, with the terror that Macbeth showed earlier, and which Banquo saw.

Shakespeare is telling us to watch what happens in these thirteen seconds because it's important: it is the first subtle step in a dance between these two men that will finally end with Macbeth hiring assassins to murder his old comrade. These 'brothers-in-arms' are becoming yet another pair of Shakespearian 'rival brothers' – as we watch.[3]

Seemingly inconsequential passages can contain matters of great significance.

We will now continue with this scene as Angus and Ross relay the messages they bear from the King and I will continue to italicise the words that I think become important stepping-stones in the unfolding of the plot. They will help us understand the way Macbeth's mind is working, and explain why the things he says to us, in the audience, are at odds with what he says to the other characters:

> ANGUS.   We are sent,
> To give thee from our royal master thanks,
> Only to herald thee into his sight,
> Not pay thee.
>
> ROSS. And for an *earnest** of a *greater* honour,
> He bade me, from him, call thee Thane of Cawdor:
>
> In which addition, hail most worthy Thane,
> For it is thine.
>
> BANQUO.   What, can the devil speak true?
>
> MACBETH. The Thane of Cawdor lives: Why do you dress me
> In borrow'd robes?
>
> ANGUS.   Who was the Thane, lives yet…†
>
> But treasons capital, confess'd, and prov'd,
> Have overthrown him.
>
> MACBETH.   Glamis, and Thane of Cawdor:
> The *greatest* is *behind.**

This last line of Macbeth's is the very first 'aside' he makes in the play. With us, but not with Banquo, he shares his excitement about becoming king. Macbeth's use of '*greatest*' here is a direct echo of that earlier line of Ross's, 'an earnest of a *greater* honour'. Macbeth has to be thinking that Ross's words *could* mean that Duncan, having created him Thane of Cawdor, could be about to proclaim him as his heir, as the next King of Scotland, and so confirm the Witches' final promise.

What a contrast this is with that thirteen-second exchange between Macbeth and Banquo, when Macbeth seemed to be suggesting that what the Witches had said to him hadn't meant all that much to him personally, nor did he seem certain he had remembered it all accurately. Whereas here, to the audience, he is expressing excitement in *all* that the Witches have said to him. Admittedly he has now been created Thane of Cawdor and you might feel that that changes everything, but with regard to the

† five lines omitted
earnest – promise of future gain
behind – still to come

way he continues to speak to Banquo, essentially it changes nothing – as we shall see by the lines that follow. First Macbeth throws a word to Ross and Angus –

Thanks for your pains.

– then he engages Banquo again and picks up on the conversation they had been having *before* they were interrupted by the arrival of Ross and Angus:

> MACBETH. Do you not *hope* your children shall be kings,
> When those that gave the Thane of Cawdor to *me*,
> Promis'd no less to *them*.
> BANQUO.   That trusted *home*,
> Might yet enkindle *you* unto the crown,
> *Besides* the Thane of Cawdor.

Macbeth's word '*hope*' is the one he now adds to that previous line of his, 'Your *children* shall be *kings*', and is a more direct attempt to get Banquo to say what he is feeling about the situation, but which Banquo again declines; while Banquo's response, with that pointed use of the word '*you*' in the phrase, '*you* unto the crown', is essentially a repeat of how he said in that previous conversation, '*You* shall be *King*' with its trochaic assertiveness.

On the face of it, these are strange lines between the two men: Macbeth deliberately ignoring – certainly playing down – how the Witches had forecast that he should become King, and Banquo reminding him of what he seems to be paying little regard to. Interestingly, yet again, neither man will comment on, or answer, what the other wishes to know. This wary stand-off between the 'rival-brothers' deepens. And yet to us Macbeth shares his excitement about the future – the 'hereafter'.

At this moment for the audience, being ignorant of what they will learn in Scene 7, the behaviour of both men is surprising, unaccountable. But that is good: they will be trying to puzzle out what is happening – they are engaged; the audience is on your case. Whereas for you – acting these roles and knowing what is still concealed – you have to work out exactly what the characters are suggesting, quizzing each other about, or hiding from the other, and which words – sometimes seemingly minor words – they are using to try to achieve their goals, or defend their positions. If you achieve that, the play will come alive, and fascinate the audience second by second.

What we are working on in this scene is how the words the characters use are so revealing; the words they repeat; the words they pick up from each other. But equally revealing are those things they don't say – the questions that go unanswered.

The greatness of *Macbeth* lies in its deep subtlety.

So go back again and sound those lines out once more, and just see how subtle, yet probing, some of these little words are. See how much is being revealed and how much more is being concealed.

Reviewing our work on verse and breath: 'breath marks'

It goes without saying that *Macbeth* is another 'breakthrough' play. Its verse reaches new heights of intensity, depth, poetic insights, compression and knotty complexity. All of it will win our admiration, yet much of it will need unscrambling at the same time. Now as we begin to work on some of its great speeches it's time to talk again about breathing. Early on in this book I said you can't act *and* be thinking where to breathe at the same time. So remember that the 'breath marks' that I'm inserting again are primarily there to show you how the thoughts are *phrased*. Learning how the thoughts are expressed in this way, by 'topping up' your breath before the new line, will both enable you to achieve clarity *and* also help you to be at one with the emotions that lie behind the words that Shakespeare 'heard' his characters saying; because we reveal our emotions in part by where and how we breathe. So the 'breath marks' should be there only while you rehearse – as you work to bring the speeches off the page. It will only sound natural in performance if you *no longer need to remind yourself where they are.*

Reviewing our work: Macbeth's first soliloquy

The speech that follows is a huge test for any actor, coming as it does less than a hundred lines after Macbeth's first entrance. You'll see my 'rehearsal breath marks' before every new line and I'm suggested some in mid-line positions as well. These mid-line ones are optional: you might need less or want more. But remember you should only *need* a mid-line breath *after* a mark of (Folio) punctuation. Which words will you 'value'? I have marked in bold those lines which I feel begin with, or contain a mid-line trochaic beat, and by definition trochees will always indicate a word of 'value'. But you'll probably find others too. It's now time, reminding yourself of all we've talked about in this chapter so far, to sound it out. The speech is cued by the conclusion of Banquo's previous speech:

BANQUO.   But 'tis strange:
   ˇ And oftentimes, to win us to our harm,
   ˇ The instruments of darkness tell us truths,
   ˇ Win us with honest trifles, to betray's
   ˇ In deepest consequence.
   ˇ Cousins, a word, I pray you.⁴
MACBETH.   ˇ **Two** truths are told,
   ˇ As happy prologues to the swelling act
   ˇ **Of** the imperial theme.

             ˇ I thank you gentlemen:

   ˇ This supernatural soliciting
   ˇ **Cannot** be ill; **cannot** be good.ˇ If ill?
   ˇ **Why** hath it given me earnest of success,
   ˇ Commencing in a truth? ˇ I am thane of Cawdor.

   ˇ If good? ˇ why do I yield to that suggestion,
   ˇ Whose horrid image doth unfix my hair,
   ˇ And make my seated heart **knock** at my ribs,
   ˇ Against the use of nature?

          ˇ Present fears
   ˇ Are less than horrible imaginings:

   ˇ My thought,ˇ whose murder yet is but fantastical,
   ˇ Shakes so my single state of man,ˇ that function
   ˇ Is smother'd in surmise, ˇ and nothing is,
   ˇ But what is not.

Macbeth: Act 1, Scene 3

At the end I'm suggesting that seven short intakes of breath in these final three and a half lines *might* work to give us the 'sound' of Macbeth's physical panic. And those last seven words –

                  ˇ and nothing is,
   ˇ But what is not.

– need a controlled delivery (remember never to rush monosyllabic words). Also allowing yourself to breathe before the final four words will clarify the antithetical paradox.

What could be simpler than these seven words? Yet if we rushed them, or failed to balance up the first four syllables against the second four (separated as they are simply by a breath – which no one should notice), how much would be lost.

The opening of his speech, ignoring Banquo's warning –

> ˘ Two truths are told,
> ˘ As happy prologues to the swelling act
> ˘ Of the imperial theme.

– is a virtual repeat of what Macbeth said earlier after that speech of Ross's –

> Glamis, and Thane of Cawdor:
> The *greatest* is *behind*.

Clearly Macbeth is unaffected by Banquo's warning as to what the Witches have told him, and redoubles his trust in his own interpretation of Ross's previous speech:

> ROSS. And for an *earnest* of a *greater* honour,

and a few lines later Macbeth, having previously interpreted Ross's use of the word 'greater' to his own 'wished-for' outcome, now picks up on Ross's word 'earnest' (a promise of something yet to come) when he says:

> Why hath it given me *earnest* of success

The elation with which this speech has opened is followed by two things that terrify him. A 'suggestion' – meaning here a prompting to do something evil – and a 'horrid image' which he fears he's being seduced by. Macbeth's hair is standing on end; his heart is beating wildly against his ribcage. Later he becomes fixated ('rapt' is Banquo's word) by watching himself murdering someone, which he acknowledges is terrifying him more than any actual imminent danger in the physical world could ever do. Somewhere the speech is 'hijacked' by this 'horrid image'. Does it happen within these following lines, or does it *begin* to rise up within him, just before them?

> ˘ This supernatural soliciting
> ˘ Cannot be ill; cannot be good. ˘ If ill?
> ˘ Why hath it given me earnest of success
> ˘ Commencing in a truth? ˘ I am thane of Cawdor.

But it's subtle – it's only in the lines that follow these that his body goes into panic. However, I'm rather taken with the fact that it's not a comma, but a somewhat unusual semi-colon after 'Cannot be ill;' (in fact it's the only Folio semi-colon in the whole scene), and I'm going to suggest that this 'horrid image' rises *as* Macbeth says it, with the semi-colon giving us this slightly weightier moment after it.

The challenge of the speech is: will we believe that what you *say* is happening to you is *actually* happening to you? That after the joyous beginning, the 'horrid image', in which he sees himself killing someone, becomes for you a reality, and that before our eyes your body goes into meltdown?

But even so – to react in so *extreme* a way – is that not still puzzling?

Perhaps something he says later might help us dive deeper still into this mystery. At the end of this scene, you may remember, Macbeth says by way of excusing his strange behaviour to the others:

> my dull brain was wrought
> With things forgotten.

Maybe these two half-lines suggest that there is more in it than that. Maybe Macbeth had *buried* this murder-pact deep in his psyche and, if so, this might explain how these feelings of terror seem to take him unawares.

Why did Shakespeare withhold that vital piece of evidence until Scene 7?

But wouldn't the play be a better one if Shakespeare had let us know about the murder-pact earlier? The answer has to be a resounding 'No'. The play thrills us *because*, as we shall see, it develops at such a headlong pace, allowing the Macbeths no time to consider fully what they are doing. Once the Witches have told Macbeth that he 'Shalt be king hereafter', a time-bomb begins ticking – though maybe we should say that the time-bomb began ticking once that murder-pact was made, though ticking so quietly that Macbeth was no longer conscious of it. Now it's become audible – it's all he can hear.

Shakespeare has an unfailing instinct as to how each of his plays should begin. He knows when to conceal motives and when to reveal them. So he only allows us to hear about the murder-pact when he does, because to release such details earlier in the Act would have undermined the onward rush of the story, which *alone* makes credible *why* the events unfold as they do. To have brought husband and wife together earlier in the play, so we could have heard them discussing these plans, would not have allowed us to meet them for the first time, isolated from each other.

Seeing them on their own, allows them, through their soliloquies, to reveal to us all their hopes and fears. We don't meet Lady Macbeth until Scene 5 – we don't even know that Macbeth is married until Scene 4. In Scene 3, which is what we have been looking at so far, Macbeth has simply revealed to us that something is terrifying him – and that should capture all our attention. If we had been told what that was, we would be the wiser, but we'd be less involved – less on the edge of our seats. But, as should now be clear, for the actors, it is essential that they know what as yet the audience doesn't.

Now it's time to go over the soliloquy again.

My guess is you found it difficult, if not impossible. A speech like this doesn't ever just drop into your lap. You'll need to go over it, and more deeply *into* it, on many, many occasions, until you feel the words are becoming yours, and that you have a taste of exactly what horrors and misgivings Macbeth is being assailed by. Whatever speech you are working on, find times in the day when you are alone, and can say it out loud to yourself – as you fall asleep at night, as you are waiting for a train.[5]

Reviewing our work on prose: Macbeth's letter to his wife

Before Macbeth is taken into the King's presence (Act 1, Scene 4), he finds time to write a letter to his wife telling her something of his encounter with the Witches and what they have said to him. By the time she reads it, Macbeth will have watched Duncan (far from being about to nominate him as the next King of Scotland) proclaiming his own son, Malcolm, as his heir. Immediately after this Duncan tells Macbeth – and this is probably the 'greater honour' that Ross was actually referring to in Scene 3 – that he wishes to spend that night as Macbeth's guest, at his castle in Inverness. Read out the letter he wrote to his wife now, but remember that Lady Macbeth as yet doesn't know that the King is already on his way:

> *Enter* MACBETH'S WIFE *alone with a letter.*
> LADY. They met me in the day of success: and I have learn'd by
>   the perfect'st report, they have more in them, than mortal
>   knowledge. When I burnt in desire to question them
>   further, they made themselves air, into which they
>   vanish'd. Whiles I stood rapt in the wonder of it, came

missives from the King, who all-hail'd me Thane of
Cawdor, by which title before, these weird sisters saluted
me, and referr'd me to the coming on of time, with hail
King that shalt be. This have I thought good to deliver
thee (my dearest partner of greatness) that thou might'st
not lose the dues of rejoicing by being ignorant of what
greatness is promis'd thee. Lay it to thy heart, and farewell.

There isn't much prose in *Macbeth*, but there is some. Besides this letter, there is the drunken Porter in Act 3, Scene 3 – he's another of our 'prose entertainers' – and for a short while after Macduff's and Lennox's entrance, Macduff 'feeds' the Porter a couple of prose cues, as if he's become this bleakly-black comic's 'straight-man'. There are some heart-wrenchingly witty prose exchanges between Lady Macduff and her son, just before they are both savagely murdered in Act 4 on Macbeth's orders. Prose also figures in Act 5, Scene 1 – generally referred to as the 'sleep-walking' scene – with Lady Macbeth now speaking in her sleep the fractured prose of the deranged. Though before she enters, the scene begins with the wary, cautious prose of the Doctor and the Gentlewoman, censoring their words lest they should reveal to each other more than they dare. Once Lady Macbeth has exited, and after she has revealed her com-plicity in all the murders done, the scene reverts to the 'sincere' sound of verse. All these prose 'uses' we have encountered before – but we have not, until now, looked in detail at one of Shakespeare's many letters.

To whom is the letter read?

In *Hamlet* when Hamlet sends a letter to Claudius informing him, in Act 4, Scene 7, that he has returned to Denmark, Claudius reads the letter out loud to Laertes. So that's easy, the letter is read by one character for another to hear, and we in the audience happily hear it at the same time. However, just before this, sailors have entered to give Horatio a letter from Hamlet. The subject matter of this earlier letter is too private for Horatio to speak it out loud in front of the men who've just delivered it, so here, rather than think-ing that Horatio speaks it to himself and we simply overhear him (which would be an odd thing for him to do) I believe he must acknowledge the presence of the audience, and, *wanting* to share its news with them, he does it in such a way that makes clear that the waiting sailors are out of earshot.

But what about characters, like Lady Macbeth, who bring a letter on stage with them and then read it out? In these situations I think you simply have to say she enters *in order* to share it with us. This leads us to ask ourselves another question, 'Who might she think "we" are?'

When we were looking at one of Hamlet's soliloquies I said he regards the whole audience as people who he's happy to take into his confidence: we are all Hamlet's 'fellows'. By contrast Lady Macbeth has no one that she would dare share her innermost thoughts with apart from her husband – and maybe not *all* of those with him either. The people she might share her thoughts with could be her parents, or other whom she holds dear – whom she likes to converse with in times of need, or joy – but who are no longer alive to give away her secrets. If so, the actress might find for herself these souls somewhere far away in the furthest reaches of the auditorium. So sound it out again, imagining that you've entered to share the news with your ancestors.

Or the speech could be addressed to their child that she will refer to later, whom we must presume is dead. And so you could try the letter again and feel what difference that makes.

Otherwise the fact that a letter is written in prose shouldn't even give us a second thought, should it? Letters are usually written in prose, so that's that. And the fact that I talk about prose suggesting that something is in some way hidden shouldn't hold true for letters as well – or should it? Well I think it should. For is it not the case that letters are always a partial account of what has happened, a spin put on events? In other words is there not something hidden here as well? In fact I think much is. Macbeth is certainly focusing on the upside of what occurred. He says nothing of his terror. But neither does he hint in any way to his wife that he's about to take action, or has even begun planning how he might eliminate Duncan.

But, as we'll discover, Lady Macbeth knows her husband better than to be taken in by the tone of his letter, as her soliloquy that follows the reading of this letter makes clear.

Reviewing our work: another verse soliloquy

Once again I have inserted these 'rehearsal-type' breath marks, plus those 'valuable' trochaic feet in bold. You must begin to work on this speech by sounding it out:

ˇ Glamis thou art, and Cawdor, and shalt be
ˇ **What** thou art promis'd:

                        ˇ yet do I fear thy nature,
ˇ It is too full o'th'milk of human kindness,
ˇ To catch the nearest way.

                         ˇ Thou wouldst be great,
ˇ Art not without ambition, but without
ˇ The illness should attend it.

                         ˇ What thou wouldst highly,
ˇ That wouldst thou holily: ˇ wouldst not play false,
ˇ And yet wouldst wrongly win. ˇ Thou'dst have, great Glamis,
ˇ **That** which cries,ˇ thus thou must do, if thou have it;
ˇ And that which rather thou dost fear to do,
ˇ Than wishest should be undone.

                         ˇ Hie thee hither,
ˇ That I may pour my spirits in thine ear,
ˇ And chastise with the valour of my tongue
ˇ **All** that impedes thee from the golden round,
ˇ Which fate and metaphysical aid doth seem
ˇ To have thee crown'd withal.

Lady Macbeth's reaction to having received Macbeth's exciting news is complex and rather strange. She seems to forget to whom she was reading the letter, and now, with her second thought-unit directs her words to her absent husband. As we saw in Chapter 6, because he is absent, she uses the 'thou' form to him throughout, though her use of 'thou' also reveals her love for him. So perhaps a more accurate way to describe what is happening here would be to acknowledge that if *ever* we are speaking to those who can't hear us, it is *because* they are also the ones we love.

Though her first thought in this speech is certainly celebratory, she follows this with a list of things about her husband's character that she finds disquieting. She admits that he is ambitious and wants to be great, but she also tells us that he is too kind, too *holy*. Love him as she does, she also wishes he was more like her – more ruthless when the occasion demands.

It could be you'll want more breath points somewhere in this speech, and you might want to sound out the opening line like this:

ˇ Glamis thou art, ˇ and Cawdor, ˇ and shalt **be**
ˇ **What** thou art **promis'd**:

But whether or not you want those extra 'breath points' in the first line, I hope you'll feel how much excitement is to be found in those 'valued' words I've just marked in bold.

I've chosen to make the phrase, '**What** thou' trochaic. Many will hear it iambically with Lady Macbeth's weight leaning on the 'thou' rather than the 'What'. But the rhythm of that 'shalt **be**' and the trochaic beginning to the phrase, '**What** thou art **promis'd**:' captures for me Lady Macbeth's initial exultant note of celebration. Though I admit, she could be exultant too if she chose to stress the 'thou'.

What's important is for *you to choose* which word in the new line is the one to go for – the trochee or the iamb: which works for you here? But whichever you choose, we are back again examining this moment between the end of one line and the beginning of the next – and how to release this moment of exultation? Something that may help you, not only with this particular thought, but with all those thousands of lines where the thought crosses from one line to the other, is to think of the sea.

I want to suggest to you that you think about a wave crashing onto the shore. Think of how just before this happens the wave first crests to its full height – and think of *that* as representing where the last stress in the old line occurs; and then, remembering how there seems to be something that we wait for – though the water is still in motion – *before* the wave spills itself against the land, and think of *this* as coinciding with the first stress in the new line.

This might help you with all such lines, because it's as if the wave itself takes a breath before its final dive onto the beach, just as you need that energising breath with which to deliver the new line. So did the wave crash onto the shore for you on 'What' or 'Thou'?

Reviewing our work on how to deal with complex passages

There are three and a half lines here which are very knotty and contain one of the first clusters of the words 'do', 'done', 'undone', that reverberate through this play – more so than in any other of Shakespeare's plays:

> Thou'dst have, great Glamis,
> That which cries, thus thou must do, if thou have it;
> And that which rather thou dost fear to do,
> Than wishest should be undone.

What exactly does it mean? It is when lines are difficult like these are, that finding how the stresses fall within the lines can be of most help. Here I'd have them fall like this:

Thou'dst **have**, great **Glam**is,
That which cries, **thus** thou **must** do, **if** thou **have** it;[6]
And **that** which **rather thou** dost **fear** to **do,**
Than **wishest should** be undone.

The second line begins with a trochaic beat, but otherwise all the rest just falls into a simple iambic rhythm, including the important stress on the 'un' of undone. (In the seventh scene Lady Macbeth will use the word 'unmake', which will be similarly stressed.) These lines are a great lesson to us all: trust that, nine times out of ten, the iambic rhythm will help to reveal the meaning, which on the page, especially when we are dealing with a lot of monosyllabic words, can escape us at first.[7] I do, however, confess these lines are still a bit cryptic. The gist seems to be that she knows that Macbeth wants something, but that he has to realise that the only way to get what he wants is to do something about it, and that something is the very thing he is frightened of doing; though if someone else were to do it instead of him, he wouldn't wish it hadn't been done.

Of course her lines would be immeasurably easier if only she would tell us exactly what it is he wants, what he actually has to do to get it, what he's frightened of, and what wouldn't he want *not* to have happened if it *had* happened. But the very fact that Lady Macbeth doesn't feel the need to speak *less* enigmatically is in itself very interesting. And now we know why that is. Even though she is talking to her husband, albeit in his absence, she could *only* speak so enigmatically to him if she were sure that he would know to what she is referring if he *was* there. And of course he does, because, as we've now learnt, they have spoken about killing Duncan – sometime in the past. If she were to have spoken more clearly in this soliloquy, that might make things easier for the audience to understand, but Shakespeare knows that to do that would betray the truth of her situation, and what is happening to her once she's read the letter.

But something has now become clearer. The letter, and her reaction to it, suggests that the murder-pact is not something they continually talk about, and Lady Macbeth probably senses from his letter that he's not intending to murder Duncan any time soon. But she has a solution: she will talk to her husband as soon as he returns from the battlefield, and she seems to be in no doubt that she will be able to instil in him the ruthlessness and the 'illness' that he lacks. It's time to sound it out again.

Was it exciting to play – and somewhat nerve-racking as well? Did you feel that you were really talking to Macbeth, though in his absence? But as if things are not ratcheted up high enough, before Lady Macbeth's speech is over, fate plays another card. A messenger now enters, virtually interrupting her, telling her that Duncan is coming to their castle that night.

The time-line leading up to the first murder

It is now that the exact sequence of events also becomes crucial to our understanding of the speed with which the plot unfolds and how the steps towards the murder are taken.[8] By the time the King invites himself and his entourage to Macbeth's castle, Macbeth knows that Lady Macbeth will have read his letter – though when he wrote it he never dreamt that the King would be sleeping under his roof that night. He would have felt he was writing about something promised to them both sometime in the future – in the 'hereafter', as the Witches have described it. Now the 'hereafter' is upon them. Macbeth decides to race home ahead of the King's party, because he knows what his wife will be thinking once she receives news of the King's imminent arrival: that tonight is the time to kill Duncan. The ticking of the time-bomb is becoming deafening.

Before he leaves the King's presence, he says in a rhyming aside, which I think takes him by surprise as a truth-confirming bolt from the blue:

> MACBETH. Stars hide your fires,
> Let not light see my black and deep desires:
> The eye wink at the hand; yet let that be,
> Which the eye fears, when it is done, to see.[9]

The word order in the final line is a bit difficult. It means 'which the eye fears to see when it is done', but Shakespeare wants to preserve its coded nature and the emotional strength of the rhyme.

And isn't this a similar thought (notice the words 'fear' and 'done') to those tricky lines that Lady Macbeth is shortly to utter?

> Thou'dst have, great Glamis,
> That which cries, thus thou must do, if thou have it;
> And that which rather thou dost fear to do,
> Than wishest should be undone.

How well she knows her husband and what he's afraid of.

Lady Macbeth now thanks the messenger that brought her the news of Duncan's arrival and immediately throws herself into another soliloquy, which takes as surprising a direction as anything that has happened yet for those of us who don't yet know about the Macbeths' murder-pact. Though probably by now some of the audience is beginning to sense what is afoot.

Read it out loud now – only mid-line breath marks now – it'll be good practice for you to imagine the ones at the beginning of the lines – the trochaic beats still in bold. The speech begins with what sounds like some black humour:

LADY.   ˇ The raven himself is hoarse,
That croaks the fatal entrance of Duncan
Under my battlements.

             ˇ Come you spirits,
That tend on mortal thoughts, unsex me here,
And fill me from the crown to the toe, top-full
Of direst cruelty:

            ˇ make thick my blood,
Stop up th'access, and passage to remorse,
That no compunctious visitings of nature
Shake my fell purpose, nor keep peace between
Th'effect, and it.

            ˇ **Come** to my woman's breasts,
And take my milk for gall, you murd'ring ministers,
Where-ever, in your sightless substances,
You wait on nature's mischief.

            ˇ Come thick night,
And pall thee in the dunnest smoke of hell,[10]
That my keen knife **see** not the wound it makes,
Nor heaven peep through the blanket of the dark,
To cry, hold, hold.

Lady Macbeth's reaction to her husband's letter has revealed she knows only too well that her husband might not be able to commit the murder without her being able to work him up to it. Once she's told the King is about to arrive at their castle she decides – and how rash is this? – that she'll have to kill the King herself – there will never be another opportunity like this one – and the time to do it is already upon them!

Reviewing our work on textual irregularities in this speech

There are no real technical difficulties in this speech, but I'd point out that while there may seem to be extra syllables in the phrases 'the crown to the toe' and 'Come to my woman's breasts', when you say these lines out loud, the 'to the' and 'to my' sound on the ear as one, rather than two syllables. This is something we'll find happening more and more in these later plays as the writing becomes more colloquial. The line:

> Under my battlements.   Come you spirits,

is missing one syllable in the middle of it (I've inserted the gap) and so gives you a moment to change your focus. Maybe with the phrase, 'Under my battlements' we should feel that you are looking down from the battlements, and then looking upwards as you try to locate the 'spirits' whose aid you want to enlist. I also like the way the Folio prints the word 'Whereever,' with an emphatic comma after it, which suggests to me something of Lady Macbeth's frustrated desires to see these spirits who she is trying to call down to her aid. Immediately after this she abandons trying to talk to the spirits, and calls upon the night to come and hide what she is planning to do – even from her own eyes.[11]

Then suddenly Macbeth is there beside her – it's another unheralded entrance in this play which is full of them. In the short conclusion to the scene between them, which we'll now look at, we have further instances of 'irregularities' – another interesting example of the way a change in the mode of address, from the 'thou' form to the 'you' form, signals a change in the emotional temperature between them. (I have marked the changes in bold.) Also there is a most dramatic half-line pause in this scene: another revealing moment of silence.

LADY.   Great Glamis, worthy Cawdor,
Greater than both, by the all-hail hereafter,
Thy letters have transported me beyond   1
The ignorant present, and I feel now
The future in the instant.

MACBETH.   My dearest love,
Duncan comes here tonight.

LADY.   And when goes hence?

MACBETH. Tomorrow, as he purposes.

LADY.   O never,
Shall sun that morrow see.   2

Your face, my Thane, is as a book, where men

May read strange matters,

                    to beguile the time,
Look like the time, bear welcome in your eye,
Your hand, your tongue: look like th'innocent flower,
But be the serpent under't.

                    He that's coming,   3
Must be provided for: and you shall put
This night's great business into my dispatch,
Which shall to all our nights, and days to come,
Give solely sovereign sway, and masterdom.

MACBETH. We will speak further.   4

LADY.   Only look up clear:
To alter favour, ever is to fear:
Leave all the rest to me.

                                      Exeunt.

1. A passionate moment: the only time in the scene she uses the intimate 'thou' form to his face. He almost always uses it to her. When we next hear her say 'thou' to him in Scene 7 it will be because she means to insult him by it.

2. After 'O never, / Shall sun that morrow see' Macbeth is (again) speechless, and the result is that a half-line pause ensues. His wife is saying Duncan is to die. Lady Macbeth sees her husband's expression change during that pause and the way she speaks to him now changes too. She uses the cooler 'you' form to him and does so for the rest of the scene.

3. Their language is like a code – the word 'kill' is never used – instead she says: 'He that's coming / Must be provided for:' and 'you shall put / This night's great business…' Their language also points up the dangerous world they live in – how walls have ears, and how spies are planted in the houses of the great.

4. Macbeth's 'We will speak further' means he wants to speak to her at greater length about all this. She seems to say that there is no need for that. But isn't it extraordinary that he arrives home to find her ready to carry out the murder without him, and yet he seems unable to begin the conversation to discuss this fully? Also, does Lady Macbeth really know herself – is she capable of murder?

Their coded language confirms that each knows what the other is talking about, but Macbeth's anxieties tell us that husband and wife are not, as yet, *thinking* as one. At the end of Scene 5, as they leave the stage, the King and his entourage enter. Shortly afterwards Lady Macbeth – rather intriguingly not accompanied by Macbeth – comes to greet them. The scene is another short one.

Then servants cross the stage indicating that a meal is being served and music plays.

Macbeth's Scene 7 soliloquy

Macbeth enters alone. In Shakespeare's day he might have indicated that he had just come from the feast by 'brushing the crumbs' off his doublet; Shakespeare's actors were adept at entering *as if* they had come from this or that activity as contemporary stage directions bear out.[12]

Macbeth has left the King, abandoning the celebratory feast, which would have been a most extraordinary thing to have done. And he now begins this important soliloquy. (It's now just marked up with mid-line breath points and the trochaic beats.)

> MACBETH. If it were done, when 'tis done, then 'twere well,
> It were done quickly:
> ˘ If th'assassination
> Could trammel up the consequence, and catch
> With his surcease, success:˘ that but this blow
> Might be the be all, and the end all.
> ˘ Here,
> But here, upon this bank and shoal of time,[13]
> We'd jump the life to come.
> ˘ But in these cases,
> We still have judgement here, that we but teach
> Bloody instructions, which being taught, return
> To plague th'inventor. ˘ This even-handed justice
> Commends th'ingredients of our poison'd chalice
> To our own lips.
> ˘ He's here in double trust;
> First, as I am his kinsman, and his subject,
> Strong both against the deed: ˘ Then, ˘ as his host,
> Who should against his murderer shut the door,
> Not bear the knife my self.
> ˘ Besides, this Duncan
> Hath borne his faculties so meek; ˘ hath been
> So clear in his great office, that his virtues
> Will plead like angels, trumpet-tongu'd against
> The deep damnation of his taking-off:
> And Pity, like a naked new-born-babe,

> Striding the blast, ˇ or heaven's cherubin, ˇ hors'd
> Upon the sightless couriers of the air,
> Shall blow the horrid deed in every eye,
> That tears shall drown the wind.
>
>   ˇ I have no spur
> To prick the sides of my intent, but only
> Vaulting ambition, which o'er-leaps it self,
> And falls on th'other.
> *Enter* LADY.

There are plenty of challenges here. As the evidence of his free-wheeling thoughts begin to stack up and overwhelm him, it's as if he understands everything – all the implications of murdering Duncan, both for himself and the entire universe, heaven included. So, as always, believe in what you are saying.

A good but really difficult exercise you could set yourself (at any time) is to find your own words for this (or any) speech – to paraphrase it, as I suggested in Chapter 2 – and then return to Shakespeare's words. It would certainly be a most useful exercise to do it here. And remember, this speech, like any of the others we've looked at, will take time to mature within you. The French call rehearsals 'les répétitions' – that's what you need to do: repeat the work endlessly.

The thought about Pity is sensational. How Pity will direct a blast of air, causing the whole world to weep over Duncan's murder, but that the tears will be universal and so eventually drown the very wind that has produced them. And Macbeth imagines Pity to be 'a naked new-born-babe', such as he craves, but will never have because of what he's about to do.[14]

Reviewing the importance of line endings

The opening lines of this soliloquy look so simple, but what exactly does Macbeth mean by them?

> If it were done, when 'tis done, then 'twere well,
> It were done quickly:

As we know by now, where a line ends is never arbitrary with Shakespeare. He doesn't just begin a new line after every ten or so syllables. He is capturing the voices of his characters as he hears them in his imagination, and the way a line ends will impact upon phrasing, emphasis and therefore meaning.

It is not an easy line to play and more often than not I hear actors instinctively sounding the lines as if they were written like this and without any comma after 'well':

> If it were done, when 'tis done,
> Then 'twere well it were done quickly:

or like this:

> If it were done, when 'tis done, then 'twere well it were done
> quickly:

It's important for us to realise that the first 'done' means, 'if it was finished and done with'. But the nub of this thought is revealed by the word at the end of the first line and that word is 'well,' and it has received further emphasis by that Folio comma, which my modern texts omit. To miss this though is to miss what Shakespeare heard – or let's say, the point Macbeth is making.

What is this thought that Macbeth is sharing with us? Let's again try to find where the pulse of this line falls.

> If it were **done**, when 'tis done, **then** 'twere **well**,
> It **were** done **quickly:**

(And note how in this line and a half, with its four 'it's, and three 'were's, and three (yet more) 'done's, only one of each of these words falls in a stressed place. This single sentence shows extreme clarity in terms of the writing and the expression of the thought.)

But what is Macbeth saying? He's admitting that it would be a good idea to kill Duncan as soon as possible *if* there were no repercussions afterwards. But, as he says a few lines later, he knows that there will indeed be repercussions.

His 'If' is already waiting in his thoughts to be answered by this 'But':

> But in these cases,
> We still have judgement here, that we but teach
> Bloody instructions, which being taught, return
> To plague th'inventor.

So he knows, right from the outset that no good can come of killing Duncan. But there is someone who doesn't know, or at least hasn't thought about the possible outcomes. That someone is his wife. So that first line ending in 'well,' is how he would begin to speak to his wife *if she were present*.

> If it were **done**, when 'tis done, **then** 'twere **well**,
> It **were** done **quickly:**

286

Yes, he is saying, if there were no repercussions then you'd be right in doing this thing and doing it tonight. So why isn't he talking to her about this rather than to us? Partly it's because they've had no time alone together since the King's arrival, but mostly it's because I suspect he finds talking to her difficult.

He is a soldier, a man of action. By the end of this scene he'll have spoken just over a hundred lines in the play, but *almost half of them* will have been spoken in soliloquy. To others, including his wife, he's not known as a talker.

In their first scene together Macbeth spoke only *fifteen words* to his wife. She spoke *nine times* as much to him. His last words in that scene had been 'We will speak further' which as we saw pointed to the fact that he was unable to speak to her there and then. Now the opportunity to speak further seems to have totally eluded him. The King is here, possibly eating his final meal.

Now Macbeth needs to finds arguments, and quickly, to counter his wife's determination to murder the King that night, by finding reasons to convince her that they should at least take time to think through the implications of this act. So one interpretation of this speech could be that it's a rehearsal of what he will say to his wife once they are together.

Or you could imagine that Macbeth is talking to his forebears, who might, in his hour of extreme need, come to his aid with some wise advice.[15] So with these choices in mind, try them both and see which one you prefer. After that we'll look at the scene that develops between them.

Will Macbeth choose to save his soul or his wife?

Lady Macbeth enters literally before he has finished speaking. The full stop after 'And falls on th' other.' is one way that the Folio indicates an interrupted speech. He never gets out the word 'side'.

> LADY. He has almost supp'd: why have you left the chamber?
> MACBETH. Hath he ask'd for me?
> LADY. Know you not, he has?

Macbeth now tells her he wishes to call a halt to the murder. But he fails to share with her any of those thoughts he had during his soliloquy. Could he have told her about Pity being like a naked newborn babe? I think not. So, while she has been urging that it has to be done tonight, he simply disagrees, saying no, it's the wrong time to do it; not that it's wrong, period. He merely offers up to her a practical, materialistic reason which maybe he thinks she'll accept.

The scene between them that follows gives us further fascinating examples of changes in the 'thou/you' forms of address.

MACBETH. We will proceed no further in this business:
He hath honour'd me of late; and I have bought
Golden opinions from all sorts of people,
Which would be worn now in their newest gloss,
Not cast aside so soon.

LADY.   Was the hope drunk,   1
Wherein **you** dress'd your self? Hath it slept since?
And wakes it now to look so green, and pale,
At what it did so freely?

                              From this time,
Such I account **thy** love.   2

                             Art **thou** afeard   3
To be the same in **thine** own act, and valour,
As **thou** art in desire?

                        Wouldst **thou** have that
Which **thou** esteem'st the ornament of life,
And live a coward in **thine** own esteem?
Letting I dare not, wait upon I would,
Like the poor cat i'th'adage.

MACBETH.   Prythee peace: 4

I dare do all that may become a man,
Who dares do more, is none.

LADY.   What beast was't then   5
That made **you** break this enterprise to me?
When **you** durst do it, then **you** were a man:
And to be more than what **you** were, **you** would
Be so much more the man.

                        Nor time, nor place
Did then adhere, and yet **you** would make both:
They have made themselves, and that their fitness now
Does unmake **you**.

[Continued over the page.]

1. She is outraged by his volte-face, and she accuses him of cowardice and of being a braggart. Though angry she begins by addressing him as 'you', as would probably be her normal way of speaking to him, but when *he doesn't answer her* she switches – repeatedly using 'thou' to him, not now as intimacies, but as insults.

2. She tells him, if this is how weak he is, the love he professes to feel for her is of no value to her.

3. She uses the 'thou/thine' words to him seven times. Five of them in stressed places. No one speaks to Macbeth like this and lives – Young Siward discovers this in the final battle when he says to him, '**Thou** liest abhorred tyrant.'

4. Finally, her words get an angry response from him, which is what she is after.

5. And then for the first time in the play it's made explicit how the pair have been plotting this assassination before the play begins. Now that he's engaging with her she'll revert to her normal way of speaking to him. And now she gives him eight 'you's. I mark them in bold, though only the last two are in stressed positions. When they began plotting Duncan's murder they had no idea as to how they might achieve it, but, she says, Macbeth had told her he would create such an opportunity. Note the stress on 'unmake'.

I have given suck, and know   6
How tender 'tis to love the babe that milks me,
I would, while it was smiling in my face,
Have pluck'd my nipple from his boneless gums
And dash'd the brains out, had I so sworn
As **you** have done to this.

MACBETH.   If we should fail?   7

LADY. We fail?

But screw your courage to the sticking-place,
And we'll not fail:

                 when Duncan is asleep,   8
(Whereto the rather shall his day's hard journey
Soundly invite him) his two chamberlains
Will I with wine, and wassail, so convince,
That memory, the warder of the brain,
Shall be a fume, and the receipt of reason
A limbeck* only:

                when in swinish sleep,
Their drenched natures lie as in a death,
What cannot you and I perform upon   9
Th'unguarded Duncan?

               what not put upon
His spongy officers? who shall bear the guilt
Of our great quell?*

MACBETH. Bring forth men-children only: 10
For thy undaunted mettle should compose
Nothing but males.

                Will it not be receiv'd,   11
When we have mark'd with blood those sleepy two
Of his own chamber, and us'd their very daggers,
That they have done't?

LADY.   Who dares receive it other,
As we shall make our griefs and clamour roar,
Upon his death?

MACBETH.   I am settled, and bend up
Each corporal agent to this terrible feat.
Away, and mock the time with fairest show,   12
False face must hide what the false heart doth know.

---

limbeck – container for distilling
quell – murder

6. Now Lady Macbeth, who has told us that her husband is 'Too full o' the milk of human kindness', and who has asked the spirits to 'Take [her] milk for gall', reminds him of the time she suckled a baby. Was it their baby boy? That has to be the simplest solution; and if so, it must have died, and from the way she speaks of it, maybe Macbeth was never at home during its short life, and never saw it.[16] And so she is saying to her husband that, had she sworn to do something, as he had sworn to kill Duncan, even if it had been to kill their baby that she loved, she would have done it.

7. By saying 'If we should fail?', Macbeth has turned a corner: life without her love and approval would be unbearable to him and he allows himself to listen to all that she has to say.

8. Lady Macbeth's words now sound as if the murder will be something they will perform together, rather than as she said previously, something that she was going to undertake alone. They work out their alibis: they will put the blame on the gentlemen of Duncan's bedchamber whom they will get drunk and drug. Lady Macbeth's language becomes seductive and intimate, marked by the proliferation of 's' and 'w' sounds, which I have marked in bold.

9. The language between them becomes erotically charged. Those two 'upon's at the line endings sound over-excited, as if Duncan's murder will arouse them sexually.

10. The lines certainly suggest that Macbeth now embraces his wife with passion.

11. With her beside him, embracing him, he feels invincible. They will get away with it. They are as one, they will have children, begin a dynasty. All will be well.

12. His final lines here mimic how *she* ended their previous scene together. 'Only look up clear: / To alter favour, ever is to fear'. Now he takes charge and creates his own concluding couplet.

And so the die is cast. The Macbeths return to the feast and we wait now for the King to be abed and asleep. My own answer to the question I posed at the beginning of this chapter – 'Why did they do it', I now offer to you: it was the love they felt for each other that finally made them do it. Macbeth kills Duncan for love of his wife, and she urges him to do it for love of him. Because being king was what he wanted, and what she felt, with all her heart, he deserved.

Reviewing the importance of the words in Macbeth

We have talked about the proliferation of the words 'do', 'done' and 'undone' in the play, but there is another 'd' word that appears more frequently in *Macbeth* than in any other of Shakespeare's plays and that is 'double'. It is one of the Witches' words, and figures in one of the most well-known lines from this well-known play. As the Witches stir their cauldron in Act 4 they chant in unison three times:

> Double, double, toil and trouble;
> Fire burn, and cauldron bubble.

You may remember from the second scene how the Bloody Captain's reporting of Macbeth and Banquo in the battle, rather surprisingly describes them as follows –

> As cannons over-charged with double cracks,
> So they doubly redoubled strokes upon the foe:

– and Lady Macbeth in the sixth scene saying as she greets the King –

> All our service,
> In every point twice done, and then done double,

– and here we have 'doubles' and 'done's' in a rather unholy alliance, together with the word 'point' which might make us think of the point of a knife, and Lady Macbeth has already talked about her knife in the previous scene.

These word-duplications suggest that all are trapped by double-talk and double-dealing.

Macbeth's language seems to take on something of the darkness of those night-dwelling Witches, as if he begins to understand and inhabit the same world as them. Here he contemplates the oncoming night in which Banquo will be murdered:

> Light thickens,
> And the crow makes wing to th'rooky wood:
> Good things of day begin to droop, and drowse,
> While night's black agents to their preys do rouse.
>
> *Macbeth*: Act 3, Scene 2

It is his mastery of language like this that bolsters his feeling of his own invincibility.

At the end of the play Macbeth will realise that the Witches have been speaking to him with double-tongues, or in other words they have been 'equivocating' with him, a word that the drunken Porter will use about one of his imaginary guests whom he is ushering on his way to hell. These are almost the last words that Macbeth says –

> And be these juggling fiends no more believ'd,
> That palter with us in a double sense,
> That keep the word of promise to our ear,
> And break it to our hope.

– so the doubling affects him too. But we should remember the very first words he says (in Scene 3) –

> So foul and fair a day I have not seen

– he seems to have picked up from the Witches rhyming lines from Scene 1:

> Fair is foul, and foul is fair,
> Hover through the fog and filthy air.
>
> *Exeunt.*

So the very words in this play seem to have a powerful life of their own, infecting and subverting the atmosphere, undermining the characters, as if they are not free to choose which words come out of their mouths. And – remember too how rhymes are closely associated with magic.

Reviewing our work on rhymes

As you'll recall, the play begins with the rhymes of the Witches: rhyming is the way they harness the power of words and make their magic. But the reason there is so much rhyme in the play is because the Witches' rhymes, like their very language, infect what others are saying as well.

At the end of the second scene on the battlefield, the King ominously rhymes 'Macbeth' with 'death':

> KING. No more that Thane of Cawdor shall deceive
> Our bosom interest: Go pronounce his present death,
> And with his former title greet Macbeth.
> ROSS. I'll see it done.
> KING. What he hath lost, noble Macbeth has won.
>
> *Exeunt.*

But we've already heard the Second Witch using the 'done / won' rhyme in that opening scene:

> When the hurley-burly's done,
> When the battle's lost, and won.

'Ambivalent' rhymes in Macbeth

The Witches' rhymes promise success: but in fact they spell out the downfall of Macbeth and his wife. Once Macbeth has murdered Duncan he and his wife are both plagued by terrifying nightmares and live in continual fear that others will now try and topple them from power.

Sometime after the mid-point in the play, Macbeth goes to see the Witches again, determined to find out what the future holds for him. The Witches conjure up for him three apparitions. The first tells him to beware of Macduff; the second, though, seems to make that warning redundant as it asserts that 'none of woman born' shall ever be able to harm Macbeth. Both these apparitions speak in rhyme (as you'd expect of anything to do with magic) respectively warning and comforting Macbeth. The rhymes seeming to say to him, *'Take note of these words: you can trust them'.*

The third also speaks in rhyme:

> Be lion mettled, proud, and take no <u>care</u>:
> Who chafes, who frets, or where conspirers <u>are</u>:
> Macbeth shall never vanquish'd be, until
> Great Birnam Wood, to high Dunsinane Hill
> Shall come against him.

Macbeth then completes the apparition's half-line with his triumphant cry of, 'That will never be:'.

And he surges on with an ecstatic speech in verse that continues to rhyme.

> Who can impress the forest, bid the tree
> Unfix his earth-bound root? Sweet bodements, good:
> Rebellious dead, rise never till the wood
> Of Birnam rise, and our high plac'd Macbeth
> Shall live the lease of nature, pay his breath
> To time, and mortal custom.

Macbeth: Act 4, Scene 1

He so needs these prophesies to be watertight, foolproof, that he uncon-sciously wills himself to continue with the rhymes, with the sound of having the right and true answer. No doubt he is comforted at the outset that his cry of 'never be' rhymes with his 'bid the tree'.

Again, like other characters we looked at in our chapters on rhymed verse, he is not actually conscious of having to rhyme: rather his uncon-scious need is driving him to keep, as it were, the world of that spell alive. And he continues, spelling out what the future holds for him; and as his rhymes unfold, his confidence grows so that what he is proclaiming, now in his own words, is the very answer he needs for his survival. He will be safe; he will sleep again; he will *have children*. For his lack of an heir has troubled him throughout the play.

The Witches had prophesised that Banquo's descendents would even-tually rule Scotland – not Macbeth's. That was why Macbeth had Banquo killed, but the assassins he hired failed to kill Banquo's son Fleance at the same time. So this now becomes the final question he asks of the Witches at the end of this still rhyming speech:

> Yet my heart
> Throbs to know one thing: Tell me, if your art
> Can tell so much: shall Banquo's issue ever
> Reign in this kingdom?

He needs just one more assurance from the Witches. He has left his ques-tion hovering at the mid-line point. They only need to complete the line with one more comforting rhyme to take away all his fears, and Macbeth has already given them the word 'ever' to rhyme with. What could be sim-pler than that? He's told them what to say and once they say it he will be safe. All they need to say is 'Never, never, never.'

The Witches do indeed complete the line. But the rhyming has now abruptly stopped; all they say is:

> Seek to know no more.

The words that Macbeth trusted in, the rhymed lines that seemed to be filled with assurances, will all eventually turn out to be delusion.

Sound out Macbeth's lines for yourself now and feel how those mount-ing rhymes continue to provide him with a growing sense that everything he desires is now falling into his hands – only to have a large part of it snatched away from him when the Witches stop playing their rhyming game.

He leaves this scene still falsely believing in his own invulnerability, though no longer believing that he'll father a line of kings. So his very next action is to have all Macduff's children killed. Like Herod, he will now try to kill all the children for fear of what they will do when they grow up. But what he fails to consider is that a wood could one day *seem* to be on the move if an army camouflages themselves with enough of its branches; and on that day too, a man whose birth has been by Caesarean section – and therefore not 'of woman born' – could face him on a battlefield, sword in hand.

So both the rhymes of the Apparitions and the rhyming speech of Macbeth still have the 'sound of having the answer', whether it's an answer that you receive from another or one that comes to you in some moment of inspiration. But when Viola said 'Prove true imagination, O prove true', she understood how an answer which sounds so positive might turn out to be a delusion, possibly even one sent to destroy you. In her case, as you'll remember, her instinctive answers proved true; in Macbeth's case they proved false.

The aftermath: *the rest of the play*

In their first two scenes together, Lady Macbeth speaks almost three times as much as her husband. Her entrance in Act 1, Scene 7, as we have seen, cut him off in mid-sentence. After the murder's done – and it turns out in the end that Lady Macbeth plays no part in the actual killing – Macbeth can't stop speaking, and here Lady Macbeth has to use all her powers to get him to be quiet, as he is in danger of waking everyone in the house and revealing to one and all their guilt. In that scene (Act 2, Scene 2) they have almost an equal number of lines.

But in their final two scenes alone together in Act 3, Lady Macbeth hardly speaks at all, having only ten lines to him, as compared with his sixty-plus lines to her.

Macbeth goes on murdering, and Lady Macbeth begins to fade from the foreground of the action. During the last two acts we'll see her only once, sleepwalking, watched over by her Gentlewoman and the anxious Doctor, as she spills all the beans, speaking in disorganised prose and confessing to all she and her husband have done. So at the end she is alone again, as she was at the beginning. But just before she leaves the stage for the last time she says to the husband she's *imagining* is there with her,

Come, come, come, come, give me your hand:

In her sleepwalking state at least, he is still with her.

And Macbeth's concern for her remains to the end. In Act 5, Scene 3 he asks the Doctor about his wife's health. And when told that her troubles are mental ones, it produces some of Macbeth's most beautiful lines.

> MACBETH. Canst thou not minister to a mind diseas'd,
> Pluck from the memory a rooted sorrow,
> Raze out the written troubles of the brain,
> And with some sweet oblivious antidote
> Cleanse the stuff'd bosom, of that perilous stuff
> Which weighs upon the heart?

There's a simplicity and a flow about these six lines – only one mark of mid-line punctuation; trochaic starts to four of them; the four yearning 'm's in the first two lines; then 'r' sounds, like the quiet roaring of a wounded lion; and then sweet 's's towards the end, grief and loss leading us to the weighty sound of the word 'weighs', like a great sigh. (When earlier, the Doctor watched Lady Macbeth sleepwalking he said, hearing her cry out, 'What a sigh is there.')

Two scenes later he hears of her death. And her death produces from him some of the most famous lines of *all* from this much quoted play. A character called Seyton brings the news after a cry has been heard off stage.

> MACBETH.   Wherefore was that cry?
> SEYTON. The queen (my lord) is dead.
> MACBETH. She should have died hereafter;

These last two lines are an example of 'mirroring'. It suggests a similar pace to these two three-beat lines and that would include the weight of any pause before Seyton speaks also being 'mirrored' by Macbeth.

> There would have been a time for such a word:

What is the word? Is it 'hereafter'? Maybe; it's the word the Witches used to him when they said he would be 'king hereafter', a word that was so exciting then, and is he now saying that this once exciting word is meaningless? Days have become simply endless repetitions, and so life and death have no meaning for him, and it's her death which has made all this clear. Now nothing remains to be 'done'.

> Tomorrow, and tomorrow, and tomorrow,
> Creeps in this petty pace from day to day,

To the last syllable of recorded time:
And all our yesterdays, have lighted fools
The way to dusty death.

Out, out, brief candle,
Life's but a walking shadow, a poor player,
That struts and frets his hour upon the stage,
And then is heard no more.

It is a tale
Told by an idiot, full of sound and fury
Signifying nothing.

It was an extraordinary marriage; they would have done anything for one another; they depended totally on each other. It's easy sometimes to feel, as Malcolm says of Lady Macbeth at the end of the play, that she was 'fiend-like', and we might take from that that it was her desire to be queen that drove Macbeth to murder. He certainly wouldn't have killed Duncan without her, but they were both equally ambitious for glory, and I don't think she could bear to see him pass up the chance to become king, because they had invested so much of their lives together dreaming of attaining it. The crime was bound up with their love. And that is what they did. That is what was done.

The 'done's continue to reverberate though the play. In vain did Lady Macbeth try to tell her husband back in Act 3, Scene 2 that 'What's done, is done.' Macbeth knew, in his soul, before the killing that that would not be the case. And with her final words in the play, Lady Macbeth, as she sleepwalks out of it, seems to acknowledge this at the very last (with another of the Folio's resonant emphases after the first comma):

What's done, cannot be undone. To bed, to bed, to bed.

Macbeth begins, not with the Witches, but when a married couple, Macbeth and his wife, wickedly dream of taking Duncan's life, and taking from him all his power, name and wealth. The play tells us that Macbeth swore to his wife that he would one day find the opportunity to achieve this. The swearing must have been preceded by other words. Maybe she said, 'Will you do this thing for us?' And maybe he said, 'I swear I will.' And was it she who then first said, 'All hail Macbeth, that shalt be King hereafter'?

We don't have this scene in the play. Some things are too private for plays, especially when the women's parts are all being played by boys. Maybe Shakespeare knew that this scene happened when they were in bed together, and that the whole play grew from that bad seed. But

Shakespeare doesn't need the scene: the moment is referred to, after all, later in the play.

And if we know, and if we are right, that the whole play moves forward from that moment, and if we play all these intentions with accuracy, then our audiences will also 'know' what happened all those years ago, somehow, without having to be shown it.

We are leaving *Macbeth* now, and as we might feel when leaving a theatre, after being shaken to the core by a great production of this play, what a blessing it is to be returning to the fresh air, to the world of the living, to where goodness outweighs evil. So with Shakespeare – his final plays are a return to the light. What is possibly his very next play, *Antony and Cleopatra,* while still being another tragedy, is bathed in a glorious light, and its movement is light as well. We will look at it briefly in our very last chapter – but for our penultimate chapter we are headed into a world of romance.

Sixteen

The Winter's Tale

Refining Our Work

Now bless thy self: thou met'st with things dying, I
with things new born.

The Winter's Tale: Act 3, Scene 3

Towards the end of his working life Shakespeare wrote four plays that are sometimes collectively described as Romances. These plays – *Pericles*, *The Winter's Tale*, *Cymbeline* and *The Tempest* – are neither fully comedies nor fully tragedies but a mingling of the two.

After the moral ambiguities of his 'problem plays' and the intensity of *Othello*, *Lear* and *Macbeth*, these Romances take us into an entirely different world. While *Macbeth* was inward-looking and enclosed, these Romances are its opposite: frequently filled with individuals alone, lost and travelling on dangerous journeys to far away places. A man is eaten by a bear; a statue seems to come to life. There are scenes of high comedy filled with rogues and fools. Gods intervene and move the action forward; while one child dies, many other children who were thought dead are found alive again. Love turning to hate and then seeking forgiveness, is a theme common to most of them. In all of them, families are reunited against all the odds.

And yet these plays are not like fairy stories; the worlds of these plays are grittily real, filled with the subtlest twists and turns of the characters' thoughts, feelings and reactions. If there were to be a common purpose behind their compositions it would be to show how the miraculous can manifest itself in our everyday lives. While *Macbeth* seems weighty with the nightmares that Macbeth and his wife carry through the play, in these Romances, the repercussions of the actions of the leading characters, though just as complex, move outward into a world that ripples and vibrates in surprising ways, as a result of those actions.

Collectively, the Romances represent a further 'breakthrough' in Shakespeare's writing, and *The Winter's Tale*, with its subtle, yet hauntingly beautiful verse, will stand as our example of this final development. It's right that we only come to it now because earlier we would not have been ready to deal with all the qualities it possesses. And it's fitting too, that as we come towards the end of this book, we focus on one of Shakespeare's final masterpieces. However, I also want to use this chapter as a way of *refining* all the work we have done together.

The story of The Winter's Tale

We have dipped into *The Winter's Tale* a couple of times before. I outlined the story of how Leontes, King of Sicilia, falsely accuses his wife Hermione of adultery with his old friend Polixenes and puts her on trial, having already commanded that the daughter that she has given birth to in prison, and which he is sure is not his, should be abandoned and left to die in some desert place, out of his kingdom. In the middle of Hermione's trial, news is brought that their other child, their son Mamillius, who had recently fallen sick, has suddenly died. Hermione collapses and shortly afterwards she too is pronounced dead. As if awaking from a dream, Leontes knows that he has been mistaken; but it is too late: through his own sick fantasies he has lost his whole family. He vows there and then, in that courtroom, to make daily visits to the graves of his wife and son and to continue to do so for the rest of his life.

At this point – and we are not quite halfway though the play yet – we leave the kingdom of Sicilia and journey to Bohemia, where we follow the fortunes of the baby girl that Leontes has ordered to be abandoned, far from all habitation. The babe is left by one of Leontes's courtiers, in the middle of nowhere, in the midst of a terrible storm. But by pure chance, a shepherd, looking for two of his lost sheep, finds the baby instead. Then sixteen years pass, during which the child, Perdita, grows up as the daughter of that Bohemian shepherd, while, back in Sicilia, Leontes continues to grieve for all he has lost.[1]

Act 5, Scene 1 brings us back to Sicilia with Leontes entering accompanied by his courtiers; perhaps they are returning from one of their daily visits to the graves of his wife and son. The courtiers are trying to persuade him that enough is enough, and after sixteen years this incessant mourning should now come to an end. We'll just look at the opening two speeches from this scene. Cleomenes, one of the King's courtiers is pleading with him:

> CLEOMENES. Sir, you have done enough, and have perform'd
> A saint-like sorrow: No fault could you make,
> Which you have not redeem'd; indeed paid down
> More penitence, than done trespass: At the last
> Do, as the heavens have done; forget your evil,
> With them, forgive your self.
>
> LEONTES.   Whilst I remember
> Her, and her virtues, I cannot forget
> My blemishes in them, and so still think of
> The wrong I did my self: which was so much,
> That heir-less it hath made my kingdom, and
> Destroy'd the sweet'st companion, that e'er man
> Bred his hopes out of.

The Winter's Tale: Act 5, Scene 1

On the face of it, these two speeches might seem rather unremarkable. Well, the Romances are not packed full of memorable soliloquies or other 'purple' passages. Folks who might happily be able quote you chunks from *Hamlet*, *Henry V* or *Macbeth* might not be able to quote you a single line from any of the Romances. And indeed these two speeches have much in common with the type of language we find in the Romances generally. Whilst what motivates the leading characters in these plays can be as obscure and deeply buried as anything we found in *Macbeth*, their language is generally more direct, the words and phrases often commonplace, colloquial, the stuff of daily life.

Look at the phrases that go to make up those dozen lines quoted above: 'you have done enough'; 'at the last'; 'forgive yourself'; 'I cannot forget'; 'still think of'. These are all phrases that we still hear today, spoken casually or meaningfully, as we go about our daily lives, and Shakespeare's lines are so frequently made up of phrases such as these, though never more so than in this group of plays with which he brought his writing career to a close.

Refining our work on 'phrasing'

How we 'phrase' anything is one of the most important aspects of our work as actors, because if we can learn to 'tune into' the phrasing as Shakespeare heard it, then, in our *own individual ways*, we will be able to make his characters live again *as he intended*. Just as some motoring enthusiasts might think it essential to understand how each part of their car functions, and how these parts act together, before they take it out on the road, so I want us to strip these dozen lines of verse down to their simplest components, to single words and short phrases. Only once the parts are identified, and seen for what they are, will we begin to connect them up, and only then shall we see how Shakespeare fires these words into life.

So don't as yet try to make connections between any of these phrases, just savour the words as I've printed them below, line by line, each to be repeated three times – though each time you repeat them, vary the way you say it – each time let the words touch a deeper part of you:

> Sir, Sir, Sir,
>
> you have done enough, you have done enough, you have done enough,
>
> and have perform'd / and have perform'd / and have perform'd
>
> a saint-like sorrow: a saint-like sorrow: a saint-like sorrow:
>
> no fault could you make, no fault could you make, no fault could you make,
>
> which you have not redeem'd; which you have not redeem'd; which you have not redeem'd;
>
> indeed paid down / indeed paid down / indeed paid down
>
> more penitence, than done trespass: more penitence, than done trespass: more penitence, than done trespass:
>
> at the last / at the last / at the last
>
> do, as the heavens have done; do, as the heavens have done; do, as the heavens have done;
>
> forget your evil, forget your evil, forget your evil,
>
> with them, with them, with them,
>
> forgive your self. forgive your self. forgive your self.
>
> Whilst I remember / Whilst I remember / Whilst I remember
>
> her, and her virtues, her, and her virtues, her, and her virtues,
>
> I cannot forget / I cannot forget / I cannot forget
>
> my blemishes in them, my blemishes in them, my blemishes in them,

and so still think of / and so still think of / and so still think of

the wrong I did my self: the wrong I did my self: the wrong I
did my self:

which was so much, which was so much, which was so much,

that heir-less it hath made my kingdom, that heir-less it hath
made my kingdom, that heir-less it hath made my kingdom,

and / and / and

destroy'd the sweet'st companion, destroy'd the sweet'st companion, destroy'd the sweet'st companion,

that e'er man / that e'er man / that e'er man

bred his hopes out of. bred his hopes out of. bred his hopes out of.

Aren't all these phrases so easy to say, and after you've repeated each of them three times don't they all seem to be rather ordinary, if not entirely modern? And yet these are phrases that Shakespeare himself would have said on countless occasions in his own daily life. It's worth remembering how simple Shakespeare's vocabulary can be and in part this is the point of this exercise. Though it's central aim – and it's a useful exercise to do with any Shakespeare part you are tackling – is to make the words he uses become familiar in your mouth and on your tongue – though when the words and phrases are as simple as these are, this exercise will be quickly mastered.

However, these phrases are without meaning until we begin to link them together to create some *thoughts*. (And it's interesting to note how a thought *is* essentially bringing two things together.) Now as you sound out the following thoughts, remember how the phrases that make up these thoughts are ones that you are already totally familiar with:

Sir, you have done enough,

and have perform'd a saint-like sorrow:

no fault could you make, which you have not redeem'd;

indeed paid down more penitence, than done trespass:

at the last do, as the heavens have done;

forget your evil,

with them, forgive yourself.

Whilst I remember her, and her virtues,

I cannot forget my blemishes in them,

and so still think of the wrong I did my self:

which was so much, that heir-less it hath made my kingdom,

and

destroy'd the sweet'st companion,
that e'er man bred his hopes out of.

So now the thoughts that Shakespeare's two characters – Cleomenes and Leontes – want to express are coming into focus. But some vital ingredient is missing and that is how in this particular moment Shakespeare heard *how* they were expressing these thoughts. We do not as yet hear their voices and so detect *how* they are feeling. So what is missing? Do you know?

The answer is that as yet we cannot hear how they were shaping those thoughts and therefore where they were *breathing*. So we must now insert the 'breath marks' into those lines above, as Shakespeare heard them.

Sir, you have done enough,
and have perform'd ˇ a saint-like sorrow:
no fault could you make, ˇ which you have not redeem'd;
indeed paid down ˇ more penitence, than done trespass:
at the last ˇ do, as the heavens have done; forget your evil,
ˇ with them, forgive your self.
Whilst I remember ˇ her, and her virtues,
I cannot forget ˇ my blemishes in them,
and so still think of ˇ the wrong I did my self:
which was so much, ˇ that heir-less it hath made my kingdom,
and ˇ destroy'd the sweet'st companion,
that e'er man ˇ bred his hopes out of.

And now we hear these two men as Shakespeare heard them. After the opening statement, all but one of these thoughts is expressed in two parts ('with them, forgive your self' is the one exception) and the difference this makes is that those thoughts expressed in two parts are spoken with more emotional care. An unbroken thought tends to sound confident, even boastful, whereas the other sounds shaken and shot through with whatever emotions the characters are feeling.

Now of course Shakespeare didn't put in 'breath marks'; instead he wrote in lines of verse that correspond to our breathing and so as we now return to our twelve lines *as Shakespeare wrote them*, we shall see that those 'breath marks' that I inserted above all coincide with the beginning of a new line.

CLEOMENES. Sir, you have done enough, and have perform'd
ˇ A saint-like sorrow: No fault could you make,

ˇ Which you have not redeem'd; indeed paid down
ˇ More penitence, than done trespass: At the last
ˇ Do, as the heavens have done; forget your evil,
ˇ With them, forgive your self.

LEONTES.   Whilst I remember
ˇ Her, and her virtues, I cannot forget
ˇ My blemishes in them, and so still think of
ˇ The wrong I did my self: which was so much,
ˇ That heir-less it hath made my kingdom, and
ˇ Destroy'd the sweet'st companion, that e'er man
ˇ Bred his hopes out of.

Before you sound out these lines, keep hold of everything that you felt about the simplicity of those phrases, and what you felt as the thoughts began to come back together again.

Feel Cleomenes's desire to help Leontes, and the sensitivity with which he tries to achieve that. And remember it is where his lines break that will most reveal to you *how* he is trying to persuade with care and understanding.

Feel the continuing rawness of Leontes's grief and how he can't accept what Cleomenes is suggesting. And *his* line breaks will reveal, though in small and subtle ways, the agony he lives with on a daily basis.

Choose that first stress in each new line; it will also help to make your speeches sound more vivid, more spontaneous, more creative.

And I think it's worth reminding you once more of the image of a wave, cresting before it slaps itself onto the shore. The way Shakespeare's lines follow each other is just as natural an action. You could say it's as if the wave takes a 'breath' before tumbling onto the land. So Cleomenes's first thought 'crests' on 'per*form'd*' and 'slaps' its emphatic marker down onto the word '*saint*':

CLEOMENES. Sir, you have done enough, and have perform'd
ˇ A saint-like sorrow: No fault could you make,

You may feel you need to insert some mid-line breath points as well, and were you to do so in the middle of this first line say (and I'm certainly not saying you should) you still need to take another one before the new line:

Sir, you have done enough, ˇ and have perform'd
ˇ A saint-like sorrow: No fault could you make,

Now go back and sound these two speeches out.

I hope you felt that our painstaking approach to these simple yet beautiful lines has paid off. I think four of these lines begin with a trochaic stress. But I'm not going to say which, as you should be making your own choices now. And your choices are equally valid.

For instance, look at Leontes's last eight words. Do you phrase them like this:

> that e'er man
> **Bred** his hopes **out** of.

Or like this?

> that e'er man
> Bred **his** hopes **out** of.

I don't know which I'd choose; probably one day one, one another. And yet – as this chapter is about refining our work – I want to take this a stage further. This phrase – and in the end the phrases are paramount – would suffer no loss of identity if you chose both these words or *neither*. There are ways that you wouldn't want to colour this phrase – you would never want to lean on the word 'hopes' or the word 'of', but, and especially because we are dealing here with a monosyllabic phrase, any of the other four options would be possible. The word that is always valued is the word 'out'. And in that simple, common word, Leontes is remembering, with a certain intimacy, the wife who is no longer with him.

Frequently in Shakespeare the 'phrase' will throw the underlying rhythm of the verse line, and it'll do so in order to capture some particular emotion in the voice of the speaker. But the line, as it were, understands this, and yields.

The line is always ready to receive these contrary, un-iambic, stresses.

We should let these Romances be a reminder to us of how, once broken up, these texts, which can look so set and formal on the page, are like mosaics: simply composed of words and phrases, which together become the thoughts which drive the action forward. I talked about the text being like a mosaic of phrases very early on in this book, so the close attention we have been giving to the phrases we found in those two speeches from *The Winter's Tale* is something that we can apply to all our work on Shakespeare, whether the plays are early or late in terms of their composition. But with the Romances, while the language can occasionally be clogged and complex, we'll also find in many other places that a directness and a new ease of expression has crept into his work, and though he is still writing about rulers and characters of power, he shows us them off their guard, frequently lost as to what to do, having to deal with problems that could confront any one of us. But before I ask you to sound out those twelve lines again there is something else to consider.

Refining our work on 'breathing'

I want to make a simple, though an important suggestion, about the way you take those breaths – either mid-line, or before the new line: try to take them quite quickly.

When I first talked about breathing in this book I pointed out that the line length has this correlation with what we normally say on one breath, and so for those 'end-stopped' lines it was easy to feel that the new line needed a new breath, or as I prefer to call it, 'a topped-up breath', in order to say it. But once Shakespeare realises that the sounds that reveal the disruption of all emotionally charged speech are the sounds of our breathing afresh in mid-phrase, his writing changes, and thoughts begin to overspill his lines. So we 'top up' our breath before the new line to be at one with what Shakespeare heard, and by doing this we can replicate the emotions that he's written into his lines, *and* achieve *clarity*.

However, we need to remember that for the characters themselves, they probably wish they were *not* so emotional – emotion just gets in the way of what they want to solve and sort out – and so in our playing of these characters we should do what we all do in life, which is to try to minimise the effect of these emotional interruptions, and in order to replicate this, we should not let ourselves take these breaths too leisurely.

Breathing quickly – snatching a breath – may sometimes put us into a place that feels less than easy... but that is also the point. Shakespeare, more often than not, writes to capture *unease,* and we don't want to dissipate the effect of this by taking our time over our breathing and ending up sounding too calm. We still should want to get to the end of any thought that we might be expressing, despite the 'emotional' difficulty of so doing.

So give yourself this task: sound out the twelve lines again; watch out for my 'breath marks'; and (now I've added some optional mid-line ones as well) make sure your desire is to get to the end of your thoughts as soon as is possible, by giving yourself no more time than is necessary for those new breaths:

CLEOMENES. Sir, you have done enough, and have perform'd
ˇ A saint-like sorrow:

                    ˇ No fault could you make,
ˇ Which you have not redeemed; ˇ indeed paid down
ˇ More penitence, than done trespass:

                              At the last
ˇ Do, as the heavens have done; forget your evil,
ˇ With them, forgive your self.

LEONTES.   Whilst I remember
ˇ Her, and her virtues, I cannot forget
ˇ My blemishes in them, ˇ and so still think of
ˇ The wrong I did my self:

                        ˇ which was so much,
ˇ That heir-less it hath made my kingdom,

                                   ˇ and
ˇ Destroyed the sweet'st companion, ˇ that e'er man
ˇ Bred his hopes out of.

I hope you got on all right and avoided keeling over by hyperventilating! If you survived and felt a slight sense of the urgency of the moment, and even if you felt somewhat 'wound-up', then you were probably doing it right and had found the way to 'refine' our breathing technique.

Refining our work on 'thoughts'

In *The Winter's Tale* Shakespeare is drawn to moments – important moments – which are fleeting and delicate and arise seemingly out of the smallest of incidents. Here's a soliloquy by Leontes, in which the 'form' of Shakespeare's verse captures as sudden a series of *thought-shifts* as anything we have seen from him yet.

Leontes is unable to sleep. He is in limbo, wanting to be able to put his wife on trial and so revenge himself on her, both for the adultery with Polixenes he believes her guilty of and, as he now thinks, for her part in a plot to have him assassinated. But he's having to wait, both for Hermione to give birth in prison where he's incarcerated her, and for his messengers to return from the oracle at Delphos with the judgement that he's confident will seal Hermione's fate by proclaiming her guilt to all. Now you should sound this out, watching out for the *thought-shifts*:

LEONTES. Nor night, nor day, no rest:

It is but weakness

To bear the matter thus: mere weakness,

if

The cause were not in being:

part o'th'cause,

She, th'adultress: for the harlot-king
Is quite beyond mine arm, out of the blank
And level of my brain: plot-proof:

but she,

I can hook to me:

say that she were gone,

Given to the fire, a moiety of my rest
Might come to me again.

The Winter's Tale: Act 2, Scene 3

It's that 'if' perched at the end of the second line that I especially want you to notice. That 'if' is the outcome of a terrible thought that has suddenly surfaced. But as yet it is unarticulated; it is still beyond words. But with the next breath he is able to express it. Or it could be he has to breathe more than once before he can express it, because it is such a terrible thought. And when he does express it, he does so, *choosing* his words (especially the first stress on the word 'cause') with caution.

'The *cause* were not in being' really means: 'If Hermione and Polixenes were both dead'; but because he is trying I suppose, to keep us in the audience on his side, he uses this more neutral word 'cause' (or 'the action before the court'), rather than naming them, and making clear to us exactly what's in his heart. But immediately he realises he's wrong-footed himself – so he back-tracks – of course he can't get at Polixenes: Polixenes is safe at home in Bohemia. Yet Leontes ploughs on with more abandon, revealing his murderous feelings towards the pair, though it is only Hermione that he can get his 'hook(s)' into and only she that can be given to 'the fire'.

Then a servant enters and Leontes calls out, possibly disturbed by the interruption to his thoughts:

LEONTES. Who's there?

SERVANT. My lord.

LEONTES. How does the boy?

SERVANT. He took good rest tonight: 'tis hop'd
His sickness is discharg'd.

LEONTES.   To see his nobleness,
Conceiving the dishonour of his mother.
He straight declin'd, droop'd, took it deeply,
Fasten'd and fix'd the shame on't in himself:
Threw-off his spirit, his appetite, his sleep,
And down-right languish'd.

                              Leave me solely:

                                                        go,
See how he fares:

                    Fie, fie, no thought of him,
The very thought of my revenges that way
Recoil upon me: in himself too mighty,
And in his parties, his alliance; Let him be,
Until a time may serve. For present vengeance
Take it on her:

                    Camillo, and Polixenes
Laugh at me: make their pastime at my sorrow:
They should not laugh, if I could reach them, nor
Shall she, within my power.

There is no stage direction in the Folio to show where this servant finally exits, but we don't need one because it's clear from the text that it happens at the colon in the middle of this second line:

And down-right languish'd. Leave me solely: go,
See how he fares: Fie, fie, no thought of him,

But look again at that second line – no longer divided into 'thought-units' – and the words 'he' and the 'him' within it. Do you see they refer to two different people? The 'he' is Mamillius, but the 'him' is Polixenes, which is another example of these sudden thought-shifts, which Shakespeare doesn't make clear, but trusts that the actor will clarify it for him. That is what Shakespeare hears Leontes say, and the actor will find a way to say it so the audience will understand what he means.

The soliloquy forges on – Mamillius is forgotten about – and Leontes is back with his fixations that are anchored on his wife and his friend, and now Camillo, his former chief advisor, who was responsible for getting Polixenes out of the country, is brought into the mix. And, as with all soliloquies, it is so revealing: we are here in the presence of a paranoiac; that much is clear. And it's all originally set in train by that 'if' we saw earlier teetering at the line's end. It's a wonderful example of how Shakespeare is able to use the 'framework' of the text to capture the sounds of Leontes's mania, indeed his very breathing, so that we hear it as Shakespeare heard it over his shoulder four hundred years ago.

Now I think you should put both those sections together, and as you sound it out find a way to make that 'he/him' line clear. One way to do this would be to imagine that when 'your' Leontes first makes mention of Polixenes (calling him 'the harlot-king') he fixes him in his 'mind's eye' as being in a particular part of the auditorium, which he returns to, to scowl at again, with that tricky 'him'.

Another 'thought-shift': the origins of Leontes's jealousy

Earlier, in the play's second scene, there is another – and as far as the plot is concerned an even more vitally important – 'thought-shift': Leontes, seemingly out of nowhere, begins to believe that his wife and his best friend Polixenes are lovers. (We should remember that Hermione is about to give birth, and Polixenes has been staying with them for the last nine months.) Some prefer to believe that Leontes's jealousy had been slowly growing before the play begins, but it seems to me to happen suddenly, before our eyes, and I feel that the text supports this.

We have already read the lead-up to this moment in Chapter 6, where Hermione tries to encourage Polixenes to stay with them longer, after Leontes has failed to persuade him to change his mind about departing the next day. We noted at that time how Hermione uses the 'thou' form to Leontes, when she is declaring how much she loves him, but only because he is out of hearing. To his face, certainly when with others, she always uses the more formal 'you' form. Leontes has left Hermione and Polixenes together, though is probably watching them from a distance. When he approaches them they are talking quite intimately, and because Leontes's first line to them is a shared line, coming in over what his wife is saying, it's quite likely that he hears some of what they are saying as he approaches them – maybe he even interrupts her.

And although they are speaking in all innocence, out of context her final words could sound rather odd. Read it out loud now and see if you can sense why Leontes might find this to be so.

HERMIONE.   yet go on,
    Th'offences we have made you do, we'll answer,

> If you first sinn'd with us: and that with us
> You did continue fault; and that you slipp'd not
> With any, but with us.

LEONTES.   Is he won yet?

HERMIONE. He'll stay (my lord).

LEONTES.   At my request he would not:

> Hermione (my dearest) thou never spok'st
> To better purpose.

The Winter's Tale: Act 1, Scene 2

And with that the moment seems to be over: it's as if nothing much has happened, but in fact everything has changed. What did you notice here?

The royal 'we'

Maybe you thought that if Leontes only hears the last couple of lines as he approaches his wife and Polixenes, he would not know what his wife means by the word 'us'.

Hermione is actually using the word 'us' quite normally to refer to herself and Polixenes's wife, and she's using the word 'you' to refer to Polixenes and Leontes. She is saying that if Leontes and Polixenes only ever had sexual relations with their own wives then they have committed no offences. But Leontes might have felt her use of 'us' was the way a queen might sometimes speak to refer to *herself*.[2]

(Leontes also uses the 'royal we', as when in Act 2, Scene 1 he berates his courtiers for daring to suggest Hermione is innocent:

> Why what need **we**
> Commune with you of this?
>   inform your selves,
> **We** need no more of your advice…)

Leontes might have thought he'd overheard Hermione saying something about herself and Polixenes when she wasn't. And Leontes's line 'Is he won yet?' seems to interrupt Hermione because it sounds as if she's not got to the end of what she might be intending to say. (As I said in the chapter on Folio punctuation, the full stop after 'but with us.' could indicate such an interruption.)

However, probably even more important is what is to come, and yet it seems so slight. She tells her husband that Polixenes will stay longer, to which with another shared line Leontes replies:

At my request he would not:

There's something naked about this line: as if he has been shocked by what he's been told. Then he recovers himself and congratulates his wife on her achievement. But you see the colon at the end of this line: this wonderfully open-ended mark, like an open mouth that has come to a stop and is no longer speaking, but has not yet come to any sort of conclusion. My modern text substitutes a full stop, which fails to suggest that it might be from this colon that Leontes's deranged suspicions seem to grow.[3]

Within a minute, as Hermione and Polixenes walk away from him, Leontes is saying to their backs, 'Too hot, too hot:' and in less than another minute he finds himself wondering if his son, Mamillius, who is standing with him, is actually his son or not.

Dealing with 'difficult' speeches: refining our work on 'thought-units'

Once Hermione and Polixenes have withdrawn we come to the following speech which is admittedly 'difficult'.[4] So we'll do what we always do and divide it up into 'thought-units' and see whether that can't help us with this 'difficulty'.

It begins with father and son talking together:

LEONTES. Art thou my calf?

MAMILLIUS.   Yes, if you will (my lord).

LEONTES. Thou want'st* a rough pash,* and the shoots* that I have
        To be full, like me:
                        yet they say we are
        Almost as like as eggs;
                        Women say so,
        (That will say any thing.)
                        But were they false
        As o'er-dy'd* blacks, as wind, as waters; false
        As dice are to be wish'd, by one that fixes
        No bourn* 'twixt his and mine; yet were it true,
        To say this boy were like me.

want'st – lack
pash – head
shoots – beard, tuft
o'er-dy'd – re-dyed
bourn – boundary

Come (Sir Page)
Look on me with thy welkin* eye:

Sweet villain,
Most dear'st, my collop:*

Can thy dam*, may't be

Affection?*

thy intention* stabs the centre.

Thou dost make possible things not so held,
Communicat'st with dreams

(how can this be?)

With what's unreal: thou coactive* art,
And fellow'st nothing.

Then 'tis very credent,
Thou may'st co-join with something,

and thou dost,

(And that beyond commission) and I find it,
(And that to the infection of my brains,
And hard'ning of my brows.)

The plays of Shakespeare are peppered with references to the 'horns' that appear, metaphorically, on the heads of all men whose wives are unfaithful to them, or, as is almost always the case, on the heads of those who mistakenly believe this to be their situation. And as terrible to those who suffer from the fear of those horns, is the hilarity of others who see them so afflicted. So Leontes's 'hard'ning brows' at the end of this speech (and the 'shoots' at the beginning) are referring to the plight of cuckolds who imagine horns growing on their heads for all to see.

There are some quite difficult words here as you'll see from the number I've glossed. Even so what Leontes is saying might still be difficult for us to grasp. But we have found similarly obscure passages elsewhere, and what we should remember is that Shakespeare is always intent on capturing what he hears his characters say; and for him to make them speak more coherently would be false to the situations in which they find

welkin – sky blue
collop – flesh and blood
dam – mother
affection – sexual desire
intention – powerful urges
coactive – needing a partner

315

themselves. Leontes is lost in a nightmare and that is what he is expressing. But as long as you've worked out where the 'thought-units' are, and what the words mean and what these characters are *trying* to work their way through, you should be able to take us with you on that journey

However, it's the passage from 'Can thy dam, may't be / Affection?' that causes the most difficulties. So, when all else fails we need to set ourselves the task of paraphrasing what Leontes's speech – full of stops and starts, as it is – is saying. My paraphrase goes like this – though once you've read my attempt see if you can't improve upon it:

'Can your mother… is it possible… Desire… you work upon us to our very core… you achieve the impossible… act upon us in our dreams… how can this happen?… with something that's imaginary… you're able to make us believe we're making love to someone though no one is actually there.' And from this Leontes argues that, if 'desire' has the power to do this, it will even more readily draw someone to an actual partner, which is precisely what he believes (though mistakenly) has happened between his wife and Polixenes.

The absence of any punctuation after the phrase 'may't be' is the way the Folio sometimes indicates an interruption, even a self-interruption. The question mark after the word 'Affection' is one of those sudden exclamations, not a real question; the colon after 'what's unreal' is an emphasising colon in the middle of this thought, used to highlight how extraordinary this thought is.

Now try the speech again and see if an understanding of all the words and the separation of the thought-units, together with how the Folio punctuation works, can make your journey through this much-argued-about passage an exciting but trouble-free one.

Refining our work on 'thou' and 'you'

In Chapter 6 we saw how, as his suspicions about his wife developed early in the play, Leontes switched from addressing her lovingly with the 'thou' form, to the cooler 'you' form, and then on to the 'thou' of insult and abuse. Similarly, once he has brought his wife to trial, he uses the 'you' form to her at the beginning of the session but before long his language reverts to the 'thou' of aggression, even within the same speech, here suggesting it's her silence that infuriates him. Sound this speech out now and see if you can feel if her refusal to answer anything, provokes in you that run of 'thy', 'thee' and 'thou':

LEONTES.   **Your** actions are my dreams.
    You had a bastard by Polixenes,
    And I but dream'd it:

                As **you** were past all shame,
    (Those of **your** fact are so) so past all truth;
    Which to deny, concerns more than avails:

                          for as
    Thy brat hath been cast out, like to it self,
    No father owning it (which is indeed
    More criminal in **thee**, than it) so **thou**
    Shalt feel our justice; in whose easiest passage,
    Look for no less than death.

The Winter's Tale: Act 3, Scene 2

Hermione refuses to be cowed by her husband and announces that she wants to be judged by Apollo: she demands that the Oracle that has come from Delphos should be read out. The court grants this, and the Oracle affirms Hermione's innocence. But Leontes refuses to accept the truth of it. His denial of its worth is followed immediately by the shocking news of Mamillius's death, and by Hermione's subsequent collapse and removal from the court.

Leontes, in panic, now admits that he has been mistaken in all his wild suspicions, and it is Paulina who, having accompanied Hermione's inert body off stage, now returns to tell the court what has happened to her. We have not mentioned Paulina yet, though she is one of the most important characters in the play and has the longest female role in it. She was married to Antigonus, who in the next scene will meet his gruesome end, being eaten by a bear, on that Bohemian seacoast.[5]

Paulina enters incandescent with rage; she no longer uses the 'you' form of address to the King, as she would have always done before, even though she has been outspoken and red with rage with him on a previous occasion.[6] Now she enumerates all his crimes in a magnificently searing, barely controlled, twenty-five line speech, in which she uses the 'thou' form to him ten times, at the end of which she tells him that Hermione is dead. And even if she's aware that he's beginning to look devastated by all that has happened, she doesn't flinch from delivering her final judgement on him as the 'thou's continue:

PAULINA. But, O **thou** tyrant,
Do not repent these things, for they are heavier
Than all **thy** woes can stir: therefore betake **thee**
To nothing but despair.

A thousand knees,
Ten thousand years together, naked, fasting,
Upon a barren mountain, and still winter
In storm perpetual, could not move the gods
To look that way **thou** wert.

Let's just take a moment to look at what is actually said in those last four lines of hers because it's another reminder that we should always assume that characters speaking blank verse mean what they say, rather than thinking that that's just the sort of thing people say in plays. We must take it literally: if five hundred naked, fasting people were to pray continually on the top of a mountain in a winter storm in relays for ten thousand years, the gods would still not forgive Leontes for what he's done.

In playing this scene we have to find a way to make Paulina's use of 'thou' to the King seem the most outrageous insult that any subject could offer to their sovereign. Kent, in his anger, does this to King Lear and is immediately banished for it.[7] And we saw in Chapter 13 that Helena in *All's Well that Ends Well* also uses 'thou' to the King of France – she initially gets away with it, the King is so much in her thrall – it's only later that the repercussions of her audacity return to haunt her. And Paulina gets away with it here because Leontes knows she has every right to speak to him in this way.

But then, with only about twenty-five lines left before the end of the scene, comes a change. And it is this which makes the next section so extraordinary. Paulina stops speaking. Leontes encourages her to go on lambasting him, but an attendant lord angrily tells Paulina:

you have made fault
I'th' boldness of your speech.

Clearly he's talking about her use of the insulting 'thou' form to the King. But Paulina's rage is spent, and she answers the lord's rebuke:

I am sorry for't;
All faults I make, when I shall come to know them,
I do repent:

Alas, I have show'd too much
The rashness of a woman: he is touch'd
To th'noble heart.

> What's gone, and what's past help
> Should be past grief:

And then amazingly, she tries to undo all she has done – reverting to the 'you' form as she does so – and in so doing Shakespeare reveals such an insightful, moving, and psychologically true representation of how in crises we can be bounced from one extreme to another – though still, being Paulina – even as she asks for forgiveness, even as she says she will not talk about the souls who have been lost, she names them again: and the result is almost unbearable to watch:

> Do not receive affliction
> At my petition; I beseech **you**, rather
> Let me be punish'd, that have minded **you**,
> Of what **you** should forget.
>
> Now (good my liege)
> Sir, royal sir, forgive a foolish woman:
> The love I bore **your** queen (Lo, fool again)
> I'll speak of her no more, nor of **your** children:
> I'll not remember **you** of my own lord,
> (Who is lost too:)
>
> take **your** patience to **you,**
> And I'll say nothing.

So these final nine lines of hers have to be worked as strongly in an attempt to pull Leontes back from the pit of despair, as her thirty-odd lines that preceded it had driven him to the brink of it. Have a go at it now.

Both tasks should be emotionally draining, though the intervention of that attendant lord creating, as it were, the lull in the storm when the raging winds drop, give Paulina a breathing-space, before they start blowing again from the opposite direction.

I have called this section 'Refining our work on 'Thou' and 'You'', but it's really Shakespeare who is refining *his* work here in his ability to reveal to us these shattered lives in all their agony. How does he do it? Well, as whatever story he is working on matures within him, whether for him it's a gift, or a curse, these characters he is writing about must 'become' a part of him: he *feels* as they feel; he *suffers* as they suffer; he *joys* as they joy. But it's even more extraordinary yet, because he's able to feel for all of his characters *at one and the same time.*

Shakespeare *is* Leontes and Paulina – yes, and that emotional attendant lord as well.

The first performance of all these plays happens within him – that's how I think he does it.[8]

Finally put those speeches of Paulina's together, and if you have a full text beside you, take it from Paulina's re-entrance, so as to include that first run of ten 'thou's, 'thee's and 'thy's. Sound them all out again and *feel* how these changes in the mode of address can help you to see and understand the emotional shifts that the characters make – one to another.

Refining our work on prose in The Winter's Tale

Just when all seems lost, something is recovered. As Leontes and Paulina leave the scene, bowed down by their grief, and Antigonus has lost his life after abandoning the baby, they are soon replaced by a simple Bohemian shepherd, who is looking for his lost sheep in the middle of a storm, and he stops to share his predicament with us. What happens is that he'll not find his sheep; instead he'll find Leontes's abandoned baby daughter Perdita. The point seems to be that only a good shepherd would be out on a day like this, and that if he hadn't been doing his best to find his sheep, the baby would never have been saved.

The Shepherd is one of our 'prose entertainers' (see above, page 117). He'll speak in verse when things get serious, but he prefers chatting away to us in a witty way, complaining, as he is here, about the young men of the neighbourhood (my slashes once again marking the thought-units):

> They have scared away two of my best sheep, which I fear the
> wolf will sooner find than the master; if any where I have them,
> 'tis by the sea-side, browsing of ivy. / Good-luck (and't be thy
> will) what have we here? / Mercy on's, a barne? / A very pretty
> barne; / A boy, or a child I wonder?

The Winter's Tale: Act 3, Scene 3

I think it's clear that what happens here is that he thinks he's spied one of his lost sheep. The baby all swaddled up in woollen shawls looks, as it lies there on this stormy day, like a sheep that has fallen and can't get up. He approaches the pale shape with his crook and discovers a child. Now there is no stage direction in the Folio to indicate when he sees what he thinks he sees, but the text suggests to me that his line,

> Good-luck (and't be thy will) what have we here?

is his response to what he's just spotted. However, many modern texts add a 'helpful' stage direction about him 'seeing the baby' *before* he says this line, in so doing they obscure from us what's actually happening: hiding from us the joy the Shepherd initially expresses, thinking he's found one of his sheep, only for him to experience an even greater joy, once he realises he's saved a baby's life.

The Shepherd's son now turns up, The son, or 'Clown' as he called in his speech-headings, tells his father how he's seen both Antigonus, the courtier who had been ordered to abandon the baby being eaten by a bear, and the ship that brought Antigonus to Bohemia sinking with all hands. But he's so aghast at the two sights that he saw at one and the same time, that he tries to keep both his reports running concurrently. His speech finishes:

> But to make an end of the ship, to see how the sea flap-dragon'd
> it: / but first, how the poor souls roared, and, the sea mock'd
> them: / and how the poor gentleman roared, and the bear
> mock'd him, / both roaring louder than the sea, or weather.

Now standing side by side, these two 'prose entertainers' become a double act, sparring off each other to our amusement – the father now getting in on the act:

> SHEPHERD. Name of mercy, when was this boy?
>
> CLOWN. Now, now: / I have not wink'd since I saw these sights: /
>   the men are not yet cold under water, nor the bear half
>   din'd on the gentleman: / he's at it now.
>
> SHEPHERD. Would I had been by, to have help'd the old man.
>
> CLOWN. I would you had been by the ship side, to have help'd
>   her; there your charity would have lack'd footing.
>
> SHEPHERD. Heavy matters, heavy matters: / but look thee here
>   boy.

And, as the Shepherd continues, comes the line that becomes the play's hinge:

> Now bless thyself, thou met'st with things dying, I with things
> new born.

> *The Winter's Tale*: Act 3, Scene 3

Our 'good' Shepherd, though, turns out to be as human as the rest of us; he and his son discover that a box has also been left beside the baby and it's filled with gold. And once they've found the gold they can't get home fast enough. With the baby safely in his arms, the Shepherd says to his son, who is holding the box in his,

> Let my sheep go: / Come (good boy) the next way home.

And as the two characters leave the stage, suddenly made rich by this turn of events, the play swings from death to life and heralds in the great comic, country scenes of Act 4.

But before we lose sight of these Bohemian shepherds, I want to draw your attention to something else that has just happened. And that is that a Sicilian king, Leontes by name, though he doesn't know it yet, has had his life and soul 'saved' by the actions of these humble inhabitants of some faraway country, who on this day, simply decide to do the right thing. This is what I meant earlier in saying that the actions of the leading characters in these Romances move outward, having unforeseen consequences in the wider world. We are all connected, one with another, and Shakespeare writes about this too.

Fully a quarter of *The Winter's Tale* is written in prose, most of it accounted for by the comic scenes in Act 4, where another great 'prose entertainer' appears, the rogue Autolycus, who fleeces the shepherds and their friends of their purses, but finally turns out to be another character whose actions, unintentionally, help to bring the play to its final resolution. The play had also begun with a short prose scene between Camillo, Leontes's chief advisor, and Archidamus, a Bohemian lord, accompanying his King, Polixenes, on his visit. Their prose exchange reveals the careful fencing of two experienced courtiers discussing the nature of the nine-month visit that Polixenes has made to Leontes, and their language becomes a screen 'hiding' some unease they are feeling, but not overtly expressing. Their disquiet may have arisen out of the excessive entertainment that Leontes is providing for his oldest and best friend, whom he hasn't seen since childhood, as if the situation had an underlying precariousness about it. And maybe Leontes's son Mamillius is already looking frail. The scene between these two men ends with their discussion of the young boy:

> ARCHIDAMUS. You have an unspeakable comfort of your young
> Prince Mamillius: / it is a gentleman of the greatest
> promise, that ever came into my note.
>
> CAMILLO. I very well agree with you, in the hopes of him: / it is
> a gallant child; one, that (indeed) physics the subject,

makes old hearts fresh: they that went on crutches ere he
was born, desire yet their life, to see him a man.

ARCHIDAMUS. Would they else be content to die?

CAMILLO. Yes; if there were no other excuse, why they should
desire to live.

ARCHIDAMUS. If the King had no son, they would desire to live
on crutches till he had one.

Exeunt.

The Winter's Tale: Act 1, Scene 1

These last lines of prose amount to a quarter of the entire first scene. And
I wonder why it ends like this. It is the visitor who introduces Mamillius
into their conversation – does he feel some anxiety about this young boy?
And the words that follow are about 'hopes' and death and what would
happen if Leontes had no son. Are the two men actually concerned for his
wellbeing?

**Prose, which by its nature hides things from us, prompts us to ask these
questions.**

Prose is also the form in which the penultimate scene is written, in which
three Gentlemen all try to outdo the others in the reporting of the news
that's just broken: that Leontes has found his long-lost daughter, Perdita.
And prose is the form in which such competitive language can be most
fittingly captured. These gentlemen are much more concerned with how
well they are performing, rather than having any real feeling for the news
they are reporting. For them the miraculous has become a media opportunity. Here is a taste of the gentleman who was able to see most of what
went on:

> GENT 3. One of the prettiest touches of all, and that which
> angled for mine eyes (caught the water, though not the
> fish) was, when at the relation of the Queen's death (with
> the manner how she came to't, bravely confess'd, and
> lamented by the King) how attentiveness wounded his
> daughter, till (from one sign of dolour to another) she
> did (with an Alas) I would fain say, bleed tears; for I am
> sure, my heart wept blood. / Who was most marble,
> there changed colour: some swooned, all sorrowed: / if
> all the world could have seen't, the woe had been
> universal.

The Winter's Tale: Act 5, Scene 2

The effect of their prose on us is that it reveals how self-opinionated these Gentlemen are, yet it also gives us an *understanding* of the extraordinary scene they have witnessed. But most importantly the prose shields us from experiencing the emotions of the scene at first hand, with the result that we will be open to the emotions that *will* be released in the final scene when, once again verse – sublime, simple, shared-line verse – takes over. In the earlier play *Pericles* another king finds the daughter he thought was dead in one beautiful emotional verse reunion, and shortly after that is reunited with his supposedly dead wife – and this second scene, also in verse, cannot then match the emotions of the first. So Shakespeare, in this later play, has learnt to do it better.

The Winter's Tale: *the final scene*

Maybe this is the most perfect and wondrous scene that Shakespeare ever wrote, and if you've never read the play you should set aside a couple of hours to do so, and feel the full emotional force of the play's conclusion. For in a relatively short scene, all the characters, including Leontes, now reunited with his lost daughter Perdita, come to view the statue of Hermione that, we are told, has recently been completed, and is in the keeping of Paulina, who, it turns out, also owns an art gallery. Everyone is amazed by how lifelike the statue appears, though Leontes feels it looks distinctly older than Hermione as he remembers her; but he weeps to see her and to see his daughter gazing on the mother she never knew.

And then the miracle happens: Paulina asks Leontes if he would like the statue to move, and come and take his hand; Leontes, heart-in-mouth, assents. Music plays, and after some urging by Paulina, the statue leaves its plinth and descends towards the astonished Leontes. Paulina, stage-managing the whole affair, gently helps Leontes overcome his astonishment, saying to him:

> PAULINA.   do not shun her,
> Until you see her die again; for then
> You kill her double: Nay, present you hand:
> When she was young, you woo'd her: now, in age,
> Is she become the suitor?
>
> LEONTES.   Oh, she's warm:
> If this be magic, let it be an art
> Lawful as eating.

And with those simple though such heart-filled words, the couple who have been lost to each other for sixteen years, take hands, embrace, and as we are told, 'she hangs about his neck.' Shakespeare has brought her, who seemed dead, to life – she who was cold as stone is now warm; and once she has seen Perdita – her lost one – we will, once again, hear her voice.

We have one short chapter left before we take leave of each other, and there I want to show you how, as it seems to me, Shakespeare believes in his heart that the whole of creation is bound together in some lively dance; and, as his writing makes clear, it is through our actions and our imaginative forces that nothing that *is* is without some kind of life, if *we* invest it with sufficient meaning and significance.

Seventeen

Sounding Shakespeare

PROSPERO.   I'll break my staff.
Bury it certain fathoms in the earth,
And deeper than did ever plummet sound
I'll drown my book

The Tempest: Act 5, Scene 1

The Tempest is the last play that Shakespeare wrote as sole author, but it is followed by *The Two Noble Kinsmen, Henry VIII* and a lost play called *Cardenio* – all of which were probably collaborations with the younger playwright John Fletcher.[1]

Those words of Prospero's quoted above come towards the end of the play as he renounces all his magical powers. He is going to throw his book of spells into the deepest part of the ocean. A 'plummet' is a lead weight used for measuring the depth of the sea, but Prospero is going to throw his book into an even deeper place – too deep to be measured. The word 'sound' here means something like 'investigate' or 'search' – so not at all like the way I have often used the word in this, *my* book, when I have asked you to 'sound out' this or that passage from one of Shakespeare's plays.

However, it could be said that we have in *our* way also been 'sounding out' Shakespeare, as we have gone in search of him, and have been trying to investigate why he writes in the way he does. Shakespeare, for his part, 'sounds' out the whole human race, as he tries to understand *us*, and then he asks us as actors to 'sound' *him* out so that others might understand what he has discovered.

Before we part company, let us look at Shakespeare at work one final time together.

But in order to feel confident that we are able to see what he does, we have to do what we did in the very first chapter of this book, and catch him when he is again using someone else's text on which to base his own. So we are going to end as we began, by looking again at Shakespeare's use of some of North's translation of Plutarch. But this time, not from his life of Brutus, but from his life of Mark Antony. Once again we will see how closely Shakespeare is following his source, but this time our main interest will be to see what he *adds*.

The passage is Plutarch's description of when Cleopatra arrived on her barge, on the river Cydnus, to meet Mark Antony for the very first time. Plutarch doesn't put these words into any character's mouth, as he did with that speech of Lucilius's in *Julius Caesar* – both in Plutarch and in North this is pure narrative. But as Shakespeare is writing a play, he has to find a character to give these lines to. And his first stroke of genius is how he chooses to give Plutarch's breathtaking picture of Cleopatra's arrival to the most cynical and least 'poetic' of characters in *Antony and Cleopatra* – Enobarbus, Antony's general. We met him earlier trying to disrupt that meeting between Antony and Caesar in Chapter 8.

So over the page is North's translation of this passage from Plutarch, which was first printed in 1579, when Shakespeare would have been fifteen years old.

I have divided it up into sections comparable with Shakespeare's 'thought-units' so that we can compare the Plutarch with Shakespeare more easily.

1.   She disdained to set forward otherwise, but to take her barge in the river of Cydnus;

2.   the poop whereof was of gold, the sails of purple,

3.   and the oars of silver, which kept stroke in rowing after the sound of the music of flutes, hautboys, citherns, viols, and such other instruments as they played upon in the barge.

4.   And now for the person of her self, she was laid under a pavilion of cloth of gold of tissue, apparelled and attired like the goddess Venus, commonly drawn in picture:

5.   and hard by her, on either hand of her, pretty fair boys apparelled as painters do set forth god Cupid, with little fans in their hands, with the which they fanned wind upon her.

6.   Her ladies and gentlewomen also, the fairest of them, were apparelled like the nymphs Nereides (which are the mermaids of the waters)

7.   and like the Graces, some steering the helm, others tending the tackle and ropes of the barge,

8.   out of the which there came a wonderful passing sweet savour of perfumes, that perfumed the wharf's side, pestered with innumerable multitudes of people.

9.   Some of them followed the barge all alongst the river's side: others also ran out of the city to see her coming in. So that in the end, there ran such multitudes of people one after another to see her, that Antonius was left post-alone in the market-place, in his imperial seat, to give audience:

Plutarch's *Life of Mark Antony*
As translated by Sir Thomas North

ENOBARBUS. The barge she sat in, like a burnish'd throne   1
    Burn'd on the water:

               the poop was beaten gold,   2
    Purple the sails: and so perfumed that
    The winds were love-sick with them.

                  The oars were silver, 3
    Which to the tune of flutes kept stroke, and made
    The water which they beat, to follow faster;
    As amorous of their strokes.

               For her own person,   4
    It beggar'd all description, she did lie
    In her pavilion, cloth of gold, of tissue,
    O'er picturing that Venus, where we see
    The fancy out-work nature.

             On each side her,   5
    Stood pretty dimpled boys, like smiling Cupids,
    With divers colour'd fans whose wind did seem,
    To glow the delicate cheeks which they did cool,
    And what they undid did.

AGRIPPA.   Oh rare for Antony.

ENOBARBUS. Her gentlewomen, like the Nereides,   6
    So many mer-maids tended her i'th'eyes,
    And made their bends adornings.

               At the helm,   7
    A seeming mer-maid steers: The silken tackle,
    Swell with the touches of those flower-soft hands,
    That yarely frame the office.

             From the barge   8
    A strange invisible perfume hits the sense
    Of the adjacent wharfs.

           The city cast   9
    Her people out upon her: and Antony
    Enthron'd i'th'market-place, did sit alone,
    Whistling to th'air: which but for vacancy,
    Had gone to gaze on Cleopatra too,
    And made a gap in nature.

           Antony and Cleopatra: Act 2, Scene 2

It's clear to see that Shakespeare is following the Plutarch/North account very closely; there are some thirty identically shared key-words (mostly nouns) and twenty-five of these are in the same order as North has them. But unlike those identical run of words we noticed between North and Shakespeare in that speech from *Julius Caesar*, apart from the phrase 'cloth of gold of tissue', here everything else is reshaped and magically transformed.

Antony and Cleopatra was probably written just after *Macbeth*, and so is another comparatively late play. So we have, as we'd expect, beautifully phrased movements between one line and the next, and I can't resist marking in a couple of stresses in the passage that follows, though along with the 'breath marks' I should be now leaving *all* this to you:

> On each side her,
> Stood pretty dimpled boys, like smiling Cupids,
> With divers colour'd fans whose wind did seem,
> To *glow* the delicate cheeks which they did *cool*,
> And what they *undid did*.

The last of these lines with its 'undid' reminds me of *Macbeth* and all the 'done's' and 'undone's' we found in that play; also the line before is so beautifully organised with its first stress on 'glow' and the last on 'cool'. But this is such a different play to *Macbeth*, and though nearly half as long again, it is not weighty at all, and my remembrance of it from when I directed it at the Globe in 1999 (though we were called Masters of Play then, rather than directors) is, as if it were bathed in a golden light, and that the play moved fleetly from scene to scene. I suspect though this had much to do with Mark Rylance's luminous performance as Cleopatra in this 'all male' production.[2]

Hear those 'b' sounds in those opening lines, which sound so seductive and brooding:

> The barge she sat in, like a burnished throne
> Burn'd on the water:

And in those final lines we have those multiple 'a's', filling the mouth with such open sounds, which are themselves interrupted by those three guttural 'g's' giving a contrasting toughness to the passage – seeming to say that this Cleopatra is a force to be reckoned with: a force of nature.

> Whistling to th'air: which but for vacancy,
> Had gone to gaze on Cleopatra too,
> And made a gap in nature.

But there is more, much more, and those last three lines should give us a clue. And the clue is that the 'air' is behaving as *if* it had feelings and desires of its own: the 'air' would, if it could, have deserted Antony to go and gaze on Cleopatra too. And *this* is what Shakespeare adds. He takes the bare facts from North and everything he adds is to give these bare facts *life and movement*.

Just as we saw when Romeo first met Juliet, Shakespeare makes the entire picture of this event come alive; then I described it as his instinct for animating the inanimate and here, marked in bold, I want to show you how it happens again, but on an even greater scale:

> ENOBARBUS. The barge she sat in, like a burnish'd throne
> Burn'd on the water:
>
> the poop was beaten gold,
> Purple the sails: and so **perfumed that**
> **The winds were love-sick with them.**
>
> The oars were silver,
> Which to the tune of flutes **kept stroke, and made**
> **The water which they beat, to follow faster;**
> **As amorous of their strokes...**
>
> On each side her,
> Stood pretty dimpled boys, like smiling Cupids,
> With divers colour'd fans **whose wind did seem,**
> **To glow the delicate cheeks which they did cool,**
> **And what they undid did...**
>
> At the helm,
> A seeming mer-maid steers: **The silken tackle,**
> **Swell with the touches of those flower-soft hands,**
> **That yarely frame the office.**
>
> From the barge
> A strange invisible **perfume hits the sense**
> **Of the adjacent wharfs.**
>
> **The city cast**
> **Her people out upon her:** and Antony
> Enthron'd i'th'market place, did sit alone,
> **Whistling to th'air: which but for vacancy,**
> **Had gone to gaze on Cleopatra too,**
> **And made a gap in nature.**

Like a painting by Van Gogh, everything is alive, everything contributes, everything has *feelings*. The winds are 'in love' with the perfumed sails on

Cleopatra's barge; later they 'play' an amorous game with Cleopatra herself, arousing and cooling her simultaneously as they fan her cheeks. The oars have 'become' music-lovers; the river Cydnus 'discovers' that to be beaten by the strokes of her oars is so seductive that the river 'races' in order to keep up with her barge; the silken tackle on the barge becomes 'aroused' and 'swells' as her gentlewomen take them in their hands. Even the wharfs have senses, being able 'to smell' the perfumes that waft out from this 'burnish'd throne'; the city too is like a living creature, 'urging' its population out to where Cleopatra can be gazed upon; and were it not against the rules of nature, the very air, filled with similar desires, 'would like' to be able to follow where the people have gone.

But the vision belongs to Enobarbus. Enobarbus it is who sees how the winds and the river, the oars, the tackle and the wharfs and the city itself are all alive and have meaning *because* of Cleopatra. His speech makes us believe not only in the reality of the *wonder* of what he saw, but by association, his speech gives to Cleopatra a goddess-like stature, making it clear that she is the cause that every 'thing' is so excited and aroused.

In Shakespeare's plays, not only can he bring the statue of a dead queen back to life, but stones move and trees speak, and tapers try to peep under eyelids to see a sleeping woman's eyes.[3] This is one of the ways his stage becomes a *living* space in which his actors can move with conviction. He creates scale and excitement by taking us to extremes. Look what he does with Plutarch's description of Cleopatra herself, as translated by North.

> And now for the person of her self, she was laid under a
> pavilion of cloth of gold of tissue, apparelled and attired like
> the goddess Venus, commonly drawn in picture:

Here it almost sounds as if she were dead, rather than being this spirit that was making everything around her vibrate with life. Initially I smile at Shakespeare's phrase that she 'beggar'd all description', because clearly the Plutarch/North description of her is itself most beggarly. But then I realise that Shakespeare's phrase, 'beggar'd *all* description', taken literally, is in itself so wonderfully extreme: *anything* you could ever say about Cleopatra would come too short. But not content with that, Shakespeare takes up his own challenge, and triumphs by saying that Cleopatra outshines all those paintings of Venus we have ever seen, even though we know these are all more beautiful than any real woman could ever be. So Cleopatra surpasses both art and nature:

> For her own person,
> It beggar'd all description, she did lie

In her pavilion, cloth of gold, of tissue,
O'er picturing that Venus, where we see
The fancy out-work nature.

So now I'm going to ask you one last time to turn back the pages and sound out this, our final speech – Enobarbus's description of Cleopatra's arrival on the river Cydnus.

This book can have no real ending because there is no end to 'sounding out' Shakespeare. All I have wanted to do is to share with you the thoughts that I've had after many years of living with, and listening to, his lines. And *looking* at them too, for we must use our eyes as well as our ears, because his scripts are as fascinating as any code or cipher. And our work together has also been about trying to crack that code.

I'm not at the end of my 'sounding' of him quite yet, neither in that word's sense of 'investigating' him, nor in the sense of encouraging the sound of his words to continue to reverberate around me. But I expect you could be just at the beginning of yours, and hopefully you will uncover many more of his secrets. Each time I come back to one of his plays I find something new and unexpected that whacks me between the eyes! But if you intend to continue to 'sound' him out, I'd like to pass on to you something that I heard Maria Callas, the great opera singer, say in a TV documentary:

Take trouble to really listen with your soul and with your ears –
and I say soul and ears because the mind must work, but not
too much.[4]

She was answering the question as to how she found her way into a role, and how she came upon the appropriate physical manifestations of the character with which to bring that role to life. And she said it was the conductor Tullio Serafin who gave her this advice – urging her to listen to the music with her soul as well as her ears. So we should do the same: we should listen to Shakespeare not with our ears alone but with our souls too.

We have come a long way together, but there will always be more for us all to discover.

Sounding out Shakespeare is the work of a lifetime: and then some.

Appendix

My Comments on the Duologue in Chapter 7

As I'm hoping you will also have done, I have now divided this scene up into thought-units. I have also marked in bold those places where the iambic beat gives way to some variation, and marked the changes of the 'forms of address' in bold italics.

CLAUDIO. Now sister, what's the comfort?

ISABELLA.   Why,   1
    As all comforts are: most good, most good indeed,

    Lord Angelo having affairs to heaven
    Intends you for his swift ambassador,
    Where you shall be an everlasting lieger;

    Therefore your best appointment make with speed,
    Tomorrow you set on.

CLAUDIO.   Is there no remedy?

ISABELLA. **None**, but such remedy, as to save a head
    To cleave a heart in twain:

CLAUDIO.   But is there any?   2

ISABELLA. **Yes** *brother*, you may live;   3

    There is a devilish mercy in the judge,
    If you'll implore it, that will free your life,
    But fetter you till death.

CLAUDIO.   Perpetual durance?

1. The first line 'Now sister, what's the comfort? Why,' is short: it's missing two syllables. Isabella is 'thrown' by the directness of Claudio's question and his use of the word 'comfort' *dis*comforts her. So there's a momentary 'hesitation' before her 'Why'. I also think the comma after 'Why', giving emphasis to that word, momentarily increases her unease, till she finds how to *use* his word 'comfort' in her next line. And so as she reaches for the word 'comfort' the first two syllables in the line, 'As all', become somewhat compressed – virtually sounding as a single unstressed syllable – though they 'ruffle' the line in an interesting way.

2. Notice now the sequence of 'shared lines' as Claudio begins to press his sister for more information, which she seems reluctant to give him. His shared lines should sound like interruptions.

3. A more obviously short line. What did you think happened here? I'm sure that Claudio makes some audible reaction to this piece of news – relief of course – which then Isabella has to cope with. Claudio's continuing questions continue to unsettle Isabella.

ISABELLA. Aye just, perpetual durance, a restraint
    Though all the worlds vastidity you had
    To a determin'd scope.

CLAUDIO.   But in what nature?

ISABELLA. In such a one, as you consenting to't,
    Would bark your honour from that trunk you bear,
    And leave you naked.

CLAUDIO.   Let me know the point.

ISABELLA. Oh, I do fear *thee* Claudio, and I quake,   4
    Lest thou a feverous life shouldst entertain,
    And six or seven winters more respect
    Than a perpetual honour.

                    Dar'st thou die?

The sense of death is most in apprehension,
And the poor beetle that we tread upon
In corporal sufferance, finds a pang as great,
As when a giant dies.

CLAUDIO. Why give you me this shame?   5

    Think you I can a resolution fetch
    From flow'ry tenderness?

                 If I must die,
I will encounter darkness as a bride,
And hug it in mine arms.

ISABELLA.   There spake my brother: 6
    There my father's grave
    Did utter forth a voice.

               Yes, *thou* must die:

Thou art too noble, to conserve a life
In base appliances.

             This outward sainted Deputy,
Whose settled visage, and deliberate word
Nips youth i'th head, and follies doth enew
As falcon doth the fowl, is yet a devil:

His filth within being cast, he would appear
A pond, as deep as hell.

CLAUDIO.   The precise Angelo?

ISABELLA. Oh 'tis the cunning livery of hell,
    The damnest body to invest, and cover
    In precise guards;

4. Claudio's run of questions, and now a demand for clarification, begins to scare Isabella – this is not how she thought he would behave and she begins to shake. Also we have here our first change in the 'form of address'. Brother and sister would normally address each other as 'you', but now Isabella begins to say 'thee' and 'thou' to Claudio. In her fear, which is real, it's as if she now begins to try and comfort him, as she might have done when he was a young child, to whom it would be normal to use the intimate 'thou' form.

5. Did you spot that these two short lines are an example of 'mirroring'? Claudio 'mirrors' her line, angry at the way she's 'baby-talking' him about beetles and giants. And with his instinctive use of the 'mirroring' technique he now gains the upper hand in their conversation.

6. Here are three half-lines. Which two form a full line? The Folio prints 'There spake my brother: there my father's grave' as one complete line, leaving the earlier 'And hug it in my arms' as a single short line. But this lineation doesn't make sense to me. I feel Isabella would be so delighted by the courage of Claudio's brag that she'd want to express her joy at once. So I'm suggesting that her initial words, 'There spake my brother' complete his line, and I have therefore printed 'And hug it in mine arms. There spake my brother:' as a shared line. Then I believe she follows that up by embracing *him* in *her* arms – the colon possibly indicating this action. Their silent embrace accounts for the shortness of 'There my father's grave', so the pause (for the embrace) comes before this half line, which we hear once the embrace is completed. I have marked that last '**thou**' in bold again, not because she has again changed her mode of address, but because she is using the 'thou' form in its other guise: she's no longer treating him as a child, now her 'thou's' are a sign of the love she feels for her brave 'saviour' of a brother. And his apparent courage now gives her the confidence to tell him exactly what offer Angelo has made to her.

                 dost thou think Claudio,
If I would yield him my virginity
Thou might'st be freed?

CLAUDIO.   Oh heavens, it cannot be.

ISABELLA. **Yes**, he would give't thee; from this rank offence
So to offend him still.

                  This night's the time
That I should do what I abhor to name,
Or else thou diest tomorrow.   7

CLAUDIO. *Thou* shalt not do't.

ISABELLA.   O, were it but my life,
I'd throw it down for **your** deliverance   8
As frankly as a pin.

CLAUDIO.   Thanks dear Isabel.

ISABELLA. Be ready Claudio, for your death tomorrow.

CLAUDIO. **Yes.**

              Has he affections in him,   9
That thus can make him bite the Law by th'nose,
When he would force it?

                  Sure it is no sin,
Or of the deadly seven it is the least.

ISABELLA. **Which** is the least?   10

CLAUDIO. **If** it were damnable, he being so wise,
Why would he for the momentary trick
Be perdurably fin'd?

                Oh Isabel.   11

ISABELLA. What says my brother?

CLAUDIO. **Death** is a fearful thing.

ISABELLA. And shamed life, a hateful.

CLAUDIO. **Aye,** but to die, and go we know not where,

To lie in cold obstruction, and to rot,

This sensible warm motion, to become
A kneaded clod;

               And the delighted spirit
To bathe in fiery floods, or to reside
In thrilling region of thick-ribbed ice,

To be imprison'd in the viewless winds
And blown with restless violence round about

7. Three more half-lines, which the Folio ranges left, so again we have to make a judgement about which lines form a shared line, and where the moment of 'hesitation' occurs. I think it occurs after Isabella's 'diest tomorrow'. Claudio cannot answer her straight away and hesitates. To make his hesitation less obvious, and to try and bind himself to what he's now about to say, he uses the '**thou**' form to her for the only time in the scene – it's as if he's taking an oath that he will not *allow* this to happen, and his language becomes biblical. His 'Thou shalt not do it', like 'Thou shalt not commit adultery' becoming another divine commandment. But his hesitation implies that the contrary thought – 'might you do it for me?' – has flashed through his mind.

8. Isabella has noticed her brother's hesitation and her form of address now reverts to the more reserved 'you' form. There is another syllable missing after 'As frankly as a pin', with suggests that there is the tiniest of moments before Claudio responds to the way his sister has said that she would willing sacrifice her life for him, but not her virginity. This line has a double feminine ending and I scan it like this:

    As **frank**ly as a **pin**. **Thanks** dear Isabel.

    Isabel having three syllables, but here pronounced with only one stress on the first of the three.

9. Another short line – 'Yes. Has he affections in him': and his 'moment of silence', coming after his 'Yes', is on account of this new thought that is just striking him.

10. Isabella's line is obviously short, but I think something happens here other than another silence. Claudio simply seems to ignore her question, and continues to pursue his own line of thought. I think what we have here is a virtual 'overlap': we hear what she says, but Claudio continues as if her question is irrelevant and not one he wants to waste time in answering.

11. Quite a lot happens here. The line 'Be perdurably fin'd? Oh Isabel' scans the name Isabel differently from before. Now as he cries her name out in his agony, it is stressed **Isabel**, and Isabella fearing what is to follow, pauses before her line, 'What says my brother?' The next two lines employ the tit-for-tat 'mirroring' technique, as Isabella scorns his fear and weakness, which pitches us into Claudio's speech about death.

The pendant world:

or to be worse than worst
Of those, that lawless and incertain thought,
Imagine howling,

'tis too horrible.

The weariest, and most loathed worldly life
That age, ache, penury, and imprisonment
Can lay on nature, is a paradise
To what we fear of death.

ISABELLA.   Alas, alas.

CLAUDIO. Sweet sister, let me live.   12

What sin **you** do, to save a brother's life,
Nature dispenses with the deed so far,
That it becomes a virtue.

ISABELLA.   Oh you beast,
Oh faithless coward, oh dishonest wretch,
Wilt **thou** be made a man, out of my vice?   13

Is't not a kind of incest, to take life
From thine own sister's shame?

                    What should I think,

Heaven shield my mother play'd my father fair:
For such a warped slip of wilderness
Ne'er issu'd from his blood.

                    Take my defiance,
Die, perish:

                    Might but my bending down   14
Reprieve thee from thy fate, it should proceed.

I'll pray a thousand prayers for thy death,
No word to save thee.

CLAUDIO.   Nay hear me Isabel.

ISABELLA. Oh fie, fie, fie: 15

Thy sin's not accidental, but a trade;
Mercy to thee would prove it self a bawd,
'Tis best that thou diest quickly.

CLAUDIO.   Oh hear me Isabella.   16

12. Claudio's line is clearly short, but what happens here? Maybe he's thrown himself down at her feet – hanging on to her skirts? You decide, but something of that sort is called for by the shortness of the line and I feel that Shakespeare has imagined some physical action. He now begins to plead with her to save him and with his next line his form of address has now returned to the deferential 'you'.

13. Isabella is horrified and as this speech develops, her more reserved use of 'you' transforms into the 'thou' of insult and anger.

14. Rhythmically the most unusual line, and it unsurprisingly occurs at one of the most emotionally intense moment in the scene. I would define it as a triple trochee with a break after 'Die'. So the stresses would be as follows:

   Die, ^ perish: **Might** but my bending **down**

   And Isabella's speech ends with her saying she wouldn't save him, even if all she had to do was simply to kneel down to do so. Instead, she says she will pray a thousand prayers for his death rather than saying a single word on his behalf. (I know this is probably obvious, but it's so easy to accept lines like this as the sort of things characters say in plays, and to forget that that is what – in this moment – she means.)

15. Although it looks like we have a short line here, I think once again we have an overlap and Isabella's 'Oh fie, fie, fie:' comes in over Claudio's interjection and flows into the rest of her speech.

16. Probably with her last words, though there is no stage direction to suggest this, Isabella is leaving, and this produces a shared hexameter, or a line with six stresses between them. And I'd have it scan like this:

   'Tis **best** that thou **diest quickly**. Oh **hear** me **Isabella**.

   I'm allowing one syllable to disappear, as it were, in the saying of the line: I'm going to count 'that thou' as one syllable. But then you will see we have two unstressed syllables in the middle of the line. It is an 'epic caesura' between the two speakers. What is that smallest of gaps about? It's suggesting that he doesn't absolutely come in on cue. That gap may be the moment when Shakespeare imagines that she tears away from him, *before* he cries out after her, before the scene between them apparently results in a final parting of their ways.

Acknowledgements

Several people have helped me in the writing of this book and I'd like to acknowledge them here.

I began writing in earnest in the early months of 2010 while I was teaching at Mary Baldwin College in Staunton, Virginia.[1] I had thought that my task would be a simple one: to describe all that I had been sharing with actors and students over the past twenty years. But to my surprise, the act of writing provoked new thoughts, new questions. Foremost among these I became increasingly conscious of a connection between a line of Shakespeare's verse and the way we breathe during speech. Eventually I discussed this with Globe Education, and their research department, early in 2011. Their response was generous: they funded a short research project which I was able to undertake with three actors later in that year, and much of what we discovered there has found its way into the pages of this book.[2]

There are a handful of books and articles that have been of particular help to me. These include *Shakespeare's Metrical Art* by George T. Wright and *Shakespearian Punctuation* by Percy Simpson (now sadly out of print I believe). I also learnt much from reading both John Jones's *Shakespeare at Work* and John Southworth's *Shakespeare the Player*. Only last year I found Penelope Freedman's *Power and Passion in Shakespeare's Pronouns* which filled in some gaps in my understanding. Many years ago I came across a dissertation by Dorothy L. Sipe which convinced me that Shakespeare's choice of words, and word-order, reveals the value he places on iambic rhythms. Two articles taught me more about the way we breathe: Alison L. Winkworth's article (with others) 'Breathing Patterns During

Spontaneous Speech', published in the *Journal of Speech and Hearing Research* (February 1995), and Ann MacLarnon and Gwen Hewitt's 'Increased Breathing Control: Another factor in the evolution of human language', printed in *Evolutionary Anthropology* 13 (2004). Finally I can no longer do without having beside me *Shakespeare's Words* by David and Ben Crystal.

On a more personal note there are some colleagues who have encouraged me and furthered my understanding of Shakespeare. The debt I owe to Peter Hall, I have touched upon in my Introduction. A few years later in 1995 Richard Eyre, then Artistic Director of the National Theatre, gave me the opportunity of running a series of Shakespeare workshops at the National Theatre Studio, and this indirectly led me to the Globe. Others include the late actor and director John Southworth, and my dear friends Nigel Frith, and Jan and Laurence Carter, the theatre critic Michael Billington, and the actor Michael Elwyn. Also I want to pay special tribute to my wife, the actress Penelope Beaumont, who has read this book on more than one occasion; and who, thankfully, has always been prepared to challenge my ideas, and has therefore played a large part in shaping them.

Finally, I acknowledge a huge debt to my most supportive editor and publisher Nick Hern, and his colleague Nick de Somogyi. Together they have helped me sentence by sentence, chapter by chapter, and it is true to say that if this book possesses any of the qualities of clarity and readability much of it is down to them.

End Notes

1. An example of a line that is usually changed from that found in the Folio comes from Act 5, Scene 1 of *The Winter's Tale*. Leontes is saying to Paulina that were he to marry again, his dead wife would come back to haunt him. Here, as Paulina agrees with him, are the following two speeches in the Folio:

   PAULINA.   Had she such power,
      She had just *such* cause.
   LEONTES.   She had, and would incense me
      To murder her I married.

   But most modern editions remove that second 'such' of Paulina's (that I have italicised) on the grounds that the line now has one syllable too many, and that the printer probably just repeated the 'such' from the previous line in error. And so the altered 'shared line' between the two characters reads in the modern version like this:

   She had just cause. / She had, and would incense me

   What now happens to the line is that it's become rather ugly, with both speakers similarly stressing the word 'had' one after the other. But *The Winter's Tale* is a late play of Shakespeare's and at this stage in his writing he very frequently begins a line with *two* unstressed syllables, which is what I think happens here. So the doubling of the word 'such'

344

in the Folio has the effect of making Paulina stress the word 'just' (rather than 'had') and in so doing the word 'just' also changes its meaning. It is no longer, as in the modern edition, an adjective meaning 'a justifiable cause', but an adverb meaning 'precisely such cause'. The shared line in the Folio sounds perfectly natural and rather beautiful – and in my view should be allowed to stand.

Introduction

1. The occasion was a talk Peter Hall gave to the Broadway company of his production of *The Merchant of Venice* in 1989. Dustin Hoffman was playing Shylock. I was working with Peter as his Associate Director.

2. It would be good to have a copy of the Complete Works within reach just for your own interest. The plays from which I am going to ask you to read passages not found in this book are *Much Ado About Nothing*, *All's Well that Ends Well*, *The Winter's Tale* and *Macbeth*.

Chapter 1

1. The Lord Chamberlain's Men, the company Shakespeare belonged to, had been playing at The Theatre, on the north side of the City, but were unable to renew their lease. So in 1599 they dismantled the building and, reusing the timbers from it, built the Globe on the other side of the river. The first Globe was burnt to the ground during a performance of Shakespeare's *Henry VIII* in 1613, but a second Globe, this one built with a tiled, rather than a thatched roof, was built the following year. The present reconstructed Globe, the brain-child of the American actor Sam Wanamaker, was fully opened in 1997. What makes the Globe different from most other theatres is that almost half the audience stand to watch the play, and the entire audience is lit throughout the performance; so the actors see the audience, as clearly as the audience see them

2. The Folio prints 'honour'd' to indicate the word is here pronounced with two syllables – as we'd say it today. But occasionally Shakespeare might want the word to sound with three syllables and then the Folio would print 'honoured' – as we'd spell it today – though it should then be pronounced 'hon-our-èd'.

3. The first line of Lucilius's six-line speech seems to call for some stress on the first syllable 'Safe' which together with the stress of the first syllable of 'Antony' makes it a somewhat unusual line, though not one that will cause us any difficulty when it comes to saying it.

4. Christopher Marlowe was born in 1564, the same year as Shakespeare. His first great success as a dramatist was with *Tamburlaine* in 1587, which may have been the first play to have been written in iambic blank verse to be performed in one of the main public theatres. Earlier plays – some in blank verse – had been staged in private theatres.

5. T.S. Eliot, who wrote successful verse plays in the middle of the last century, said in a lecture delivered in 1950 that 'the verse rhythm' (in a play) 'should have its effect upon the hearers, without their being conscious of it.'

Chapter 2

1. The Blackfriars Theatre in Virginia is a reconstruction of the indoor theatre that Shakespeare's company took possession of in 1608/9. At the original Blackfriars, candles lit both stage and auditorium alike, and in Virginia today this company proudly proclaim how they still 'do it with the lights on!' While their 'candles' are electric, the Globe will open its own reconstruction of a Jacobean theatre in 2014, and there the candlelight promises to be genuine. It is to be named 'The Sam Wanamaker Playhouse'. (See End Note 1, Chapter 1.)

2. Antony's line is short. 'Where is he?' only has three syllables. And it's deliberately so, and is Shakespeare's way of *writing in a pause*. And it is in that pause, before Lucilius speaks, that the soldiers realise they have captured the wrong man.

3. Here are the colours I gave to each of these 'thought-units'. But remember that there is no absolute right and wrong way to go about this exercise. 1: amazement/assertive; 2: milder/nostalgic; 3: bitter; 4: like a teacher; 5: warning; 6: developing the warning in a wider way; 7: like 4 but a different lesson; 8: softer/emotional; and 9 (after the King doesn't take up the offered moment to respond to her speech): confidently and generously inviting the others to join in the discussion.

4. All these fancy words are just a useful shorthand. But if they worry you (and I can have too much of them myself) here are some consoling words from Montaigne's essay on 'The Vanity of Words' – a work that Shakespeare is likely to have read himself. 'Do but hear one pronounce Metonomia, Metaphor, Allegory, Etymology, and other such trash-names of Grammar, would you not think, they meant some form of a rare and strange language? They are titles and words that concern your chamber-maid's tittle-tattle.' (From Florio's English translation of Montaigne's *Essays*, 1603.)

Chapter 3

1. Kyd is most remembered for his play *The Spanish Tragedy* and it might be that his great melodrama took the public stages by storm even before Marlowe's *Tamburlaine*.

2. We may today feel that Hermione's trial is taking place inside a court-room, but she herself tells us otherwise. Indeed plays at the Globe theatre to this day frequently give us a sense that a scene is taking place *in front* of a building, to which, and from which characters come and go.

3. The authorities would close the playhouses when the number of weekly deaths from the plague seemed to warrant it.

Chapter 4

1. Alexander Pope in his *Essay on Criticism* (1711) describes how 'The Sound must seem an Echo to the Sense.'

2. This line is short. It has nine syllables, though we probably 'hear' only eight, with the word 'happier' sounding as two rather than three. But whether eight or nine, the line has this brief pause written into the middle of it.

3. The Folio usually prints words like 'myself' or 'yourself' as two words – 'my self' and 'your self', with the stress falling on the word 'self' – and in so doing seems to be referring to a deeper part of 'our selves' than when the two words come together as one, as is customary in our usage today.

4. These lines are called 'epic caesuras'; you will find out more about them in Chapter 6, pages 96–100.

5. The mid-line comma frequently indicates a place where the iambic is replaced by a trochaic foot. To see more examples go to Chapter 6, pages 89–90.

Chapter 5

1. Though the opening line of *Julius Caesar* – 'Hence: home you idle creatures, get you home:' – might have seemed a doubtful beginning to some. The playgoers might have imagined that the authorities were closing the theatre down and actually asking everyone to leave!

2. The difference between the punctuation of the First Folio and some modern texts is striking. My modern version of Hamlet's speech changes about two-thirds of all the Folio's punctuation marks. In particular it adds eleven more exclamation marks to the Folio's two. Generally speaking, modern versions slow up the whole speech.

3. When I was playing Hamlet at Ipswich Theatre in 1976, this was one of the many insights given to me by the director John Southworth.

4. In a production directed by Richard Eyre at the Royal Court.

5. As it might be when Macbeth asks for guidance when he soliloquises as whether or not to kill Duncan. (See Chapter 15, page 287.)

Chapter 6

1. Nick de Somogyi has drawn my attention to 'Orson Welles's acting habit of all but interrupting his collocutor's line, biting it off, as it were, and overlapping his dialogue' – a technique which is similar to the effect that Shakespeare's 'shared line' aims at. Welles himself was a great actor and director of Shakespeare, both on stage and film, and it's conceivable that he developed this technique from his understanding of how Shakespeare's 'shared lines' worked. There are actual 'overlaps' in Shakespeare's plays too, and I suggest (see the end of Chapter 2) that one occurs between the Duke of Gloucester and Henry VI towards the end of *Henry VI, Part Three.*

2. Actually this first 'shared line' is somewhat of an exception. There is an extra unstressed syllable in the middle of this line: 'To *tell* me *truly*. Good *madam pardon me*.' So the 'ly' of 'truly' and the word 'Good' are not stressed. A line like this is called an 'epic caesura' (see Chapter 6, pages 96–100). The effect of such a line is to create the slightest of pauses in the middle of it. So here Helena comes in *almost* on cue, but not as quickly as she might.

3. Epic caesuras are rare in Shakespeare's early plays, but quite common in his later ones. However, they appear with greatest frequency in a group of plays – all written around the years 1602–5: *Troilus and Cressida, All's Well that Ends Well, Measure for Measure, Othello* and *King Lear*. It's as if for a time, Shakespeare was frequently drawn to this rhythm whenever he wanted a mid-line break.

4. I think there are six – though possibly seven!

5. More conciliatory because, by completing a line and thereby creating a shared line, you are giving the previous statement a greater measure of regard. You, and whoever you are speaking to, are breathing as one; taking in what they have said, and moving on from it. 'Mirroring' by contrast sounds out a strong alternative opinion. Also note how the first of these three pairs of 'mirroring lines' begins with a 'mirrored' trochaic beat.

6. There are two texts of *Richard III* – it's one of the plays for which we have a Quarto version as well as the Folio, and interestingly (and confusingly) there are literally hundreds of minor, and not so minor differences between them. Here the Folio has 'That shall **thou** know hereafter'. I used to think that the Quarto's 'That shall **you** know hereafter' seemed to make more sense, because Anne was moving away from her insulting use of 'thou' to Richard, to the cooler, more polite 'you' form with which she ends the scene. However, in working on the play at the Globe in 2012, with Mark Rylance as Richard and Johnny Flynn as Lady Anne, I began to think that if the Folio were to represent Shakespeare's second thoughts, then her reverting to 'thou', and using it as a 'come-on' for this one line, could make this fascinating scene all the richer. And that is how we eventually played it.

Chapter 7

1. The Folio uses open-ended inverted commas as a way of marking proverbs and moral maxims – or 'sentences' as they used to be called. As Percy Simpson explains in his *Shakespearian Punctuation*, 'a favourite device to call attention to them was the use of inverted commas at the beginning, but not at the end, of the line.'

Chapter 8

1. In 1999 when I joined the Globe, Mark Rylance felt that as the role of the director of the play was so demanding, it would be better if, as in the world of opera where a musical director works alongside the theatrical director, the role was divided at the Globe along similar lines. In Mark's time the theatrical director was known as the Master of Play, and the one whose role was to listen out for the text was originally called Master of Verse. After a few years I was allowed to change this title to Master of the Words, because I wanted a title that would acknowledge how much prose Shakespeare wrote. Once Mark left the Globe at the end of the 2005 season, these titles became a thing of the past.

2. While these Clowns don't speak in blank verse, they frequently sing songs and recite rhymes.

3. Sir John Falstaff appears in *The Merry Wives of Windsor* and both parts of *Henry IV*. The Epilogue to *Henry IV, Part Two* seems to suggest that Falstaff will also appear in *Henry V*, but if so Shakespeare changes his mind, and instead has his death movingly reported in the middle of Act 2.

4. The word 'humour' was something of a buzz word in 1599 when *Henry V* was written. In the previous year Ben Jonson had written his play *Every Man in his Humour;* it had been performed by the company that Shakespeare belonged to, and Shakespeare himself was one of the actors in it. In Jonson's play, the main characters are ruled by one dominating characteristic, or 'humour', and Shakespeare is clearly influenced by this. His character Nym – who appears in *Henry V* and *The Merry Wives of Windsor* – uses the actual word 'humour' in almost every other sentence that he utters, and so this becomes *his* dominating characteristic.

5. The Folio and most modern texts do not print this line as verse. Probably Shakespeare manuscripts were often unclear where a passage of prose ended and verse took over, and so errors such as these frequently occur. But the rhythm is verse and that is all that matters – and with it, the emotions pour into the scene.

Chapter 9

1. Lines from one of the Commendatory Poems prefixed to the 1647 Folio of the plays of Beaumont and Fletcher.

2. From the opening sentence of Percy Simpson's *Shakespearian Punctuation,* first published in 1911. A view he himself absolutely disagreed with.

3. The substitution of 'o'erdone' for 'over-done' in this passage occurs because this editor is here following *Hamlet* as printed in the Quarto of 1604/5. I prefer the rhythm of the Folio's 'over-done'.

4. The first line is not a full pentameter – something happens between Guildenstern's and Rosencrantz's exclamations. An excited sound from Hamlet maybe.

5. *King Lear* is another of the plays which was also published as a Quarto (1608). And several of the lines quoted here are only found in the earlier Quarto version and not in the Folio. Maybe they were deliberately 'cut' from the Folio to keep the play moving forward, and thus not allowing Lear even a moment of rest – incessant journeying being one of the main ingredients of this play. But today these Quarto lines are usually included in any staging of the play. (The opening line of the Quarto passage I've printed here is clearly missing the word 'she' – hence the square brackets around it.)

6. Matthew, Chapter 10, verse 29.

Chapter 10

1. Beatrice also has ten lines of rhymed verse when she is alone at the end of Act 3, Scene 1, after overhearing that Benedick loves her.

2. Most editions remove the full stop after 'Claudio' and substitute a comma, but this is a highly difficult and emotionally fraught moment for Benedick, and the full stop could indicate that he breaks off in mid-sentence – which is how the full stop is sometimes used in the Folio – before regaining his composure and completing his speech.

3. This line of Benedick's is printed as verse in the Quarto, but as prose in the Folio. Either might have been Shakespeare's intention. If it is prose (as here) then Benedick I suppose becomes unnerved by what Beatrice is saying, and in throwing the verse rhythm attempts to cover his anxiety with a somewhat panicked attempt at wit. Also, maybe oddly, both Quarto and Folio print 'deceived' – though most modern editions print 'deceiv'd' indicating that these editors feel it should be pronounced as two syllables rather than three. However, if the Quarto is right and the line should continue as verse, it's a verse line with only four stresses in it. If it is prose then maybe 'deceived' should be pronounced rather pedantically with three syllables. For I believe, though I think many don't, that in prose these words printed with an 'ed' ending should on occasions be pronounced with an extra syllable. When Lady Macbeth is sleepwalking and speaking prose (see Chapter 15) the Folio gives her, 'Fie, my lord, fie, a soldier, and affear'd?', though at the top of this same speech her famous phrase 'Out damned spot:', it is not printed damn'd, but damned – and I think in performance 'damned' with two syllables might sound better.

4. The Folio probably incorrectly gives this line to Leonato. But I suppose it is just possible that Leonato, in his anxiety about whether Beatrice and Benedick will ever be able to seal the knot, takes his niece by the hand, and gives her to Benedick to be kissed as he, Leonato, is saying this line.

5. Time is always elastic in the plays of Shakespeare. From scene to scene the plays move forward with speed. But when you come to the end of a play, looking back over it, the feeling you have is that you have been with these characters over a longer period a time. (It is therefore usually a waste of time to try and pin down too absolutely how much time has elapsed scene by scene.) However, it seems Beatrice overheard

that Benedick loves her on the day before Hero's aborted wedding, and Benedick probably overheard that Beatrice loves him, earlier on the same day or the day before. For the audience these considerations matter not at all while they are watching the play, but for those of us who put the plays on, sometimes we need to draw some conclusions from these facts. And here we can safely say that since they both overheard what they overheard, they haven't met each other again until now.

6. Beatrice's line is in verse rhythm with a missing beat before the final 'farewell'. So we hear from her a rare 'sound of sincerity' with a break before that final word.

7. In Beatrice's two speeches filled with her frustration at not being a man, we have five Folio exclamation marks: a wonderfully appropriate occasion on which to use them.

8. Though in her rhymed soliloquy at the end of Act 3, Scene 1, she uses the 'thou' form when speaking to Benedick in his absence. See Chapter 6, pages 84–5.

9. The absence of any punctuation here is one of the ways the Folio marks an interruption by another speaker.

10. Though it could be said by using the word 'lechery', he speaks more insightfully than he is aware of.

11. Though *As You Like It* and *Henry IV, Part Two* both have Epilogues written in prose, and *Love's Labour's Lost* ends, after a song, with an enigmatic prose statement, possibly spoken by Don Armado: 'The words of Mercury are harsh after the songs of Apollo: You that way; we this way.'

12. For the percentages of blank verse, rhymed verse and prose to be found in Shakespeare's plays which I sometimes mention, I am indebted to tables I have found in *The Complete Pelican Shakespeare,* edited by Alfred Harbage. I also use the tables of lines that deviate from the pentameter found in George T. Wright's *Shakespeare's Metrical Art.*

Chapter 11

1. I have italicised the *'not'* to indicate it receives more stress than the final 'hit' in the line, and yet the 'hit'/'wit' rhyme will still sound out.

2. Some editors emend the Folio's 'fire' to 'fires' to make the rhyme with 'liars' absolute.

3. In some editions this scene is counted as being Scene 5, rather than Scene 4. This is because the original texts usually don't mark scene divisions and some editors choose to divide Scene 4 into two different scenes.

4. I was told by an Australian actor that when he was young he and his friends would say 'jinx' if anyone had inadvertently rhymed. When I was young we had to shout out the name of a poet.

5. *Albion* by Peter Ackroyd, Chapter 20.

6. 'Within' in this stage direction means 'from backstage'. Behind the back wall of the acting area in an Elizabethan theatre was the 'tiring-house' from which the actors entered and to which they exited. The word 'tiring-house' means the place where they got changed into their costumes – that is, where they 'attired' themselves – and this back wall looked like the front of a building, and anything happening inside it could be said to be happening 'within'.

7. *Love's Labour's Lost* has more rhymes, but because it is a longer play than *A Midsummer Night's Dream,* proportionally it has less.

8. The Duke of Gloucester, one of the sons of Edward III, and therefore one of Richard's many uncles, had been one of a group of lords who had tried to restrain what he saw as Richard's despotism. Richard had had him imprisoned at Calais, which is where he met his death.

9. Shakespeare wrote ten History plays and eight of them form a continuous cycle from the deposition of Richard II to the death in battle of Richard III, spanning a period of about a hundred years. But the last four plays in the sequence – the three parts of *Henry VI* and *Richard III* were actually written first – before *Richard II,* both parts of *Henry IV* and *Henry V.* The two plays standing outside this cycle are *King John* – an early play, and *Henry VIII* – a much later play that Shakespeare wrote in collaboration with the younger playwright, John Fletcher.

Chapter 12

1. There are quite a number of people who question whether Shakespeare was the writer of the plays that were printed bearing his name. Their uncertainty is based much upon the fact that Shakespeare didn't go to university, and while whoever wrote these plays certainly drew inspiration from many books, in Shakespeare's will, no books are mentioned. Many suggestions have been made as to who might have written the plays anonymously, using the name Shakespeare as a front, the most common being the Earl of Oxford and Francis Bacon. I feel whoever wrote the plays has to have had an intimate and continual exposure to theatrical life and practice, so I am happy to take it on trust that Shakespeare, the actor and 'sharer' (co-owner), was also the author of these plays that the world at large believes him to have written.

2. Besides the 'public theatres' such as the Globe, there were also 'private theatres' situated at Court, the Universities, and the Inns of Court. These sometimes put on a more serious and intellectual repertoire of plays, and in 1561 *Gorboduc,* a play in blank verse pentameters, was acted before the law students at the Inner Temple. It's a worthy effort, but has none of the fire and danger of Marlowe's plays written some quarter of a century later.

3. Pistol, a character Shakespeare creates when writing *Henry IV, Part Two,* and who also appears in *Henry V* and *The Merry Wives of Windsor,* speaks as if he is permanently living out his life in one of Marlowe's dramas. He frequently speaks nonsense, but his vocabulary often manages to impress some – for a while.

4. An unusually long line that editors usually emend, but I enjoy the bouncy rhythm of it.

5. The Folio (and Quarto) print 'sworn', but the Second Quarto emends this and prints 'swore' and as this is a chapter on rhyme, I have followed suit.

6. I have remembered this advice against rushing monosyllabic lines ever since reading John Barton's acclaimed *Playing Shakespeare.*

7. A short line indicating a pause before the three principal characters left alive make their final statements.

8. I am indebted to George T. Wright in his *Shakespeare's Metrical Art* for pointing this out to me.

9. In *As You Like It*, the character Phoebe falls in love with Rosalind who is disguised as a boy, and expresses her passion in this couplet, while at the same time referencing Marlowe's early death:

> Dead shepherd, now I find thy saw of might,
> Who ever lov'd, that lov'd not at first sight?

Chapter 13

1. *Pericles,* written about 1608 has a large amount of rhyme in it, mainly because Shakespeare uses the fourteenth-century poet John Gower to be his Chorus in the play, and fittingly he speaks in rhymed verse throughout.

2. We know from what the Sea Captain has told Viola in the second scene that Olivia's father died a year ago and her brother shortly afterwards. All we know about Viola, and her brother Sebastian, is that they come from somewhere called Messaline, and are of a noble family. But as to whether they have left any estates behind them, we are ignorant.

3. When I was Master of Play of *Hamlet* at the Globe in 2000, with Mark Rylance in the title role, we put this idea into practice. Performed in this way Shakespeare's scripts come to resemble film scripts, with scenes dissolving or 'fading' from one scene into the next. And it's a device that audiences accept totally.

4. Shakespeare always understood how by expressing ourselves, by speaking, we are able to ease some small part of the emotional burdens we are carrying. In *Richard III*, Queen Elizabeth, whose two sons have been murdered by Richard, says that words are – 'Poor breathing orators of miseries, / Let them have scope, though what they do impart, / Help nothing else, yet do they ease the heart.' (Act 4, Scene 4.)

5. When I was about to direct *The Comedy of Errors* at the Blackfriars Theatre in Virginia in 2008, I felt I needed to understand more about twins, and I came across a wonderful book, *Identical Strangers: A Memoir of Twins Separated and Reunited* by Else Schein and Paula Bernstein. Shakespeare had twins himself, Judith and Hamnet, though tragically the boy Hamnet died aged only eleven.

6. This line momentarily breaks the sequence of couplets. Presumably a line which would have rhymed with 'there' is missing from the unique Folio text.

7. These two rhyming lines are a good illustration of how sometimes, while making the rhyme 'work', you need to make sure that the thought, moving through the two lines, doesn't become dislocated. Here you have to 'set up' the word 'when' so that we hear how it rhymes with 'men', but you also have to account for the fact that the line breaks where it does. The solution is to realise that the second line needs that 'highlighting' that will be given to it if you 'top up' your breath before it, and fill the second line with the assurance that such a phrase demands.

8. It can be a risky business to say 'thou' to a king. In the first scene of *King Lear*, Kent is so angry with Lear that he starts to 'thou' him, and gets banished for his pains.

9. The director was John Dove; the actors were Sam Cox as the King of France and Ellie Piercy as Helena.

Chapter 14

1. The Folio omits the word 'round' from this line, but it is there in the Quarto.

2. We know Shakespeare wrote for specific actors because the texts sometimes, rather than prefacing some lines with the name of the character, give us the actor's name instead. What has happened in these circumstances is that the printer, following Shakespeare's manuscript, has come across a passage where Shakespeare has written the actor's name, rather than the character's, at the 'speech heading'. One example comes from a scene from *Much Ado About Nothing*, where the Folio has printed the name 'Kemp', the name of the famous clown of Shakespeare's company for whom the part of Dogberry – whose name should have been printed there – was specially written.

3. The 1604/5 Quarto of *Hamlet* is also very lightly punctuated and scholars have concluded the likelihood of this having been printed directly from Shakespeare's manuscript copy.

4. I am indebted to John Jones's fascinating book *Shakespeare at Work* for drawing my attention to the *Thomas More* manuscript and for his convincing attribution of those parts of it that seem so 'Shakespearian'.

5. As I have acknowledged elsewhere, I have learnt most of what I know about the punctuation of Shakespeare's time from Percy Simpson's *Shakespearian Punctuation*.

6. The boys that played the women's parts would have been apprenticed to one of the adult actors, from whom they would have received training. Richard Burbage was Shakespeare's leading actor for whom he wrote the parts of Richard III, Hamlet, and probably all his other major serious roles; and Burbage's apprentice, Nick Tooley, might well have played the part of Rosalind.

7. The Arden Shakespeare's *Twelfth Night* edited by J.M. Lothian and T.W. Craik (1975). Arden 3's 2008 edition deviates from the Folio's punctuation considerably more. It gets rid of five rather splendid colons, adds a further unnecessary comma to the 1975 edition's tally, and starts a new sentence with the phrase, 'She pined in thought,'.

8. The Folio is available on the web. But if you want actual copies, the Globe Theatre has produced a number of hardback Folio facsimiles, and more titles are being produced each year. Also the Nick Hern Books Shakespeare Folios have many of the key plays now in print – these editions faithfully reproduce the Folio's punctuation and spelling on one side and supply a modernised grammatical version on the facing page.

Chapter 15

1. The assassination of Caesar in *Julius Caesar* is one major exception, and Othello's murder of Desdemona another.

2. One of the major characteristics of *Macbeth* is the shortness of its scenes. Only six of the twenty-nine scenes are over a hundred lines in length, and this gives to the play a feeling of the characters being constantly overtaken by events and having little time for reflection or consideration.

3. We must remember that Banquo has been seduced by the Witches too, and it proves to be fatal for him, as for Macbeth. After the murder of

Duncan he never reveals his suspicions about Macbeth, feeling, no doubt, that if he did, it might jeopardise the promises that the Witches made to him and his offspring.

4. I find this line of Banquo's strangely placed. I would like it to come *after* Macbeth's next line, 'Two truths are told,'. I say this because the lines, 'In deepest consequence' and 'Two truths are told', make a perfect 'shared-line', and it makes more sense for Macbeth to come in immediately with his response to Banquo's doubting of the 'truth' behind the Witches' words. It's true that we are about to go into Macbeth's first soliloquy, and to make this moment work he would have to be moving away from Banquo *as* he says this line – a line which it would be perfectly fine for Banquo to overhear. Then before (or even with) Macbeth's next line, Banquo could move back to the others saying his line, which we barely *need* to hear, though having something spoken to cover his move, would make the moment more realistic. But it's impossible to see how this might have been printed in the text to explain such an arrangement. But it is for this reason that I have put Macbeth's 'Two' in bold, indicating a mid-line trochaic beat.

5. I frequently go through Hamlet's soliloquies in my head, or out loud. I played Hamlet almost forty years ago, have directed it twice, seen it countless times, and only the other day, I realised a new connection, and a clearer meaning behind some words in the 'To be or not to be...' soliloquy.

6. I would be tempted to change this difficult line and a half – 'Thou'dst have, great Glamis, / That which cries, thus thou must do, if thou have it;' to 'if thou'**dst** have it;' and avoid the change of tense between the beginning and end of the thought. I think it's quite likely that Shakespeare originally wrote 'thou'dst' and the Folio misread the manuscript. (Others have suggested this emendation before me.)

7. In *All's Well that Ends Well*, Act 3, Scene 4, the Countess has this monosyllabic line:

> Might you not know she would do, as she has done,

It might at first be difficult to see where the stresses fall in these eleven words; but again the basic iambic pattern, plus a trochaic first foot reveals all:

> **Might** you not **know** she **would** do, as she **has** done,

8. You have to be careful though and avoid trying to pin down Shakespeare's 'time-lines' too precisely. Time in Shakespeare is elastic, and with almost all the plays we have a feeling that scene by scene events are moving fast. Whereas when we arrive at the final scene, we feel that we have been living with the characters over a much longer space of time. In *Hamlet*, for example, by the end of the play Hamlet is thirty; at the beginning of the play he seems a teenager. Shakespeare does this deliberately; we experience the excitement of the play progressing with speed, yet the characters are allowed to mature and develop as well.

9. I have added the comma after 'done', which I think could be of help to the actor.

10. With all the repetitions of the words 'done' and 'undone' in this play, it makes me smile that Shakespeare here (and only on this one occasion) uses the word 'dunnest' (meaning darkest or murkiest).

11. Again we see a similarity between what she says about not wanting to see: 'That my keen knife see not the wound it makes,' and what Macbeth has said at the end of the previous scene: 'Let not light see my black and deep desires:'. How alike they are in many ways.

12. One of my favourite stage directions comes from the anonymous play *A Yorkshire Tragedy* in which the actor is directed to '*enter as if thrown from a horse*'.

13. The Folio has 'this bank and school of time', which a few editors have defended. But most change 'school' to 'shoal', which was first suggested by the Shakespearian critic Lewis Theobald (1688–1744).

14. The play suggests that Macbeth becomes impotent after the murder. He cannot sleep and he says in Act 3, Scene 1, 'Upon my head they plac'd a fruitless crown / And put a barren sceptre in my gripe, / Thence to be wrench'd with an unlineal hand, / No son of mine succeeding:'

15. Talking to your forebears is not such a fanciful idea. In *Henry V*, the King is urged to 'Look back into your mighty ancestors: / Go my dread lord, to your great-grandsire's tomb, / From whom you claim; invoke his warlike spirit,' (*Henry V: Act 1, Scene 2*).

16. The notes sometimes tell us how Lady Macbeth had a child by a previous marriage, but as this earlier marriage is ignored by Shakespeare, we have to search out other answers for this missing child.

Chapter 16

1. Perdita means 'the lost one'.

2. Cleopatra in Act 3, Scene 7 of *Antony and Cleopatra* refers to herself as 'we' when she says 'why should not we / Be there in person', telling Enobarbus she herself has every right to take part in the military action against Caesar.

3. There are two possible ways to play this vitally important line. Either Leontes simply says it straight to his wife, or he might say it as an 'aside' to the audience. The colon sometimes seems to indicate a change of focus, and so here could mark the moment when he turns back, from having spoken to the audience, and now attempts to cover his shock as he congratulates his wife.

4. One critic called it 'the obscurest passage in Shakespeare' (M. van Doren, *Shakespeare*, 1939).

5. Bohemia has no seacoast, but the source story Shakespeare was following – *Pandosto* by Robert Greene (1588) – has a reference to 'the coast of Bohemia'.

6. Act 2, Scene 3 when Paulina attempts in vain to get Leontes to accept the baby Perdita as his.

7. See end note 8 to Chapter 13.

8. Of course we know so little about Shakespeare's life that everyone who writes about him falls into conjectures of their own. John Aubrey (1626–97) in his *Brief Lives* was one of the first to gather scraps of information together about Shakespeare's life, and he has left us some tantalising bits of gossip to puzzle over. One such tells us, 'He was not a company keeper, lived in Shoreditch, wouldn't be debauched, & if invited to writ; he was in pain.' These statements are not the easiest to interpret, but John Southworth in his book *Shakespeare the Player* distrusts the punctuation and interprets these last words as meaning that Shakespeare would be in pain *when* he was writing. This interpretation strikes a chord with me, because whenever I conjecture about how Shakespeare is able to write as he does, it seems to me that he must first become obsessed by what ever story he is about to dramatise. These obsessions are then fuelled by the characters within them, who tell Shakespeare, as it were, *why* they

are doing what they are doing – and eventually he hears all that they are saying. Finally the only way Shakespeare can get these voices out of his head is to write them down, and leave it to the actors to bring them to life.

I suspect many writers work in the same way. Katherine Mansfield writing to John Middleton Murry about her short story *The Stranger* records: 'I've *been* this man, *been* this woman. I've stood for hours on the Auckland Wharf. I've been out in the stream waiting to be berthed. I've been a seagull hovering at the stern and a hotel porter whistling through his teeth. It isn't as though one sits and watches the spectacle. That would be thrilling enough God knows. But one IS the spectacle for the time.' (Quoted in Katherine Mansfield, *Selected Stories*, Oxford World's Classics, edited by Angela Smith.)

Chapter 17

1. John Fletcher (1579–1625) became the leading dramatist of the King's Men (the name of Shakespeare's company after the accession of James I) after Shakespeare's death. Fletcher is for ever associated with the dramatist Francis Beaumont with whom he also collaborated.

2. Antony was Paul Shelley, John McEnery was Enobarbus and Danny Sapani was Charmian. I remember them all most fondly.

3. It is Giacomo in *Cymbeline* (Act 2, Scene 2) who sees the taper trying to peep under Imogen's sleeping eyelids

4. Maria Callas, talking to Lord Harewood for the BBC, 1968.

Acknowledgements

1. Thanks not only to Mary Baldwin College, and Paul Menzer and Julie Fox, but also to Ralph Alan Cohen and Jim Warren, the founders of the American Shakespeare Center at the Blackfriars Theatre in Staunton, for whom I have directed on three occasions. Thanks too to Marlena Hobson and Paul Borzellaca who provided me with such a beautiful room in which to start writing this book.

2. Besides Patrick Spottiswoode who gave the green light to this project, I was also supported by Farah Karim-Cooper, Jamie Arden and Harper Ray. The actors were Penelope Beaumont, Philip Cumbus and Jo Herbert. To all of them, and especially to my extremely talented and long-suffering actors, my thanks.

Index of Play Titles and Characters

Index of Names